Wetter Than the Mississippi

Prohibition in St. Louis
and Beyond

by Robbi Courtaway

with a Foreword by Tom Schlafly

Reedy Press
St. Louis, Missouri

Reedy Press, PO Box 5131, St. Louis, MO 63139, USA

Library of Congress Control Number: 2008937131

ISBN: 978-1-933370-37-8

Please visit our website at www.reedypress.com.

Printed in the United States of America
08 09 10 11 12 5 4 3 2 1

cover by Kevin Belford

CONTENTS

Acknowledgments

A MISCHIEVOUS SMILE WOULD CRINKLE THE LINES IN HIS FACE, BROWN FROM HOURS spent in his garden, as he worked his ever-present toothpick with his tongue until it dissolved into splinters.

Grandpa was fun. At the railroad tracks in Neoga, the small Illinois town where he lived for a time, he helped us select choice rocks to haul back to St. Louis, which gratified my father to no end. Grandpa would stand on the tracks as slow-moving freight trains approached and hop off with perhaps fifty feet to spare, gleefully sending my younger sister into hysterics.

When he succumbed to lymphoma at age eighty-three in July 1975, Walter Courtaway departed a colorful life. He had been raised in a log cabin outside DeSoto, Missouri, with twelve siblings, spoke French in a Missouri dialect, helped shoot the family's supper and gathered tasty young weeds and morel mushrooms, and traveled from town to town by hopping freights. Later, he married a young woman from Bismarck, Missouri, became a shoe factory foreman, and raised nine children.

He also was a common criminal after 1920, as were many others when the manufacture and sale of liquor were outlawed. Grandpa home-brewed beer during prohibition and made soda pop for his kids. He sold some of the brew, and the sheriff caught up with him in Owensville, Missouri. Ever helpful, Grandpa helped the raiders pitch the bottles into the woods and aimed for the soft spots. My mother, Bernice, also felt the effects of prohibition. Her home town of Hermann, Missouri, built around the wine industry, was mired in a depression by the time she was born in 1922.

My curiosity about the prohibition years has resulted in this book. It focuses on St. Louis and vicinity and includes stories within roughly a 150-mile radius, including Boonville, Cape Girardeau, Jefferson City, and Poplar Bluff, Missouri, and Nauvoo, Springfield, Decatur, and southern Illinois. Anecdotal stories about prohibition are everywhere: These pages carry a few of them. Most who lived through the time are dead, and some don't wish to talk: They still feel the stigma of their families branded as "common criminals." The prohibition enforcement offices have long since been dismantled, the location of their records a mystery.

Invaluable to my research were the oral history memoirs recorded during the 1970s and early 1980s from the University of Illinois at Springfield and the Western Historical Manuscript Collection in Missouri. Special thanks to Thomas

J. Wood, archivist at the University of Illinois at Springfield, and his staff; Zelli Fischetti, associate director of the Western Historical Manuscript Collection in St. Louis, and staff, including the late Doris Wesley; Diane Ayotte, assistant director of the Western Historical Manuscript Collection in Columbia, Missouri, and staffers Jenny Lukomski, Bill Stolz, Peter McCarthy, Mary Beth Brown, and John Konzal; and Gary R. Kremer, Ph.D, director of the Western Historical Manuscript Collection and executive director of the State Historical Society of Missouri, and staffers Loucile Malone, Lauren Leeman, Ara Kaye, Seth Smith, Todd Christine, Sara Przybylski, Kimberly Harper, Dianne Buffon, and Rebecca Ballew.

Thanks also to Gary R. Mormino, Ph.D, professor of history at the University of South Florida; brewery historians and writers Kevin Kious and Donald Roussin; archivist Bill Popp and staff at the St. Charles County Historical Society; Susan Rehkopf, archivist for the Historical Society of University City; Director and Curator Floyd J. Sperino and Manager Cary Harvengt of the Collinsville Historical Museum; Susan Burkett, Nancy Mason,

Right: Walter Courtaway, circa 1912.

Below: The author's mother, Bernice, is second from left, shown here playing with neighbor kids in Hermann, Missouri, in the mid-1920s.

James F. Baker, Albert Winkler, Earl Maschmeier, and Paul R. Gegg of the Kirkwood Historical Society; volunteer Matilda "Til" Keil of the Old Trails Historical Society; St. Louis historian NiNi Harris; volunteer James Bielefeldt of the Webster Groves Historical Society; Della Lang, Jefferson County historian, and the Fenton Historical Society; Barbara L. Miksicek, librarian for the St. Louis Police Library, and retired St. Louis Police Chief Joseph Mokwa; Bryon Andreasen, Ph.D, research historian for the Abraham Lincoln Presidential Library & Museum in Springfield, Illinois; David Kyvig, Ph.D, distinguished research professor in the department of history at Northern Illinois University in DeKalb, Illinois; Bruce Ketchum, site administrator of the Deutschheim State Historic Site in Hermann, Missouri; Lois Puchta, archives director for the Gasconade County Historical Society; and Frank Nickell, Ph.D, director of the Center for Regional History at Southeast Missouri State University.

Thanks to Jeff Fister and the Virginia Publishing Co.; Special Collections Curator Deborah Cribbs, Assistant Director Charles Brown, and the staff of the St. Louis Mercantile Library, Bette Gorden, director of the Herman T. Pott Inland Waterways Library; the staff of the Missouri Historical Society Library and Research Center; Adele Heagney, reference librarian in charge of St. Louis–area studies, and staff at the St. Louis Public Library; Director Tom Cooper of the Webster Groves Public Library and staffers Chris Johnson, Tim Nix, Diane LeBeau, Jean Foy, Paige Shaw, Steven Barnett, and Mary Ann Rehkop; the staff of the Audiovisual and Special Collections departments at St. Louis County Library; Mike Meiners, director of the News Research Department at the *St. Louis Post-Dispatch,* researchers Matt Fernandes, Mark Learman, and Steve Bolhafner, and Hillary Levin of the photo desk; Kirkwood City Clerk Betty Montano; Maplewood Acting City Clerk Karen Scheidt; and Webster Groves Deputy City Clerk Jennifer Conrad.

Thanks to Tom Schlafly, president of The Saint Louis Brewery, Inc., and others who read a rough draft and made suggestions: Tom Cooper; Kevin Kious, and Donald Roussin; Mary Sherfy, director of marketing communications for St. Anthony's Medical Center; and my husband, Kevin Murphy.

Thanks also to Rick Biggs, Barbara J. Byerly, Jean Fahey Eberle, Ron "Johnny Rabbitt" Elz, Michael Everman, Susan Fadem, Jim Fox, Ray Griesedieck, Kathy Grillo, Esley Hamilton, Patty Held-Uthlaut, Glenn Hensley, Julius Hunter, Monika Kleban, Kim Orth, Steve Taylor, and Alexander "Fritz" Zenthoefer; and to the ever-patient Matt Heidenry and Josh Stevens of Reedy Press, LLC.

FOREWORD

EARLY IN THE SUMMER OF 2008, ST. LOUISANS WERE STUNNED BY THE announcement that Anheuser-Busch, a beloved local icon, would be acquired by the international conglomerate InBev. Politicians crossed party lines to achieve rare unanimity in opposing the transaction. Pundits and others worried about the possible loss of jobs and the impact on the St. Louis economy.

Against this backdrop, imagine the anxiety that must have gripped St. Louis in 1920, with the onset of prohibition. While InBev's reputation for cost-cutting sent ripples of worry through the community, no one talked about eliminating the brewing industry altogether in St. Louis, which is exactly what happened on January 16, 1920, when the Eighteenth Amendment to the United States Constitution took effect.

As recounted in *Wetter Than the Mississippi*, Robbi Courtaway's supremely readable story of prohibition in St. Louis, in the mid-1910s the local breweries had 9,617 employees. Another 45,000 workers were at least partially dependent on the brewing industry, including those involved in making barrels or glass bottles. All of these industries and their related jobs were affected by prohibition. To get some idea of the economic impact of prohibition on the local economy, consider what Joseph Hahn, the secretary of Local 6 of the Brewers and Maltsters Union in St. Louis, said at the time: "I think we can safely say that about 5,000 men are on the streets on account of prohibition." Moreover, the federal government, having outlawed an entire industry, paid no compensation whatsoever to the affected businesses or displaced workers.

St. Louisans weren't simply hurt in their pocketbooks. They were also thirsty. Some resorted to brewing beer and distilling spirits in their homes. Others took advantage of religious and medicinal exemptions in the law and bought liquor legally. Among the conditions for which prohibition-era physicians in St. Louis prescribed alcoholic beverages were "flu, fever, senility, debility, drug addiction (withdrawal), heart block, tuberculosis, fatigue, dyspepsia, post-measles, symptoms of ptomaine poisoning, insomnia, exposure, flatulency, exhaustion, shock, asthma, malaria, baldness, gall stone pain, chronic bronchitis, epileptic attack, neurasthenia, whooping cough, scarletina, cerebral anemia, mitral insufficiency, acute indigestion, confinement, dropsy, valvular lesion, pernicious anemia, post-operative pain, and broken arm."

The religious exceptions to prohibition permitted state prohibition directors to issue sacramental wine permits to "ministers, priests, rabbis or other church or congregational officials." Under these exceptions, members of congregations could purchase "sacramental wine" from their clergymen. Under the oversight of a mobster named "Big Maxie" Greenberg, there were purportedly Jewish congregations with dues-paying members named Sullivan, O'Brien, and Caruso.

With legitimate businesses prohibited from selling liquor, criminal gangs arose to fill the void. According to Courtaway, there were no fewer than six major gangs "that made big money bootlegging and running gambling rackets when they weren't robbing banks or knocking each other off." Among them were Egan's Rats, the Hogan gang, the Cuckoos, and the Green Ones in St. Louis and the Metro-East; and the Birger and Shelton gangs in southern Illinois.

As unsavory as these gangsters were, some of the individuals on the other side weren't much better. One of the staunchest allies of the prohibition-enforcement effort, especially in southern Illinois, was the Ku Klux Klan. According to Courtaway, "Members of the Klan were held in high esteem by many in deep southern Illinois, and they ran liquor raids in outstate Missouri and attempted to gain power in East St. Louis." She adds that liquor raids were often conducted with the approval of the local sheriff or police and allowed the Klan to persecute Italians, Catholics, African Americans, and Jews, among others.

Despite all of these raids and other enforcement efforts at the federal, state, and local levels, St. Louisans tippled happily throughout prohibition. *Wetter Than the Mississippi* opens with an account of a raid of a New Year's Eve Party at the Chase Hotel in 1922. Incensed revelers drove the prohibition agents out of the ballroom with a shower of glasses, cutlery, and plates and continued partying without further interruption until dawn.

In St. Louis and elsewhere, cocktail parties were very popular during prohibition. Courtaway's book, in which one good story follows another, is like a great cocktail party.

—Thomas Schlafly

CHAPTER 1

CUTTING TO THE CHASE

"If the raids that were made upon the hotels on New Year's eve were started when prohibition first went into effect, I venture to say that prohibition would not have lasted six months, but alas, they saw fit to make the poor the victim and what chance have they?"
—Unidentified St. Louis waiter, 1923

IN ELEGANT SEDANS THEY ARRIVED IN THE WANING HOURS OF 1922, DRESSED IN silk and broadcloth and fur-trimmed coats, and entered the gilded halls of Hotel Chase for what would be a truly unforgettable New Year's Eve.

More than 2,200 of St. Louis's prominent citizens had purchased tickets at $10 a plate—the equivalent of approximately $120 today—to enjoy the private party at St. Louis's exclusive West End hotel, built earlier that year at a cost of $5 million. Many also rented rooms at an additional $10 to store their wraps and private liquor stocks. Nationwide prohibition, enacted three years earlier, forbade the manufacture and sale of liquor but allowed residents to savor their stocks of pre-prohibition liquor at home.

Under crystal chandeliers in the Palm Room they sat in chairs with rich brocade upholstery, at tables with starched white cloths and gleaming place settings. Their special guest for the evening was the Paul Whiteman Orchestra, one of the most popular musical talents in the nation, which two years later would introduce to the world George Gershwin's legendary "Rhapsody in Blue."

Whiteman no doubt was pleased to visit St. Louis, then the seventh-largest city in the nation with 800,000 residents, a solid manufacturing bastion known for its red brick homes and yellow streetcars. One in every five people in the United States walked through the day in shoes manufactured in the Mound City.

If Gus O. Nations had his way, the land of the brick homes and yellow streetcars would be one with the Sahara Desert. Nations, chief of the city's prohibition enforcement agents, had pledged to make New Year's Eve 1922 the driest ever in St. Louis. But the well-to-do residents who gathered at the Chase had no intention of joining the working-class St. Louisans, African Americans and immigrants who dominated the headlines in liquor arrests up to that time.

The result was a riot: One of the agents shot three patrons, one of whom was dancing with his wife at the time, another returning from the powder room.

I

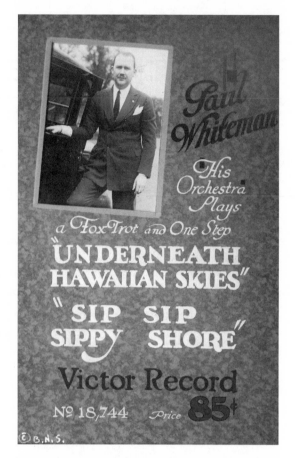

The Paul Whiteman Orchestra was one of the most popular bands in America in the 1920s, as illustrated by this undated poster advertisement for Victor Records. Courtesy Library of Congress.

The resulting mob that gathered injured an agent; sent a hail of silverware, plates, salt and pepper shakers, and entrees flying across the room; and, as many continued to dance and dine, drove out the agents in an angry wall 250 people strong as police enforcements gathered outside. The Chase fiasco galvanized wet and dry forces in a contentious battle that would continue for the rest of the decade and into the 1930s, over an unpopular law many felt compelled to break.

THE RAID

Shortly after 11 p.m. on New Year's Eve 1922, three men entered the hotel and one announced he was a prohibition enforcement agent, hotel proprietor Chase Ulman later told reporters. Ulman replied that the event was open only to guests holding admission tickets and asked if the agent had a search warrant. "Here's my search warrant," the dry agent replied, and displayed his badge.

Ulman told the agent he would cooperate only if he had a search warrant. The agent ignored him and made his way into one of the dining rooms with the other agents, stopping at each table. Eventually, they stopped at a table where two men and two women were seated and arrested O. L. Dixon, thirty, and Richard Warren, twenty-five, after accusing Dixon of pouring a drink of liquor from a flask. "Why didn't you leave your liquor at home?" asked one of the agents. "You're under arrest."

A reporter from the *Post-Dispatch* was there:

Like wildfire word of the arrests spread through the dining rooms. Those who had liquor kept it on the hip, abandoning the custom of keeping it on the table under a napkin or tablecloth.... At midnight, to the raucous cheers of more than 2,200 diners, Paul Whiteman's orchestra ushered in the New Year with the national anthem. Hundreds accompanied by singing, laying particular emphasis on the words, "The land of the free."

Around 1:30 a.m., Nations and assistants M. L. Hogg and L. H. Gatter walked in, this time with a search warrant, and headed to the Palm Room. Nations had summoned city detectives to follow him, including St. Louis Police Detective Sergeant John Glassco, but they participated mainly as spectators, the *Post* noted.

Tables of diners were located on the north and south sides of the room, and guests were dancing in the center. All of the agents were wearing hats and overcoats, and one was smoking a cigar, as they circulated among the tables, tossed napkins about, picked up tablecloths, and sniffed the contents of glasses. The *Post* described the scene:

"Take off your hat!" "Throw away that cigar!" "Get out of here and stay out!" These suggestions were disregarded by Nations and his two assistants as they progressed in their search. About 10 tables had been searched when a woman screamed and her escort punched an enforcement agent's face. One version was that the woman had asserted that one of the agents, in lifting a tablecloth to glance under the table, had raised the skirt of her gown.

Various explanations were given for the uprising. One witness was Miss Alice Busch, queen of the Veiled Prophet Ball, an elite celebration hosted annually by a group of prominent St. Louis businessmen. Busch said the trouble arose at an adjoining table when the agents lifted a tablecloth. Tulsa, Oklahoma, oilman Thomas A. Creekmore told a *Globe-Democrat* reporter the trouble began when one of the agents found some liquor on a table directly opposite the orchestra pit and began to arrest a young man at the table.

The Palm Room at the Chase. Courtesy Virginia Publishing Company and Susan Kopler Brown.

"I was dancing past the table when I noticed the officer, and that was when I first learned that the hotel was being raided," Creekmore said. "Someone hissed the officer, and then the crowd began to push forward throwing dishes and bottles. I was struck a light blow on the head by a flying water glass, which I think was thrown by a woman. I saw someone hurl a chair at the officer, and then the crowd closed around him, pushing him toward the door."

Ulman gave a third account of the disturbance:

"One officer, who appeared to be the leader of the party, addressed a remark to the occupants of a table directly in front of me," he said. "I could not hear what was said, but one of the men in the party arose and confronted the raider. Something else was said and then the officer hit the man. It was then that the melee started. The two men near me drew their revolvers and held them in their hands, at the same time continuing their search. Dishes in several instances were thrown to the floor by the raiders, who roughly pulled up the tablecloths. I did not see any liquor and do not think that the agents found any, although one of them showed me an inch of white stuff in a glass which he said was gin."

Almost immediately the dry agents were surrounded by about 200 men and women. Vigor-

An ad for Hotel Chase in the March 2, 1927.

ous demands were made by some guests that the dry agents depart at once. The agents stood their ground. Words passed. Blows were struck. Glasses, plates, silverware and water were hurled through the air. The three agents, being the only ones in the demonstrative and surging group who were not in evening dress, were shining targets.

Some women began screaming and rushing for points of safety. Some held their hands over their eyes as their escorts hurriedly led them from the dance floor. All the while the orchestra, under orders from the management, kept playing fast and loudly, in an effort to drown the noise of the excited, fighting, surging crowd 50 feet distant.

Nations would later tell officials he spent most of his time "trying to disengage myself from a drunken woman who wanted to dance with me." The surging mob, which he described as "250 drunken men," eventually got the better of him and his agents.

Other men and women watched from a safe distance. The rioting in the center of the Palm Room continued about 10 minutes, all the while there being insistent demands of guests that the prohibition agents be "thrown out." Then the crowd surged toward an aperture in the lounge room, which also was filled with guests at tables. An unsuccessful effort was made to push the dry agents from the Palm Room into the lounge room. Then the crowd surged toward the west entrance to the Palm Room, the only avenue of entrance and exit during the evening.

Throw them out! the insistent and oft-repeated demand, was being put into execution. The dry agents found themselves helpless in the center of an angry crowd, and gave ground, although they were punching and being punched. About 15 men were in the group that gave impetus to the agents' rapid retreat toward the exit leading into the lobby. The orchestra stopped playing. As the belligerents neared the exit, and while still in the Palm Room, a revolver shot was heard.

GLITZ AND GUNFIRE

A single bullet apparently ricocheted off the tile floor and hit a woman and two men. Jane Robinson, thirty-six, of 108 Arundel Place, was returning from the dressing room to her table in the west dining room when she felt a sting in her ankle. George A. Bode, Jr., twenty-seven, of Clayton and McKnight roads, son of the marshal of the St. Louis Court of Appeals, was grazed by a bullet in the right foot. And John Pazdera, twenty-eight, of 1211 Hamilton Avenue, was wounded in the left leg below the knee while he danced with his wife. Pazdera was vice president of the Consumers Grocery and Meat Company.

St. Louis police detective Edward Sullivan, who had fired the shot, told investigators he had been struck repeatedly on the head and back by flying objects. Sullivan said he and the other agents were pulled and dragged back and forth by the crowd, many of whom were intoxicated.

"The 'mob' all of this time were yelling 'Lynch them,' 'Throw them out,' 'Where is Nations?' and other things of a like nature," Sullivan observed. "I had

ON THE RECEIVING END

St. Louis police detective Edward Sullivan made the news again in 1929, this time on the receiving end of a raid. He was dismissed by the Board of Police Commissioners on October 18, 1929, after he was found present in the rear room of a confectionery raided by federal agents at 901 N. Taylor Avenue. Two agents said at the hearing that Sullivan attempted to escape when the raiders entered; Sullivan, who was in civilian clothes at the time of the raid, said he was unaware that liquor was being sold in the place and believed agents had the situation in hand, so he thought he was justified in leaving. Nonetheless, he pleaded guilty before the board of conduct unbecoming an officer and neglect of duty. He was fifty years old and a twenty-six-year veteran of the department.

gotten toward the front part of the dining room when I was attacked by several men, all of whom were striking me from the rear. I was finally knocked down and while down three or four men were kicking me in the side and back. Also one man said, 'Throw pepper in his eyes and blind him.' I managed to rise from the floor to my knees and seeing them attempt to kick me again I drew my revolver and shot at the man who was kicking me. I later learned that he had been shot in the leg. When I had gained the front door I found that I was bleeding from a badly lacerated lip; also four of my front teeth were loose, and [I was] bruised on the back and sides."

Pazdera denied he had kicked the detective. He also denied he had any liquor at the hotel and said he was dancing with a woman in his party when the crowd began shoving toward the south wall of the Palm Room.

"I saw a lady fall to her knees," he said. "I went over to help her and lifted her to her feet. As I turned around, an officer smiled at me. I said to him: 'I don't think you can do much here,' and he agreed. The crowd shoved the officers to the entrance. My wife grabbed me and said, 'Come on.' I started away. I saw a man put his hand to his hip and fire."

Harry Meyer, a waiter at the Chase, said the officer was arising from a

OTHER BUSTS (OR LACK THEREOF) ON NEW YEAR'S EVE, 1922

- Statler Hotel: two arrests
- Jefferson Hotel: one arrest
- St. Louis County roadhouses: no arrests or calls

"Although all of the roadhouses in St. Louis County were taxed to capacity New Year's Eve, and most of them remained open until after daybreak, there was not a single call for police at the Sheriff's office in Clayton," the *Globe-Democrat* reported. "Constables in the five townships of the county reported orderly crowds at every resort. Pocket flasks were very much in evidence, but as far as could be learned, there were no arrests for liquor violations by either county or federal officers. County bootleggers did a flourishing business, and the prices of moonshine were almost doubled. Bonded whisky could be obtained from many at the regular price of $20 a quart."

kneeling position when he drew his revolver from his right-hand hip pocket and fired. He then placed the blue steel gun back in his pocket. Guests from nearby hotels heard of the ruckus and headed to the Chase.

Fully as exciting as the melee in the palmroom of the hotel was the scene that was enacted at the front door after the raiders had been driven out of the establishment. A jeering crowd of 200 people, some of whom were irate diners and others who had stopped their automobiles because of the excitement, crowded around Nations and his small band, who stood with their backs to the wall of the hotel, a short distance from the door. Women and men in evening clothes over-ran the soggy lawn and others leaned out of the open windows of the hotel. The arrival of a wagon-load of police reserves from the Newstead Avenue District and Assistant Chief Rundle from Police headquarters merely added to the confusion. The crowd seemed to welcome the arrival of the uniformed men and clapped them on the back in a good-natured fashion as they mixed with the crowd.

Chase Ulman, who had not seen the search warrant, approached with his attorney and asked Nations what authority he had to enter the hotel. Nations displayed the warrant, and Ulman gave him permission to conduct a further search. "I had not quite finished," Nations replied, "but if I go back I will take more than six men."

"Take ten men, then," said Ulman.

"Not on your life," Nations replied. "I will take the whole squad, including the reserves, or I won't go."

Despite all the excitement, the festivities at the Chase continued without interruption until daylight, when "a large proportion" of the 2,600 guests could still be found dancing or sitting around tables, according to the *Globe*. Nations didn't return to the hotel that morning. He later cited public safety concerns. "When they [the mob] began throwing things and pressing toward us, I saw that, should we avail ourselves of all means of resistance we could have rightly used, many innocent people would have been hurt or killed," he later told a reporter. "So I told the men to get out as quickly and quietly as possible.

"I don't say that all the guests were drinking. Only a small part of them were. I know that some of the best people in St. Louis were in the room, and I decided it was better for us to lose and retreat than to injure any of them.

"We searched no hip pockets, but confined ourselves to examining what was on the tables. We found a number of glasses of whiskey, but they were taken from the guests. I understand that the trouble started when a number of the guests jumped upon one of the agents and took some whiskey he had found."

A Quiet Start

For all the hoopla on New Year's Eve 1922, prohibition in St. Louis had started quietly enough. Nationwide, temperance groups such as the Anti-Saloon League and the Women's Christian Temperance Union (WCTU) had campaigned for years and gradually succeeded with various counties and communities that had voted themselves dry. Abuses in the saloons of the early 1900s fueled the fire for progressive reformers and women. Evangelical Protestants, business owners concerned about productivity, and nativist Americans concerned about foreign immigrants joined the temperance forces, which branded the city's German American brewers as "anti-American" during World War I. Even members of the Ku Klux Klan supported prohibition, because it targeted the drinking traditions of immigrants, among others.

Despite heavy opposition from residents of St. Louis and vicinity, the Missouri and Illinois legislatures voted to ratify the Eighteenth Amendment in January 1919, a constitutional amendment that took effect one year later on January 16, 1920. It forbade the manufacture, transport, sale, import, and export of intoxicating beverages in the United States and was preceded by a wartime prohibition measure that took effect July 1, 1919. Congress passed an enforcement statute in October 1919 known as the National Prohibition Act, or Volstead Act, after its sponsor, Andrew Volstead of Minnesota. It set up the legislation and criminal penalties by which the wartime act and later the Eighteenth Amendment would be enforced, including the definition of intoxicating liquor as anything with more than 0.5 percent alcohol. It did not specifically prohibit the purchase or use of intoxicating liquors, though it did prohibit the manufacture, possession, sale, transport, and barter of intoxicating liquor.

A Time Like No Other

The prohibition years in St. Louis were a baker's dozen of change and conflict between the old and the new. Radio broadcasts, electricity, telephones, moving pictures, automobiles, and paved roads were ushered in, along with the world's first consumer economy and advertising-created afflictions such as "halitosis." Civil War veterans dropped like flies, and the old ways of doing things were called increasingly into question. Women exercised their newly acquired right to vote (usually in the manner of their husbands), and more daring souls questioned issues such as sexuality and birth control. St. Louis newspapers carried the lat-

CURB SERVICE

Some prominent members of St. Louis's Racquet Club in the Central West End received their refreshment on the go during prohibition, according to *The First Fifty Years: The Racquet Club*:

A casual observer interested in such things during this period could have strolled through the alley south of the club building and he might have caught a glimpse of a parked car nestled remarkably near the back of the building . . . fairly soon he would have seen a bushy-haired, white coated individual leaning through the club's window and into the window of the car, passing certain objects to the car occupants . . . a very early exhibition of curb service.

est headlines of the unearthing of King Tutankhamen's tomb in Luxor, Egypt, Charles Lindbergh's transatlantic flight, and the razing of the mansion of city father Clement Delor de Treget so that busy Virginia Avenue could be widened.

"St. Louis is suffering from an acute attack of radiomania," the *St. Louis Star* opined in January 1923, as radio sales in the city totaled $7,000 weekly, or $81,500 in today's dollars. "The other day at the counter a professor from Washington University was rubbing elbows with a mechanic in greasy overalls while nearby a Cleveland High School teacher was in solemn conference with a pudgy-faced boy in knickerbockers and a red sweater over the best kind of wire to buy for an aerial."

On that note, the 1923 technological equivalent of today's iPhone was offered for the price of rent at the Garden Court apartment house, 5330 Delmar Boulevard. Each of the sixty-four apartments was equipped with a loudspeaker, which the tenant could connect to or disconnect from a central radio receiving station. Paul Jones, manager of the property, said the station had picked up KSD in St. Louis and signals from Waco, Texas; Kansas City, Missouri; Atlanta, Georgia; and Pittsburgh, Pennsylvania.

Flappers, short skirts, bobs, permanent waves, and fast living in the manner of F. Scott Fitzgerald made for exciting headlines, but around St. Louis the pace was slower. "Short hair changed women's looks with permanents under execution-like machines holding you in your chair at the mercy of the operator," Herrin, Illinois, native Sue Spytek recalled in 1984. "Women came forth with singed hair, brittle ends, but 'in style.'"

St. Louis was a dirty, if exciting, place to live, a newfangled smoke detector at Shaw's Garden determined in 1924: Each St. Louisan inhaled fifteen table-spoons of soot every five days as a result of the soft coal used in most home furnaces. After smoke killed off what had been the finest collection of ever-greens in the United States, Garden officials in 1923 received permission from the courts to sell off fifty acres of pasture land bounded by Shaw, Vandeventer, and Shenandoah avenues and a then-roadless line that extended Alfred Avenue. They used the money—$250,000 from the realty company of Cyrus Crane Willmore—to purchase land in Gray Summit on which they built eight green-houses the following year for the garden's precious orchids.

Like their counterparts across the nation, St. Louisans took time out for a newfangled tile game known as Mah-Jongg, catchy new crossword puzzles, and the song "Yes, We Have No Bananas." Dance marathons were popular until city health commissioner Max Starkloff nipped them in the bud for health reasons. He shut down a steamy affair at Cinderella Hall, at Cherokee Street and Iowa Avenue, as the event entered its eighty-sixth hour at 4 p.m., September 5, 1928. The grueling dance had begun four days earlier with fifteen couples; at the end, two couples split a prize of $750. The promoter, Danville, Illinois, clothing store owner Harry J. Silverberg, lost $600.

The dance marathon and Mah-Jongg crazes faded away, and in 1925 Dr. J. H. Hoover predicted the same fate for the crossword puzzle. Hoover, head of the Teachers College psychology department in Cape Girardeau, had few good things to say about crosswords when he spoke to a student organization on "The Psychology of the Cross-word Puzzle." The hobby outlived him.

MAKING HEADLINES

The Chase fiasco made the front page of *The New York Times* on January 2, 1923: *"Bullets, Chairs and Tableware Fly in Riot As St. Louisans Run Dry Squad Out of Hotel."* Only the New Year's Eve events in San Francisco came close: two dry agents were knocked unconscious by flying bottles during the raid of a drinking establishment.

St. Louis's melee was followed by a lawsuit from one of the wounded patrons, a mass meeting of citizens to protest the enforcement of the Volstead Act in St. Louis, condemnation of the revelers by local Methodist officials and prohibition supporters, demands for Nations's dismissal, and a scandal involving a promi-nent temperance official with the Anti-Saloon League. An ongoing debate ensued over Fourth Amendment (search and seizure) rights, godlessness, and lawlessness that included the Anti-Saloon League, the Association Against the Prohibition Amendment (AAPA), the Ku Klux Klan, a federal judge, and assorted clergy.

Wayne Wheeler, general counsel of the Anti-Saloon League in Washington, D.C. Courtesy Library of Congress.

Missouri's state prohibition director, William H. Allen, and the St. Louis Police Department each investigated the raid and concluded their men behaved appropriately. Prohibition agents Hogg and Gatter were whisked off to special assignments outside St. Louis. Ulman accused Nations of leading an illegal and unconstitutional raid on his hotel; Nations cited Ulman as the only hotel proprietor who refused to cooperate with prohibition agents in their New Year's raids about town.

The mass meeting was organized by former U.S. District Judge Henry S. Priest, a Westminster Place resident and former president of the Missouri Bar Association who also was president of the AAPA. The AAPA supported modification of the prohibition amendment to allow beer and light wines. Priest was joined by a committee of some of St. Louis's leading businessmen, who introduced resolutions calling for the resignation of Allen and Nations.

Dry attorney Charles M. Hay, who later would run for the U.S. Senate, penned a letter on January 6 to Wayne B. Wheeler, general counsel of the national Anti-Saloon League in Washington, D.C. He implored Wheeler to get in touch with federal prohibition commissioner Roy C. Haynes, the top man in U.S. prohibition enforcement, and "warn him against being misled by any of the influences here." He accused the AAPA and the "wet press" of seeking to arouse public sentiment against the officers who arrested "the maudlin bunch of drunks who committed these outrages."

"A large number of our most prominent and influential citizens, belonging particularly to the upper-crust of our city, assembled at the Chase Hotel, the most fashionable and expensive hostelry in the city on New Year's Eve," Hay wrote. "He [Nations] found a large number of drunken guests and much liquor in evidence. He said the condition prevailing there was the worst that he had found anywhere in the city."

Hay wasn't the only angry dry. Shortly before the mass meeting, Priest received a letter signed "Ku Klux Klan. Chartered."

"Advise the twenty-five gentlemen you have in mind that the meeting will not take place for two reasons, one of which is that almost the entire aggregation represented at the Hotel Chase New Year's Eve was un-American and lawbreakers, and second that not one of them can come into a court of law with clean hands," the letter read. "You need have no fear if you come to the conclusion that you want to be a 100 per cent American and that in the future you will uphold rather than tear down the laws of our government."

Priest, who countered that his group *was* 100 percent American, went ahead with the meeting.

Before it began, however, thirty-three congregations of the Methodist Episcopal Church, South, in St. Louis pledged their support of Nations and Allen. One of the ministers, the Reverend Marvin T. Haw, characterized the Chase revelers as "the mob in decolette" and "parlor bootleggers."

"Officers of the law of the great United States and of the city of St. Louis were hurled from a place made sacred to revellers by $10 per plate," Haw told the congregation of the Shaw Avenue Methodist Episcopal Church on January 8. "Had it been on Sixth street, where the common people were seated at $1 a plate, it would not have been questioned that the Government had the right of inspection, but this was on King's highway and the price was $10 a cover. This always is the philosophy and the attitude of the children of privilege."

Haw compared the New Year's revelers to those at the feast of Belshazzar in Babylon and said both flouted God and law and order to revel in luxuries that included wine.

"The St. Louis revelers outdid their ancient prototypes in that they formed themselves into a mob and howled and fought like savages," Haw said. "Look, St. Louis, on your wounded police, lying prone and battered and besmeared amid the palms of your great West End hotel, and tell us who sinned."

Likewise, the Reverend W. C. Shupp, superintendent of the Missouri Anti-Saloon League, attacked the AAPA as a "mouthpiece of the big breweries" in a speech the same day at Elmbank German Methodist Church, 4433 Elmbank Avenue. Shupp and his organization wielded a great deal of influence with prohibition forces. He filed tips and complaints almost daily with prohibition enforcement agents, and sometimes he accompanied them on raids. Although he was not present at the Chase on New Year's Eve, Shupp himself reportedly said of the raid, "If there had not been ladies present, my man Gatter would have shot up the place." Publicly, he denied making the statement.

"Resist or Die"

"Demand a search warrant" and "resist or die" were the rallying cries of the more than 2,200 guests, mostly men, who packed the auditorium of the Odeon Theater, at Grand Boulevard and Finney Avenue, on January 10, 1923. About two hundred people were turned away, and due to the Klan threats about fifty uniformed policemen were stationed throughout the theater.

They questioned the legality of Nations's blanket search warrant, obtained at 12:20 a.m., January 1, based on violations Nations observed at the hotel three months earlier on October 3, when he saw whiskey and wine at two tables during festivities of the Veiled Prophet Ball. Nations said it was impossible to arrest anyone during the October 3 visit because the chairs at the tables were mostly vacant.

"Gentlemen, I've often wondered how an old German could sit for an hour over one stein of beer," joked attorney Lee Meriwether, one of the speakers, "but I say to you, that the man who had that whiskey Nations saw had it on any German that ever lived."

Priest was more to the point. "No warrant has yet been issued, save by a

What the Volstead Act Prohibited

- the manufacture, sale, advertisement, barter, transportation, or delivery of beverages containing more than 0.5 percent alcohol
- home brewing of beverages containing more than 0.5 percent alcohol
- personal liquor held in warehouses and elsewhere
- hip flasks containing liquor
- the possession of intoxicating beverages, except those the owner had in his own home for his own use, which must have been purchased before July 1, 1919
- the sale of liquor stored in one's home or giving it away, except to members of one's household or bona fide guests

Sixty-sixth Congress of the United States of America;

At the First Session,

Begun and held at the City of Washington on Monday, the nineteenth day of May, one thousand nine hundred and nineteen.

AN ACT

To prohibit intoxicating beverages, and to regulate the manufacture, production, use, and sale of high-proof spirits for other than beverage purposes, and to insure an ample supply of alcohol and promote its use in scientific research and in the development of fuel, dye, and other lawful industries.

Be it enacted by the Senate and House of Representatives of the United States of America in Congress assembled, That the short title of this Act shall be the "National Prohibition Act."

TITLE I.

TO PROVIDE FOR THE ENFORCEMENT OF WAR PROHIBITION.

The term "War Prohibition Act" used in this Act shall mean the provisions of any Act or Acts prohibiting the sale and manufacture of intoxicating liquors until the conclusion of the present war and thereafter until the termination of demobilization, the date of which shall be determined and proclaimed by the President of the United States. The words "beer, wine, or other intoxicating malt or vinous liquors" in the War Prohibition Act shall be hereafter construed to mean any such beverages which contain one-half of 1 per centum or more of alcohol by volume: *Provided,* That the foregoing definition shall not extend to dealcoholized wine nor to any beverage or liquid produced by the process by which beer, ale, porter or wine is produced, if it contains less than one-half of 1 per centum of alcohol by volume, and is made as prescribed in section 37 of Title II of this Act, and is otherwise denominated than as beer, ale, or porter, and is contained and sold in, or from, such sealed and labeled bottles, casks, or containers as the commissioner may by regulation prescribe.

The Volstead Act

tyrannical government, to search you for four bottles of liquor which some man saw on a table three months before," he said.

Haynes, the national prohibition commissioner, conceded that blanket search warrants were not normally used in raids. Nations insisted he was within his rights. Days before the raid, however, Nations told a reporter that there appeared to be some question as to the validity of blanket search warrants. Meriwether urged the audience to resist all future search attempts unless the police or agents could show a warrant authorizing the search. He also questioned the jail terms for Volstead Act violators. "Why," he asked, "they are giving men six months in jail for violating the Volstead act, when every last one of us know that the policemen themselves are going in and drinking it?"

"A faint ripple of consternation agitated for a moment the lines of blue-coated officers who stood in the foyer and along the walls," a *Globe-Democrat* reporter recounted. "One policeman standing near the reporter made a wry face and winked while the crowd laughed."

"Beer-Pickled City"

Miss Fannie D. Robb, secretary of the St. Louis WCTU, blasted Meriwether's speech as "dangerous and inflammatory."

"It would incite very foolish people to resist the law," Robb said. "The whole meeting was un-American, disloyal and anarchistic."

The Reverend Charles McGehee agreed. McGehee later achieved a high standing in the membership ranks of the Ku Klux Klan and was defrocked by the Methodist Church (see Chapter 15). "When the leading men of a community urge resistance to the police the only result can be anarchy and Bolshevism," McGehee said.

Time is on the drys' side, Shupp noted in an address at Maple Avenue Methodist Church. "The brewers see that in a few short years of this sort of thing the drinkers all will be gone," he said. "Then there will be nobody left to fight prohibition."

On January 15, the ministers of the Methodist Episcopal Churches of Greater St. Louis accepted a committee report that concluded there was considerable intoxication among the guests, and that Nations and his deputies were professional and courteous in all seventeen hotels they visited on New Year's Eve. "It is apparent that hardly anything could have happened that has helped prohibition so much in this beer-pickled city of St. Louis as the honest, impartial enforcement of the prohibition law in the West End the same as on Market street by the prohibition agents, as exemplified by the Hotel Chase," Shupp wrote in the Anti-Saloon League's annual report in January 1923.

Public Opinion

As the bickering continued, the *St. Louis Star* took aim at both sides:

We have on the one hand an apotheosis of Gus Nations by the ministers of St. Louis, who are so devoted to the eighteenth amendment that the fourth and fifth mean nothing to them. On the other hand, we have the untempered rage of the ultra-thirsty, who so worship the fourth and fifth amendments that they will lay down their lives in defense of them—against the eighteenth.

Since this discussion of personal rights is put on the direct basis of legality under the constitution, why not test it squarely in the courts? The Star does not believe that the warrant under which Mr. Nations conducted his search at the Chase Hotel will stand a test, fairly applied, in federal court. Furthermore, we believe the sobriety of the nation can be promoted more effectively without such methods of law enforcement, than through them.

Readers of the *Star* lined up on both sides. "This banquet was likened to Belshazzar's feast," Peggy McS. wrote. "Another feast they forgot to mention . . . 'twas the 'Marriage of Cana' in Galilee. . . . Cana was 'dry,' if this story is true, with nothing to drink but H_2O. Of the right and great at that festal board the guest of honor was Christ our Lord, and Christ in his wisdom thought it best that wine be served to each wedding guest. And straightaway He turned the water to wine. . . ."

Joe Laman of East St. Louis disagreed. "St. Louis nearly squealed her head off about the East St. Louis race riots," Laman wrote. "She also made a big to do about the Herrin mine mob [a 1922 massacre of strikebreaking coal miners in Herrin, Illinois], and it was a case of bread and butter for them. But what was at stake for the Hotel Chase mob to fight for—a bunch of drunks who would seek the Turkish bath next day and be boiled out and rubbed down. Which mob had the most justification for its actions?"

On the Stand

Pazdera, one of the shooting victims, filed a $20,000 damage suit against Shupp and St. Louis police detective Edward Sullivan. Daniel Bartlett, the attorney for Sullivan, charged at the taking of depositions January 19 that a conspiracy was afoot at Hotel Chase to resist officers, "even to death." Bartlett alleged that the orchestra played "Hail, Hail, the Gang's All Here" as a pre-arranged signal to guests that dry officers had entered the hotel. He also pledged to "put 2,400 witnesses on the stand—every one who was a guest in the dining-rooms of Hotel Chase on New Year's Eve."

"I hope I live long enough to finish this case," deadpanned Lee Meriwether, Pazdera's attorney.

Witness Herbert H. Piou of University City said, to his knowledge, the orchestra never interrupted a waltz to play "Hail, Hail, the Gang's All Here." Piou testified that he was hit in the eye when he protested to a dry officer who had grabbed his wife by the arm and threatened to arrest her. Piou said he and his wife and two friends had a drink at home before they came to the Chase but did not drink at the hotel. "We men had a high ball, and the ladies had a glass of port," he said.

Shupp, a co-defendant in the suit, soon had larger matters to deal with after investigators for the AAPA testified that Shupp accepted a five-hundred-dollar bribe to endorse a local business owner's application for an alcohol permit (see Chapter 9). During prohibition, companies could handle and dispense alcohol for legal purposes, such as production of extracts, if they secured a permit from prohibition authorities.

One day after he testified in a deposition in the Pazdera suit, on February 1, 1923, Shupp took to his bed at his home on Raymond Avenue with a nervous breakdown. On March 17, he announced his resignation from the Anti-Saloon League, citing health concerns, and said he and his family would be moving from St. Louis to a new home in the country. A day later, Pazdera dropped his suit after Shupp agreed to pay approximately $250 of the $800 in court costs. "By dismissing the case on payment of part of the costs, they virtually confess that the suit was baseless from the beginning," said Charles M. Hay, Shupp's attorney.

Enforcement Easy-Over

Gus Nations left his post in 1924 to enter the Republican primary for state attorney general, and in subsequent years enforcement on New Year's Eve took a more low-key approach. The Hotel Chase raid still was fresh in the minds of residents by New Year's Eve 1926, which was proclaimed the most orderly celebration since prohibition began by Nations's successor, James Dillon. Names were taken, and certain persons were asked to report to the Federal Building the following Monday, but no arrests were made. Twelve bottles that had been left out in plain sight on tables were confiscated from Marigold Gardens, Bevo Mill, Mission Inn, the Gatesworth Hotel, and Congress Hotel.

A U.S. commissioner had ruled not long before that no single person could be charged with possession in an instance in which several persons were sitting about a bottle and each disclaimed ownership. "New Year's is a time when persons who ordinarily are strict observers of the law bow to a custom of ages," Dillon said. "Unquestionably there was a lot of drinking, but there was very little drunkenness."

On New Year's Eve 1928, federal agents on their tour of roadhouses seized and smashed two hundred bottles that were plainly exposed and wrote down the names of obstreperous guests, "just to scare them," Dillon said. At the Forest Park Hotel, the orchestra began playing "Hail, Hail, the Gang's All Here" as the twelve uninvited guests arrived.

By December 1930, the hotel hip flask seizures were history, federal prohibition director Colonel Amos W. W. Woodcock declared. Instead of frisking individual violators, agents were ordered to concentrate their efforts on commercial dealers.

"Nobody before or since I had the prohibition office went after the millionaires and the big hotels," Nations observed to a reporter in 1926. "They haven't forgotten [the Chase raid]."

CHAPTER 2
HOW DRY WE ARE

PERHAPS SPOT SENSED WHAT WAS AHEAD FOR ST. LOUIS, OR PERHAPS HE WAS A poor judge of speeding vehicles. The ten-year-old canine met an untimely end under the wheels of a truck at Eleventh and Gratiot streets in downtown St. Louis on June 30, 1919, the day before wartime prohibition took effect. He had been the faithful companion of Joe Biersinger, stableman at the Hyde Park Brewery, the *Post-Dispatch* eulogized:

> *It is said of dog Spot that he was almost human in some ways. For one thing he went daily from the stable to the tap at the brewery for a glass of beer, and after having refreshed himself, was prepared for a bout with anything on four legs that happened along his way.*
>
> *Continuing to predict calamitous situations as a result of the ban on liquor, despondent brewery workers who saw the dog killed declare that dog Spot possibly sensed an impossible situation in living without beer and rather than lead a mere dog's life, destroyed himself.*

ENTERING THE "TWILIGHT ZONE"

Spot could thank Congress for the various prohibition acts and declarations, of which there were several. The Lever Food and Fuel Control Act, effective in 1917, closed all distilleries in the interest of wartime food conservation and empowered the president to prohibit the manufacture of beer and wine. Under pressure from prohibitionists, President Woodrow Wilson in September 1918 issued a presidential decree that restricted the grains brewers could use after October 1, 1918, and prohibited the use of food materials in manufacturing by breweries after December 1, 1918. Wilson later amended the proclamation to permit the use of grain in the manufacture for sale of non-intoxicating liquors, such as "near-beers."

The "twilight zone of prohibition," as *The New York Times* called it, was prompted by Congress's passage of a wartime prohibition act in November 1918. It took effect on July 1, 1919, eight months after the Allied Nations and Germany signed their armistice, and prohibited the manufacture or sale for beverage purposes of beer, wine, and other malt or vinous intoxicating liquors, except for export. It left up for grabs, however, the definition of "intoxicating"

Missouri Governor Frederick D. Gardner signs the national prohibition amendment following ratification by the Missouri legislature in January 1919. Standing behind him are, from left, the Reverend Dr. W.C. Shupp, superintendent of the Missouri Anti-Saloon League; Mrs. Shupp; Miss Bessie Shupp; Secretary Williams (no first name on photo ID); Secretary of State R.E.L. Marrs; and the Hon. J.W. Thompson, superintendent of insurance for the state. Photo by Carl Deeg. Used by permission, State Historical Society of Missouri, Columbia.

and failed to provide a means by which it could be enforced.

In October 1919, the Volstead Act, the enforcing arm of the wartime prohibition act and the Eighteenth Amendment, made the definition clear: It was illegal to transport, manufacture, or sell any beverage with more than 0.5 percent alcohol. Wilson, aggravated by the drys' ambitious measures to lower the lid in advance of constitutional prohibition, vetoed the measure on October 27, 1919.

The U.S. Senate overrode the veto the next day and gave a standing ovation to Wayne B. Wheeler, America's leading prohibitionist and the general counsel for the Anti-Saloon League of America. The league, a well-heeled lobbying organization composed of dry businessmen and Protestant churches, drafted the Volstead Act and played a pivotal role in the adoption of prohibition by state legislatures.

Constitutional prohibition, or the Eighteenth Amendment, took effect January 16, 1920, though the wheels had been set in motion one year earlier: Illinois was the twenty-sixth state to ratify the amendment on January 14, 1919; Nebraska was the thirty-sixth and deciding state on January 16; and Missouri was the thirty-seventh state, also on January 16.

Between wartime and constitutional prohibition, St. Louis and some surrounding areas enjoyed varying degrees of dampness as brewers filed legal challenges as to whether beverages of 2.75 percent alcohol were intoxicating. Others braced for dry times.

FINAL FLING

Across the country, mourners held funeral celebrations for "John Barleycorn," including St. Louis's Liederkranz Club, Sunset Hills Country Club, and the University Club, which held a four-day wake. The Riverview Club hosted its funeral north of the Chain of Rocks Bridge on Saturday, June 28, 1919. It featured a real coffin filled with a demijohn of liquor, a red wig, and a suit of clothes. Wreaths of flowers, a wreath of pretzels, and a pair of skates decorated the affair. After the coffin was buried in a real grave at midnight, a quartet sang "How Dry I Am" and "Pickle My Bones in Alcohol." More than three hundred guests attended, including several city officials.

In St. Louis, the bar trade easily was surpassed by the package liquor business as residents stocked up for dry times. The owner of four saloons downtown reported $20,000 in sales on June 30, much of it in package liquor. The last night's celebration may have been too much for Joseph Klein of 1515 Mallinckrodt Street. Klein was found dead July 1 on a bench in Hyde Park, at Blair Avenue and Salisbury Street, with an empty gallon whiskey jug and pint wine flask at his side.

In East St. Louis, some saloonkeepers announced plans to try the soft drink business, although their future drink offerings weren't very soft. East St. Louis was, and would continue to be, known for the corruption of its public officials and its wide-open liquor sales.

In Boonville, Missouri, thirsty patrons spent $25,000 at the saloons June 28 and 30 and waited in line approximately fifteen minutes for a refill. "This is one reason why there was as little drunkenness as there was on the streets both Saturday and Monday," the *Central Missouri Republican* pointed out. "The crowd was so thick that a person could not get one drink right after another."

NOT ALWAYS AN OUTCAST

Liquor was a valued commodity when American Revolutionary War veteran John Sappington settled in south St. Louis County in 1805. A gallon of whiskey, worth $1.25 in precious cash, was the going rate for an acre of land, and tradition has it Sappington paid with whiskey for the nearly two thousand acres of land he purchased in what is now Affton, Sappington, and a portion of Webster Groves.

The temperance movement in America picked up speed with the efforts of the Women's Christian Temperance Union (WCTU), founded in 1874, and the Anti-Saloon League of America, founded in 1895. The support of progressive reformers and populist politicians such as William Jennings Bryan helped gain converts. "The prohibitionists had been skillful and persistent as they attacked on the two grounds of personal health and the health of society," Louis G. Geiger noted in his paper "In the Days of Prohibition: Cooper County, 1919–1934." "They hammered away relentlessly also on the social effects of drink: crime, broken homes, abused and neglected children, the poverty-ridden families of men who drank away their pay checks in saloons—the so-called 'poor men's clubs.' Although the opponents of the 'demon rum' exaggerated, blaming it for every imaginable social ill, there was more than a little truth in their charges."

The German-American Alliance of St. Louis in 1910 opened fire on the prohibition movement, attacking it as a violation of the principle of personal liberty. Many businessmen, city officials, and newspaper editors believed prohibition would succeed only in draining community tax revenues. "St. Charles derives approximately $8,000 a year in the form of saloon licenses and this would have to be made up—how?" asked a local newspaper in 1917.

But the tide of support was turning in outstate areas, due to intense lobbying by the WCTU and Anti-Saloon League and local option laws in Illinois and Missouri. In Illinois, 220 towns, cities, and villages had voted dry by 1918, including the state capital, Springfield. By 1917 in Missouri, ninety-six counties were dry and only nineteen wet. St. Louis was one of a few holdouts: In 1916, a state prohibition referendum was approved nearly statewide—even by Jackson County, which includes Kansas City. St. Louis voters furnished 127,000 votes against it, enough to turn the tide. Methodists, Baptists, and some Presbyterians favored prohibition, while most Catholics and Lutherans and some Episcopalians opposed it.

Republicans and Democrats each had their wet and dry factions, with exceptions. In big cities such as St. Louis, just about all of the politicians were wet and, outstate, many were dry. Middle- and upper-class suburbanites and small-town dwellers were usually dry, and trade unions and immigrants wet. The immigrants often were unable to vote.

THE FOREIGN ELEMENT

Fear of immigrants in general helped convince many to support prohibition. As Audrey Olson of the Sisters of St. Joseph of Carondelet pointed out, reformers had hounded St. Louis's large German population since 1846, when a local law was passed that restricted the Sunday movements of immigrants. Nativist Americans looked askance at the Germans' Sunday picnics, festivals, and beer garden gatherings. "The law they passed prohibited the only means of public transportation from operating after 2 p.m.," Olson noted in a dissertation. "One Sunday on a Fourth of July in the 1850's, Heinrich Bornstein and his liberal German followers led a parade to the picnic grove. They formed lines at six o'clock in the morning in order to avoid a clash with the native Americans and the Irish who threatened to break up the parade, and to avoid any interference with church services. . . . After reaching the picnic grounds without any serious mishap, they listened to their Fourth of July orators and spent the rest of the day enjoying gemutlichkeit. The following day the English press moaned over the godlessness of the 'Dutch.'"

Many evangelical Protestants regarded drinking as sinful, while beer and wine were culinary traditions in German, Italian, and eastern European households, many of them Catholic.

"Everything that has been said about the Mexicans and the Muslims today was said about the Poles and Greeks a hundred years ago," said Gary R. Mormino, author of the book *Immigrants on the Hill: Italian-Americans in St. Louis, 1882–1982* and professor of history at the University of South Florida. "This is an old theme in American history, the fear of outsiders." The passage of prohibition was followed the next year by an immigration restriction act that set quotas, Mormino noted. More legislation followed, and by 1927, immigration was limited to about 150,000 per year. Between 1840 and 1920, by contrast, an average of 500,000 immigrants entered the country each year.

DENS OF INIQUITY

"Please, Father—dear Father—come home with me now.
The clock in the steeple strikes one.
You said you were coming right home from the shop,
As soon as your day's work was done.
Our fire is all out, and our house is all dark,
And Mother's set watching since tea.
Poor brother Ben is so sick in her arms,
And no one to help her but me."
—Old temperance song

The saloon, oft-cited in temperance literature and songs, could play havoc with a workman's salary, sobriety, and health. In worst-case scenarios wives and children were beaten, homes were broken, families left destitute. Even well-run operations were criticized for their connections with machine politics. "Rural America viewed alcohol as primarily a problem of urban life where drinking took place in saloons," David E. Kyvig observed in *Daily Life in the United States, 1920–1940.* "There, rural dwellers believed, saloon keepers encouraged drinking to excess, workers spent wages that should have been going to support their families, political machines influenced voters, prostitutes and gamblers plied their trades, and immigrants gathered to discuss the homeland, speak their native languages, and carry on old customs that slowed their progress toward becoming good Americans. These negative images help explain why the largest, most influential prohibitionist organization called itself the Anti-Saloon League of America."

In 1881, the editor of the *Paris (Missouri) Monroe County Appeal* outlined the abuses of the local saloon: "The *Sturgeon Leader* says they have four saloons in that village and that they are doing good business," the *Appeal* intoned. "This may be so, but we'll bet a cent that their customers are not doing very well, or at least their families are not in as good fix as the saloon keepers. Did you ever think about what a darned fool the average dram drinker is? He spends two or three dollars a week at the saloon, the saloon man and his family dress well and ride in a carriage, while the poor devils who keep them up wear old clothes, live on sow-belly and walk, if they go at all. If this picture ain't true, we hope to go to heaven in a week."

The quintessential saloon-buster, Carrie Nation, was raised in Cass County, Missouri, and endured an unhappy life. She was married briefly to an alcoholic physician who died just six months after the birth of their daughter, and she entered into another unhappy marriage before she took to dismantling bars at the turn of the twentieth century. As her fame grew, Nation took to selling purse-sized copies of the nickel-plated hatchets she used in her saloon-wrecking career, and she later preached the cause of prohibition onstage at theaters on the eastern vaudeville circuit.

A crowd of five hundred gathered on the night of July 5, 1901, after Nation was stopped by a bartender and patrolman as she headed for the front door of the Oheim Brothers' saloon on Walnut Street in St. Louis. She upbraided police for not putting down the liquor traffic as she was conveyed by patrol wagon to the central district station. Nation later left for Crawfordsville, Indiana, where she was to stand trial for attempting to wreck a saloon.

St. Louis—along with Leavenworth, Kansas—had a bar named for Car-

Post-Dispatch *newsboys pose in 1910 at their headquarters, next door to a saloon at Tenth and Cass streets in St. Louis. Courtesy Library of Congress.*

rie Nation in those days, and drinks that packed a wallop were named for her, Robert L. Brown observed in *Saloons of the American West*. She also inspired folks such as a Mrs. Veatch of Keytesville, Missouri, who in 1904 exacted revenge on a restaurant keeper who sold her son intoxicating cider, causing him to get drunk. Mrs. Veatch "compelled a restaurant keeper, at the point of a revolver, to roll a keg of cider onto the walk, where she busted out the head of the keg with an ax, and who was later arrested for disturbing the peace," a local newspaper reported. She was found guilty in Squire Wheeler's court and fined twenty dollars and costs.

On the Meramec River in present-day Kirkwood, the four saloons of the popular Meramec Highlands resort area made it off-limits to many Kirkwood kids, Kirkwood historian and author James F. Baker observed in his book, *Glimpses of Meramec Highlands.* The area was characterized by God-fearing middle-class residents as a "den of iniquity."

"During portions of the late 1800s and early 1900s, neighboring Kirkwood was a 'dry' town with no saloons allowed within city limits," Baker wrote. "As a result a number of saloons, such as Repetto Saloon at the Highlands, sprung up within easy traveling distance for 'thirsty' Kirkwood residents.

"The character of the Highlands' drinkers prior to the arrival of the streetcar

Carrie Nation. Courtesy Library of Congress.

lines has not been well documented. However, once the masses from the city discovered the cheap streetcar fares to the resort, drinking became more frequent and customers more boisterous. A July 27, 1902, entry in the *County Watchman* noted the arrest of a streetcar rider, 'filled with "fighting whiskey" at Meramec Highlands.'"

In 1929, a *Post-Dispatch* reporter remembered a couple of decades earlier when the St. Louis levee was lively with the arrival of packet boats and the bustle of businesses, hotels, boarding houses, stores, and saloons—five in one block alone. "There was Burke's place on Washington avenue and Levee street and a great many other Irish names over bars along the street," the reporter wrote. "Within these places the boatmen drowned their cares with old-fashioned lager, good whiskey and the many wines and vintages which were displayed prominently behind the bars. All this resulted in much gayety and occasionally in brawls, but seldom in anything of a serious nature."

Closer to prohibition, shootings and misdeeds in St. Louis saloons were reported frequently in newspapers. On January 6, 1920, former Democratic politician and professional bondsman Charles Thompson's saloon was raided at 1048 N. Vandeventer Avenue. Twenty warrants charging burglary, larceny, highway robbery, and receipt of stolen property were issued against Thompson's bartender and others. One day earlier, Dan Hammond, a bartender in Terry Jackson's saloon at Mississippi and Chouteau avenues, was fatally shot after he interfered in a fight. The twenty-three-year-old Hammond had been cited for

A saloon on Ste. Genevieve's Main Street, circa 1891. Courtesy Missouri State Archives.

gallantry in action one year earlier while serving with U.S. armed forces near Remonville, France.

While on the mark in some instances, the rap on saloons was undeserved in others, especially in neighborhoods with large immigrant populations. Many German beer saloons were considered as innocuous as the corner grocery and attracted entire families who sang and played cards and other games. An editorial writer in the early years of the twentieth century described beer gardens in St. Louis in David Detjen's book *The Germans in Missouri, 1900–1918:* "They sit in family and friendly groups, talking away the hours before bedtime," he wrote. "Some patrons have their supper in these gardens. The men smoke and . . . drink a little beer. The women generally drink pop and lemonade. . . . The people who go to the scores of little summer gardens do not get drunk."

Former U.S. Senator George H. Williams, R-Missouri, testified before a House committee in 1930 that the pre-prohibition saloon in St. Louis was a respectable family tradition. Saloons were owned by influential members of the community who, like their customers, were good citizens who attended church regularly. "It was an employment agency, a political clearinghouse, a place for social networking," Mormino said. "It wasn't just a place you'd go and drink. Every neighborhood in St. Louis had saloons. To be sure, alcohol created tremendous problems for Americans. It's no accident that the most fervent [temperance] advocates came from the Great Plains and the Midwest. Women were especially victimized by abusive husbands, but this did not seem to be a problem [for Italians] on the Hill."

Immigrant workers in the Atlas Portland Cement Company's new mill town of Ilasco, Missouri, caught the attention of native-born temperance advocates in the early years of the twentieth century. The Romanian, Slovak, Italian, Hungarian, and other residents found drinking offered a temporary escape from cultural isolation, family separation, and loneliness, noted Gregg Andrews, author of *City of Dust: A Cement Company Town in the Land of Tom Sawyer.* In a town without a bank, saloonkeepers fulfilled a financial service by cashing paychecks and making short-term loans to patrons. For the purchase of a nickel beer, they also provided a free lunch. "For many workers, this became a major daily source of food," Andrews wrote. "Alcohol reformers like Rev. Thomas Wallace complained about the number of children entering Ilasco's saloons each day, but many of these children may have gone there, in part, to take advantage of their father's 'free lunch.'"

PATRIOTIC PLUNDER

Wartime fervor gave the prohibition movement its final push toward victory, noted G. K. Renner in the *Missouri Historical Review*. "It had the effect of adding one more cause, patriotism, to the many emotional factors already fueling the movement and it reinforced the more rational arguments in favor of the greater efficiency of the working man and soldier as well as a new one: saving food," Renner wrote.

PORTRAIT OF A SALOONKEEPER

When Joseph L. Schuler, St. Louis's "marrying justice," passed away on December 7, 1929, the *Post-Dispatch* ran a colorful obituary of the long-time justice of the peace and his earlier days as owner of a saloon opposite the Four Courts at the southeast corner of Eleventh Street and Clark Avenue downtown. Schuler was described as a kindly, dapper man whose haunts were anything but dirty. In fact, of the row of saloons that lined Clark, Schuler's was considered one of the two best, along with Schweickardt's at the southwest corner of Twelfth and Clark. "He was a dispenser of counsel with his beer, of aid with his free lunch," the *Post* noted. "Jury warrants and witness fees were cashed in Clark avenue saloons which were the rendezvous of lawyers, reporters, attaches of courts and police headquarters, visitors to the adjacent jail. More than once a winning attorney stood the drinks for judge, jury, and opposing counsel. "Some of his 'sales appeal' was quiet and decency, due in part, to the Schuler disposition, but possibly more to the frequent presence of the Schuler women-folk. And political St. Louis knew Mrs. Schuler's pies well and favorably."

Public resentment and harassment of German American residents and institutions peaked during World War I. Outstate, residents of Hermann, Missouri, and other German strongholds were regarded with suspicion and outright harassment, even though they had sent their share of soldiers to war. In St. Louis, the St. Louis Symphony stopped performing the works of German composers, Berlin Avenue in the Central West End was renamed Pershing, Kaiser Street in south St. Louis was renamed Gresham Avenue, and many German customs came to an end. "On the citizens' level self-appointed 'Hun-Watchers' listened for pro-German remarks on streetcars, in the streets and parks, and at work, seeking ammunition for prosecution under the Espionage Act or for vigilante action," James Neal Primm noted in his history of St. Louis, *Lion of the Valley.* "William Stiefer, a streetcar motorman, was forced by his co-workers to stand on a table and give three cheers for Wilson and three for America, curse the Kaiser, and kiss the American flag. He was alleged to have predicted a German victory and to have carried a newspaper that reported the capture of some American troops."

The greatest aid to the temperance movement, Renner noted, was the German background of the brewing interests. "They were vulnerable on this point and opened themselves to further criticism by buying influence in newspapers and intervening in newspaper campaigns," he wrote. "They were probably no worse in this respect than the prohibitionists, but the latter could easily identify their activities with a good cause, whereas the brewers could not avoid the opposite label."

Savvy brewers such as August A. Busch hedged their bets. Busch's father, Adolphus, had taken prohibitionists seriously from the beginning and referred to them as the "long-haired men and short-haired women of the temperance movement." In 1916, Busch instructed his department heads to plan for eventual conversion of the plant, valued at $30.8 million. But he also did his best to convince the public that the company was patriotic and that beer was a temperance drink. The brewery launched items such as Malt-Nutrine, a nutritional supplement for new mothers, and Bevo (from *Pivo*, the Bohemian word for beer), a checked-fermentation product containing less than 0.5 percent alcohol. Busch also opened the Bevo Mill at Gravois Avenue and Morganford Road in south St. Louis in 1917 to prove that a classy restaurant could be operated without a bar, if good food and drink were served at the table. The windmill-reproduction restaurant was built with forty-eight-inch-thick exterior walls of stone and stucco at its base, embedded with rocks collected at the Busch home, Grant's Farm. Waitresses dressed in Dutch clothes and wooden shoes served customers on opening day. It became a popular dining spot, though it failed to prevent prohibition.

An advertisement for Bevo, Anheuser-Busch's near-beer.

Anheuser-Busch discontinued the production of Bevo near-beer at the height of its popularity in December 1918 due to "patriotic duty," a large ad in the *Chicago Tribune* explained. The manufacturing shutdown was in response to the proclamation by President Wilson, which required brewers to cut the alcohol content and the use of "foodstuffs," or malted barley, in the product, said brewery historians Kevin Kious and Donald Roussin.

The United States Brewers' Association and its Missouri counterpart, the St. Louis Brewers' Association, were active in Missouri. The St. Louis organization began its efforts in 1881 when it circulated an anti-prohibition pamphlet, and it kept up the momentum during the 1910, 1916, and 1918 state referendums.

Closer to the passage of the Eighteenth Amendment, the Missouri chapter of the Association Against the Prohibition Amendment (AAPA) became active. Composed mostly of business and professional men, it had been founded nationally in 1918 by Captain William H. Stayton, a Washington lawyer and former naval officer who had no financial interest in liquor or political aspirations. The AAPA, which favored the continued legalization of beer and light wines, commissioned a tearjerker of a play in St. Louis called *The Passing of Hans Dippel*, which portrayed a goodhearted saloonkeeper whose business was ruined by the drys.

The drys painted the AAPA as a trade organization representing mostly brewers, which they saw as the bane of society. Others agreed with the tem-

The Bevo Mill in south St. Louis during construction in 1916.

perance goal but never believed that light wines and beer would be outlawed. When they realized their mistake it was too late. Others in the working-class and immigrant communities had no say, and many in rural areas were used to "dry" conditions locally. "Consumers were inherently difficult to organize, one prohibition scholar suggested, particularly since they assumed that the liquor industry, with its wealth and apparent influence, could easily protect itself," David E. Kyvig noted in his book *Repealing National Prohibition.*

On a Roll

The teetotalers were on a roll in areas such as Howard County, Missouri, which had voted itself dry in 1908 and again in 1912 by local option. Despite their gains, temperance advocates felt a continual annoyance from their Cooper County neighbors in wet Boonville, also known as the Vine Clad City. "Were it not for the booze in Boonville, New Franklin like other towns we have read about could boast of not having any use for a calaboose [jail] since local option has predominated but until booze has been eliminated from Boonville we cannot conscientiously make this statement," wrote the editor of the *New Franklin News.* "Then too it is rather embarassing for those of us who are total abstainers because when you are seen going to Boonville some good old sister is sure to make the remark that so and so is going to Boonville to get tanked up."

Founded largely by ministers, the Anti-Saloon League had focused on the abuses in saloons initially, then directed its efforts toward a larger audience. "Moderate drinkers and total abstainers, who balked at the idea of absolute prohibition, were willing to admit that the American saloon had become a noisome thing," wrote Peter Odegard in his book *Pressure Politics: The Story of the Anti-Saloon League.*

During the Wilson administration, the organization shifted its focus to complete prohibition and, from early on, was a success. The league had begun an appeal to manufacturers and businessmen for contributions by 1910, and by the time of prohibition it was firmly entrenched from a financial and lobbying standpoint. To the surprise of many, the Eighteenth Amendment was ratified quickly. "The grip held by the Anti-Saloon League over the state legislatures was never better illustrated than the manner in which these bodies obeyed the command to ratify," noted the 1919 *Year Book of the United States Brewers' Association.* "In vain were suggestions made that the lawmaking bodies were without instructions from the people on this important question," recalled St. Louisan Horace Gruman in 1927: "If a person ever let it be known that he was a 'wet,' he was marked as a pro-German and working against the goverment."

By the time the American Women's Council of Justice called a mass meeting on prohibition in January 1920, it was too late. The Eighteenth Amendment was the work of "hysterical women and emotional men," Mrs. Thomas Swinney, president of the council, told a crowd of one thousand people at the Odeon at Grand Boulevard and Finney Avenue in St. Louis. She was joined by ninety-year-

FASHIONS ON A BENDER

In her *Post-Dispatch* women's page column, "Maxims of a Modern Maid," Marguerite Mooers Marshall spoke of upcoming "dry styles" and of hopes that husbands would loosen their purse strings on fashions for their "better halves," now that they wouldn't be spending it on booze. "Now that home entertaining will be the rule—for the obvious reason that almost every one at present has something at home to entertain with—women will wear more beautiful and elegant frocks than they have chosen in years," Marshall opined. "The setting will be perfect, and the wearer of a lovely evening gown will know that every other woman present will be able to study and analyze her costume to its last flawless detail. So the standard in dressing will be higher."

old Emilene Tucker of 3840 Windsor Place, who called prohibition "a great mistake." "As I view it," said Miss Emille Sweeney, secretary of the organization, "prohibitionists are divided into three distinctive classes. They are the parents whose son, through their own fault, has become a drunkard; the reformed drunkard, and the misguided persons, who trace the great evils to drink."

"The theory that man mistreats his wife and children just because he drinks is without foundation," she added. "A man that does that would do it if he never touched liquor. If the millions that are being spent by the Anti-Saloon League were given to the poor instead of being used as they are, a greater good could be accomplished."

THE END

By midnight on January 16, 1920, everyone was dry, at least in theory. The WCTU hosted a service of praise and thanksgiving that morning at the YWCA at 1411 Locust Street in St. Louis.

"Gloom Day," as one of the Washington, Missouri, papers called January 17, followed more hoarding, more stocking up, more funerals for John Barleycorn, in the style of the previous summer. Some men in Washington were accused of making stills out of their wives' cookstoves, and tears were shed at Pete Bopp's Courthouse Buffet in Clayton. At nearby Autenrieth's bar, the beer barrel "spit" at 10:30, and a barrel of the near-beer Bevo was tapped in its place. "Many of the celebrants gulped it down under the impression it was the real thing, but the old "beer hounds" could not be fooled and they ordered bottle beer or switched to whiskey and soda," journalist and author Dickson Terry reported in *Clayton: A History.* "But these cost 25 cents and the working man could not afford it so they wended their way home muttering about a cold, hard world and a country that would take your personal liberty away."

They needn't have fretted too much. By August 1920, 60 percent of St. Louis's 1,023 saloons would still be open, many operating as soft-drink parlors. Half of them sold liquor in violation of the law.

A Missouri State Penitentiary inmate, working at the governor's mansion, took a final fling with alcohol after stealing a bottle of perfume and some hair tonic that belonged to Governor Frederick Dozier Gardner and his wife, Jeannette. Gardner, apparently, had nothing more palatable to steal. The prisoner was captured "several miles from town, very sick and very drunk, and quite willing to return to the confines of the cold, gray walls," Mrs. Gardner said.

In Peoria, Illinois, formerly the largest distilling center in the nation and the fourth city for production of malt liquors, some manufacturers turned to the production of smokeless gunpowder from solvents of celluloid and butanol. On a more somber note, Joseph Lyttle, vice president of St. Louis's oldest grocer, David Nicholson at 13 and 15 N. Sixth Street, announced February 6 that the business would close that spring, as prohibition made operations unprofitable. Founded in 1843, the business specialized in rare, unusual, and imported liquors and liqueurs. Across town, in the tap room of the University Club, some thirty-five members sipped tea out of china cups and munched wafers. There was no "treating," or buying rounds, and there were few repeat orders, waiters reported.

The city's drunk tank and its five cells were closed in the old city hall building at Eleventh and Market streets. Only two guests had been entertained there in the twelve days after prohibition took effect. The three turnkeys and three policemen on staff had been biding their time playing pinochle, Police Chief Martin O'Brien reported on January 28. Future guests were taken to the police holdover or the city hospital.

Arrests were slow, at first. Frank T. Digges, chief enforcement agent for Missouri, said thirty deputies had roamed from saloon to saloon in St. Louis on January 17 but found no violations. Henry Koch, the first violator of constitutional prohibition, pleaded guilty February 2 to selling intoxicating drinks on January 19 at his former saloon at 220 S. Fourth Street and was assessed a $500 fine by U.S. District Judge Charles Faris. By his comments, Faris did not appear to be thrilled with the law. But he had a job to do, he said on January 23 as he fined Galvino Lange, who had pleaded guilty to selling a drink of whiskey at his saloon at 6655 Manchester Avenue, on September 1, 1919, to a policeman disguised as a streetcar motorman. "No matter what we may think of the law, it is the law, and we must abide by it," said Faris, who would dole out many more sentences as the years progressed. "I will not be disposed to deal so leniently as this with cases of violation of the constitutional enforcement law."

Julius A. P. Lillie, a twenty-nine-year-old German immigrant, just couldn't take it. Lillie, caretaker of the clubhouse of the American Car and Foundry Company in Fenton, had been despondent over the advent of prohibition, his wife told police. At 4 p.m. on January 31, 1920, he ended his life with a gunshot to the head.

More Precious Than Gold

Liquor thefts were common as prohibition took hold. Mrs. John Antosiak, wife of a former saloonkeeper, was knocked down by four liquor thieves who emerged from the basement of her home at 4615 S. Compton Avenue in St. Louis on

February 7. The robbers carried away ten cases of whiskey half-pints, eleven cases of whiskey quarts, and three cases of beer valued at $2,108.

The *Webster News-Times* told of four gallons of whiskey, a case of champagne, and a fifteen-gallon cask of wine stolen from the home of Dr. F. J. Guilbault at 614 Mildred Avenue. Burglars entered the basement by forcing open a window. "This should be a warning to the 100 or more Websterites who have barrels and cases of the heavier than water product to have a special alarm installed in their cellars," warned the *News-Times*. Yet another Websterite, this one anonymous, had his liquor stolen before he got it home. He had invested in a barrel of the best whiskey from friends in the liquor business for $600. Although he guarded it carefully on the trip home, he opened it to find water, then readily available for 10 cents per thousand gallons, the *News-Times* reported on January 9, 1920.

On February 10, burglars depleted the "private stock" of Morris L. Friedman, president of the Friedman Loan & Mercantile Co., at 4212 W. Pine Avenue. They broke through four doors and picked a patent lock before they reached the wine cellar in the basement. They carried away five cases of champagne and ten cases of whiskey valued at $1,500 and couldn't wait to sample it. A bottle half-filled with whiskey was found in the area between the garage and a fence. Later that year, on August 13, thieves with a more cosmopolitan bent made off with a trunk containing Russian socialistic literature from the basement of J. Reifler, 7325 Clayton Avenue. To make the read more comfortable, they also took twenty-two bottles of wine, a three-gallon jug of whiskey, a one-gallon jug of whiskey, a quart bottle of Prunelle brandy, two bottles of champagne, and a lady's tan coat.

With tongue firmly in cheek, a *Post-Dispatch* editorial writer questioned the next step for his "prohibition friends." "We direct their attention to the pretzel," read the January 15 commentary. "Is there anything inherently vicious in the pretzel? they may ask. Possibly not. But its traditions, environment, association are sinister. One might say, bar sinister. In the pure, delectable world which the prohibition philosophy conceives, there is no niche for the pretzel. . . . 'The pretzel must go.'"

LUBRICATING THE LAW

Taylorville, Illinois, attorney Samuel Taylor recalled in 1986 the story of an Irish American attorney named John Hogan in pre-prohibition days. Hogan, the story went, came out of a local Taylorville saloon at 11 a.m. and met a society lady. Taylor, born in 1910, recounted her reaction: "'Why, Mr. Hogan, do I see you coming out of a saloon at eleven o'clock in the morning?' John tipped his hat and says, 'Well, Mrs. So and So, you wouldn't want me to stay in there all day, would you?'"

CHAPTER 3
HOMETOWN HOOCH ADVENTURES

ONE NIGHT, AS HE AND HIS JOURNALIST FRIENDS SAT AROUND DRINKING HOME brew, a photographer for the local newspaper told his tragic story. "He was an excellent photographer and a diligent worker, yet we all knew that he had been fired and sent forth in disgrace from a newspaper in another city," explained Dickson Terry, a St. Louis author and journalist, in a 1964 article for *St. Louis Magazine*. "But we didn't know why. . . ."

The photographer, it seemed, had started a new batch of home brew in his darkroom, which was directly above the publisher's office. He went out of town and was gone longer than expected. One day the publisher noticed something dripping. "The sun was shining and there wasn't a cloud in the sky," Terry wrote. "He returned to his work, and about then the plaster separated itself from the ceiling, and the publisher's desk was flooded with home brew. We were saddened by the photographer's fate, but at the same time we always felt it was worth it. A job was just a job, but in those days home brew was considered one of the essentials of life."

Despite prohibition, liquor remained an essential of life in and around St. Louis. Home-brewed beer brightened up early meetings of the Richmond Heights City Council, and whiskey helped pay the fare to ride the river ferry near Alton, Illinois. Even college professors in Columbia, Missouri, indulged in the illicit fruits of the Volstead Act. "The story is told of a University professor who received regular shipments of wines and liquor from another county under the label of 'books,'" journalist Irene Taylor wrote in the *Columbia Missourian*. "The freight agent of the railroad called him one day and said, 'Your shipment of books is leaking. What shall I do with it?'"

Prohibition brought the Great Depression to the city of St. Louis a decade early, historian NiNi Harris noted. St. Louis was the city that made Missouri the seventh-largest state in the nation in the production of beer. The Depression also came early to the wine-growing German communities around the Missouri River and the grape-growing areas of Illinois.

During the early years of prohibition, the bottom fell out of the post–

World War I economic boom and cut by nearly two-thirds the prices farmers received for their goods at a time when most communities were rural. St. Louis County, for instance, was home to 10,480 milk cows and 20,000 hogs in 1925. One St. Louis County Farm Bureau member, C. F. Overfield, kept an award-winning flock of four hundred white leghorn chickens at his home at 717 Lilac Avenue in Webster Groves. "The farmer is now getting pre-war prices, but his dollar is only worth 38 cents as compared with the pre-war prices of things he must buy," explained the *St. Louis County Watchman-Advocate* in 1922. And his income dropped: He received only 40 cents for a bushel of corn in 1921, for instance, compared with 70 cents a bushel in 1913.

In Illinois, the value of all crops during the ten-year period from 1921 to 1930 dropped to $371,542 from $503,437 in 1911–1920. They dropped again, to $271,268, from 1931 to 1940.

Those conditions did not improve much as the twenties progressed, while the prices farmers paid—for feed, fertilizer, machinery, transportation, and taxes—continued to climb. Some farmers lost their land, and the value of Missouri farm property dropped 40 percent by the late 1920s. In St. Louis County, the number of farms decreased from 3,735 on January 1, 1920, to 3,089 on April 1, 1930. In St. Louis City, there were 244 farms on January 1, 1920, and 46 on April 1, 1930.

"To supplement the family income a lot of [residents] turned to this moonshining and bootlegging," Jefferson County historian Della Lang noted. Others—especially those in ethnic communities—refused to give up the beer, wine, and cider that had been the backbone of family traditions and get-togethers. "These people were proud to be Americans, but prohibition, that was not American," Harris summed up the outlook. "They just did not accept it . . . the issue was not obeying the law: it was, how are you going to survive the law?"

Longtime Illinois legislator Martin B. Lohmann used the term "wetter than the Mississippi River" to describe Tazewell County during prohibition, but the moniker applied equally to St. Louis and much of the bi-state area. "That early-morning mist hanging over the valleys of Jefferson County, that wasn't mist at all; it was smoke rising from the moonshiners' still," Lang observed.

Booze—and boozing—were so prolific that after he injured his nose in 1924, attorney Carl M. Dubinsky felt the need to explain to those in the St. Louis Municipal Courts Building who asked about the adhesive tape he wore over the bridge of his nose. "I fell on a washstand and broke it," read a card Dubinsky handed to the curious. "Doctor says my profile will not be changed. Was sober."

From 1914 to 1919, St. Louis Health Commissioner Max Starkloff reported, City Hospital treated 8,181 alcoholics. From 1920 to 1925, it treated 14,254, an increase of slightly more than 74 percent. "There is no such thing as prohibition in St. Louis," Starkloff observed; "that is, if one wants liquor and has the price, it can be obtained."

HOME IS WHERE THE BREW IS

Booze and basements were a popular pair around town, as vaudeville performer Bert Williams crooned in a popular song, "Everybody Wants a Key to My Cellar":

> *I've got a secret hidden there: I guard it with my life;*
> *There's only one mistake I made: I told it to my wife.*
> *Now everybody wants a key to open my cellar, my cellar, my cellar*
> *Folks who never even gave me a tumble, even perfect strangers are beginning to grumble,*
> *'Cause they all want the key to open my cellar, I'd like to see 'em get one, let 'em try*
> *You can have my money, yessir, take my car, take my wife if you want to go that far*
> *But nix on a key to open my cellar, if the whole darn world goes dry.*

Soda pop and cakes of yeast were pleasant byproducts of home-brewed beer, said Matilda "Til" Keil, a native of Richmond Heights, Missouri, and a longtime volunteer with the Old Trails Historical Society in Manchester. "My parents had come from Europe, and we made our own wine from the grapes we raised and made beer at our house," Keil recalled in 2005. "When the bottles were being washed, my parents always cautioned us not to rattle the bottles. If a policeman would hear them rattle he might come in and find us making beer and we would be arrested. Our home-made brews were not served to every guest. My parents were selective in serving only to those who also made home brews. The wine and beer was consumed by even the children in our family and wine was very important on religious holidays. I do not think that we got drunk or made drinking alcoholic beverages a big deal."

Keil's favorite drink was the non-alcoholic root beer, made with canned malt syrup, sugar, water, and fresh cakes of yeast and aged in five-gallon crocks covered with a cloth. "We children loved to scoop out the syrup which clung to the sides of the empty malt syrup cans, and there were always extra cakes of yeast for the children," she said.

In the Irish-American Dogtown community in St. Louis, the men in the

George Schuppe. Courtesy Oral History Collection, Archives/Special Collections, Norris L Brookens Library, University of Illinois at Springfield.

family enjoyed homemade ale. Sometimes they would drink it on their front porrches in delighted defiance of the prohibition law, an early resident recalled.

Many communities had a bootlegger or gangster or two living in their midst as well. "Prohibition made millionaires out of ordinary gangland punks," retired journalist and public servant George Schuppe recalled in the 1970s. "The gangsters didn't want prohibition repealed because it would deprive them of the main source of their wealth." One such punk was Whitey Doering, a member of Egan's Rats, who reportedly lived in the 1200 block of Sunset Avenue in Richmond Heights. The home later was torn down to make way for U.S. 40 (I-64).

Olivette also was a liquor-producing center during prohibition, Barbara Kodner noted in *Olivette: Chronicle of a Country Village.* "Some of the biggest vats and stills in the community were located where Stacy Park is now—the land there was rented by the moonshiners before the reservoir was built," she wrote. "These people dug the basements out beneath two old houses on the property, using teams of mules, then used the basements to house the vats used to cook the mash. The mash drained into a nearby pond [Bock's Pond], a favorite swimming hole until the mash got knee-deep. The moonshiners lived in the houses above the vats, and grew sugar cane for their fermentation process—at a time when a large purchaser of sugar would be under suspicion."

Not far away was University City's Gables Tearoom, now a day care center at 7315 Olive Boulevard, a Tudor Revival–style building designed in 1931 that was believed to have served illegal liquor. In 1932, according to a book prepared by the Historic Preservation Commission of University City, neighbors complained about "the Gables employing an orchestra and catering to dance crowds until two a.m." Even though prohibition made liquor sales illegal, University City was one of the first cities to prohibit liquor sales on or around school property in 1921, after some students became drunk during a farewell party for a University City High School student who was moving away. The participants apparently retreated between dances "to a machine that stood in front of the house 'to cool off,'" a *Post-Dispatch* reporter explained. Those who attended a subsequent meeting of the League of Women Voters and the Parent-Teachers' Association learned that whiskey often was brought to dances and social functions at the high school.

DOWN BY THE RIVER

Then as now, drunk drivers and speeders threatened the peace of the Oakville–Mehlville–Concord Village community, and some of them were gangsters, Jean Fahey Eberle noted in a history of the area, *A Starting Point*. The rural area also became a dumping ground for a stolen car or the occasional dead body, along such thoroughfares as Cliff Cave, Grimsley Station, and Ringer roads.

"The November 22, 1931 edition of the *St. Louis Globe-Democrat*, reported that Ernest Dohack, while out hunting, found a body near Hollywood Beach on the Meramec River," Eberle wrote. "Such crimes, in addition to other illegal activities like gambling and bootlegging, had little effect on the farmers and businesses in the OMC area."

The Meramec River hosted a number of bootleg joints and, reportedly, visits from vacation-seeking gangsters affiliated with Chicago's Al Capone. "A more dangerous result of drinking was noticed for those swimming at the Meramec River beaches," James Baker observed in his book *Glimpses of Meramec Highlands*. "Numerous drownings occurred each year, caused in part by alcohol consumption which clouded judgment and slowed reflexes."

The Meramec Highlands resort area converted from saloons to "restaurants," "cafes," and speakeasies during prohibition, Baker said. Law enforcement officers received payoffs from sellers and manufacturers of the illicit alcohol in return for protection, he said. For instance, Edward Shifflett, a bartender at Beccard's Grove, usually received a tip-off that prompted him to pour out the booze. "Though a payoff arrangement made by the operators of the speakeasy usually worked, on one occasion, due to a late tip, Shifflett hadn't disposed of all the liquor," Baker wrote. "He was arrested and sent to St. Louis County Jail. He recalled that day, 'I had gotten rid of all but one bottle when they caught me.'"

Beccard's Grove was a tavern with outside dining just south of present-day Repetto Drive in Kirkwood, frequented by Bonhomme Township Republicans, Baker noted. The Highlands also was said to be frequented by gangsters. "When they tore down one of the houses for I-270, they found machine guns under the floorboards," Baker said he was told. "Whether that's an urban legend or a fact, I don't know."

In Fenton, a christening for the new Highway 30 bridge across the Meramec in October 1925 (closed in 2007) featured Missouri Governor Sam Baker, several dignitaries, several thousand people, and plenty of red, white, and blue bunting. But the guest of honor—a bottle of wine reserved for the ceremonies—mysteriously disappeared.

"If that sounds a little strange, remember the country was in the midst of prohibition at the time," Della Lang wrote in her book *River City: The Story of Fenton, Missouri.*

Farther south, crowds also flocked to the clubhouses set up on the banks of the Big River, where Reden's Cottage Park opened in 1927 with a dance floor and bathing beach in Morse Mill, Lang noted. One of the most fashionable speakeasy locales was the popular Morse Mill Hotel, where "high rollers" came to gamble, drink, swim, and dine. Names on the guest register included aviator Charles Lindbergh, movie idol Clara Bow, and St. Louis executives. It was at Rockford Mill on the Big River in 1929 that the Jefferson County sheriff arrested the proprietor of a four-hundred-gallon-per-day, 180-proof still.

The hills, creeks, and open land stretching from Antonia to Pevely were perfect for illicit distilling operations. Many "moonlighters" from urban areas, particularly Italian Americans, rented—or simply used—old barns and land, Lang said. Locals also were in on the action: Richard Dalton, former president of Fenton Bank, recalled twenty or more speakeasies in the area. A number of microbreweries in Jefferson County also peddled their goods.

"They opened a lot of soft drink parlors in those days," Lang said. "I think they were fronts for whiskey and beer." These included Margaret Murphy's general store in Murphy. "Even the stores sold it through the back door," Lang said. "You had to know when the supply came in, so you'd get it fast. Nobody wanted to get caught with it. In Murphy, Mrs. Murphy sat a broom on the porch. That signaled the home brew was in."

There were some dry areas, notably Hillsboro, a city history noted. Residents in the close-knit French community of Old Mines and in the vicinity around Valles Mines made their own brew, as they had for years, Helen Valle Crist and Norma Hoelzel observed in their respective histories of the areas. "Brewing one's own had been going on in this vicinity for over a hundred years . . . first by the French living in Ste. Genevieve County (from which part of Jefferson County was derived) and also by many of the German immigrants living throughout our area," Hoelzel wrote in *Valles Mines, Missouri and Vicinity*. "During the winter, it was common for someone in the community to invite the neighbors in for Saturday night dances . . . having moved the furniture out of a room or two of a log home . . . someone was always available to play a fiddle or guitar . . . and the folks would dance the night away. Many shared in a bit of moonshine, guarded by the farmer in charge."

Backwoods settlers in southern Pulaski County and the Waynesville, Missouri, area between the Big Piney River and Roubidoux Creek, produced and sold fine moonshine whiskey. They had been making it since they arrived from Kentucky and Tennessee in the nineteenth century, Steven D. Smith noted in his book *Made in the Timber: A Settlement History of the Fort Leonard Wood Region.* "Declaring distilling an illegal activity probably only made it taste better to the average antiregulation, antigovernment backwoodsman," Smith wrote.

SCHOOL SOCIAL

At age five, journalist and columnist Clarissa Start attended Froebel Elementary School, 3709 Nebraska Avenue, and lived across the street with her Aunt Lil and Uncle Howard. She'd often visit her Aunt Olie's for dinner, and her "big kid" Uncle Len would play dominoes with her and walk her home after dinner. "I assumed this was the highlight of his day," Start recalled in her 1990 memoir, *I'm Glad I'm Not Young Anymore*, "but later I learned he'd stop off at the saloon for some prohibition brew."

Some drinks were served in the vicinity of the schoolhouse, and some were even served inside. Representatives of Laclede School's Social Center were barred from the building, at Goodfellow and Kennerly avenues, in 1923 after janitor Elmer Henry reported he'd found nine whiskey bottles after a recent meeting of the social club. Several weeks of lively controversy and denials of flask ownership followed, and eventually a committee of the St. Louis Board of Education allowed the members back in the school.

In February 1923, officials of the Salvation Army Industrial Home for Men, 13 N. Third Street, reported that drink accounted for the greatest number of down-and-out men at the home. "Since the passing of the Eighteenth Amendment, Major [C. A.] Soderholm says there is an appreciable falling off in the number of men who come to grief through drink, yet drink still is by far the greatest contributing factor," the *St. Louis Star* reported. "On the other hand, family troubles figure more and more in the stories that the down-and-outers tell."

GRAND AND GRIPS

As a boy, Jim Fox lived one block south of Tower Grove Park on Hartford Street in South St. Louis. "We lived next to a cop, and my dad [Arthur] would serve him home brew," recalled Fox, a journalist and newspaper columnist, now eighty-seven. "I knew liquor had been barred from manufacture and sale, but sale was the key . . . I was convinced one day this cop would blow the whistle or something and my dad would wind up in the pokey." Jim's mother, Eva, made the brew, and it aged for approximately ten days before the task fell to Jim to bottle the stuff. One time it didn't turn out quite right, and he unwittingly served "essence of critter" to his brother-in-law, Robert Patrick Eyenatten. "My brother-in-law, now deceased, was a great beer drinker," Fox explained. Somehow a cockroach crawled or fell inside the bottle, and when Fox siphoned the beer through a tube it killed the unfortunate creature. Eyenatten drank the contents with gusto. "Of course, with the last gulp he took, the cockroach came floating out," Fox said. "He took it without batting an eye, he was so dedicated to home brew."

At Union Station in downtown St. Louis, law enforcement agents looked for signs of "whiskey grip" when travelers released their bags. "If the owner eases the grip or suitcase on the granitoid, as he would if it contained eggs, that is a pretty good indication of bottles within," a policeman told the *Post-Dispatch* in February 1920. "Men are not so careful with grips that contain only clothing. They drop them without any ceremony.

"To make sure, it is well to speak to such a man. If he is carrying liquor, he will usually have drunk enough of it to give an odor to his breath. That odor gives sufficient reason for searching his hand baggage. In the case of baggage which is set down on the ground before we see it, it is sometimes possible to tip it with the foot, as if by accident. If it rattles, we nail it." A day earlier police had nailed fifty-six-year-old Joseph Cameron of Detroit, whose fragile suitcase was found to contain six quarts of whiskey.

Bases Loaded

A liquor war of smaller scope was waged in the locker room of the St. Louis Cardinals, between general manager Wesley Branch Rickey and a few of his players. Rickey served in 1931 as local chairman of an Allied Forces for Prohibition campaign by local and national temperance advocates. "A pious Methodist who wouldn't go to the ballpark on Sunday (but assiduously counted gate receipts on Monday morning), Rickey was also a relentlessly determined man who'd played briefly in the American League (as a light-hitting catcher), coached baseball and other sports to pay his way through Ohio Wesleyan College and the University of Michigan law school, and then fought off tuberculosis," author Charles Alexander wrote in *Rogers Hornsby: A Biography.* "Seeking to build upon the virtuousness supposedly gained from the legal prohibition of liquor, Rickey even banned cigarette smoking (while he continued to puff his cherished cigars)."

In June 1926, playing manager Rogers Hornsby brought Grover Cleveland Alexander to the team. Formerly a pitcher for the Chicago Cubs, Alexander began drinking heavily after he returned from World War I, and the previous winter had attempted to shake his habit in a sanatorium in Dwight, Illinois. "I knew Alex liked his highballs. He liked to go out and drink with his friends, and he had a lot of friends," Hornsby was quoted by Peter Golenbock in *The Spirit of St. Louis: A History of the St. Louis Cardinals and Browns.* "But he never showed up drunk [on a day he was scheduled to pitch], and I don't think we could have won the National League pennant that year without him."

Hornsby played a cat and mouse game with Alexander to stem his drinking, and he didn't appreciate that Rickey had arranged for a federal prohibition agent to snoop after Alexander and other drinking players during road trips. One day during batting practice he observed

Alexander crouched over third base, staring into the plate, as two ground balls and a line drive whizzed by him. "Hornsby let out a howl and said, 'Where in the hell did he get it?'" recalled player Bill Hallahan, a rookie at the time. "Meaning the booze, of course. 'Get him out of here before he gets killed.' . . . He ordered a search made and they found it, all right. In old Sportsman's Park in St. Louis, there used to be a ladies' room not far from the corridor going down to the dugout, and that's where he had stashed it, up in the rafters of the ladies' room. One of those little square bottles of gin."

Prohibition had adverse effects on ethnic and fraternal organizations in South St. Louis, such as the German Turnvereins, NiNi Harris noted in *Bohemian Hill: An American Story.* One popular gathering place, the German American Liederkranz Club building at Grand and Magnolia avenues, was sold only six months into prohibition for an undisclosed six-figure sum to the Alhambra Grotto, an organization whose membership consisted of Masons. "The Liederkranz Club, with its comparative small membership, had larger quarters than were needed, according to its officers," noted a newspaper account. "The difficulty of meeting the heavy expense was greatly increased when prohibition came, as the barroom had been the chief source of revenue."

Harris recalled stories of residents crossing the river from Carondelet to East Carondelet, Illinois, to purchase illegal liquor. "Again, with illegal activity, it's hard to confirm," she said. "[Prohibition] took a huge industry and turned it over to the criminals. The communities where people brewed their own were actually much safer."

PUNKS' PARADISE

Just north of downtown was a mishmash of neighborhoods that would later be known as Murphy Park and O'Fallon Place. The area was settled by waves of immigrants, beginning with the German Catholics in the vicinity of Eleventh and Biddle streets and the German Protestants in the Carr Square area, Norbury Wayman wrote in his *History of St. Louis Neighborhoods: Old North St. Louis & Yeatman.* The first Irish immigrants colonized the area that later became St. Patrick's Parish around Sixth and Biddle, and another Irish group settled what later became known as Kerry Patch in the vicinity of Eighteenth and O'Fallon streets near Cass Avenue. Other Germans settled north of Cass Avenue in an area known as

Little Paderborn. "After 1870 large numbers of Poles settled in the Kerry Patch area supplanting the Irish," Wayman wrote. "The German Protestants around Carr Square began an outward migration in the 1880's and were succeeded by Orthodox Jews. An Italian community [Little Italy] began to emerge near Seventh and Carr Streets after the turn of the century. By 1920 the area north and west of downtown assumed a polygot [*sic*] character of mixed nationalities including immigrants from Russia and the Balkan countries."

As was true in other big cities, ambitious Italian, Polish, and Jewish men in their twenties dominated the bootlegging trade. These same men, because of their immigrant background, found it difficult to obtain jobs in legal oc-cupations, noted David E. Kyvig in *Daily Life in the United States, 1920–1940*. They often developed and managed large and complex business organizations, and competition was fierce. "While bootleggers fought and sometimes even killed one another, customers remained almost entirely untouched," Kyvig wrote. "They received the care and consideration essential in any successful retail busi-ness, particularly one dependent on repeat purchasers."

From Kerry Patch and Little Italy emerged the Egan, Hogan, and Green Ones gangs, each of which cornered a share of the lucrative bootleg liquor market and left a slew of casualties in its wake. The northern part of the Jewish ghetto overlapped Kerry Patch, Walter Ehrlich noted in *Zion in the Valley: The Jewish Community of St. Louis, Volume II.* In spite of the area's reputation as a dangerous ghetto, most residents remembered minor crimes. "Typical reminiscences went something like this: 'I'm sure so-and-so was a *gonif* [thief]; he always flashed a roll of big bills,'" Ehrlich wrote. "Or 'gambling was going on in the back of so-and-so's store all the time. But everybody knew it and it wasn't a big deal.' Or 'everybody knew that Nissel, the *shammas* [sexton] of the *shul* down the street, or Rabbi so-and-so of such-and-such *shul,* was a bootlegger on the side, but he didn't bother anybody and was a harmless fellow.' Or 'we all knew that so-and-so had ties with the Italian mafia gangsters, so we just steered clear of him.' So the crime was there, as in other immigrant communities, but it was not publicized. Nor was it a driving factor in Ghetto life. The residents just lived with it."

It was in a saloon at 3167 Easton Avenue—now Dr. Martin Luther King Drive—in December 1921 that prohibition enforcement agent Louis Gualdoni sensed there was something anatomically incongruous about the legs of saloon-keeper Alfred Capasso. Gualdoni's subsequent bust coined the term "sockleg-ger." "There was a hardness there which muscles hardly ever attain," noted a reporter. "Capasso was searched and 10 two-ounce bottles of a liquid believed to be whisky were found sticking in the tops of his socks."

DR. TICHENOR AND LIGGETT & MYERS

In the African American community, as in many other communities in St. Louis, some residents signed a sobriety pledge with the Women's Christian Temperance Union (WCTU). Among them was the grandmother of Julius Hunter, a broadcast journalist and author. Hunter's grandmother died in 1978 at the age of 102. "She never had a touch of alcohol in her 102 years, she said," Hunter recalled. "But she did take a little of something called Dr. Tichenor's Antiseptic. It said very clearly on the bottle 'for external use only.' It was about 70 or 80 percent alcohol and the remainder, 20 percent or so, oil of wintergreen."

"There was another product that was popular in the black community—I guess all over—and it preceded the Fuller Brush people," Hunter added. "This was called Watkin's Products. Watkins vanilla and lemon flavoring in particular are easily 70 to 80 percent alcohol. My grandmother cooked with that; she made cakes and pies with it. I don't know if she was aware how much alcohol it contained."

Speakeasies flourished in the black community during prohibition, and parties at home also were popular. In his book *Honey Island*, Hunter writes of his aunt Willetta Williams, who went to St. Louis to live with her aunt Lillie B. and Lillie's husband, Wes Pfeiffer. Weekend get-togethers at the Pfeiffers' centered on a popular card game called bid whist, plenty of jazz and rhythm and blues music on the Victrola, and a tableful of food at midnight. "And never mind prohibition," Hunter wrote. "There was plenty of bootleg booze to go around until the silly Volstead Act was repealed."

Lillie B. worked at the Liggett & Myers tobacco processing plant, 4241 Folsom Avenue at Vandeventer Avenue, where she managed to get Willetta a job.

GETTING A BUZZ ON . . .

Even insects couldn't escape prohibition, residents learned when some Brentwood honeybees began weaving home in a drunken stupor. "Each evening upon return of the bees a terrific odor has been noticed by the owners of the hives," reported the *St. Louis County Watchman-Advocate* in October 1923. "It is assumed that the bees hang out at somebody's sour mash and have sipped of the forbidden substance until they become unmanageable. Fear is held forth that the bees will consume their winter's supply now—they go wild, simply wild over it. The case has been referred to the newly appointed Marshal of that town."

The work stripping tobacco leaves made Willetta sick to her stomach, but she was most horrified by the practices of some red-eyed co-workers with swollen, blackened hands, who appeared to be "high" on something. "The new hire soon found out that the workers—both men and women—would, during this prohibition era, take home with them the sweet and pungent swill of secret ingredients in which the huge tobacco leaves were 'cured,'" Hunter wrote. "The stuff made an intoxicating liquor." The plant foreman turned a blind eye to the pilfering of the toxic sludge, which was sold by some L&M employees for 25 cents a bottle, Hunter noted.

LEMONADE STAND

Virtually a whole neighborhood took the prohibition lemon and turned it into lemonade, so to speak: the Italian American residents of the Hill. "Among the supreme ironies of the dry crusade was the monetary gain made by Italians, one of the very groups the zealots sought to protect from demon rum," Gary R. Mormino wrote in *Immigrants on the Hill.* "While bootlegging was scarcely limited to practitioners with names ending in vowels, Italians certainly pursued the art with more zest than other contemporaries." Unlike many of their brethren in Little Italy, "few Hill Italians took the risks or paid the price to become pezenovante [big shots]," he wrote. "Moonshine meant the difference between poverty and middle class." The setting was perfect, Mormino said. Their protective, insular community was guided by the ancient Italian code of omerta, or silence; many residents had experience back in the old country making wine or grappa, a crude brandy; and they managed largely to stay free from protection rackets and gangland influences. "Most of all was the nutty idea, they would claim, that the government was trying to enforce a really stupid law," said Mormino. "They're just not going to abide by this."

New homes built and existing ones renovated, automobiles and nice clothes and furnishings, and powerful political and social organizations would typify the community's progress by the time the Volstead Act was repealed in 1933. When it had begun, there were few voters and no political machine. Mormino referred to the case of a young man from the Hill who worked at a local hospital and earned many times his weekly pay by selling liquor to the doctors and nurses. The man used his profits to buy a new home and take his family, with six children, on an extended vacation to Italy.

QUEENS OF THE SUBURBS

Webster Groves and Kirkwood were nineteenth-century railroad suburbs in St. Louis County that fought it out for the prestigious title "Queen of the Suburbs." Both enjoyed a fashionably dry status at the time of prohibition. Many middle- and upper-class residents belonged to the WCTU or the Anti-Saloon League. There were plenty of drinkers, however. "My own father made a very good home brew, and we had a cabinet down in the basement where you would pick up the door, and when you would let it go it would automatically close," Kirkwood resident Albert Winkler recalled. "He made a batch one time that was a little too wild, because it blew off the door." Some prematurely bottled batches of home brew would blow the caps off, and the noise was said to sound like gunshots. "One preacher said that when he went around to visit people in their homes, he'd be embarrassed, because they would be sitting there talking about spiritual things and these explosions would go off in the basement," Winkler recalled.

By 1925, a problem with sewage disposal prompted a number of Sugar Creek neighborhood residents to rent or sell their property "to seemingly modest people of allegedly honest trades who invariably turned out to be bootleggers," resident Philip Gronemeyer noted in June Wilkinson Dahl's *A History of Kirkwood, Missouri, 1851–1965*. It was scandalous, but hardly new. As early as 1922 the WCTU had complained about the illegal sale of liquor in Kirkwood, Dahl wrote. "Word of mouth has it that there were two such [bootlegging] operations on Dougherty

LAST LAUGH

The editor of *Reedy's Mirror*, St. Louis's William Marion Reedy was a giant in the national literary world and a hearty drinker. After he died on July 28, 1920, Reedy had the last laugh on prohibition, Orrick Johns wrote in *Time of Our Lives: The Story of My Father and Myself*:

Around the coffin on tables were empty bottles and glasses. At its foot were a bartender and a gangster praying, and back of them stood a couple of gamblers and gang politicians, the wives of a few of his friends, and, somewhat apart from them, a group of light ladies. They were strange surroundings for a man of brilliant intellect whose body lay in the coffin. Reedy's funeral was an affair of state, which all of the world and the underworld of St. Louis attended.

Ferry Road at approximately 1970 and 1920," longtime Sugar Creek resident Doris Danna noted. "The old brick house at 1920 was still standing until sometime
in the '60s when the police caught a 'chop-shop' operation there, run by a notorious character from north St. Louis county." To the south, just east of Meramec
Highlands, a Craftsman-style stone cottage was said to enjoy a lively though illicit
existence. Its status would be elevated to landmark restaurant after J. H. and Mary
Toothman opened the Green Parrot Inn there in 1938. "Before my grandfolks
moved here and bought the place, it was a speakeasy," said Louis Toothman of
Kirkwood. "On weekends the people from St. Louis would get off at the train
station at Meramec Highlands, come up here, and eat and have a drink. There
was a little cubbyhole for the still in the basement, and a little secret passageway
for people to escape out of the building. My grandmother always said there were
bullet holes in the walls in her apartment and downstairs."

Bootleg gangs congregated just outside Kirkwood, in the African American community of Meacham Park in unincorporated St. Louis County, William
Speckert recalled in 1998 in *Meacham Park: A History*. The gangs were controlled
by a local sheriff and other law-enforcement types, he said. "You belonged to the
cartel or you would be in jail," Speckert said. "That's the way the ball bounced."

On at least one occasion, a "luxuriously furnished residence" in the high-
class section of Kirkwood at 541 South Clay Avenue turned out to be a profitable liquor factory for three enterprising Italian American tenants. Ross Maggio,
Jim Banano, and Matio Ardizzone rented the place for one hundred dollars a
month (twelve hundred dollars today), drove a "handsome sport model Nash"
and a Dodge truck and appeared to be the successful grocerymen they represented themselves to be. That is, until prohibition agents raided the place on August
3, 1923. Authorities secured a search warrant after they were alerted by readings
on the home's water meter, which showed tremendous quantities of water were
used. Most of the home appeared to be respectably and elaborately furnished.
A secret compartment in the basement, however, revealed mass quantities of
hooch: fifty to seventy-five cases of gin with fake labels, ten five-gallon cans of
grain alcohol, fifty pints of whiskey, glycerine, gin flavorings, and five hundred
bottles and labels of all kinds.

Five female representatives of the WCTU who turned out for the trial were
disappointed to see the defendants discharged for lack of evidence, but they
perked up when Constable Louis Hollman and Marshal Frank G. Weiss offered
to let them help smash up the liquor. "Although the women insisted that the work
of destroying the liquor—or the 'Carrie Nation Hatchet Party,' as Mrs. Minnie
Radcliffe called it—be held right away, they were finally convinced that it would

take some time to complete the task, and as it was near noon time then the work would interfere with many of their noonday meals, and possibly with previous engagements of the afternoon," the *St. Louis County Watchman-Advocate* reported. "So this afternoon [Friday, August 24] was agreed on." The party was held at Constable Hollman's home on Clinton Avenue and was attended by Radcliffe, state organizer of the WCTU; Mrs. J. H. Pierce, county vice chairman; Mrs. H. Schroeder, welfare chairman; and members Mrs. J. J. Rowe and Mrs. John Wilson.

In Webster Groves, the police reports were relatively mild. "Ed ___ of ___ N. Elm called the office and said his father was drunk and disturbing the peace," Officer Frank Lenz reported on March 7, 1923. "I went up there and gave him a good talking to and he promised to behave." There was more than met the eye, as the *Webster News-Times* alluded. "Moonshining in these sunny days of parched throats is not confined to the ancient habitat of mountaineers," intoned an article from January 30, 1920. "It is apt to be in your neighbor's aristocratic cellar."

In an interview with students from Webster Groves High School in the 1970s, longtime Webster resident Wallace Rinehart said his family home was dry, even though his father had been opposed to prohibition. "We had liquor in our home before prohibition, but he said, 'Soon as that law was passed, we were not going to have a drink in our house,' and we didn't," Rinehart said. "Now, some people did, but my family just didn't believe in it."

Others did believe in it. On a wild Saturday night in July 1925, police seized sixty-three bottles of home brew at Josephine White's home at 661 Cornell Avenue in north Webster, following complaints that intoxicated revelers were disturbing the peace.

There always was the occasional drunk. Roy Biessan was found sleeping on a street in Old Orchard, Webster Groves, in April 1923, with a half-pint of "white mule" or clear moonshine whiskey in his pocket. Biessan, alias Roy Brown, was sentenced by Justice of the Peace William E. Gould to thirty days in jail for possession of liquor.

Occasionally some heavy hitters surfaced in sedate suburbia. In July 1925, what may well have been the entire Webster police force—Chief Andrew McDonnell and officers Lenz, Whalen, Piper, and Neil—raided a booze factory in a home at 227 Hazel Avenue. They arrested the home's owner, J. W. Anderson, listed in the city directory as a magazine agent; and J. S. Bartels. They confiscated twelve bottles labeled "Gordon Gin—Made in London," ten quarts of whiskey, labeled Scotch Whisky, a partly filled barrel of moonshine whiskey, and some wood alcohol.

Tops in Town

Despite popular reports that America was awash in illicit booze, evidence indicates that consumption of alcohol decreased by at least half during prohibition, David E. Kyvig noted in *Repealing National Prohibition*. Some wanted to abide by the law; others simply couldn't afford illicit booze. A quart of beer alone cost an average of 80 cents—the equivalent of nine dollars today—and represented a 600 percent increase from 1916, at a time when the average family income was about $2,600 per year. Hence, Kyvig said, the more prosperous upper and middle classes tended to violate the alcohol ban more frequently than the working classes.

On October 22, 1924, liquor thieves dynamited a stone liquor vault twenty-five by fifteen feet, with walls two feet thick, at Hazelwood, the summer home of attorney Samuel W. Fordyce on Graham Road, three miles north of Natural Bridge Road. Their haul was five hundred dollars worth of pre-prohibition liquor.

Nothing lasts forever, especially fine liquor. In 1925, a federal grand jury in New York began investigating a nationwide bootleg syndicate that shipped liquor in trunkload lots to twenty thousand customers in seventy large cities in twenty-nine states. Every member of the St. Louis Country Club was on the ring's prospective customer list, and a number of prominent St. Louisans had received trunkload consignments of the illicit goods. Tracing the buyers was difficult, because it was common practice for the buyers to use fictitious names and addresses.

Highbrow or lowbrow, bootleggers boasted a booming business in St. Louis County in 1922, according to Gus Nations, prohibition enforcement agent in charge of the Eastern Missouri District. "The situation in St. Louis County is also slightly improved, but I am convinced that there is still more moonshine whisky made in St. Louis County alone than in all the rest of the state combined," Nations said. Nations and William H. Allen, state director of prohibition enforcement, acknowledged that Missouri's seventeen prohibition enforcement agents, including two assigned specifically to St. Louis, were inadequate to cover the state's thirty-nine counties. "With a force of twenty-five agents working continually in St. Louis I could clamp down the lid so tightly that the city would be bone dry," Nations said. He never got the chance.

St. Charles and Outstate

By March 1927, St. Charles County was giving St. Louis County a run for its money in booze, according to James Dillon, deputy prohibition administrator

Main Street Celebration, St. Charles, July 17 through 22, 1922. The view is south on Main Street from near Monroe Street. Courtesy John J. Buse, Jr., Collection, 1860–1931, Western Historical Manuscript Collection-Columbia, Missouri.

for the metropolitan area. Dillon characterized St. Charles County as the most "still-infested county" in the state. He told a *Globe-Democrat* reporter that he received numerous tips from local farmers, but in most instances the raids that followed were unsuccessful because the stills had been moved to some other locality. At the same time, a grand jury was investigating an alleged lack of prohibition enforcement by county authorities and the failure of the sheriff's office to communicate satisfactorily with the prosecuting attorney.

On North Second Street in the Frenchtown neighborhood, liquor merchants kept watch for prohibition agents, noted Richard Vinson of the Frenchtown Museum. "During prohibition, tavern owners stationed a spy on the old [Highway] 115 Bridge," Vinson said. "When the federal agent came across, the spy would signal and all the liquor would go under the counter, and soda pop would go on top."

A number of locales today are so named because they were used for illicit bootlegging activities during prohibition. One is Whiskey Spring in Quail Ridge Park, a former farm and 250-acre open space park at the southeastern edge of Wentzville. The spring reportedly was used to distill whiskey during prohibition. Another, the Ballast Pits Hunting and Fishing Club, served as a hideout of sorts during prohibition, where members came to dance and some hid their booze in the trees.

Mouse Martini, Anyone?

A young Glenn Hensley.

As a boy, Glenn Hensley and his parents lived for a time with his grandfather, I. J. Holt, in Stanberry, Missouri. In that small town was an abandoned, three-story building once used to assemble barn-protecting lightning rods, or so he was told. One day, he and his buddies decided to explore the place. "So we got together there late one Sunday evening when all the other more respectable townspeople were sleeping off their heavy, small-town noon meals," Hensley recalled. "We had explored and found a basement window that could easily be swung open on long-unused hinges. So with our play clothes on, we inched that window open far enough so we could crawl through it. A dark, moldy basement was empty of anything of interest, so we wandered up the steps. Nothing special on the ground floor, so up we went. Same thing on the second floor, but WOW, we 'jackpotted' up on the third floor.

"There before our eyes appeared what we thought might be a mini-distillery. We saw a big iron pot full of gooey mash stuff, a batch of pipes, a burner, a flue, and a jumble of glass gallon jugs. We didn't really know what we'd found, but we figured we better get out of there FAST.

"However, before departing we left one small bit of devilment. We dumped into the vat of mash three dead mice we found on the floor. If it was a 'booze-making' set-up, we decided a little extra protein wouldn't hurt it."

Particularly in rural areas, enforcement efforts tended to focus on immigrants, minorities, and low-income residents. Among them were the Romanian, Slovak, Italian, and Hungarian immigrants of the mill town of Ilasco, Missouri, three miles south of Hannibal. "Attitudes in nearby Hannibal and New London toward Ilasco's immigrant prohibition violators were particularly vicious," author Gregg Andrews wrote in his book *City of Dust: A Cement Company Town in the Land of Tom Sawyer.*" Hannibal had its share of raids, including one notable affair at a residence on Hill Street in 1928 in which three hundred gallons of moonshine were confiscated.

In Columbia, the staff of the University of Missouri botany department were forced by prohibition to detail in excruciatingly bureaucratic fashion the types of alcohol—and the amounts—they used to preserve specimens, or any other liquors they might have lying about the classroom. Outside class, enterprising students found there was money to be made. "One group had the problem of making the green corn liquor they obtained fit to drink," journalist Irene Taylor wrote. "They scouted around and found a traveling salesman who agreed to have a keg of the liquor strapped to the back of his roadster. When he returned to Columbia a month later the stuff was aged enough to consume. The traveling man was invited to the party and left a few days later with another keg. Some students worked their way through school by selling bootleg liquor, particularly during the football season."

At the University of Missouri–Rolla, even prohibition couldn't stop the beer that flowed during the annual Saint Patrick's Day parade and celebration, which had begun in 1908. In Cooper County and Boonville, Missouri, as in other locales, residents dabbled in home brewing.

"Much of the home product was a poor substitute for the real thing, often cloudy and with a considerable deposit of yeast on the bottom of the bottle," Louis Geiger wrote in a paper, "In the Days of Prohibition, Cooper County, 1919–1934." "Some was so 'wild' that the entire contents of a bottle would go up in a geyser of foam when uncapped. It was told of one Stony Point farmer, who, trying to recapture the good old days when threshing crews were treated to a keg, that he served an entire crew of some twenty men out of a single foaming bottle."

In the shadow of the Capitol in Jefferson City, Missouri, moonshiners and bootleggers vigorously plied their trade. In May 1924, prohibition agents used twenty sticks of dynamite to blow up a still seven miles southeast of Jefferson City. Run by a gasoline engine, pump, boiler, and water tank, the several-thousand-gallon mash operation was said to be the largest ever found in Missouri. In November 1929, federal prohibition agents made seventy-two arrests in two days.

Bootleggers also could be found in the vicinity of the construction site of the hydroelectric Bagnell Dam in the Ozarks, where laborers earned 35 cents an hour and worked nine hours a day beginning in 1929. While some of the corn liquor was made locally, most of it was hauled in, laborer Curtis Beach recalled in 1981. "There was plenty of it, but you had to buy it and then hunt a place to drink it," Beach said.

Members of the Missouri Legislature in session at Jefferson City and students of Missouri University found a special oasis in Westphalia, a little German community in Osage County "which has shown but little evidence that the eighteenth amendment ever was on the statute books," the *St. Louis Globe-Democrat* noted in 1933. A Westphalian judge and banker, Ben Schauwecker, maintained his innocence after serving a year in prison for selling liquor from his home. "I sold wine and beer and whiskey, yes, but that's not wrong," he told a reporter in 1931. "We don't respect that prohibition law."

In Washington, the local newspaper published an article on etiquette, "How to Act Around the Soda Fountain," but it wasn't necessary. Illegal stills flourished in Franklin and Warren counties, and a large-scale whiskey distilling effort began on Boeuf Island and produced more than three hundred gallons of moonshine daily. Federal agents dynamited the still on June 12, 1933.

Land of Lincoln

In East St. Louis, Illinois, organized crime fought for control of the city's bootleg liquor market, and the new commission form of government, under the surface, was as corrupt as the ward-based government it replaced, Andrew J. Theising observed in *Made in USA: East St. Louis.* Booze and graft were just about everywhere. "Madison and St. Clair counties became notorious for their bootleggers, gamblers, and racketeers," Ernest Kirschten noted in his 1960 history of St. Louis, *Catfish and Crystal.* "Even today their taverns do not cater to Ladies' Aid fish fries."

Graft also made its mark in Herrin, Illinois, settled by immigrant families who worked in the coal mines. Herrin was kept in flux, sometimes violently so, by the rise of unions, gangsters trying to become "kings of the road," and Ku Klux Klansmen living in the vicinity of bootleggers, Herrin native Sue Spytek recalled. "Widowed women left with several children and no income because of coal mining accidents were compelled to 'take in washings,' sewing, keeping boarders for $15 a month room and board, or invest in an underground business of making home brew and moon-shine to sell to boarders after pay day," Spytek wrote in 1984.

Two coal miners were arrested in February 1923 and placed in the Belleville jail for hawking their moonshine for army surplus from Scott Field. Michael Daneff and Theodore Janden, who lived near the Shiloh mine, were arrested by deputy sheriffs. Ninety percent of the arrested men's trade was with soldiers stationed at the post.

Lieutenant James A. Healey, field intelligence officer, said officers found a complete still at the Daneff home, along with eighty-five gallons of moonshine whiskey and seventy gallons of mash. They also found army blankets, shoes, shirts, rubber army overcoats, a brown government sweater, and other items. A similar haul was found at the Janden home. "When the boys became short of funds and could not purchase the liquor with cash they just stole some of the army property and traded it for the liquor," Healey said.

Carl Wittmond grew up in Brussels, Illinois, on a peninsula surrounded by the Illinois and Mississippi rivers. Born in 1905 to the family that operated the Wittmond Hotel in Calhoun County, Wittmond became a Democratic politician and state legislator and was instrumental in opening a state-operated ferry across the Illinois River and promoting construction of the Great River Road along the Mississippi River. On Saturday nights during prohibition, dance halls and outdoor platforms would be established in the woods, and periodically the operator would go broke, Wittmond recalled in 1983. "Oh, they'd have a good band and dance and have a stand or two where you could buy soft drinks," Wittmond said. "You couldn't buy any hard drinks then. But there would be a bootlegger there in those days. And they made more money, I guess, than anything else." Nightspots were numerous, Wittmond added. "Yes, we used to think that was smart to stop in some place and if you knew your way in to get around the back way or if somebody knew you," he said. "I traveled around quite a bit, and I knew all the honkeytonks around. And I'd take some local people with me. They thought I was somebody because I could get in. . . . If you didn't have a pint of whiskey with you, you couldn't even cross the river half the time . . . part of the fare. Oh yes, if you didn't have a drink for him, why, he'd be disappointed."

Locals made home brew, and outside the county was a large distillery that was raided once or twice, but Wittmond said he was never much of a drinker. His father, of German ancestry, always had beer and whiskey available at home, he said. "I could have had all I'd want to drink but I just didn't want to drink," he said. "I used to argue that with Governor [Adlai] Stevenson years ago. He was trying to regulate people's morals and you sure get in trouble. If you just tell somebody they can't do something, that's when they want to do it."

Lloyd "Dude" Coffman. Courtesy Oral History Collection, Archives/Special Collections, Norris L Brookens Library, University of Illinois at Springfield.

Carl Wittmond. Courtesy Oral History Collection, Archives/Special Collections, Norris L Brookens Library, University of Illinois at Springfield.

BAKERS' BOOZE AND MINE NUMBER FIVE

Farther north in Roodhouse, retired pharmacist Lloyd Coffman told of a number of "blind pigs" or saloons. Then a booming railroad town in west-central Illinois, Roodhouse had a couple of bakeries, and Coffman worked in one as a baker's apprentice. "One time I remember I was working with a baker, and some of them bakers were bad to drink," Coffman recalled in 1983. "This guy's name was Archie Moran, Irish as Paddy's pig, you know. Had some saloons that were bootleg places during prohibition . . . we had some places over here on Palm Street that sold bootleg whiskey. He'd go in the back door of the thing . . . and I keep waiting for him, waiting for him, you know. I know that bread was getting ready to take out, you know. I mean he never came." Coffman hurried back and tried to salvage the goods himself, but at least a third was too burned to sell.

In 1932, he received a pharmacy degree and became joint owner of Smith's Drugstore in Roodhouse, where the ingredients for home brew were big sellers. "Darn near everybody" had home brew, he said. "You had to buy it somewhere," Coffman said. "And . . . people didn't think anything of it. The people would be standing there when one of the preachers would be buying some bottle caps or yeast or something.

"It was a farce. Prohibition was a farce in the United States. You cannot, I've thought about this a little, you cannot enforce any law that public opinion is against . . . and public opinion was sure in hell against prohibition, you see."

To the east, Benld was the home of a well-known bootlegger named Dominic Tarro, who eventually met a tragic end in the Sangamon River (see Chapter 8). It also was the boyhood home of Avinere Toigo, born to Italian immigrants in 1902, who was briefly employed in the area's coal mines while in high school. He later became a state government employee. "Benld never knew prohibition existed," Toigo told an interviewer in the early 1970s. "Benld was a wide open town. They had not only bootlegging [but also] gambling and other vices. The distilling of liquor took place along Cahokia Creek. The creek furnished the water, and the hills furnished the gravity of feeding the mash from the hillside to the still. The distilled product was then put in five-gallon cans and the liquor was hauled through Benld at night, and those of us who were interested and knew that it was happening could hear the rattling of the tin cans—five-gallon tin cans."

There were four coal mines around Benld, and the distillery was known as Mine Number Five, Toigo said. It didn't last long, because a prohibition agent misstepped and fell into the vat, and the investors sustained a huge loss and had to close up shop, he said. Despite the bootlegging, there was less crime in Benld than in other communities, and residents considered it their right to make liquor, he said. "Fact of the matter is when someone would be arrested or pinched for bootlegging, he would be sent off to jail for maybe thirty days; when he came back they would hail him, 'Hey, Frank, how was college?'" Toigo said. "They were almost a hero and they would continue to be respected in the community."

LIKE THE UNTOUCHABLES

Vineyards were populous in the hilly areas around the coal mines of Collinsville, and many of its German, Italian, Lithuanian, and other residents took a dim view of prohibition. "Collinsville was a prohibition town," said Floyd J. Sperino, museum director and curator of the Collinsville Historical Museum. "We often find homes and garages that have caves inside, still to this day, where they made the home brew." Sperino speaks from experience. His grandmother, Josephine Sperino, operated a speakeasy to make ends meet. "We had places where liquor was illegal, taverns and places like grandma's," said Sperino. "The gang in Chicago would fight with bootleggers down here; one time they came in cars with machine guns and killed the bartender here." Sperino's dad took him to see the bullet-riddled tavern. Young Floyd wanted to stick his fingers in the holes, but his father wouldn't let him. "I just wanted you to see," he said. Gangsters Al Capone and Buster Wortman were spotted on Collinsville's streets from time to time, he said.

Long after prohibition ended, Sperino and his wife, Bernice, operated a flower shop for twenty-five years in the old Jacob Farber building downtown. One night a storm tore off a section of the roof and damaged the floorboards. When they were pulled up they revealed two huge distilling vats, apparently used during prohibition, that had been filled in with dirt. The furnace had been walled off from the rest of the basement with concrete blocks.

Stills and bootlegged wine were common, longtime Collinsville newspaperman Karl Monroe told an interviewer in 1973. "The people who were doing it bribed public officials, they bribed federal prohibition agents, they were outside the law so that their activities couldn't be protected by the law," Monroe said. "So they became targets for other bootleg type gangsters who hijacked their trucks and tried to steal their stuff, tried to move in on their territories. And we had the regular things, like you saw on the *Untouchables* in the movies. There were rather a large number of murders and attempted murders right around Collinsville. We had a feeling that this was kind of a battleground for some of these gangs. It was a curious thing. Although these things went on around you, they didn't really affect the law-abiding people."

All in all, it was a wild time, Monroe said. "There were a lot of stills and there were raids," he said. "And you'd walk uptown and see a soft drink parlor, which is what they called saloons in those days. They weren't supposed to sell hard liquor and they'd be padlocked by the prohibition people. And there were numerous places like that uptown. It was an interesting period. The Fleischmann Yeast Company trying to keep its big yeast stock moving . . . went on radio with regular programs in which they touted the medical benefits of eating chocolate-flavored yeast. And I was a believer. I used to save my pennies and buy my little box of yeast and eat chocolate yeast, which tasted very soapy."

Like those in many other communities, the city fathers in Madison, Illinois, passed their own ordinance to ensure compliance with the Eighteenth Amendment and raise local revenue as well, Ron Stern noted in *A Centennial History of Madison, Illinois, 1891–1991*. Those who manufactured, gave away, or sold intoxicating or fermented liquor could be fined between one hundred and three hundred dollars. "There were some curbs on the openness of drinking," Stern wrote. "However, saloon owners and drinkers ran circles around the law and enforcement officials."

In Glen Carbon, Freda Burian's family cooked whiskey in the basement and supplied Arksmith's Tavern at Glenn Crossing. The bootleg whiskey was stored in a large hole underneath her bed. A rug covered the hole in case prohibition agents paid a visit. "We got tipped off about a raid one time," recalled her son,

For years, few were aware of the distilling operation concealed in the basement of the Jacob Farber building in Collinsville, Illinois. Courtesy Floyd Sperino and the Collinsville Historical Museum.

Vernon "Bud" Burian, in 1989. "So we dumped all the mash in a neighbor's pasture. His chickens ate the mash and got drunk. Mom and me had to pick them all up and carry them home."

BEST BREW ANYWHERE

The best home brew in the country was made in Pekin, Illinois, by a German immigrant named Raymond Worrel, said Martin Lohmann, a Pekin resident and longtime state representative and state senator. Lohmann, who was approaching middle age when prohibition began, helped Worrel and two other German Americans become naturalized citizens. Despite the law, the saloons were wide open, he said. "In Tazewell County we were wetter than the Mississippi River," Lohmann told an interviewer in 1979. "You see, these Germans like their beer. We had a brewery here in Pekin, you know the Pekin Brewery . . . you could get a case of beer for fifty cents. Dozen bottles. Get a small pony-keg for a dollar."

"And they didn't stop or slow down during prohibition?" asked the interviewer, Cullom Davis.

"Oh, no," Lohmann replied.

CHAPTER 4

BREWING DISASTER

OTTO F. STIFEL WAS A SHELL OF HIMSELF BY AUGUST 1920. FORMERLY AN EASY-going man, a fan of horseracing and baseball, he now was nervous and smoked cigarettes constantly. That he had just won the Republican primary for Missouri's Eleventh Congressional District—handily, over three other candidates—seemed of little consolation. Stifel's son, Carl, and brother-in-law, Edwin Conrades, considered sending him to a sanitarium to recuperate.

Beer had been a big part of Stifel's life. He had trained in the brewer's art in Germany, his parents' homeland, and in 1908 organized Stifel's Union Brewery at Michigan and Gravois avenues in south St. Louis. For many years, life was good: He was one of the organizers of the St. Louis Federal League Baseball Club and owned a horse farm in Valley Park, on the outskirts of St. Louis County. Popular with those of every social stripe, Stifel also liked to helped people "on the quiet." "No person in distress ever appealed to Otto Stifel and failed to get food for his family and help in finding profitable employment for himself," a friend told the *St. Louis Star.* "He could not bear to see suffering of any kind without doing something to relieve the sufferer. On his daily arrival at his brewery office, usually at 10 a.m., he always found several old men, cripples and pensioners of his, many of them getting from him a regular daily allowance."

Those days were gone. St. Louis ranked among the top four brewing cities in the nation before prohibition ruined the industry. Stifel closed his brewery, in which he had a million dollars invested, and put $500,000 into a plant to manufacture oleomargarine, an enterprise he knew little about. He had been pressed for funds for some time, but there was no benefactor to help him. Disagreements with his family over finances continued to mount, and appeals for assistance to several "choice Masonic friends" had fallen on deaf ears. He wrote a series of rambling suicide notes to the public and to members of his family. The public note blamed prohibition for his difficulties. He left the notes in his bungalow at the farm in Valley Park and on August 17 had supper with the farm superintendent, Edward Paubel, and his wife. Paubel then drove him to Barrett's Station to see an old friend, E. C. Mahanay. Stifel's mood lightened when he saw the six gentlemen sitting around Mahanay's store.

Otto F. Stifel's

Union Brewing Co.

Gravois and Michigan Avenues

"Give all the boys a fine cigar," Stifel said, as he paid for the stogies and took one for himself. They discussed his congressional nomination, and the conversation turned to contracts and friendships. He asked Mahanay what he would do to a fellow in whom he had lost confidence. "I would tell him to go to hell," Mahanay said. Stifel laughed.

The next morning, after breakfast with the Paubels, Stifel caught the 7 a.m. train to St. Louis and returned to the farm three hours later, alone and depressed. He picked up a revolver, placed it in his mouth, and pulled the trigger. Paubel entered Stifel's bungalow at noon to call him to dinner and found the brewer dead, just sixteen days short of his fifty-eighth birthday. Stifel was one of two local brewers who committed "the Dutch act" as a direct result of prohibition. A corruption of the word *Deutsch*, or German, the phrase was used by police to describe the suicides of local brewers in the early years of the twentieth century. William J. Lemp, Jr., was the second, in December 1922.

Left Holding the Bag

Although the brewing industry ended for good in 1920, a gradual decline had been underway, noted Donald Roussin and Kevin Kious, brewery historians and writers for the American Breweriana Association, National Association Breweriana Advertising, and Brewery Collectibles Club of America. "While sales may have grown some for a few years after that, for most breweries things started to go downhill around 1912 or so," Kious noted. "Consumption was not increasing due to prohibition laws, anti-saloon ordinances and the like. Around 1917 the Feds threw a bunch of conservation measures on grain and fuel use that further hampered the breweries. They never had time to get back on their feet when they were hit with the Eighteenth Amendment."

St. Louis's commercial beer plants turned out 3 million barrels in 1917. That's not so impressive today: In 2006, Anheuser-Busch alone turned out 125 million barrels of beer worldwide. But it was a big deal then; St. Louis's beer production in 1914 amounted to $26.8 million, or more than a half billion dollars today. By contrast, the post-prohibition beverage industry would reach a peak of $8.57 million in 1923 before sliding to $4.88 million in 1929. "Prior to national prohibition, the beer business was the fourth most important industry in St. Louis, as measured by the value of the product," Ronald Jan Plavchan observed in *A History of Anheuser-Busch, 1852–1933*.

In the mid-teens St. Louis brewers paid $5,402,000 yearly to 9,617 employees, invested more than $1 million each year in new buildings and machinery, and paid more than $4.2 million annually in federal and local taxes and water licenses, according to the January 1916 issue of *The American Brewer* magazine. Another 45,000 workers were estimated to be at least partially dependent on the brewing industry, such as those in the cooperage or barrel-making trade or the glass bottle industry. All together, brewing was a $140 million industry in St. Louis.

"I would judge that, in St. Louis, 4,000 are unemployed as a result of prohibition," Joseph Hahn, secretary of Local 6 of the Brewers and Maltsters Union in St. Louis, wrote in a letter to Hugo Koehler, president of the Independent Breweries Company. "Figuring the wage of these men at $5 per day or $20,000 per day, which is the purchasing power that has been destroyed, thereby causing unemployment in other Industries, I think we can safely say that about 5,000 men are on the streets in St. Louis on account of prohibition."

The average brewery worker stayed out of the headlines and made it through the prohibition years in non-brewing occupations. By 1928, only 1,200 men remained in Local 6 of the Brewers and Maltsters Union, and few of those had steady employment, secretary Joseph J. Hauser reported.

Those still employed with the unions found concessions were necessary. In November 1924, 150 men working in Anheuser-Busch's corn products department accepted wage cuts of $1.20 to $4.80 per week, which saved the company $2,500 yearly. All men were employed by one of five brewery workers' unions. General superintendent August A. Busch, Jr., had told a union committee that the wage contracts would not be renewed unless the reduction was accepted in the corn products department. A refusal would mean that the plant would be run on an open shop basis, he said, meaning it would be open to non-union employees.

Only seven of the twenty-one St. Louis breweries operating at the time of prohibition were still manufacturing beverages in 1928. That year, fourteen British journalists toured the city in an airplane and visited a state-of-the-art shoe factory and the Anheuser-Busch near-beer plant. The shoe factory failed to excite them, but they were impressed by the Busch operation. Of particular interest was the statement that Americans once consumed 6 million barrels of beer each year, but were then drinking only 1.3 million barrels of near-beer. They asked the amount of compensation given by the federal government to the liquor industry when the lid went down and appeared amazed by the answer: "None."

August A. Busch.
Courtesy Library of Congress.

The Lemp Legacy

Once a worldwide supplier of beer, the William J. Lemp Brewing Company attempted to maintain its presence in the marketplace with the near-beer brands of Tally and Cerva. Substantial overhead and other costs led the owners to stop production of Cerva in June 1919, author Stephen Walker noted in *Lemp: The Haunting History*. The brewery's failure to keep up with technological advances didn't help. "Their brewery profits had made them quite wealthy, so the individual members of the Lemp family apparently lacked any real incentive to keep their giant firm afloat during those trying times," Walker wrote. "William J. Lemp, Jr., the brewery's third and last president, had long since given up on the return of beer, and abruptly closed the great plant." Its sale was announced in the December 1921 issue of *The Brewers' Journal*, eight buildings on 30.5 acres of land that originally cost more than $7 million. The asking price was $1.5 million.

Six months later, the sprawling brewery was auctioned off in parcels for a total of $588,500—literally pennies on the dollar—and some of it became

William J. Lemp, Jr.

Alswell, Lemp's three-story Bavarian retreat in south St. Louis County, was designed to look like a Swiss chalet. Courtesy of Harold and Clifford Zelch.

part of the International Shoe Company factory. Though he was only fifty-five, Lemp's physical and mental condition declined. At 9 a.m. on December 29, 1922, he fatally shot himself twice in the chest at his office at 3322 S. Thirteenth Street. He had just sent out his stenographer, Olivette Berscheck, to confer with an architect who was working on plans. "On the way she heard a noise as though someone had dropped a board on the floor," wrote a reporter for the *St. Louis Star.* "She thought nothing of it at the time. When she returned to Lemp's office she found the body on the floor." Police checked Lemp's pockets for a note but found none. They found $130 in currency and silver, and a gold watch, gold cigar case, and gold cigarette case.

A pillar of the community, Lemp held a director's chair in many companies and belonged to the Merchants Exchange, the Glen Echo and St. Louis country clubs, the Liederkranz Club, and the Masons. He lived with his second wife, Ellie, in Alswell, his Bavarian-style retreat in south St. Louis County that overlooked the Meramec River. His brother Charles maintained a farm on Christopher Drive in Oakville, and another brother, Edwin, lived on a Kirkwood estate he named Cragwold.

Co-workers said Lemp had been very nervous and on the morning of his death complained he could not get warm. Several times he rose from his desk and stood beside a steam radiator. August A. Busch, a close friend as well as a competitor, told a reporter he had seen Lemp about a week before his death. "At that time he seemed cheerful and there was no indication that he was worrying either about the business situation or anything else," Busch said. "He was a hard worker and personally looked after the operation of his farm. He was a fine fellow and it is hard to believe he has taken his own life."

Even in death, William Lemp couldn't catch a financial break. Alswell, built at a cost of $125,000 in 1914, was auctioned by his estate in May 1925 for $118,500 to a Chicago real estate dealer. Draperies, fixtures, rugs, and statuary went with the deal, as well as the 192 acres surrounding the home. Lemp's estate, valued at less than $1 million in 1923, was divided between his widow and his son, William J. Lemp, III.

By the end of the decade, Lemp—once the country's nineteenth-largest brewer and a worldwide supplier of beer—largely was forgotten, save for an occasional mention of animals lost from Edwin Lemp's menagerie. "Two black African swans, rare birds, disappeared Sunday from a lake at the home of Edwin A. Lemp, financier and former brewer, near Windsor Springs, St. Louis County," the *Post-Dispatch* noted on October 24, 1929.

GIVE UP OR RIDE IT OUT?

Not all brewers viewed prohibition as an insurmountable obstacle. They pledged to ride it through and displayed at least some confidence that the situation wouldn't be permanent. Many secured licenses to brew near-beer, or beer with less than 0.5 percent alcohol, which was legal under the Volstead Act. Some also made soda or food products that ultimately were used in the home-brew process, such as malt syrup and yeast. Among them was Anheuser-Busch, although August A. Busch was said to be dismayed by the illicit use. "If you really want to know, we ended up as the biggest bootlegging supply house in the United States," August Busch, Jr., was quoted by Peter Hernon and Terry Ganey in their book, *Under the Influence: The Unauthorized Story of the Anheuser-Busch Dynasty.* "Every goddamn thing you could think of. Oh, the malt syrup cookies! You could no more eat the malt syrup cookies. They were so bitter. . . . It damn near broke Daddy's heart."

Anheuser-Busch—once a 150-building enterprise that covered seventy city blocks—stopped brewing beer in October 1918. It sold off half of its property in unused buildings and other real estate, made glucose, corn sugar, corn oil, and livestock feed, and manufactured a frozen eggnog product, Anheuser-Busch ice cream, and a chocolate-covered ice cream bar called Smack, a forerunner of the Eskimo Pie.

Easily the most divergent of the St. Louis brewers, Anheuser-Busch converted its Old Wagon Shop into a manufacturing plant for truck and motorcoach bodies, manufactured a special refrigerated truck body suitable for hauling ice cream and other perishable foods, built diesel engines for U.S. submarines, owned a coal company and the Hotel Adolphus in Dallas, Texas, and operated a tiny railway known as the St. Louis and O'Fallon. In 1926, it secured a permit to resume the manufacture of Malt-Nutrine, an alcoholic tonic for new mothers originally produced by the brewery about thirty years prior to prohibition. It also produced Bevo near-beer, carbonated coffee and tea drinks called Caffo and Buschtee, respectively, Busch Extra Dry Ginger Ale, and a beverage syrup known as Grape Bouquet. "My good daddy called us in his office shortly before prohibition went into effect," August Busch, Jr., recalled in 1970. "He looked out the window, at the brewery, and he said, 'You all can afford to ride this out, to retire, but in my book prohibition is a challenge and we owe it to our employees to keep going.' Brother and I swore that come hell or high water we would keep it going."

A ten-ton-capacity baker's yeast plant was installed in 1926 that required the services of an additional 150 employees. By that time, the number of employees had dwindled to 1,800 from 7,000 in 1920. An estimated 25,000 people in the brewing and dependent industries had relied on Anheuser-Busch for their livelihood prior to prohibition.

A Soft Market

The promise of a magic "beer pill" in 1919 never materialized for struggling St. Louis–area brewers. "So long as the citizen of this great free nation cherishes his inherent right to take a swallow of water after a pill, that long may he have his beer," proclaimed the February 15 edition of *The Brewer and Maltster*, which announced the development of a beer pill by the Pabst Brewery. "These little life savers are intended for conversion into lager after being placed on the tongue—a mouthful of water and a shake of the head does the trick."

Wagner Brewing Company of Granite City ventured for a short time into the ice and soft drink business. In 1923, the ice plant was taken over by the Granite City Ice and Fuel Company for a sale price of one hundred dollars, which

ALMOST BEER

Many breweries at the outset of prohibition marketed a checked-fermentation near-beer or a dealcoholized beer product, according to brewery historians Donald Roussin and Kevin Kious:

Old Appleton—Appleton
Bluff City—Special Brew
Lemp—Cerva, Tally
Anheuser-Busch—Bevo, Busch Lager, Budweiser
Schibi—Tipling
Mascoutah—Masco
Griesedieck—Hek
Falstaff—Falstaff
Western—Stag (later bottled by Falstaff)
New Athens—Jiffy
Schott—Helvetia Delicio
Stecher—Oasis
Columbia—Alpen Brau

included all brewery buildings and equipment, Roussin and Kious noted. In the early 1930s, the brewery buildings were used as a commissary by a local relief organization. In East St. Louis, the Central Brewing Company made it in the ice and soft drink business until 1931, when the brewery sold in a foreclosure sale for $63,000, a sum that included a beer depot in nearby Granite City and an old saloon in Mount Olive. A similar fate befell the Hannibal Brewery, which also produced non-alcoholic beverages for a time, but folded. Around 1925, the city of Hannibal rented the property to Stark Nursery.

In Washington, Missouri, another Busch brewery—founded in 1855 by John Busch, brother of Adolphus—survived prohibition. The John B. Busch Brewery sold the trademark rights to its cereal beverage, Buscho, to Anheuser-Busch, went into the ice and soda business, and was believed to have manufactured potato chips at some point. It later became a distributor for Anheuser-Busch products.

The old Fischbach Brewery on Clay Street in St. Charles, Missouri, had installed a new cold storage plant and thirty-five-ton ice machine shortly before prohibition. That equipment found a new use when it was converted into the St. Charles Dairy in 1919, and the successful enterprise sold milk and twenty-five flavors of ice cream. However, Jacob Fischbach, president of the former brewery, was fined $1,500 in 1925 after federal agents found 180 barrels of beer in his brewery, author Steve Ehlmann wrote in *Crossroads: A History of St. Charles County, Missouri.* "Deputy United States Marshal Tom Elton, a former St. Charles boy, came here this afternoon from St. Louis and went to Fischbach's Brewery on Clay street where he dumped 180 barrels of real beer into the sewer in the basement of the brewery," the *Daily St. Charles Cosmos-Monitor* reported in January 1925. "This beer was made before the days of prohibition and was being deal-coholized to make beverage, when the company lost its permit about a year ago. The beer had been in charge of the Government since that time, and in dumping it into the sewer this afternoon the Deputy U.S. Marshal carried out the orders of the court. Sheriff [John] Grothe says he was at the brewery when the beer was opened up and it was all soured, the odor being sickening."

The Bluff City Brewery in Alton, Illinois, survived prohibition by selling ice, a bottled near-beer, and a popular root beer. Another Alton brewer, Reck, folded in 1919 after a brief foray into the ice business. Its owner, Anton Reck, followed the business in death, at the age of eighty on June 26, 1922. "A couple of years later, it was rumored that the Reck brewery was going to be sold, either to the recently organized Alton Ice and Beverage Company, or to a group being formed by some men from Joliet, Illinois, which reportedly planned on making near beer, fruit syrups, and soft drinks," Roussin and Kious wrote in an article in the *American Breweriana Journal.* "Supposedly the latter group had also made an overture towards buying a Peoria brewery which had been shut down for making real beer. A bit of reading between the lines could lead to the conclusion that this story was really one about bootleggers showing interest in operating at the former Reck's brewery."

The shuttered Klausmann Brewery already was in the hands of bootleggers when things went awry. On September 25, 1930, an exploding still caused $1,500 damage to the abandoned brewery on Lorentz Avenue near South Broadway. Inside, firemen found two stills and eight 2,500-gallon mash vats. Traffic over the Jefferson Barracks streetcar line on Broadway was delayed by forty-five minutes. The building, which had recently been rented, was owned by the St. Louis Brewing Association.

Anheuser-Busch

Near-beer Mecca

The Griesedieck family had established the Griesedieck Beverage Company in 1917, but they nearly lost the company in 1920 due to financial difficulties. That year, to help buy back the company, and with the popularity of Anheuser-Busch's Bevo near-beer in mind, Joseph "Papa Joe" Griesedieck and his son, Alvin, organized and issued stock in a new company, Falstaff Corporation, with offices on Forest Park Boulevard. The elder Griesedieck had just purchased the Falstaff trademark from the Lemp family for $25,000, and he used the name for their near-beer.

Busch's Bevo, launched in May 1916, set an all-time record when it sold 5 million cases in 1918; the beverage was popular in areas as far away as the Hawaiian Islands and Canada. After six months of national prohibition, however, sales declined rapidly and by 1923 were negligible. This disappointment came after Anheuser-Busch invested more than $15 million in a large bottling plant and other equipment.

The profits were usurped by bootleggers selling real beer and spiked near-beer. Drinkers wanted a "kick" that the malty-tasting Bevo failed to provide.

Many breweries produced near-beer, including the Hyde Park Brewery in St. Louis. Courtesy Kevin Kious and Donald Roussin.

"War-time restriction on the use of grain, and then prohibition which stopped all brewing operations, made it necessary for the Company to change the method of producing Bevo—and this in turn changed the flavor," August Busch, Jr., wrote in 1955. "There is also pretty good proof that the vast quantities of 'home brew' produced was heavy competition for Bevo."

Sales of Budweiser near-beer also declined as the techniques of home brewers improved, though it continued to serve a purpose, Plavchan noted in *A History of Anheuser-Busch, 1852–1933.* "Anheuser-Busch officials found many consumers who like[d] the dealcoholized Budweiser simply as it was, whereas many others preferred to pour a small jigger of grain alcohol into it for that additional 'kick,'" Plavchan wrote.

At Falstaff, the brewery's namesake near-beer was an excellent mixer, Alvin Griesedieck wrote in *The Falstaff Story.* "Falstaff was one of the few 'near beers' that would successfully absorb alcohol when added in the bottle or keg," Griesedieck wrote. "Needless to say, my visits with our distributors took me to many so-called 'spike joints,' some entirely respectable, others no better nor worse than some of our less reputable taverns of today. It was not the type of business that I would have particularly selected, but in those times we could not afford to be choosey."

In addition, Griesedieck Beverage Company produced a near-beer with the unique name Hek, which referred to a beverage fermented by the Egyptians in 1500 B.C. The label carried pictures of the Sphinx and pyramids. "Likewise it was very easy to coin advertising slogans, etc., such as—'Buy Hek—by heck!', and with it all, remember, the name had a meaning, being in reality the Egyptian word for Beer," Griesedieck wrote. "All of which made interesting advertising copy."

To supplement its income, Falstaff cured ham and bacon and sold it under the Falstaff label. The brewery also produced a root beer made with real sugar and had a franchise to manufacture Canada Dry soda, recalled Alexander "Fritz" Zenthoefer, whose father worked for Falstaff during prohibition and for years after. Zenthoefer also worked there for many years, beginning in 1945.

Near-beer alone wasn't enough to pay the bills. The Star Brewery, sister to the Western Brewery in Belleville, Illinois, discontinued production of its Peerless near-beer in 1922 and called in federal agents to legally dump down the sewer 35,000 gallons of beer from which the alcohol had not yet been removed. "A brewery representative said that making near-beer was unprofitable because there were too many home brewers and too much sale of illegal beer!" Roussin and Kious wrote in the *American Breweriana Journal*.

For What "Ales" You

The wets petitioned the Treasury Department to issue regulations that would allow doctors to prescribe full-strength beer as medicine, as they were allowed to do with whiskey. A ruling from the Department of Justice in March 1921, signed by Attorney General A. Mitchell Palmer, permitted physicians to prescribe beer "when the use of it would aid in recovery for illness." While the order was still in its infancy, Anti-Saloon League officials and prohibition proponents went ballistic, prompting dry legislators to draft an "antibeer bill." The wets and drys lined up in the usual manner for the debate, with a few strange bedfellows. Among them was August A. Busch, who sided with the drys on the anti-beer bill. He said beer prescriptions would lead to general law-breaking and would benefit only the rich, while the poor would not be able to afford the price of prescriptions. "Beer for all or beer for none," Busch said.

The anti-medicinal-beer bill, the Willis-Campbell Bill, was signed into law November 23, 1921, by President Warren Harding, who voted dry but kept plenty of liquor on hand for his parties at the White House. Disappointed brewers included the Falstaff Corporation of St. Louis, which had secured a government permit and had begun the manufacturing process for medicinal beer.

SURVIVAL TACTICS

Brewers with licenses to manufacture near-beer began with real beer, then sent it through a machine that removed the alcohol. This led to an ongoing temptation for brewers to skip the dealcoholization process, Roussin and Kious said. "Not every brewery bootlegged, but quite a few of them did," Roussin said. "It kind of goes back to the German mentality that beer was your birthright."

For many it was critical to survival, added Major Walter A. Green, former chief prohibition investigator, in a 1926 article. "Prohibition enforcement experts believe that 90 per cent of all brewers must cheat all or part of the time, or go out of the business," Green wrote. "That is only opinion, to be sure, but it is indicative. Add to this anything you like for the incalculable but enormous amount of near-beer that is needled [injected] with alcohol somewhere along the line after it leaves the brewery, and you have a possible total which will upset any idea that there isn't much 'kick-beer' to be had.

"The drys, of course, soft-pedal on the number of criminally active breweries," Green added. "But the number is very large, and the output is a satisfying flood to the thirsty."

For a short time after prohibition began, Falstaff and a half-dozen other breweries in St. Louis pulled down the window shades and made real beer on certain days, until prohibition enforcement agents in St. Louis put a stop to the practice, Zenthoefer said. "Jellyroll Hogan (a gangster and politician—see Chapter 8) would come with the trucks and haul the beer away," Zenthoefer said. "He would distribute it to the saloons."

In April 1925, Hogan and Falstaff president Joseph Griesedieck were indicted for conspiracy to violate the Volstead Act by shipping a carload of beer to Jefferson City in April 1923. The charges later were dropped by Judge Charles B. Faris because both Griesedieck and Hogan had testified before a grand jury investigating beer protection rackets. Faris ruled that the interrogation of a person by the grand jury barred the indictment of that individual on any charge connected with the offense on which he was questioned.

Officials of Anheuser-Busch were said to have spent thousands of dollars on locks each month to ensure real beer wasn't taken out of the plant. However, a brewery employee recalled August, Jr., taking beer out of the plant for his own personal use before it was dealcoholized, and other employees drank it on the job, Hernon and Ganey wrote in *Under the Influence*. "As the man in charge of brewing operations, it would appear [August Busch, Jr.'s] own attitude was one

MISSOURI BREWERIES AT THE TIME OF PROHIBITION

* denotes those that survived prohibition

Cape Brewery & Ice Company, Cape Girardeau*
Hannibal Brewing Company, South Side Brewery, Hannibal
Capitol Brewery Company, Jefferson City*
Old Appleton Brewery and Ice Company, Old Appleton*
Schibi Spring Brewing Company, St. Charles
Fischbach Brewing Company, St. Charles*
American Brewery, St. Louis
Anheuser-Busch Brewing Association, St. Louis*
City Brewery, St. Louis
Columbia Brewery, St. Louis*
Columbia Weiss Beer Brewery, St. Louis
Empire Brewery, St. Louis
Gast Brewery, St. Louis*
Green Tree Brewery, St. Louis
Griesedieck Beverage Company, St. Louis (Falstaff Corporation also
    launched during prohibition)*
Griesedieck Brothers Brewery, St. Louis*
H. Grone Brewery, St. Louis
Hyde Park Brewery, St. Louis*
Klausmann Brewery, St. Louis
Louis Obert Brewing Company, St. Louis*
National Brewery, St. Louis
Otto F. Stifel's Union Brewing Company, St. Louis
Schorr-Kolkschneider Brewing Company, St. Louis*
Stettner & Thoma Weiss Beer Brewing Company, St. Louis
Wainwright Brewery, St. Louis
Wm. J. Lemp Brewing Company, St. Louis
Sainte Genevieve Brewing & Lighting Association, Ste. Genevieve
John J. Busch Brewing Company, Washington*

ILLINOIS BREWERIES AT THE TIME OF PROHIBITION

* denotes those that survived prohibition

Bluff City Brewery, Alton*
Anton Reck Brewing Company, Alton
Western Brewery Company, Belleville (later Griesedieck-Western)*
Star Brewing Company, Belleville*
Cairo Brewing Company, Cairo
Central Brewery, East St. Louis*
St. Louis Brewing Association, Heim Brewery
Highland Brewing Company, Highland (later Schott)*
Wagner Brewing Company, Granite City
Lebanon Brewery, Lebanon
Mascoutah Brewing Company, Mascoutah
Millstadt Brewery Company, Millstadt
Rudolph Stecher Brewing Company, Murphysboro
New Athens Brewery, New Athens (later Mound City Brewing Company)*
American Brewing Company, Pekin
Gipps Brewing Company, Peoria*
Gustav Leisy Brewing Company, Peoria
Union Brewing Company, Peoria*
Dick & Bro., Quincy Brewery Company, Quincy
Ruff Brewing Company, Quincy*
Reisch Brewing Company, Springfield*
Waterloo Brewing Company, Waterloo

of benign neglect when it came to employees drinking on the job," Hernon and Ganey wrote. "The consumption of real beer on the premises was so methodical, he recalled, that he was tipped off in advance whenever a group of workers got together to toss back a few so that he wouldn't risk seeing them. August A., by contrast, insisted on strict compliance with the law. 'Daddy,' his son said, 'wouldn't let us take one bottle out of the place.'"

In one instance near-beer was needled before it left the Highland Brewery, prohibition agents from Chicago learned in 1925 after they pulled a fast one on the Highland, Illinois, company. Highland, which once turned out 75,000 barrels of beer a year, had a permit for a time to produce a non-alcoholic drink called Helvetia Delicio. "For seventy years the Highland Brewing Company has been making beer," the *St. Louis Star* reported on January 22, 1925. "Before prohibition it was real; afterwards it has been near-beer. But rumors reached Chicago that it was getting too near, the agents said." Two agents were dispatched, and they reported to Chief Field Agent Charles W. Vursell that the brewery was closed. So Vursell called his "crack brewery squad"—agents Johnson, Sandberg, and Benson—who visited the small town for two weeks. They reported back that someone had been trailing them, spies from some unknown person. They sent their automobile to a nearby town, purchased train tickets for Chicago and boarded, and got off at the town where their car had been taken. Then they high-tailed it back to Highland.

"The car creaked to a stop with its brakes set, while the three men leaped from the car to the brewery door. The door swung open. There was [Eugene] Schott, the president," Johnson said today, "with two five-gallon cans of alcohol, trying to empty them. Back of him was Rolla Newdecker, his clerk, with three one-gallon glass jugs of the same stuff. Newdecker had the corks out and one jug was partly emptied."

A LITANY OF LAWBREAKERS

Drys in St. Louis kept the authorities informed of the renegade brewers in town. In June 1921, Bessie M. Shupp, secretary of the Anti-Saloon League, wrote a letter to Missouri Governor Arthur M. Hyde. "Father is out of town today, but asked me to write you giving you the names of the breweries down here that are breaking the law," wrote Shupp, daughter of Missouri Anti-Saloon League superintendent W. C. Shupp. "They are the Louis Obert Brewing Co., 12th and McGirk Sts., the Griesedieck Bros. Brewing Co., 19th and Shenandoah Sts., and the Hyde Park Brewing Co. Most every saloon here is now selling the products of one or more of these breweries."

A complaint by W. C. Shupp led to the second raid in three weeks on the Obert Brewery in late September 1921. A truck loaded with ninety cases was seized in front of the brewery, which had been operating quietly since 1876 in the shadow of the nearby Anheuser-Busch Brewery. Earlier, on September 8, 1921, agents headed by E. J. Hoover raided the plant and confiscated a truck loaded with 178 cases of bottles with a 4.1 percent alcohol content. "St. Louis Bakers' Association—All Goods Delivered Promptly," read the sign on the truck. "Whether or not the Obert family directly sanctioned the bootlegging is unknown," Roussin and Kious wrote. "However, as the Obert Brewery was still tightly held by the family, it is hard to believe that they were not at least indirectly involved with the making of intoxicating brew.

"Despite the Federal raids, the Obert Brewery managed to keep its manufacturing license in hand, and its doors open until 1927, when the financial failure of the company accomplished what Federal Agent E. J. Hoover could not. The lights in the brewery would be turned off for the next six years."

Obert was not alone. A litany of lawbreakers made headlines, including Schorr-Kolkschneider in St. Louis and Old Appleton in outstate Missouri; and in Illinois the Mascoutah Brewing Company in Mascoutah, Griesedieck-Western Brewery in Belleville, Rudolph Stecher Brewing Company in Murphysboro, and the New Athens Brewery in New Athens. The Missouri River was the ben-

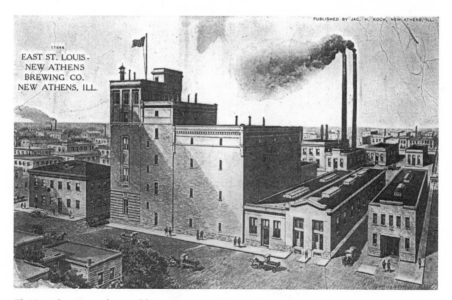

The New Athens Brewery before prohibition. Courtesy Kevin Kious and Donald Roussin.

eficiary of 925 barrels of beer on July 19, 1923, generously supplied by prohibition agents. It had been produced by the Moerschel Brewery in Jefferson City and had contained more alcohol than the law allowed.

Beer Barons Five Years Running

Operated by well-to-do brothers Ben and George Probst, who inherited the old-time brewery from their father, New Athens's name was changed in 1920 to the Probst Pure Products Company. This was fitting because the company manufactured pure, unaltered beer from 1921 to 1926 while it managed to escape prosecution. Despite periodic raids, charges in five cases were dismissed due to "insufficient evidence" by the U.S. district attorney from East St. Louis, William O. Potter, and federal judge George Washington English of Illinois's Eastern District. English's son, George W. English, Jr., was one of the attorneys who represented the brewery in two of the court cases. The other attorney was Charles B. Thomas, a "friend of the Court" and the recipient of many favors at the hands of English, according to the *Post-Dispatch*, which had launched an investigation of English in 1925 (see Chapter 14). "For years corrupt federal and state agents took advantage of the brewery's hospitality by holding drinking parties there," Roussin and Kious wrote in an article in the *American Breweriana Journal*. "It also became fairly common knowledge that a large Belleville speakeasy was obtaining a steady supply of real beer from New Athens."

In 1923, prohibition agents seized a carload of 550 cases of real beer on a siding track of the Southern Railway Company in East St. Louis. The agents traced the contraband to the New Athens Brewery and informed Potter. Six months later, after Assistant U.S. Attorney General Mabel Walker Willebrandt inquired about the case in a letter, Potter charged the Probst Pure Products Company with violation of the Volstead Act. "Several terms of court passed without the case being considered and finally, on October 6, 1925, Potter, with the Government's files of the case under his arm, appeared before Judge English and remarked: 'Another case of insufficient evidence, your honor,'" the *Post* reported. "'Veery well, case dismissed,' answered the Judge, and another Government failure was written on the court docket."

Potter also was presented evidence of an alleged protection scheme involving Griesedieck-Western Brewery in Belleville. He nol-prossed, or failed to prosecute due to insufficient evidence, a charge that the brewery allegedly paid five thousand dollars in protection money to an unidentified government department. Brice Armstrong, a dry enforcement agent, testified to the charge before a U.S. Senate investigating committee in 1924. H. L. Griesedieck, president of Griesedieck-Western, denied the allegation. Eventually, Potter was not reappointed, and English resigned rather than face an impeachment trial before the U.S. Senate for "high misdemeanors." Potter, said to be worried over his failure to be reappointed, killed his wife, two children, two grandchildren, and himself at his Marion, Illinois, home in 1926.

The Probst brothers finally were indicted in 1925, and English's successor, federal judge Walter C. Lindley, presided over the case in federal court in East St. Louis. In December 1926, ten people and the Probst Pure Products Company were found guilty of conspiracy to violate the Volstead Act by the manufacture and sale of real beer. They included Belleville saloonkeepers Antone and Philip Wolf, beer truck driver Arthur Gass, and brewmaster William Schreiber, each of whom was sentenced to a year and a day at Leavenworth. Ben and George Probst stayed out of jail on a series of appeals but finally were sentenced in 1928 to ninety days in the Franklin County Jail at Benton and fined one thousand dollars. In short order, however, a local newspaper revealed the Benton jailer allowed the brothers to drive his son's car and to lounge on the lawn outside the building on warm days. Federal judge Fred L. Wham ordered them moved to the Vermillion County Jail at Danville. In 1933, George Probst resurrected the brewery as the Mound City Brewing Company.

ALCOHOLIC TO THE CORE IN OLD APPLETON

Located at the edge of the Ozark Mountains, Old Appleton, Missouri, was for many years the home of the Old Appleton Brewery, which survived prohibition in part by bootlegging real beer in enterprising fashion. Roussin and Kious in 2003 interviewed ninety-three-year-old Louis Meyer, who has since passed away. Meyer's father, Theodore, and grandfather, Ignatz, ran the brewery for close to a half-century. "Interestingly, Louis learned to operate a car during the early days of Prohibition by driving the autos of St. Louis bootleggers from the Old Appleton Brewery grounds to some out-of-the-way location, such as a farmer's barn," Roussin and Kious wrote in *American Breweriana Journal*. "Once there, he would stuff the vehicles, usually equipped with false compartments, with bottles of Old Appleton beer packed in cloth bags that had been stashed at that location in advance. After a little practice, he could pack the equivalent of 25 cases of beer into the modified cars before driving back to meet the owner.

The Old Appleton Brewery in 1917. Courtesy Tim Conklin.

He also chauffered nuns to Mass in between bootlegging runs, which as a kid he felt 'kind of balanced things out.'" The brewers at times used fake labels printed with the name of a Canadian brewery known as Huether's in Kitchener, Ontario, but that didn't fool the local press, which may have helped print them.

In 1928, the brewers at Old Appleton were approached by a thirty-six-year-old boxer-turned-bootlegger named Benny McGovern, who wanted the brewery to "run with me, or you're not going to run at all." McGovern, who once sold bootleg whiskey from Canada out of a florist shop, more recently had been selling inferior homebrew made in St. Louis. He also had ties to St. Louis gangsters and nearly died in 1932 after his car was machine-gunned near the intersection of Clayton and Warson Roads in west St. Louis County. He was rushed to a hospital, where a surgeon told his wife, Ann, he wasn't expected to live. He gave her a few minutes to say goodbye. "Upon hearing this, Ann rushed into Benny's room wailing, 'No way you're going to leave me here, to raise these children by myself,' all the while pounding on his chest with her fists," Roussin and Kious wrote. "Benny is said to have groaned softly during his wife's impassioned plea, which prompted the surgeon to dash back into the room and resume resuscitation efforts on his 'dead' patient! Benny was quickly revived, and eventually made a full recovery."

Old Appleton was raided at least three times during prohibition. In 1932,

Symphonic Suds

He was scheduled to perform in one of the foremost beer cities in the nation, and there was no beer to be had. So famed composer and pianist Sergei Rachmaninoff did what any thirsty gentleman would do—he begged—when he arrived in St. Louis in January 1920 to plan for his second concerto with the St. Louis Symphony Orchestra the following month. "I'll play anything you want . . . just as you declare—but on one condition," Rachmaninoff told Conductor Max Zach over breakfast at the Jefferson Hotel. "That is, that I must have a dozen bottles of genuine beer to drink while I am in St. Louis!"

Local brewing magnates, however, were turning up dry. Finally, August A. Busch came to the rescue. "You can say for me that if it isn't a penitentiary offense, I'll be glad to accommodate Mr. Rachmaninoff," Busch said. "Be sure and tell Mr. Rachmaninoff not to go to the brewery, however. Have him come to Grant farm, my home. A brewery is the last place in the world to look for beer in these days."

prohibition agents raided the brewery twice, in May and August. The first time, they confiscated six thousand gallons of real brew, which authorities said had been going to St. Louis speakeasies. The second time, they netted fourteen thousand gallons of beer valued at twenty-five thousand dollars at wholesale bootleg prices. The brewery's sewer emptied into nearby Apple Creek, where several neighbors were said to have waded out with buckets to rescue the product.

After one last raid of its brewery trucks on Missouri Highway 25, in February 1933, the brewery began making legal beer. McGovern purchased the company and renamed it the McGovern Brewery Company in 1934.

Fighting Spirit in Illinois

Established before the Civil War and known for its popular Electric Brew, the venerable Mascoutah Brewing Company changed its name to the Mascoutah Products Company with the advent of prohibition. It was deemed one of fifteen to twenty "cheating" breweries in the state, seized by the government for repeated violations of the Volstead Act and dismantled and sold, piece by piece, in 1925. Later, in the waning days of prohibition, the brewery's buildings were all but demolished by a tornado.

Rudolph Stecher Brewing Company in Murphysboro, on the other hand, survived even the infamous southern Illinois tornado of 1925 before the Feds killed it. Rudolph Stecher had founded a successful cooperage works across the street from Anheuser-Busch in south St. Louis after the Civil War and expanded into the brewing industry in Murphysboro in the late 1880s. After prohibition began, the brewery produced a near-beer, but it also continued to produce real beer illegally. After repeated seizures of real beer, the government ordered the brewery closed the same year as the tornado.

COOPERS AND THE CONTINENTAL

Prohibition decimated the cooperage industry, which manufactured barrels to hold beer, wine, and whiskey. A Searcy County, Arkansas, entrepreneur named Ed Mays was well acquainted with the destructive effects. By 1918, he had purchased the Pekin Company Stave Plant, one of the largest manufacturers of barrel staves in the country, only to have prohibition wipe out most of the market, Stephen L. Trampe noted in *The Queen of Lace: The Story of the Continental Life Building.* Mays, also a banker, brought his family to St. Louis. In 1928, he decided to build an Art Deco skyscraper at Grand Boulevard and Olive Street. At the top of the Continental Life Building he added plans for a penthouse for his family on the twenty-first, twenty-second, and twenty-third floors.

"The twenty-third floor would have been an ideal location for entertaining guests with liquor," Trampe wrote. "It was secluded and secure and would have provided ample warning for a raid because there was only one means of entry— through an elevator and two sets of doors. Given the nature of the twenty-third-floor space, there would have been better places in the building, particularly the ballroom, or the main floor of the penthouse, to properly entertain guests. The only appeal of the twenty-third floor may have been the availability of 'spirits.'" Mays, who made his initial fortune in the wine and whiskey barrel stave industry, scorned prohibition, Trampe added. "In fact, he detested the dry laws, since they put his barrel stave company virtually out of business and substantially decreased the value of his holdings," he wrote. "He was also not one to adhere to laws or regulations that inconvenienced him. In an anecdote related by his daughter, Mays had liquor on the premises during prohibition and even served a drink to one of his daughter's dates. The front door to the penthouse was also built as a classic speak-easy door, with a small panel that slid open to view any prospective visitor. It was an ornate walnut door that looked like it was inspired by an Eliot Ness newsreel."

Filling the Void

The outlook wasn't all grim in St. Louis. By 1929, St. Louis's industrial district was seventh in the nation in manufacturing, with $1.542 billion in products, James Neal Primm noted in *Lion of the Valley*. "Other industries filled the vacuum left by the temporary loss of the brewing giants," Primm wrote. "Despite the relative decline of wholesaling nationally, the city's jobbing trade set new records in the 1920s, and light manufacturing, especially the making of shoes and women's clothing, was booming. Electrical manufacturing, represented locally by the Century, Moloney, Knapp-Monarch, Emerson, and Wagner firms, had grown rapidly since the 1890s; and Ford and General Motors had found that St. Louis's railroad connections and large trade territory made it an ideal location for their assembly plants."

Spelunking for Spirits

Some of St. Louis's splendid German beer gardens drifted away with prohibition, while others died a peaceful death before dry times hit. Schnaider's, Schoenlau's, Koerner's, Kammerer's, and Cherokee all are memories today. "The beer gardens became family gathering places on balmy afternoons with waiters running among the outdoor tables with foamy pitchers of beer and edibles," a reporter wrote in 1964. "Perhaps the most famous of them all was Uhrig's Cave, an underground cavern at Jefferson and Washington. This refuge from the summer heat could handle 3,500 persons at a time. Besides beer, patrons could enjoy entertainment ranging from light opera to vaudeville. And many a top star of old played the cave." The first entertainment spot in St. Louis to use electric lights, Uhrig's held band concerts and picnics in the early days and drew audiences of three thousand at its peak in the mid-1880s, Hubert and Charlotte Rother noted in *Lost Caves of St. Louis.*

Part of the estate of prominent physician Dr. William Beaumont, the cave was purchased by brewer Joseph Uhrig in 1852, Mary Bartley observed in *St. Louis Lost.* As the cave was fine for ageing and lagering but proved too cold for comfortable beer sipping, Uhrig built an above-ground beer garden and dance

Schnaider's Beer Garden was located on St. Louis' near South Side in the vicinity of Lafayette Square in the late 1800s.

hall. "In 1881, a saloon keeper named Tom McNeary leased the cave site and then bought it for $50,000 in 1884," Bartley wrote. "McNeary rearranged the beer tables to provide seating for 1,600, hired the Spencer Opera Company, and gained worldwide fame as a sponsor of light opera. He added three separate music pavilions so that his customers could be entertained nonstop by relays of fine orchestras. Phalanxes of waiters served his cave-cooled beer, wine, and large platters laden with food. No detail was overlooked—there were 'retiring women' to help the ladies with their wraps and groomsmen to attend the carriages of those who drove there to enjoy the music and fresh air."

St. Louis writer and poet Orrick Johns recalled visiting the cave in his memoir, *Time of Our Lives:*

> In the garden, set with tables on the bare ground, a stock company played light opera during the summer. It was at Uhrig's Cave that I first heard the "Mikado," with Lillian Berry and Frank Moulan, "Pirates of Penzance," "Martha," "Bohemian Girl," the "Chimes of Normandy." The manager was a tall, lean Irishman, with a beautiful accent, a deep campaign color, and a military moustache, a man known in theaters all over the country, and with a name no boy could forget: Billy Blood. He was a friend of the family and treated the boys like favored guests. After the performances at Uhrig's Cave, Billy Blood and members of the company joined their friends among the regular patrons at the beer tables, and the talk often lasted until the early morning hours. There I also first had pointed out to me old Adolphus Busch, Marse Henry Watterson, Billy Reedy, the Lemps, of "Falstaff" fame, and other local characters.

The Coliseum

The commercial cave fizzled in 1903 and subsequently served as a roller-skating rink, a bowling alley, and a mushroom farm; a multipurpose building called the Coliseum was built over it. In 1928, Herbert Hoover delivered the keynote speech of the Republican National Convention in the large hall. Underneath, however, the cave was long vacant—or so everyone thought until prohibition enforcement agents followed a tip and discovered a large distillery forty-five feet underground at Jefferson Avenue and Morgan Street on June 25, 1926. In an area two blocks north and half a block west of the Coliseum, they found two two-hundred-gallon-capacity stills, along with a section of the cave walled up to serve as vats for twenty-four thousand gallons of whiskey mash, forty feet below street level.

Whoever set up the stills did so piece by piece and installed electricity and an exhaust fan. Several chairs and piles of sacks were laid out as though for beds, and two hundred empty five-gallon tins were found near the still. Agents also found twenty-seven five-gallon cans of an excellent-quality, uncolored alcohol.

Police arrested four men, including a German immigrant, two African Americans, and Lawrence W. Foster, owner of the Foster Hauling Company. Foster, who lived over the garage, said he had sublet part of the building used for general storage purposes to another man, but the officers were unsuccessful in finding him.

CHAPTER 5

A BRIGHT AND SHINING LIGHT

HE WAS "A BRIGHT AND SHINING LIGHT" OF THE PROHIBITION CRUSADERS, A Farmington-raised newspaper publisher, and Missouri's labor commissioner under Governor Arthur M. Hyde from 1923 to 1924. His younger brother, Gus Orvel Nations, was chief of the state prohibition enforcement forces in Missouri's Eastern District.

Heber Nations rode with the local sheriff on more than one hundred raids on bootleggers in Cole County as a member of a group known as "The Four Horsemen." He published the *Jefferson City Daily Post*, where, in February 1925, a temporary restraining order sought by nearly every physician in Jefferson City ended the paper's practice of printing the names of persons who received prescriptions for medicinal whiskey. Such prescriptions were legal during prohibition.

So it made national headlines when, on May 29, 1925, Heber Nations was convicted in federal court in St. Louis of taking bribes to protect the Griesedieck Brothers Brewery Company. The beer protection scheme also involved the state's food and drug commissioner, Charles S. Prather: Both Nations and Prather were political appointees of Republican Governor Hyde. The troops of temperance expressed unwavering support of Heber Nations. Three times he was convicted of conspiracy to violate the Volstead Act, and three times the convictions were overturned in the U.S. Circuit Court of Appeals and new trials ordered In October 1933, U.S. District Attorney Louis H. Breuer dismissed the charge against Nations, observing beer had been legalized and "the Eighteenth amendment is now on its last legs."*

---

*The appeals court reversed Heber Nations's first conviction on the grounds that Judge Charles Faris should have disqualified himself when asked by Nations's attorneys to do so, on an affidavit by Nations charging the judge was prejudiced against him. The second reversal was due to a prejudicial statement made by the district attorney in his argument to the jury. The third reversal was because evidence admissible in the second trial was not admissible in the third, the court decided, because "a connecting link of evidence was lacking," i.e., a government witness at the second trial failed to appear at the third trial.

Heber Nations. Courtesy the St. Louis Post-Dispatch.

Ice-Cold Beer Bust

During prohibition, some public officials in Missouri took bribes, or "protection" payments, to look the other way as liquor producers and sellers engaged in an illegal trade. While investigating this trade one frosty morning in February 1924, federal prohibition enforcement agents planned to raid the Griesedieck Brewery but were beaten to the punch by Gus Nations and five of his state agents. They seized seven hundred to eight hundred cases of beer and took into custody Raymond Griesedieck, secretary-treasurer of the brewing company; J. Edward Griesedieck, superintendent; and forty-three employees. Nations's men reportedly had to draw their revolvers to keep several of the workers from running away.

That Griesedieck was raided wasn't big news: The brewery had been raided and fined in the past for producing real beer. In December 1923, however, information had been leaked to the *St. Louis Post-Dispatch* that Griesedieck was manufacturing and selling real beer under the protection of two state officials. Reporters from the *Post* turned over their findings in January 1924 to federal prohibition officials, who launched an investigation and learned the brewers were not happy with the price they were paying of one dollar per case for "protection."

The Griesedieck Brothers Brewery prior to prohibition. Courtesy of Kevin Kious and Donald Roussin.

Gus Nations, it was learned later, knew rumors had circulated of a protection scheme, and made the raid to demonstrate that the Griesedieck plant wasn't getting protection from him. Investigators soon released the names of Prather and Heber Nations. Prather had been in trouble with the law before: He had been charged in May 1922 with operating a still at Bloomfield, Missouri, but the case was dismissed in the circuit court there. Prather resigned his post in March 1924 and was indicted in April 1924. Initially, he maintained his innocence; he later pleaded guilty in U.S. District Court, as did the Griesedieck Brewery as a corporate defendant. Heber Nations resigned as the state's labor commissioner just before his indictment in May 1924. He claimed his actions were part of a plan to catch the Griesedieck Brewery making beer and joked with reporters after he posted bond. "I suppose I would look better with handcuffs on," he said.

Prosecutors alleged Griesedieck paid Heber Nations through Prather to use alleged influence over his brother, Gus, to keep prohibition agents away while the brewery manufactured full-strength beer. Investigators confiscated a small notebook, bound in red leather, from brewmaster Edward Wagner that listed sixteen occasions over the previous nine months when some seventeen thousand cases of real beer left the plant. U.S. District Judge Charles Faris ordered the brewery closed for a year.

Gus was suffering from appendicitis in Bethesda General Hospital in March 1924 when investigators implicated his brother and Prather. "Show me a man who will say he ever gave Gus Nations a nickel for protection or ever got a nickel's worth of protection from him, and I will show you the biggest liar in America," Heber told a reporter when he came to St. Louis to visit his brother. He declined to comment on his own guilt or innocence.

Gus Nations was legal adviser to the director of prohibition in Missouri, acting head of the prohibition field forces, and acting prohibition department group head for St. Louis when he resigned in June 1924. He entered the race for the Republican nomination for attorney general but was defeated.

Asked about the Griesedieck scandal, L. F. DeHart, state prohibition director for Missouri, expressed his confidence in Gus during a visit to Bethesda Hospital. Gus Nations was never charged, or implicated in trial testimony, with any wrongdoing in the case. "I am positive he has had nothing to do with any graft in the fulfillment of his official duties," DeHart told a reporter. DeHart was then asked if his confidence in Gus Nations extended to his brother, Heber. "Well, you know, I told a reporter in Kansas City that the worst trouble with Gus was that he had Heber for a brother," De Hart said. "That was a sort of a joke, but you can judge for yourself from that."

Klan Connections

Heber Nations was no stranger to controversy. In February 1924, he had arranged a meeting of the Ku Klux Klan in the Missouri State Capitol at which the Reverend Z. A. Harris of Blackwell, Oklahoma, spoke on "Americanism and the Ku Klux Klan." The meeting was scheduled, Nations said, in response to a "slurring reference to the klan" by a speaker for "a secret religious organization." The speaker was Peter Collins, a nationally known sociologist who discussed the need for "Catholic and Protestant, Jew and Gentile, [to work] together like brothers for the upbuilding of the home town." The secret organization was the Knights of Columbus, a Catholic men's club.

Though he would claim only to be a friend of the Ku Klux Klan, Heber Nations likely was an influential leader in the organization, along with the other Horsemen: Jefferson City Sheriff L. C. Withaup, Jinx Coffelt, and Phil Berry. A rival newspaper, the *Jefferson City Tribune*, referred to Heber as "the most prominent Klansman in Missouri" and one of the leaders of the Klan, which included "more than 1000 of the best citizens in Jefferson City, and which has exerted a powerful influence for law and order." By his own account, Heber Nations

*Raymond Griesedieck. Courtesy Ray
Griesedieck of Griesedieck Brothers
Brewing Corporation.*

enjoyed a close friendship with Klansmen and an intimate knowledge of the group's structure and activities.

An enforcement agency known as the Prohibition Unit was established at the outset of prohibition, but its network of state and federal enforcement agents was extremely limited. Local police forces and sheriffs were expected to assist the agents, but they had other duties, and their liquor-control efforts often were lackluster. Citizens in many communities across Missouri were dissatisfied with prohibition enforcement, and local Klansmen often pitched in as vigilantes (see Chapter 15).

The Horsemen conducted raids of suspected liquor producers and establishments and published photographs of the confiscated stills in the *Daily Post*, often with a story on the raid. A competing newspaper told of a raid on twelve Jefferson City soft-drink parlors in June 1924 by Heber Nations, who was identified in the story as a prohibition enforcement officer. The crusade against liquor was part of a larger, cultural and religious battle by many native-born Protestant citizens and dry leaders against what they considered the sinful and destructive influence of immigrants, many of them Catholics and beer-drinking Germans. These views were embodied in an editorial cartoon published in the *Daily Post* in July 1926. It portrayed Uncle Sam dumping into Europe a melting pot of aliens with tags attached to their bodies: "alien insane," "alien criminal," "alien degenerate," "alien unfit," "alien vicious," and "alien incurable."

IN THE BLOOD

Both Heber and Gus Nations were of strong opinions, and were willing to back them with their fists if necessary. A Jefferson City newspaper reported one altercation in May 1917, when Heber pummeled a young man who had come out of a pool hall. "I can't discuss the provocation, because it seriously concerns other people," Heber explained at the time. In July 1923, Gus pushed *Post-Dispatch* reporter Ray Webster from a courtroom in the Federal Building in downtown St. Louis at a hearing on the revocation of a druggist's permit to sell medicinal whiskey. Outside, the two engaged in fisticuffs over Webster's right to cover the hearing.

Heber was the first of seven siblings born to Sarah McFarland Nations and Gilbert Owen Nations, also of strong opinions. Gilbert, descendant of a pioneering Anglo-Saxon family in Perry and Ste. Genevieve counties, served as a schoolteacher and school superintendent and later as a lawyer and probate judge. "He stands uncompromisingly for clean politics and the rights of the people," noted *The History of Southeast Missouri*, published in 1912. He was an elder in the Christian Church, ran for president on the ticket of the American Party, a nativist political organization, and authored several publications critical of the Catholic religion: *Blight of Mexico; or Four Hundred Years of Papal Tyranny and Plunder; The Canon Law of the Papal Throne; Papal Guilt of the World War; Papal Sovereignty, the Government Within Our Government;* and *The Political Career of Alfred E. Smith.*

Sarah Nations' piety and the family's avoidance of liquor impressed Gus Nations early on. "I have never either used it or served it and there has been none in my family in four generations," he wrote in 1929. "I have been an advocate of prohibition since I learned my prayers at my mother's knee."

During his teens, Gus served for three years as president of the Young People's Branch of the state WCTU, which boasted five thousand members. He attended the Christian University at Canton and became editor of the *Arcadia Valley Enterprise* at age nineteen. He later became an attorney, and in 1916 he served as a district delegate to the Progressive National Convention in Chicago, where he forged a friendship with future governor Arthur Hyde. He was named chief prohibition agent in St. Louis in 1922.

Heber Nations graduated from the Cape Girardeau State Normal School, by 1912 was married and working in real estate in Flat River, Missouri, and in 1916 served as a lieutenant with the Missouri National Guard on the Mexican border. By 1917, he was divorced, had three young children, and served as a Jef-

ferson City correspondent for the *St. Louis Post-Dispatch*. A year later, he married
Alma Conrath, member of a prominent German-American Protestant family
in Jefferson City. Beginning in 1921 he published the *Daily Post*, where his crusading reporting style was criticized on more than one occasion: Jefferson City
Mayor Cecil W. Thomas referred to Heber in 1924 as "a menace to the peace
and tranquility of this city" for what he described as malicious attacks on certain political candidates, citizens, and institutions.

Under Heber Nations, the *Daily Post* provided thorough coverage of local
religious activities, rendered opinions on Christianity and salvation, featured the
escapades of local drunks on the front page, and denounced the "ruthlessness"
of prohibition's opponents and wet newspapers. Read one editorial, in part:
"After prohibition has become an established fact, and an enforced law, and the
thirsty writers have acquired a taste for buttermilk, they will read with shame the
old files containing their vicious assaults on the fundamental law of the land."

A Tale of Graft

News of the trial shared space with headlines for Dayton, Tennessee, science
teacher John T. Scopes, who was indicted for teaching evolution in Tennessee
in violation of state law. Heber would editorialize in 1927 for a similar anti-
evolution law proposed in Missouri (see Chapter 16), but for now he was a defendant, along with Charles Prather and the Griesedieck Brewery as a corporate
defendant. All pleaded not guilty on the morning of May 25, 1925. After a jury
had been selected, however, both the brewery and Prather switched their pleas to
guilty of conspiracy to violate the prohibition law. Prather, who hailed from the
southeastern Missouri town of Advance, spoke with a Southern drawl in a low
voice. He appeared nervous and ill at ease. In the audience, a hundred women,
each wearing the white ribbon of the Women's Christian Temperance Union
(WCTU), lent their moral support to Heber Nations. Behind the scenes, the
Anti-Saloon League had sent out a pamphlet of propaganda calling for the
charges against Nations to be dropped.

Raymond Griesedieck, this time identified in newspaper accounts as vice
president and manager of the brewery, served as the government's chief witness.
Griesedieck, of 3847 Flora Place in St. Louis, told the attorneys he dealt only
with Prather. He said Prather explained that Heber Nations was already doing
business with one brewery in St. Louis, and he didn't want two brewers testifying against him in case anything blew up. "I had received a telephone call from
a friend [in April 1923] saying that Heber Nations wanted me to meet a friend

A postcard view of Twelfth Street, with the Jefferson Hotel in the center, between Washington Avenue and Locust Street.

of his at Hotel Jefferson," Griesedieck testified. "I went to the hotel and met Prather and we went to his room. We talked about general topics and then about putting out beer. Mr. Prather asked if I would be willing to put out beer if the brewery was protected . . . Mr. Prather explained that Heber Nations could control Gus Nations. He said Heber had got Gus his job, that Gus was just a kid and didn't have a mind of his own, and that he would do what Heber told him. He said Heber could tell Gus to leave town, and Gus would go. I asked what this arrangement would cost, and he said $1 a case of beer. I said I would have to think it over. Mr. Prather called me up a week later, and I told him I thought $1 a case was a high price, but that I was going to run and try it."

Griesedieck said he made the payments—of $1,020 or $1,040 each time—in cash at the Jefferson or Claridge hotels, usually the Jefferson. "When we were making beer I would meet him in the morning and again in the afternoon," Griesedieck said. "I paid him as the beer was made."

Griesedieck said he paid between $10,000 and $13,000 for protection. Prather set the sum at $8,000 to $9,000 and said Heber Nations received two-thirds of the take. "Every dollar Griesedieck paid went to you, didn't it?" asked Nations's attorney, Patrick H. Cullen. "Not every time," Prather replied. "Sometimes Heber would have an adjoining room, or a room on the same floor of the hotel. I'd just leave the money on the table. After Griesedieck had gone I'd call Heber in. He'd take the money and give me one-third."

"But Heber Nations was never, at any time, present when the money was paid. Is that correct?" Cullen asked.

"Yes, that is correct.'"

Later, Prather said, he had reason to believe Griesedieck was holding out on him. Prather had bought a drink of near-beer in Westphalia, Missouri, and was told by the bartender he ought to be in St. Louis, drinking real beer at Parisi's and Buck Keenan's saloons in St. Louis. Prather confronted Griesedieck, who replied he had never sold to those places and suggested they be made to patronize him, or raided. "I told Heber, and he told me, a few days later, that the places had been raided," Prather recounted.

Brewmaster Wagner, of 4010 Magnolia Place, testified that beer of 5 percent alcoholic content was made at the brewery on seventeen different dates beginning May 15, 1923. Work began at 7 a.m. on the days when the beer was brewed, and between one thousand and fourteen hundred cases of beer were hauled away in trucks later each day.

The brewery had a permit to manufacture cereal beverage, or near-beer, at the time it was violating the law. To make cereal beverage the brewery made regular beer of 4.5 to 5 percent, then dealcoholized it by reboiling and evaporation.

Louis Sklarey of Newark, New Jersey, a former federal agent of the prohibition intelligence unit, testified that he had "shadowed" Prather and Griesedieck shortly before the brewery raid. On February 7, 1924, he said, he watched Prather, who was seated on a lounge in the Hotel Jefferson lobby. "Raymond Griesedieck," he said, "came up to the desk and the clerk pointed out Prather to him. He walked over to Prather and they both went upstairs in the elevator at 2:05 p.m. Seventeen minutes later Griesedieck came down and left the hotel." A listing from the Hotel Jefferson register showed Heber Nations or Prather or both in attendance on more than thirty occasions from April 1923 to February 1924.

The day before the raid, on February 20, 1924, Prather said he collected one thousand dollars from Griesedieck in St. Louis and returned home to Advance, where he owned a hardware store with his brother. The next day the brewery was raided by Gus Nations.

On the afternoon of February 22, Prather said, Heber Nations telephoned from Jefferson City and told him the brewery had been raided and the *Post-Dispatch* was publishing a story that two state officials were involved in protecting the brewery. Nations told Prather he wanted to see him "right away." Prather took the train to St. Louis and was unable to reach Griesedieck, so he took a night train to Jefferson City and arrived there about 1:40 a.m. "I called Heber at his home immediately upon arrival there and he told me to come to his house,"

Prather said. "I went out and we talked it over and agreed I should go back to St. Louis right away and attempt to get Griesedieck to stand pat and not say anything and we would be whatever possible assistance we could to him."

Unable to reach Griesedieck in St. Louis, Prather and Heber Nations developed a "plan of defense": Their actions were for the purpose of making a case against the brewery for Gus Nations. Prather told his questioners he had never been in the brewery or met Ray Griesedieck until Heber Nations arranged the meeting in the Hotel Jefferson.

Former Prohibition Agent Louis J. Gualdoni testified that on the Sunday following the Griesedieck brewery raid, he met Heber Nations at Grand and Lindell boulevards at Heber Nations's request, and Nations asked him to watch the case and learn what he could. Several weeks later, he said, Nations telephoned him again and asked to meet him at Seventeenth and Pine streets. Gualdoni drove there and took Nations for a ride. "Heber wanted me to say that he and I had got the Griesediecks to run, so Gus could catch them," Gualdoni testified. "I told him, nothing doing, that I wouldn't make any such statement." It was his last conversation with Nations, Gualdoni said.

A Different Story

"I should say not," was Heber Nations's reply when he was asked whether he took money received by Prather from Griesedieck. Nations told investigators he wanted to help his brother catch the brewery in law violations, because a local politician was trying to make trouble for Gus Nations. He said he explained this to Prather, who at the time was a friend, and asked Prather to help him "lay a trap" for the brewery. Since Prather as state beverage inspector had official supervision over the brewery's output of cereal beverage, he reasoned, he would be able to obtain the needed information. However, Mabel Walker Willebrandt, assistant U.S. attorney general in charge of prohibition cases, pointed out that Prather was not beverage inspector at the time of the conversation, because a law that transferred beverage inspection duties to the food and drug commissioner did not become effective until June 1923.

Heber testified he had no knowledge of Prather taking money from Griesedieck. He said after Gus Nations and his men raided the brewery on February 21, 1924, he asked Prather if he had taken any money. He said Prather replied that he had not.

Heber Nations sat "well forward in his chair" and spoke in a loud, clear voice in the witness chair at the Federal Building downtown. A small but physically strong man and a flashy dresser, he often emphasized his statements by bringing his hand down with a loud slap on a nearby railing. He was thirty-six and had lived in Jefferson City for eleven years. Nations said he had known Prather for four years.

The trap for the brewery was laid on an eastbound Missouri Pacific train headed to St. Louis from Jefferson City in late April 1923, Nations said. "I asked Prather if he would agree to help me in a difficult situation which confronted me," Nations said. "I told him that my brother, Gus, who was then group chief of prohibition agents at St. Louis had asked me to help him get some confidential information about the Griesedieck Brewery. I explained to Prather why it was necessary for Gus to get the information for which he had asked me. Gus had had a row with the brewery over the reissuance of its permit to operate.

"I told Prather that a prohibition agent named Baker had caught the brewery making beer by hiding under a truck at the brewery while it was being loaded. I told him how Baker had hid there until finally Mr. Wagner, the brewmaster, had come to the wagon after the last case had been loaded and had told the driver to drive like hell.

"I told Prather of the political pull that the brewery had and how Mr. Dyott [John C. Dyott, special assistant U.S. attorney general, of St. Louis] . . . had refused to prosecute them in one instance and in another had let them off with an insignificant fine. I told him how following a raid three temporary permits were issued to the brewery under which it continued to operate. I told him that it was absolutely vital that Gus catch that brewery. I said, 'You know that "Hank" Weeke [a Republican politician] and those St. Louis bums are after Gus . . . they're after him constantly in Washington and from every angle. . . . I want you to help me by going down to this brewery and meeting all these people. Get on friendly terms with them and find out when they are going to run.'"

Both Heber Nations and Prather agreed on one point, that at Nations's request Gualdoni had contacted Griesedieck and asked him to meet Prather at the Jefferson Hotel. Gualdoni also testified to this. "Did Prather at any later date tell you of the operation of the brewery?" Cullen asked. "No," Heber Nations replied. "He never did tell me he had found anything unlawful. I was a little anxious about this matter and I pressed him frequently for the information I had asked him to get, but he seemed to be doubtful about the whole proposition. He told me on one occasion he had had real beer at the plant, but I understood he'd just had a drink or two. He never told me the brewery was putting beer out for sale."

In evidence was a letter signed by M. H. McFarland, a superintendent with the Missouri Bureau of Labor Statistics in St. Louis, dated February 18, 1924: "Dear Heber: Thursday and Friday will be the days. Hoping this information will be what you want I am, Sincerely, M. H. McFarland." Nations said he showed Prather the letter and explained he had sent a man to learn when the beer was to be delivered at Keenan's and relayed the information to Gus.

Another letter, allegedly written from Heber to Gus Nations and sent to Kansas City on February 19, 1924, was said to have prompted Gus Nations to hurry back to St. Louis to raid the brewery on February 21. It was a torn piece of paper, with the dates and some of the words rubbed off, and it had been pasted on another sheet of paper to hold it together. It was addressed to "Spat," apparently Gus's nickname. "The information I wanted to bring you ought not to wait until Friday but could not give it over the phone tonight. The breweries run when you are out of town. I also have infor— [the page was torn] Griesedieck Thursday or Friday. You should slip back quietly." The letter appeared to be signed, "Lovingly, Heber," but tears in the page made the closing phrase illegible, a reporter noted.

Heber Nations confirmed he met late one night with Prather after the Griesedieck raid. He testified Prather was worried about his involvement and told him, "You got me to help you catch that brewery and now that bunch is after me. They are powerful enough to frame me, to send me to jail. I should never have mixed up in it. Now they'll blame everything on me." Heber said he reassured Prather that he had nothing to fear, and he asked Prather if he received any money from Griesedieck. Prather, he said, replied, "Of course not."

"Why did you send him to Griesedieck after that conference?" Willebrandt asked.

"I did not," Heber Nations said. "I didn't know he went to Griesedieck."

Nations recalled his final conversation with Gualdoni. "I called him up and asked him what information he had for me, and he said he had none, that he didn't want to get mixed up in it," Heber Nations testified. "I told him, 'Gene, that's good work we did.' He said, 'Don't say we. I didn't have anything to do with it. I am a friend of those boys. I didn't know that was what you wanted.'"

Gus Nations corroborated Heber's testimony that he had asked Heber to help him catch the Griesedieck Brewery violating the law. He denied that Heber had knowledge of the dates when he and his agents were out of town. He said, as far as he knew, he told Heber on only one occasion that he was going out of town, and that was on the trip to Kansas City, when Heber wrote the letter that called him back to raid the brewery.

Prohibition Agent M. L. Hogg, formerly one of Gus Nations's agents and in May 1925 a group chief in Kansas City, testified that Gus Nations was active in the enforcement of the prohibition law and was constantly raiding places where liquor was sold.

A Disgrace Worse Than Death

Both Nations brothers showed signs of emotion and wiped their eyes as their attorney, Patrick Cullen, declared in his closing arguments that the enemies of law enforcement had attempted to inflict on the Nations brothers a disgrace worse than death. Heber, he said, would "cut off his right arm" rather than involve his brother Gus in a criminal plot as implicated in Griesedieck's and Prather's testimony.

Defense Attorney Charles G. Revelle, former Missouri Supreme Court judge, questioned the testimony of Prather and Griesedieck, "whose word you are asked to accept, to send an honest citizen to prison. What a miserable spectacle, to have against this man the testimony only of two confessed criminals.

"If Heber Nations was protecting the Griesedieck brewery, and if he learned that the intelligence unit was coming to raid it, why did he not inform Griesedieck, instead of calling Gus Nations to make a raid?"

Dyott asked if it was not better to do as Prather had done, to tell the truth and seek to atone for the wrong. He also questioned, given Prather's meeting with Griesedieck in April 1923, why there was no prosecuting action until ten months later. Heber Nations betrayed the confidence of his younger brother, Dyott claimed.

Willebrandt called Heber Nations's story "bluff." "Prather, who was in as deep as anyone, got the first information of the crash from Nations," she said. "They conferred at night, and Prather came to St. Louis to try and get Griesedieck to sit tight. That was a natural thing to do, and it was natural also that Prather, at first, should attempt to bluff the thing through with denials. Heber Nations is still clinging to the theory of bluff."

She also questioned the notion of a frame-up. "But if it were a frame-up, why should not Griesedieck testify that he himself had dealings with Nations?" she asked.

After twenty-seven hours of deliberation and a request for additional instruction from Judge Faris, the jury voted for conviction at 3:50 p.m. on Friday, May 29. The night after the verdict, Heber Nations slept in a cage in the office of the U.S. marshal on a cot supplied by the government and a mattress and pillow sent in by Gus Nations. Gus also sent in his brother's meals, including a breakfast of grapefruit, ham and eggs, bread, and coffee the next morning. He ate lunch at the City Club, where he was a member, and later went for an automobile ride with Gus, who was his only visitor that day. "I slept like a top last night, as a man with a clear conscience can," Heber Nations said Saturday morning. "My faith in God and in the ultimate result is unshaken and unshakable. While the present situation is humiliating to my family and friends, I feel that I am only an incident in this stupendous contest."

Heber Nations showed no emotion as Faris sentenced him to eighteen months in Leavenworth Prison and fined him $3,333. The Griesedieck Brewery was fined $10,000. Prather was fined $500, and his sentence was suspended while he testified for the government at Nations's successive trials.

"The Greasy Hand of Boodle"

The reliably wet *Post-Dispatch* wasn't kind to the fallen dry. Read an editorial published that Saturday:

> *He was the model of the political clergy, the pride of the Anti-Saloon League, and the pet of the WCTU. His newspaper in Jefferson City was the recognized organ of high morality and law enforcement.*
>
> *Under Nations's cloak of righteousness, however, was the greasy hand of boodle. He had an itching palm. He used his vociferous professions of high moral purpose and civic righteousness to betray his cause and cheat the State. . . . He stabbed the cause to which he professed the greatest devotion.*

"The long arm of Uncle Sam" prevailed, despite the drys' propaganda, the *Jefferson City Tribune* observed:

> *As one of the "four horsemen" [Nations] rode forth a hundred times to find and wreck whiskey stills and drag the offenders off to jail. With an automatic in one hand and a stinging pen in the other he made merciless war upon those who by disregard for the law, the prohibition law, were undermining the government of the United States. He was regarded as a scrapper. He was the boss Klansman, the 100 per cent reformer. . . . Some say that the fall of such men handicaps law enforcement. . . . The very fact that this government weeds out the despoilers is proof that the law is still supreme. . . .*

More of the Same

The newly convicted Nations was back with the Four Horsemen on June 4, 1925, for a raid on Anton Haselhorst's farm near Tin Town, Missouri, in southeastern Polk County. They confiscated two gallons of wine and a barrel of mash. Withaup defended Nations' involvement when he discussed the raid with a reporter, but unfavorable comments from many Jefferson City residents effectively reduced the Four Horsemen to three.

When sociologist Peter Collins returned to Jefferson City in November 1926 to give another lecture for the Knights of Columbus, Heber Nations threatened to bring in a Klan lecturer to rebut the remarks. By this time the *Tribune* referred to Nations as an ex-Klansman.

That same year Heber's newspaper published an editorial, "Consider the Sun Dial," which advised readers to adopt the sundial as a life motto: *No one has learned the art of life who has not trained the mind to forget every experience from which it may derive no advantage. When the lesson of the mistake is learned, forget the mistake. The hours of shadow make no record on the sun-dial.*

"Not only has this fight been tremendously expensive to the government, but it has been ruinously so to me," Heber Nations commented on appeal after his third conviction in January 1930. "The savings of a lifetime has been wiped out. . . . The proved loyalty of thousands of friends is of sustaining power in this further trial . . . I thank God for the sturdy health and the clear conscience which have enabled me to stand up under three disappointments. . . ."

Though his dry supporters were less vocal after Heber Nations's first conviction, many considered him a brother in arms and did not waver in their support. The Reverend Walter M. Haushalter, pastor of the First Christian Church in Columbia, praised Heber for his "moral courage by virtue of his previous work in raiding suspected places" and maintained the conviction was a frame-up by those who opposed Nations's efforts to enforce the prohibition law.

"This is not only my opinion but also that of the Missouri Anti-Saloon League," Haushalter said.

More than two decades later, in Heber Nations' obituary, the *Sikeston Herald* offered a similar view: "It was believed by many the indictments were prompted by an effort on the part of liquor forces to impede the prosecution of the illicit liquor trade."

Mabel Walker Willebrandt was not impressed by the drys' show of support. The second woman to serve as assistant U.S. attorney general, Willebrandt was known for her successful prosecutions that "put teeth in the 18th Amendment," as the *New York Times* put it. She earned the name "that Prohibition Portia" from Democratic presidential candidate Al Smith because of her eloquent speeches for President Herbert Hoover.

Willebrandt had been angered and frustrated by the torrent of protests, letters, and propaganda churned out by the Anti-Saloon League prior to the Heber Nations trial. Some of the literature was read by prospective jurors in the

Griesedieck case (see Chapter 9). She described her experiences in St. Louis in "When the Anti-Saloon League Went Wet," the tenth installment of a series of articles on prohibition enforcement published in the *New York Times* in 1929. "I bear for the Christian men and women who have worked with passionate zeal for the prohibition cause the most sincere respect," Willebrandt wrote. "I have never, however, seen a more flagrant example of misuse of influence and power than the Missouri Anti-Saloon League exhibited in the Nations trial. . . .

"Through his extensive affiliations, political and otherwise, Nations was given the 'moral support' of thousands of people who honestly believed he was the victim of persecution. Notwithstanding this fact, however, he was twice convicted by juries."

REBUTTAL

Gus Nations took offense at Willebrandt's statement that she "had to fight the Anti-Saloon League to remove a popular agent," which he took to mean himself. Nations sued her and the Current News Features Company for libel, charging that the articles falsely accused him of attempting to obstruct justice during the prosecution of his brother in 1925. He also took issue with the statement by Willebrandt that she had to fight the Anti-Saloon League as it fought to protect Heber Nations, who, she said, "was helping to flood his territory with high-powered beer."

He replied to Willebrandt in a lengthy article in the *New York Times* in August 1929. He maintained that she let the Griesedieck brewery off on multiple occasions:

The Griesedieck brewery was first caught violating the law June 11, 1921. The corporation was fined a paltry $250 and all the individuals who should have gone to prison were released by Mrs. Willebrandt. In 1922 the brewery applied for reinstatement of its permit . . . I disapproved it. Heavy political pressure was brought to bear at Washington and my superior ordered a change in my recommendation. I refused. . . . Two United States Senators put on the pressure at the capital and the permit was issued over my protest. . . .

The Griesedieck brewery was twice caught in flagrante delicto and more than eighty men apprehended before my brother was indicted. Mrs. Willebrandt each time intervened to prevent the punishment or prosecution of a single one of the eighty persons arrested. The Griesedieck brewery was raided by me the second time upon information obtained and furnished me by my brother, Heber Nations, whose only interest was that of a citizen who wanted the law enforced. . . .

I leave to candid minds the question of why Mrs. Willebrandt twice released every officer and employee of this lawless brewery, and has sought to prosecute only the man who caught them.

Since my retirement from the government service I have seen beer unlawfully carried out of

Will Rogers. Courtesy Library of Congress.

a St. Louis brewery seven times. But in the light of the record of Mrs. Willebrandt in the handling of prosecutions, neither prohibition agents nor citizens dare to interfere.

Even humorist Will Rogers weighed in on the Heber Nations case and subsequent lawsuit. "As long as Gus Nations works for Prohibition, and his brother for the Griesedick [*sic*] Brewery, just so long will he be in argument with Mabel," Rogers observed.

In 1933, a jury before Federal Judge Robert P. Patterson cleared Willebrandt of the libel charge after twenty-six minutes of deliberation.

In Closing

Heber Nations sold the *Daily Post* in 1927, ran an insurance office for some years, and for a short time published the *Missouri Republican,* "to serve the best interest of the Republican party." His wife, Alma, hosted meetings and garden parties of the Capital City Republican Women's Club. Heber taught Sunday School at the First Christian Church of Jefferson City for many years and worked to revive and organize churches in small communities. The church newsletter in January 1946 reported that Nations had been ill, but he recently returned to teach. "The Young People are glad to have him back in the Department," reported the *Church Bell.*

For the last five years of his life he suffered from a heart ailment, and at age fifty-nine on the morning of March 11, 1948, Heber Nations was found dead in his bed from a heart attack. His pallbearers included Jefferson City Mayor James T. Blair, Jr., and Missouri Governor Phil M. Donnelly. None of the Jefferson City newspaper obituaries mentioned the Griesedieck beer scandal.

Gus Nations earned a reputation as the "stormy petrel of prohibition enforcement in Missouri because of his militant tactics in conducting raids and making arrests," according to the *Globe-Democrat*. He prepared and wrote more than 2,500 cases and said he never lost a case. Later he served as legal counsel for the Anti-Saloon League, where his request for an injunction in 1933 to restrain the sale of 3.2 percent beer was denied in Cole County Circuit Court.

In 1925, he was charged with using the mail to defraud, in connection with the operations of the Federal Home Building Corporation of St. Louis, of which he was counsel and director. He was cleared of the charges, which he called a plot by "vicious interests" to ruin him in return for his efforts to run down bootleggers. For years, he maintained a law practice in St. Louis and served as board member and newspaper editor for the Lawyers Association of the Eighth Judicial Circuit of Missouri. On December 21, 1942, at age forty-nine, he died of heart disease at St. Luke's Hospital. He was survived by his wife, Mabel, and five children, three of whom still lived in the family home in Webster Groves. One, Gus O. Nations, Jr., became mayor of Webster Groves in 1960.

Mabel Walker Willebrandt served as assistant U.S. attorney general in charge of prohibition cases from 1921 to 1929. Considered a champion of women and the poor, she also supervised the Bureau of Federal Prisons and established the prison for women at Alderson, West Virginia, which was considered a model institution and gained fame years later during the incarceration of domestic diva Martha Stewart. Willebrandt later practiced law and for a time had offices in Washington and Los Angeles. She and her husband, Arthur Willebrandt, were divorced in 1924, and a year later she adopted a two-year-old daughter whom she raised with the help of friends. At age seventy-three, in April 1963, she died of cancer in Riverside, California. At her bedside was her daughter, Mrs. Henrick Van Dyke of Seattle.

Raymond Griesedieck died on July 12, 1930, at age forty-two, of peripheral neuritis complicated by heat prostration. He had testified for the government at the Nations trial but did not enter a plea, and his case was still pending at the time of his death. Griesedieck Brothers Brewery went on to manufacture legal beer after prohibition ended, and GB beer was a popular brand that could be found at Sportsman's Park in St. Louis in the 1940s and 1950s. After a hiatus of some years, GB beer again is being produced by Griesedieck descendants.

CHAPTER 6

YOUR AVERAGE JOE

IT COULD PACK A WALLOP COMPARED TO THE OLD-STYLE BREWERY BEER. AND IF THE proportion of ingredients wasn't perfect, it resembled the depths of the Mississippi River for all the sludge it contained. Most households in St. Louis and beyond were not without a stock of home brew in their basements in what was a family affair. Parents made soda for the kids; the kids helped cap the brew. "A lot of people who were knee-high to a crock in those days remember mother's warning: 'If you don't behave, I'll tell your father and he won't let you put the caps on,'" *Globe-Democrat* staff writer Beulah Schacht recalled in 1964. "Maybe it was delicious and maybe it was just better than nothing, but whatever it was, it was good for a laugh now and then when a batch backfired. Sometimes in the middle of the night everybody in the house would be awakened by what sounded like an invasion of Egan's Rats and their tommy guns."

More enterprising souls, and those out for profit, experimented with wine and distilled liquors such as bathtub gin. Distilled spirits could be dangerous, depending on the alcohol used. Home brew was relatively safe and widely used. It had been made for years in many German households, where it was known as *heim gemacht*.

HOME IS WHERE THE BREW IS

"There were very few homes in town that were without their home brew or something similar," Gilbert W. Killinger recalled in 1976. "It was a matter of buying a can of malt, a few pounds of sugar, and a yeast cake and setting it in a big crock and letting it go . . . sometimes it was bottled too young, as they called it, and the bottles did explode and knock the caps off."

WAS IT GOOD?

"Well, in comparing it with beer today, no, it wasn't," said Killinger, a lifelong Collinsville resident, journalist, and former mayor. "But at the time it tasted pretty good."

Left: Gilbert Killinger. Courtesy of Oral History Collection, Archives/Special Collections, Norris L Brookens Library, University of Illinois at Springfield.

Below: A still in the collections of the Collinsville Historical Museum in downtown Collinsville, Illinois.

Wild batches that remained intact had to be held carefully when opened or the bottle would scoot across the yard, spewing its contents like a Fourth of July firecracker, Killinger observed. "As the years passed and memories of brewery beer faded and a new generation of drinkers who had never tasted it came into the market, home brew became the alcoholic beverage of choice of many Cooper County [Missouri] drinkers," Louis G. Geiger noted in 1992. "It had about twice the alcoholic content of the commercial product."

The alcohol content of any fermented product is directly related to the amount of sugar in it, and budding home brewers likely followed the adage "more is better," brewmaster James Ottolini said. "Odds are, I would say, it probably was higher in alcohol," said Ottolini, head of brewing operations at Schlafly Bottleworks in St. Louis. "When you chop up a sugar molecule, you turn it into two other things, alcohol and carbon dioxide."

There are two other reasons drinkers may have regarded the brew as high powered, said Ottolini, who oversees the production of bottled and keg beer for a five-state area. If the product fermented too fast, it produced "off flavors" that imparted a strong taste to the brew. And if the amateur brewer used simple sugars such as molasses, they could produce another type of alcohol called fusel alcohol, which resulted in light-headedness. Another by-product was acetone, which could make the drinker positively loopy.

The phenomenon of exploding bottles was caused by sugar that had not fermented, as well as weak bottles, Ottolini noted. "They put a little extra sugar in it [for carbonation], shook it and capped it," Ottolini said. "You can start to imagine the quality control issues in one's kitchen."

A couple of years after repeal, a friend of journalist Dickson Terry discovered a couple leftover bottles of home brew in a fruit closet in the basement.

"Misty eyed, we raised our glasses in silent toast to a strange and unforgettable time," Terry wrote in 1964. "It tasted just the same, but somehow it didn't taste as we had remembered it. . . . The only thing we could say was that it was better than no beer at all."

Malt Mania

Grocery and hardware stores around town carried the items needed to make home brew. The key ingredient was malt extract or malt syrup, essential to fermentation, which filled an entire store aisle. As a boy growing up in Kirkwood during prohibition, Albert Winkler was impressed by the size of the malt display at the local A&P store on the southwest corner of South Kirkwood Road and Jefferson Avenue. "The display was the biggest thing in the store when I was a kid," Winkler said. "Cereal or nothing else was in abundance like the malt was: Everyone knew what they were buying it for."

Shops dedicated to malt and hops sprang up, and other stores carried them as well. "I had it big, sold a lot over [at] Smith's Drugstore," Lloyd E. Coffman, a pharmacist from Roodhouse, Illinois, recalled in 1983. "We had Mound City's malt. That was a popular one. Blue Ribbon and White Banner, and Miller's High Life. . . . I had Fleischmann's yeast. I kept it in a refrigerator. Had bottle caps, one hundred in a box, and a bottle capper, and bottles . . . people didn't think anything of it. The people would be standing there when one of the preachers would be buying some bottle caps or yeast or something."

Anheuser-Busch offered its Budweiser Barley Malt Syrup, plain or hop-flavored, at a discount to employees. The three-pound hop-flavored, light or dark, sold at three dollars for six cans, or the two-and-a-half-pound plain, light or dark, at $2.40 for six cans. ". . . an ideal body building food, sold to bakers and grocers throughout the United States and Canada, for food purposes," Anheuser-Busch vice president and general manager August A. Busch, Jr., wrote in a 1929 memo.

This easel-backed, cardboard ad for Budweiser Barley Malt Syrup was a promotional piece found in stores. Courtesy Kevin Kious and Donald Roussin.

J. Willard Conlon. Courtesy of Oral History Collection, Archives/Special Collections, Norris L. Brookens Library, University of Illinois at Springfield.

The notion that the syrup was used for food purposes was a subterfuge, noted J. Willard Conlon, a retired federal employee from Springfield, Illinois. "Any recipe will show you that a tablespoon full of that malt would flavor a large batch of bread, whereas it was sold in about a three-pound can, you see," Conlon explained in 1972. While manufacturers could stress the product's baking abilities, they could not even intimate that it made better home brew, Roland Krebs noted in *Making Friends Is Our Business: 100 Years of Anheuser-Busch.* "Hence it was not at all uncommon for one home-brewer to tell another that his last 'batch of cookies' had turned out beautifully," Krebs wrote.

Many who lived through the time insist home brewing was legal if it was used only for personal consumption, not for sale. Newspaper articles of the day and prohibition scholar David E. Kyvig said otherwise; both federal and state dry laws banned the manufacture of alcohol. Whether it always was interpreted that way is unclear. Home brewing for one's own use was a popular defense in a number of prohibition cases, including one filed by the State of Missouri in September 1925 against Henry Goerecke and Mike Simon. Deputy sheriffs had arrested the men the previous May at Goerecke's home on Spencer Place in Wellston and seized fifteen gallons of mash, a bottle of wine, and home brew:

a twelve-gallon crock, eighty quarts, and seven cases of the brew. Goerecke's defense was that he made the beer for his own use: A St. Louis county jury deadlocked after five hours of deliberation.

In most instances, home brewers weren't bothered unless they tried to sell the stuff or caused a ruckus with drunken parties. "There was never any thought that you'd be bothered by the police or the law or anyone else, unless—it would be just like now—unless you were a nuisance," Conlon said. "In other words, if people got to quarreling and fighting and there was loud and boisterous talk, or you were offensive to passersby or someone else, the police would certainly put a stop to it. But just for the circumstance that you were drinking some liqueur on the premises, you'd never be bothered. On more than one occasion, I've played poker with and sat around the table in company with police officers who were not on duty—however, on one or two occasions they were in uniform."

Everett Tuttle of Springfield, Illinois, made home brew for guests, not for sale, though he made the mistake one summer of keeping the stuff in the attic, just above the side entry door of his home on East Monroe Street. His wife, Mae, opened the door one steamy day for a bill collector, and the hot air found its way to the attic. "That home brew all bursted, and that brew all come down that wall," Mae Tuttle told an interviewer in 1985. "That was my most embarrassing moment!"

Have You Tried Our . . .

There were endless variations on the home brew formula. Some home chefs added potato peelings and/or rice. Others used cups or syringes to "needle" bottles of commercially made near-beer with grain alcohol. "When I went to medical school [at Washington University] we had it easier because those of us [who] worked in the laboratory could get laboratory alcohol and we could put it in," recalled Dr. Emmet Pearson of Springfield, Illinois, in 1983. "They [breweries] made near-beer, they left a little area in the top of the beer open for air so you [could] fill that with alcohol, and you had real good beer." An intern at Barnes Hospital, Pearson earned his beer money by selling a pint of blood each month.

Home brewers and professional bootleggers alike often made wine. (See Chapter 7.) Many residents left the making of distilled liquor to the "experts"— some of them not so expert—and some used other creative means of obtaining alcohol. Those who were truly desperate could buy alcohol-based food extracts, such as lemon, or even canned heat, known as Sterno, which was grain alcohol in a semisolid, jellylike base. "Now if you buy a can of that Sterno and you take an old felt hat and put this goo in there and then squeeze it through so that the liquid will drain through and be filtered through the hat, what's coming out of there is really pure alcohol, and you can drink that," Conlon said. "There was just a lot of that done, really."

Wine of pepsin, which contained 25 percent alcohol and was available in drugstores and some soft drink parlors, was another alternative to hard liquor. In Jefferson City, two men were arrested for drunkenness after imbibing it in 1920. Another was Jamaica ginger extract, a patent medicine known as jake, sold in drugstores.

SPIRITED PURSUITS

An ant was gazing longingly at the carcass of a dead horse, and a bootlegger's car passed and a jug of liquor bounced off the car and broke. The ant took one drink of the stuff, grabbed the dead horse by the tail and shouted, "Come on, big boy, we're going home."
—From the Wyconda (Missouri) Reporter-Leader, *April 2, 1931*

Bootleggers distilled clear whiskey, known as "white mule," and "bathtub gin," which was frequently made in quantities that necessitated using a bathtub. Whiskey wasn't so difficult to make, recalled Larry Mantowich, who made his own once with sugar, yeast, and rye at a friend's house in the Lithuanian community of Springfield, Illinois. It took all night to cook, he said, and one could get drunk from the fumes.

When prohibition began, bootleggers could get thirty to fifty dollars a gallon for whiskey, Mantowich said, and it cost them twenty or twenty-five dollars to make six or seven gallons. As time went on and others learned to make the product, the prices dropped, he said. Conlon recalled that one could buy a gallon of white mule in the Springfield, Illinois, area for four dollars. He said he knew people who made their own beer and wine, but few attempted to distill because the result could be bought cheaply and easily.

Supply and demand determined price. After federal prohibition officers made their largest raid ever in Jefferson City, Missouri, in November 1929, "good corn" whiskey was commanding $3 a pint, up from $1.50 to $2. Liquor by the gallon that previously sold from $5 to $8 was bringing prices of $15 to $20. "The Christmas and Thanksgiving supplies are about ruined," an alleged seller told the *Columbia Missourian.*

Lincoln C. Andrews, assistant secretary of the treasury in charge of prohibition, testified before a Senate committee in 1929 that an estimated 1.7 million stills operated throughout the country. "Consider the fact that a man with an ordinary wash boiler may make in a day a profit of nearly $2,400," said Senator James Reed of Missouri. "Consider that millions of people are convinced they have a right to buy the product of the wash boiler—consider these facts and you have a situation where the violation is inevitable.

"MAKING WHISKEY IS SIMPLER THAN MAKING BREAD."

Reed then told the committee how to make it. "It can be produced by so primitive an equipment as a tea kettle and a little corn, or rye, or potatoes, or anything that contains starch or sugar," he said. "Fermentation is a natural process; distillation is simply the separating and condensing of alcohol produced by fermentation. Whiskey can be made in any home in the land."

Some of it was awful, said Tom English, a resident of southern Illinois who worked in a bank in Eldorado in the 1920s. "The poorest I ever tasted, we got that at Equality [a town in deep southeastern Illinois] one night," English recalled in 1979. "And we went down there and got that stuff, got a bottle from him [a man named Meadows] and come back to Eldorado. Boy! That was the worst I ever saw. You could pour it in the palm of your hand and it had enough alkali in it to make a lather." He rubbed his hands together. "I never did get home that night."

Occasionally, the stuff was noteworthy. A *Post-Dispatch* reporter's description of one raid by the St. Louis County sheriff sounded more like a food review than a police story. The raid was in the basement of a bungalow at 1701 Annalee Avenue in Brentwood. "Not ordinary moonshine but an amber liquor of pleasant bouquet filled the five ten-gallon charred oak kegs found on a truck outside and kegs more recently filled which stood on end near sugar sacks," he wrote in July 1929. "And the sugar sacks explained the quality, according to Sheriff Al Lill. Instead of the ordinary coarse corn sugar, a good grade of granulated beet sugar was used." The driver of the truck, forty-year-old Edward Cole of 726 Clara Avenue, was charged with transportation and possession of whiskey. Fifty barrels of mash were destroyed, and fifteen hundred pounds of sugar were sold, with proceeds going to the school fund.

Bathtubs and Bootleggers

Bathtub gin was made with grain alcohol, which continued to be used by factories and laboratories during prohibition for legitimate purposes and was often "diverted." "People—the owners and some of the employees—would divert some of this to their own personal use," Conlon said. "And bathtub gin was when people would take, say, a gallon of this grain alcohol and they would dilute that with a gallon or more of water. They always describe it as distilled water, but in practice, it was nothing but tap water put to it. And then at the drugstore you could buy juniper juice and add three or four drops of that juice out of an eye dropper and taste it as you go along and stir it, and pretty soon it makes pretty respectable gin. . . . You could do it in a dish pan or anything else. But there's no question but what a good deal of the drink that was sold as gin was literally mixed in a bathtub. . . . They also flavored some of it with anise seed to give it a licorice taste. Various flavors were added."

An otherwise law-abiding milkman in his twenties, Edward Daegele joined the bootlegging forces while working for Woodlawn Dairy in Kirkwood. He bought "white lightning" from a bootlegger in gallon jugs, then went to the dairy barn on Woodlawn Avenue north of Manchester and hid them in the loose hay. "He cut it with water so it wouldn't be too unreasonably strong, and he peddled it on the side, decanting into small containers," recalled his son-in-law, Paul Gegg of Kirkwood.

From time to time, bootleggers needed help. Everett Tuttle of Springfield, Illinois, then earning a paltry nine dollars a week, was offered twenty dollars by a bootlegger friend to fix his sink and remove the drain trap. "That was the longest night of my life, I think," Mae Tuttle recalled in 1985. "We had our tiny baby. We drove up in front of this home brewer's place and Everett took his monkey wrench and stuff and went into this bootlegging place to fix this sink so that it [the home brew] wouldn't sit in the trap. Oh, I was so scared sitting out in front that the police would come while he was in there fixing the trap."

Back To the Farm

Because the production of moonshine is aromatic, budding bootleggers often found the farms, fields, and woods of St. Louis and Jefferson counties—and beyond—perfect sites for their new businesses. It was a regular back-to-the-barn movement, journalist and author Dickson Terry recalled. "In fact, tumble-down barns were at a premium, they looked so innocent," Terry wrote. Each maker had a special recipe for his moonshine, so named because it was safest to make at night, and easiest when the moon provided some light, Jefferson County historian Della Lang noted. "The salesmen often concealed small decanters of sample whiskey in their boots, hence, the name 'bootleggers,'" she said. "Words like hooch, White Mule, White Lightning, Wildcat booze, Tanglefoot, Mountain Dew, bathtub gin, etc., became household names during prohibition. Since Jefferson County was known for its natural springs, wooded areas, plenty of land, and its proximity to St. Louis, the area immediately became a popular place for the moonshiners to set up shop."

Shortly after prohibition ended, local carpenters were given a job rehabbing a Fenton-area home that obviously had been used to distill booze, Albert Winkler recalled. The house sat high on a hill with a view a mile distant. A rug on the living room floor covered a trap door, which opened to a basement where a ring of discoloration could be found on the plastered walls. It had a ventilating system, and the basement could not be seen from outside the home. "That basement was the equivalent of a small swimming pool," Winkler recalled.

It could be dangerous to intrude on moonshiners in the woods. The settlers of southern Pulaski County, Missouri, turned their tradition into a profitable

Mae Tuttle. Courtesy of Oral History Collection, Archives/Special Collections, Norris L Brookens Library, University of Illinois at Springfield.

enterprise during prohibition, and unwanted visitors risked becoming part of the natural landscape, Steven D. Smith noted in his history of the Fort Leonard Wood region, *Made in the Timber*. "Even the authorities made a profit off Prohibition," Smith wrote. "On court days after a trial, the canning jars seized as evidence during an arrest were taken out to the street and their contents emptied, giving the center of Waynesville a distinctive odor. Then the jars were lined up on the courthouse lawn and sold. They were, of course, bought by moonshiners."

In Jefferson County, one of the first stills discovered was in the summer of 1920 on Old Gravois Road near Brennan Road, where a St. Louis man had rented a farm from local resident Bill Hilgert with the pretense of starting a hog farm, Lang said. Soon, the neighbors noticed "some rather odd behavior for a hog farmer." Three or four men roamed about, but never did any work. Each day at 10 a.m., two men got into a car and headed toward the city, accompanied

PEACHY KEEN FOR MOONSHINE

William A. Smith had a farm in rural Ste. Genevieve County, with hogs running in a wooded, fenced area across a road from the farm. Each evening he would leave food by the fence for the next morning's feeding. One evening he left peach peelings, seeds, waste from canning, and fruit that dropped on the ground in sacks by the side of the road, said his nephew, Paul Gegg. The next morning the sacks were gone. Smith put sacks out the following evening, and they disappeared again. Soon after, the sacks reappeared, and inside was a quart jar of homemade white lightning with a dollar bill rubber-banded around it. Smith served the high-powered drink to company and began putting out all kinds of fruit until he ran out later that fall. "That fall he's out walking the fences . . . and some guy shows up," Gegg recounted. "The guy was carrying a shotgun and said, 'Get off my property.' Uncle Will said, 'Wait a minute. This is my property.'"

There wasn't much point in calling police, as the nearest sheriff was twenty miles away, Gegg said. Uncle Will backed off, although he owned the property. Later, Uncle Will found the still in a tunnel in a sandstone bluff with a little branch of water nearby. "The next year he put sacks out there, but nothing ever developed," Gegg said.

by a third man on a motorcycle. Neighbor Eugene Murphy caught a whiff of a strong odor one warm summer evening and notified Charlie Bouzek, the local deputy, who found the still, Lang recounted. Bouzek drove into St. Louis to notify federal authorities, who promised to look into the matter. When they didn't show the next day, Bouzek and the sheriff made the raid on their own, but it was too late. "They uncovered one hundred empty whiskey barrels, twenty-five empty sugar sacks, which had held three hundred pounds each, empty raisin boxes, and some yeast packages," Lang said. "The nearby creek reeked of the smell of whiskey. The moonshiners had obviously spotted Bouzek, or got a tip that they were going to be raided, and dumped the booze. Oh, yes, they did find three pigs on that 'hog farm.'"

A Basement Business

City dwellers made a surprising amount of hooch in crowded metropolitan areas, despite the distinctive odor involved in distilling. "I was born on the corner of Lexington and Biddle [in Little Italy] in 1917," St. Louisan John Favignano recalled in 1973. "My father had a grocery store at that time, and like most old Italian people they all dabbled in bootlegging. I mean, you can talk to any of them and they might tell you they didn't but I know for a fact that at least 90 percent of them did, see."

The Italians in the Hill community of south St. Louis used small-scale bootlegging to create a better future for themselves, noted Gary R. Mormino, author of *Immigrants on the Hill.* "It's a pretty protective, insular community; that's one of the reasons it worked there," said Mormino. "Since you didn't have gangs dispensing this, you literally had to go door to door."

Unlike the rivalries found in some other communities, the Lombards (northern Italians) and Sicilians (southern Italians) worked together, Mormino noted. The Sicilians manufactured the booze, while the Lombards owned the establishments that sold it, some with fronts as soft drink parlors or candy stores.

Some residents outfitted their entire basements for use as stills and vats. In one raid, police found a still and a vat with twenty thousand gallons of mash—the equivalent of a large, in-ground swimming pool—at the home of Peter Torretta at 2213 Sublette Avenue. Police reached the vat through a trap door in the living room floor and used a city fire truck to pump out the mash.

One local bootlegger bought such ample quantities of chicken feed from Ralston-Purina that he was invited to an agronomy lecture, Mormino wrote.

While some basements were outfitted with vats and stills, others were turned into makeshift speakeasies.

"Another grocer was nicknamed the 'Sugar Baroness' because she convinced suppliers that the tons of sugar she ordered each month were used to make candy."

According to many elderly residents, Mormino said, a fire that destroyed St. Ambrose Church in January 1921 began when a vat of moonshine exploded in the church rectory. "Even if the story is apocryphal the fact that so many people believe it is true authenticates the legend," he said.

Down By the River

Creek areas and rivers offered nooks, cane breaks, and deserted islands that were popular bootlegging spots. In 1929, a deputy sheriff seized a thirty-foot launch containing 550 gallons of alcohol in five-gallon cans near Herculaneum, Missouri, and arrested its sleeping occupant, George Hall, thirty-five, of Valmeyer, Illinois. Hall said he was to receive fifty dollars for delivering the cargo—picked up near Valmeyer—to a man named Murphy in St. Louis. The following year, a 150-gallon still in a wooded clump along the Mississippi River near East Carondelet led prohibition agents to arrest Joseph Zinselmeier, who lived across the river at 8214 Minnesota Avenue in Carondelet.

In St. Charles, Catfish Island was a well-known holdout for moonshiners and generated a community picnic of sorts when a still on the island blew up, making the spoils available to any who got their boats there fast enough. An unnamed deserted island in Firma, Missouri, twelve miles northwest of St. Charles, yielded a still and six thousand gallons of mash to raiding prohibition agents in March 1927. The 130-gallon still belonged to an O'Fallon, Missouri, man.

Referring to the "bootleg navy" plying the waters of the Mississippi and Missouri rivers in small, fast river boats, chief federal prohibition agent James Dillon wrecked four stills in a two-day attack on river moonshiners in March 1927. In addition to the Firma still, Dillon raided one on Pelican Island near Alton, Illinois, and dynamited a whiskey- and beer-making plant capable of turning out three hundred gallons of whiskey a day. The plant represented an investment of approximately forty thousand dollars. "Only the telltale smoke-stack showed through the thick willow banks when Dillon approached," wrote a *Globe-Democrat* reporter. "It had been carefully camouflaged, and even the bare spot in the shore used to land boats and barges, had been covered with willows to make the landing invisible. . . . A lone hound stood on guard when Dillon arrived, but was soon on friendly terms when the agents started to feed him his master's eggs, several dozen being found in the bunkhouse." Dillon also raided stills on Little Viney Island—twenty miles upstream from Alton, Illinois; Maple Island, directly across the Mississippi from Alton; and Mobile Island, three miles downstream from Alton.

Federal prohibition administrators grappled with methods—including high-powered launches and airplanes—to stem the tide of bootleg liquor man-ufactured along the Mississippi, Missouri, and Ohio rivers. They were largely unsuccessful. Among other advantages, moonshiners could see them well before they landed, and they had plenty of time to destroy the evidence or escape.

CASH CAVERNS

Other enterprising bootleggers used caves instead of riverbanks. One, a newly dug and well-furnished cave on the John Martin farm near Lamine-Chouteau Springs in mid-Missouri, housed a still capable of turning out sixty gallons of whiskey a day, Louis Geiger noted. One of the operators, Leo Stanfield, said he had been hired by Martin to dig and furnish the cave and was paid five dollars a day to operate the still. A judge in the case cited a lack of corroborating wit-nesses, and neither Stanfield nor Martin was brought to trial.

"Because of the labyrinthian network of underground caverns with hidden or little-known entrances in St. Louis, a lot of stuff could be and was made and stored in these little caverns," author and St. Louis radio personality Ron "Johnny Rabbitt" Elz noted. "They were under Benton Park, Chouteau-Jefferson going way south on Broadway, way north too. It was the main reason Lemp and Anheuser-Busch moved where they did, because of those caves."

"In the vicinity of Sidney and Twelfth Street, a lot of these houses, built in the 1860s, '70s, and '80s, had sub-basements and became ideal places to manufacture this stuff," Elz added. "I don't think there were many big, big operations. A lot of these places nobody will ever know about because they got away with it. It wasn't terribly expensive to put together a place to make home brew or a distillery."

To Market, To Market

From hearses to florist vehicles, cars with secret compartments or "farm" trucks with a thin layer of vegetables on top, bootleggers managed to get their goods to their customers. To do it right, though, the vehicles had to be retrofitted and equipped with heavy-duty springs to hold the heavy liquor. Floyd Sperino of Collinsville, Illinois, recalled one "flower" truck that was a front for booze hauling. "The funeral homes were involved in the whiskey trade at the time, too," Sperino said. "The hearses were used to haul the mash in and the whiskey out of the city."

Sometimes they went to great extremes, retired Springfield, Illinois, engineer Anthony Massaro recalled in 1979. "They were taken into shops, and a liner would be placed inside of the car conforming to the shape of the car. And it was filled up with alcohol. So if you were stopped, you didn't have anything there. Although somebody observed, 'The inside of this car seems to be a little bit narrower than the average car.' And it paid those people to go to those extremes. . . . But later they were transporting it by trucks."

One such St. Louis truck escaped notice until it caught fire on a hot day in August 1924 in east central Illinois. The truck, which appeared to be loaded with tomatoes, was abandoned by its two occupants when flames headed up the windshield. Residents of a Decatur neighborhood threw dirt on the fire to extinguish it, and the truck was towed to police headquarters, where it was found to contain 280 gallons of grain alcohol in five-gallon containers under fourteen crates of tomatoes. The truck had Missouri plates and a St. Louis license and was labeled Metropolitan Truck Service.

One of the largest rumrunning operations in the Midwest involved fifteen hundred gallons of whiskey, gin, and alcohol distributed between Indianapolis,

Tom English. Courtesy of Oral History Collection, Archives / Special Collections, Norris L Brookens Library, University of Illinois at Springfield.

Chicago, Louisville, and St. Louis in automobile loads of one hundred to five hundred gallons, some of which originated in St. Louis. The case went to federal court in Indianapolis, Indiana, in the fall of 1927 and included ninety-nine indictments and fifty-eight guilty pleas. Several Italian Americans were indicted, including Anthony Sansone, a wealthy fruit merchant from St. Louis.

Edward Kelsey, a rumrunner turned paid government informant, said Sansone followed him once from St. Louis to Collinsville when he had a load of alcohol in his car. Once there, Sansone was paid. "Hijacking [pirating liquor from other illegal sellers] was so bad in those days that we demanded a safe convoy through St. Clair and Madison counties before we paid for the stuff," Kelsey explained. Sansone took the stand in his own defense and denied he had sold any liquor since 1925, when he pleaded guilty to bootlegging and was sentenced to a year and a day in jail.

Even at home, bootleggers found inventive hiding places for their goods. Retired banker Tom English recalled buying liquor one cold night from a southern Illinois bootlegger named Dave Mack.

"He reached and got a tile spade and went across the road in front of the house," English told an interviewer in 1979. "Down so many rows and up the corn like that. He stuck that tile spade down, the ground was froze. Stuck that tile spade down. Chunked over a great big frozen chunk of ground. Got her out. He'd had it buried in the corn field."

BRINGING IT BACK FROM HAVANA

The sun, a great ball of gold which seemed suspended just above the water, slipped from sight as we entered a pretty bay and followed a wide channel into a bayou. Dead trees, strangled by the Spanish moss, were silhouetted against the darkening sky. The channel widened out like a lake, now narrowed to the width of a small river. Darkness came swiftly. Now and then we could hear a loud splash as some huge living thing, turtle or alligator, slid from a log or the bank, into the water. We ran without lights.

"How do you pick your way through this water without lights?" I asked.

"Know every inch of the way," was the response.

Harry T. Brundidge, reporter for the *St. Louis Star*, composed this narrative from his travels into Louisiana from Cuba in 1925 with rumrunners from a St. Louis syndicate. Brundidge gave no clue as to the group's identity but said its members came together because of rising bootleg prices and dwindling supplies of American whiskies:

A base was established in New Orleans and three large schooners, twenty-five or thirty smaller boats, motor trucks, garages and warehouses were leased or purchased outright. Interests in "cover-up places" were purchased in St. Louis and Kansas City, these places in many instances being small poultry, fruit and feed businesses, to which concerns liquor was consigned.

Since then, motor trucks have traveled between New Orleans and St. Louis bringing thousands of cases of whiskey and two small boats, with a capacity of two hundred cases each, have made more than a score of trips up the river, unloading the contraband in St. Louis.

During the two years, losses to prohibition agents and to state and county officers have been almost negligible, but hi-jackers have taken a heavy toll. In one period of two weeks, seven trucks were lost to these pirates of the highways, and each truck was loaded with Scotch. For every dollar invested in the syndicate, a profit of $500 has been taken out.

Brundidge headed out of New Orleans on a big liner bearing the flag of Honduras, destined for Havana. There, the ship was loaded with two thousand cases of Scotch whiskey and two thousand five-gallon tins of alcohol.

We arrived at the office of the broker. What a stock of liquor! Whiskies, American, Canadian, Scotch and Irish. Brandies, cognac, benedictine, absinthe, ojen, kummel, wines, champagne—everything. It was a collection of bottled goods which, had the labels been genuine, would have made the place a drinker's paradise.

Prices ranged from $5.50 a case for the American whiskey to $10 for the brandy and $15.50 for fine scotch. The five-gallon tins of alcohol sold at wholesale for a little more than 25 cents a gallon and would be sold in the United States as "fine old Scotch" for about $100 a case, Brundidge noted. The Cuban Industrial Alcohol Company made the stuff from sugarcane and sold it cheaply; its stock-in-trade was "synthetic" whiskey, with imported bottles and bootlegged labels.

Brundidge asked his rumrunning friend how they got away with it:

"But we have the advantage, because we know who is looking for us, while the government agents do not know for whom they are looking. We know the agents and have photographic likenesses of most of them. We take no chances. Our employes [sic] know their immediate superiors and those superiors know that someone pays and directs them. But those who direct the operations have no contact with persons who deliver the goods. Consequently the agents could put thumbscrews on our employes [sic] without learning the names of the so-called "higher-ups."

Brundidge returned to New Orleans on a smaller boat, and from there rode, along with the hooch, in an undertaker's truck or "dead wagon." They reached New Orleans safely, and Brundidge found himself in a hooch plant, where the Cuban alcohol was turned into "fine old Scotch":

The process of mixing water and alcohol, adding coloring matter and flavoring, required only a few minutes. The green whiskey brought over from Cuba flavors the alcohol. The finished product, which costs the manufacturer something like 30 cents a quart, finished, is bottled, labeled and packed in this same building.

Each case of "whiskey" is doused thoroughly with a bucket of water before the lid is nailed on so that the straw packing around the bottles smells of the sea when it is opened by the consumer, who pays from $100 to $140 a case of twelve bottles for this stuff.

A large truck labeled Louisiana Drayage Company was piled high with the hooch, covered with a tarpaulin, and festooned with four or five empty chicken crates. It was manned by two rough characters, Art and Jimmie, who carried army automatics and sawed-off, repeating shotguns. Across the state line in Mississippi the truck entered a garage where the men inside removed the Louisiana license tag and the drayage sign and replaced it with a Mississippi plate and two signs that read: *R.T. Jameson. Trucking-Hauling. Vicksburg, Miss.* Gasoline and oil were added and charged to someone's account. More plate and sign changes were made at Clarksdale, Tennessee; Osceola, Arkansas; Sikeston, Missouri; and

The Municipal Free Bridge across the Mississippi River (later known as the MacArthur Bridge).

Carbondale, Illinois. They were almost home, Brundidge wrote:

> *We came down the Belleville highway to East St. Louis and traveling down State street, turned at Tenth to the Municipal Bridge, which we crossed. I knew of the police guard at the west approach and wondered whether we would be stopped. No word was said to us by the police and we moved west on Chouteau. The truck continued west and pulled up where Vandeventer and Sarah intersect. Art turned to me.*
> *"Guess we'd better leave you here," he said.*
> *"I'd like to go with you and get cleaned up," I suggested.*
> *"Nothing doing," Art said. "You unload here. You can find a place around here to clean up."*
> *A frightful looking tramp, I stood there and watched them depart. I had not noticed the signs which he had installed at Carbondale, but I looked on them now, wide-eyed. They bore the counterfeited legend of one of the largest dairy companies in St. Louis.*

"RANKEST KIND OF POISON"

Missouri Attorney General Jesse Barrett called white mule and moonshine "a brew for fools." "There would be no market for moonshine liquor if people knew what it is," Barrett told reporters in 1921. "The investigators report that it is made under the most filthy conditions. The raw materials used are soured and wormy corn and vermin-infested sugar. The vats are located in unclean barns, are open and practically level with the ground. Field rats are attracted and no effort is made to prevent them from falling into the mixture. When the vats are drained there remains a foul green slime on the sides and bottom of nauseating odor. . . . Men are daily being blinded for life, killed or made insane by drinking it."

Reports of dead animals mixed in with the mash and of lye being added to hasten fermentation were common. In *Farmin' in the Woods during Prohibition* Days, Mahlon N. White told the story of a 250-pound Poland China boar getting drunk at an Ozark still and falling into the mash box while the operators were away. They removed the hog, found drowned in the mash, several hours later and continued making whiskey from the same mash. "It didn't take long for the word to get around and it brought many chuckles up and down the Pomme River," White wrote. "The tale also had its psychological kickbacks. Sometimes when a 'client' bought a pint that didn't taste just right, they would comment in disgust: 'It's Got That Ham Flavor Again.'"

E. H. Gohlaz, chemist in charge of the food and drug division of the Missouri State Board of Health, told of cockroaches, mice, and bugs infesting the mash. "The simplest expression of a still seen by the writer consisted of a common boiler covered with a filthy blanket: the alcoholic vapors passing from the boiling liquid were retained in the blanket and wrung out of same into a bottle," Gohlaz wrote. "In another instance a torn-up mattress had furnished the necessary cotton for straining the product."

If the wrong type of alcohol was used, the effects could be deadly. "Cadaver vats containing bodies used by university students for dissection work are being drained of alcohol for bootleg purposes," noted the *St. Louis County Watchman-Advocate* in September 1922. Production of industrial alcohol—used by the chemical industry and businesses—increased from 28 million gallons nationally in 1920 to 81 million gallons in 1925.

To make this alcohol unpalatable, the Prohibition Bureau created some seventy-six formulas by 1923, ranging from harmless oil of peppermint or menthol crystals to poisons such as benzine and sulfuric acid, Charles Merz observed in *The Dry Decade*. But it got out anyway, through myriad channels. The most popular method entailed the setup of a supposedly legitimate business that used alcohol, such as the marketing of a tobacco spray or perfume or toilet articles. The majority of alcohol withdrawn for the legitimate business instead was diverted to a bootlegging use, Assistant Treasury Secretary Lincoln C. Andrews explained in 1926. Bootleggers attempted to "wash" the denatured alcohol of its contaminants or redistill it for booze. Often the denaturants included wood alcohol, a deadly substance obtained by the distillation of wood. Even whiskey distilled from scratch from raisins—which contained seeds, stems, sticks, and parts of vine—could produce enough wood alcohol on its own to cause blindness. Other contaminants came from old car radiators, which were soldered with lead and used in distilling, and lye, which made the alcohol taste more potent but could cause serious internal burns.

In April 1925, St. Louis prohibition agents closed down a poison liquor factory that supplied a three-state area including Illinois and Indiana. It was located in an old building at Tenth and Wash (now Cole) streets where denatured or rubbing alcohol was redistilled, aged in charred barrels with artificial aging devices, and labeled Old Grand Dad and Sunny Brook whiskey and Gordon & Co. gin. Earlier that month, agents had raided buildings at 5045–49 Shaw Avenue and seized two stills likely managed by the same operation. "It is believed that the Shaw Avenue and Wash Street plants were but two of a number of sources of the shipments of redistilled alcohol," noted the *Post*. "Runners" in East St. Louis transported some seven hundred barrels each month to the vicinity of Terre Haute, the sheriff there reported.

A man visited one of the agents, Ben Goode, after the Shaw Avenue raid. "I understand you are after the outfit at Tenth and Wash," the man said. "There is $2,500 in it for you if you forget it. If you accept you will be on the payroll regularly hereafter." Goode declined the offer and, dressed in old clothes, went to Tenth and Wash late one evening and lay down on the sidewalk as though he were a drunken man. He watched men unload three truckloads of denatured alcohol in five-gallon cans. During a subsequent raid, agents didn't find the operators, but on the second floor they found a two-hundred-gallon still used to redistill the alcohol. "Some things about the redistilling process were not clear, even to the experienced raiders, at the first inspection," the *Post* reported. "Hundreds of marbles, of the various kinds used by boys, 'agates,' 'chinys' and 'glassies,' some plain and some of brilliant colors were found in the place, and many of them were in use in the condenser of the still, where they had become coated with a film, apparently the poisonous substances removed from the 'rubbing' alcohol in the redistilling process."

The operation generated large sums for protection and fueled violence between the armed men who drove and guarded the trucks and robbery gangs who held up the drivers and seized the shipments. In one incident in March 1925, rumrunner Floyd Washburn of East St. Louis was kidnapped and shot twice in the abdomen. The shooting of Washburn, who was in a Paris, Illinois, hospital at the time of the Wash raid, brought officials' attention to the magnitude of the operations.

Despite the raids, there was still plenty of questionable liquor to be found in St. Louis. During the 1927 holiday season, one anonymous resident ordered large quantities and found impurities in all but one batch. He was asked by a reporter if he intended to throw out the bad stuff.

"I should say not," he replied. "A little bad liquor won't kill you and everybody expects to be sick for the next week anyway."

Deadly Drinks

Among the first to die in the area were Arthur Marquitz, a respected Meramec Highlands School Board director, and Roy Rozier, former bartender of the Hi-Point saloon in Meramec Highlands. The half-clothed bodies of both men were found in November 1919 by two women with "fast" reputations in a cottage formerly owned by Marquitz's father, author James F. Baker reported in *Glimpses of Meramec Highlands*. Homemade wine that contained wood alcohol was found in the room, along with a can of wood alcohol.

They weren't the only ones, Baker learned from historian Roy Schymos: "Railroad workers who were called 'gandy dancers' used to buy radiator alcohol and take a loaf of bread and cut off both ends and filter the alcohol so that they could drink it. Every once in a while they [railroad authorities] would find one of their bodies along the railroad—from their drinking."

The St. Louis coroner issued a warning against drinking whiskey or other intoxicants following the death of a wealthy Birmingham, Alabama, grocer in May 1920. Robert E. Collins, Jr., twenty-five years old, died suddenly at the Marquette Hotel in St. Louis while attending a convention of the Southern Wholesale Grocers Association. "It is time to issue a warning especially to the traveling public," Deputy Coroner William Dever told the press. "I understand that bellboys and others connected with some of the hotels in St. Louis are in the habit of going out and buying what they call whiskey to be resold to guests. This is not whiskey, but a home-made product and the traffic in it is one of the most dangerous things occurring in the life of the city."

Wood alcohol poisoning claimed the lives of three friends in October 1920, two of whom had started a flower fund for the funeral of the first. Thomas P. Shaw, a shoe worker, had been treated by a local doctor several times for drinking extracts, hair tonic, and other alcoholic preparations over the previous six months, and he was warned not to imbibe again. On October 20, 1920, he returned to his home on West End Place in critical condition. Dr. A. J. Raemdonck found him suffering from wood alcohol poisoning. Shaw became blind the next day and died the day after.

His friends, Henry Axtell and Edward O'Shea, took up a collection for flowers among Shaw's acquaintances, who regularly gathered at a saloon at Laclede and Theresa avenues to pitch horseshoes. They were later seen together near a certain saloon, and at 7 a.m. the next day Mary Quinlan, proprietor of a Pine Street rooming house, heard groaning in the men's room. She found Axtell dead and O'Shea in convulsions. O'Shea died a few hours later at City Hospital, at about the same time Shaw's funeral was being held. Axtell, who was fifty-two, had a wife and daughter living in Maplewood. O'Shea was twenty-six. Both were employed as packers and movers by the Leonori Storage Company at Grand Boulevard and Laclede Avenue.

During the first six months of 1922, wood alcohol caused 130 deaths and 22 cases of blindness nationwide, including four deaths in Missouri, said Mrs. Winifred Hathaway, secretary of the National Committee for the Prevention of Blindness. Those figures likely were low, she added, because relatives and friends often tried to conceal the real cause of death, and deterioration of sight from wood alcohol poisoning was frequently a gradual process.

Perhaps the most mysterious wood alcohol death involved Carrie Bruns, a nineteen-year-old Ohlman, Illinois, postal clerk, who was found dead along the highway near her home on January 4, 1929. Although authorities were convinced by her friends and family that she did not drink, visit roadhouses, or keep "fast" company, an autopsy determined she had died from the effects of wood alcohol.

Mary Margaret Ellis of St. Louis nearly lost her grandfather, John Bohan, to wood alcohol poisoning. In a memoir, "That's the Way It Was, 1914–1930," she explained that she and her brother Walter knew him as "Pal" "because as long as he lived, he was always our close pal. We loved to listen to him tell stories about Ireland and the leprechauns he said he often saw in the woods." One Saturday night Pal came home and went straight to bed, and he was taken by ambulance to City Hospital the next day. When he came home two weeks later, he had lost his memory and was almost blind, his granddaughter recalled. "The doctor said that he had drank some bad liquor that had wood alcohol in it," Ellis wrote in 1980. "He never totally recovered from this and he became like a child repeating questions and then forgetting what he had asked. We kids would lead him around the yard and talk to him for hours at a time."

In many instances, the seller of the poison liquor was never identified or brought to justice. Others were sent to prison, and Illinois's state prohibition law was one of the most stringent in the nation: It subjected bootleggers who sold poison liquor to the same penalty as if they had committed murder. In Taylorville, Illinois, John Tokoly was found guilty in 1924 of five counts of manslaughter in connection with the alcohol poisoning of five men in Pana the previous fall. He was sentenced to terms ranging from one year to life in prison on each charge. In Fulton County, John Cox was sentenced to twenty-five years in prison in 1929 for selling poison liquor.

Wet legislators waged a losing battle throughout prohibition for legislation that would forbid the government to use deadly denaturants. Dry organizations such as the Anti-Saloon League of America defended the use, saying the seller was responsible, not the government, and that some bootleg liquor was just as deadly as denatured alcohol. The Methodist Board of Temperance in 1927 urged the U.S. government to continue poisoning alcohol, since a harmless denaturant could not be found.

JAKE LEG

By the spring of 1930, a number of blue-collar workers in the southeast, including Missouri, experienced paralysis of the arms and legs caused by adulterated Jamaica ginger extract, or jake. Humorist Will Rogers wrote of the condition in March 1931:

> *First, the fingers and toes become numb; then the legs and knees become permanently paralyzed. It seldom reaches above the knees. Among yesterday's cases was a barber with a wife and two children, hands totally paralyzed; a laborer with a wife and three children will never walk again. . . . This is not to be construed as a prohibition lecture. It's really an ad for just old "corn." It only paralyzes you temporarily.*

Jamaica ginger extract had been available as a patent medicine since 1863, and an article in the November 1875 *Globe-Democrat* included it as a component in the treatment of alcoholism. The extract "is sufficiently stimulant to settle the disordered nerves for the time," the unidentified author wrote, who added that should not be taken for more than ten days. Each two-ounce bottle contained as much as 85 percent ethyl alcohol and was stronger than a drink of whiskey. "You downed the whole two ounces in one gulp and then, without taking a breath, as if you could, you followed it with Coke," Dickson Terry wrote. "But with a two-ounce bottle of that, a man was fixed, both figuratively and literally. He went around with a fixed stare, walking into posts, closed doors or anything else that got in his way."

At the outset of prohibition, manufacture and sale of the alcoholic tincture was prohibited, and only a virtually undrinkable substance known as Jamaica Ginger Extract, U.S.P., could be sold legally. It contained little alcohol and a high proportion of pungent ginger solids and was sold as a headache remedy and an aid to digestion, John P. Morgan, M.D., and Thomas C. Tulloss noted in "The Jake Walk Blues," an article in the *Annals of Internal Medicine.* Manufacturers developed less pungent, drinkable mixtures adulterated with castor oil, molasses, and other substances designed to fool the solids requirements. Others used a cheap adulterant called triorthocresyl phosphate that allowed them to undercut their competitors. It also paralyzed their customers. "The victim of 'Jake paralysis' loses control of his fingers," *Collier's Weekly* described the affliction. "The feet of the paralyzed ones drop forward from the ankle so that the toes point downward. The victim has no control over the muscles that normally point the toes upward. When he tries to walk his dangling feet touch the pavement first at the toes, then his heels settle down jarringly. Toe first, heel next. That's how he moves."

The outbreak of partial paralysis led to indictments against numerous firms, including one unnamed manufacturer in St. Louis, for conspiring to manufacture, distribute, and sell extract of Jamaica ginger for beverage purposes, the *New York Times* reported. Anywhere from twenty thousand to sixty thousand victims were paralyzed, Morgan and Tulloss wrote, and the affliction prompted no less than twelve phonograph recordings of blues and rag ballads by both black and white artists, from the "Jake Leg Wobble" to "Jake Liquor Blues." "The later, postepidemic performances reflect a whimsical, even cynical, cultural attitude that those with 'Jake Leg' were suffering the wages of sin and should not be regarded as objects of pity or sympathy," Morgan and Tulloss wrote.

Bootlegger Woes

Being a bootlegger had its disadvantages. Disgruntled customers and neighbors turned them in, cops made tracks to their doors, their stills blew up, and gangs hijacked their goods. A blown-up still sounded comical, but it could destroy a building or cause serious burns and death. Della Lang told the story of a Fen-

HOOCH HEADLINES

"Guarded Still With Shotgun and Bulldog"
May 28, 1920, *St. Louis County Watchman-Advocate*

A farm at Marquette Avenue and Watson Road offered a unique booze setup: six barrels of raisin mash buried in the ground inside a shed with a skylight that permitted the sun to warm the mash. Revenue agents arrested Nick Maravich, Derno C. Gerk, and Mike Matcavich, who resided nearby, without incident, but a bulldog at the farm leaped at one of the deputies, P. J. Butler, who struck him on the nose with the butt of his revolver.

"Whiskey Ring Is Operating in the County"
August 5, 1921, *St. Louis County Watchman-Advocate*

A whiskey ring known as the Benevolent and Protective Association of Moonshiners, with a working capital of between $150,000 and $200,000, was operating in St. Louis and the county. Sixteen prominent St. Louis County residents formed this "corporation" to deal in illicit liquor traffic. The members paid large sums as dues, based upon the amount of liquor they produced and sold. The money collected was placed in a "treasury" to pay fines and litigation costs.

"Police Find No Burglar, But 'Fall Over' Liquor"
April 24, 1922, *St. Louis Star*

Police from the Dayton Street station responded to a burglary call at 2856 Spring Avenue. They rushed into an open front door in search of the supposed robber and tripped over a large assortment of jugs and bottles. They returned with twenty-seven pints of whiskey, twenty pints of gin, fifteen gallons of wine, and Dominick Juinta, who lived in the house. Juinta said he did not own the liquor and was unaware of the burglar call.

"Huge Liquor Plant Found in Downtown Raid"
January 12, 1923, *St. Louis Post-Dispatch*

Federal prohibition agents and Fourth District police discovered a four-story brick warehouse at 109–111 Morgan Street that was converted to a factory to render denatured alcohol beverage-ready. Inside were thirty-four steel barrels filled with raw denatured alcohol, which awaited recovery. They arrested Arthur G. Whittaker, 3541 Lafayette Avenue, manager of the Greenville Construction Company and former chemist for the Missouri Chemical Works, and Bert Higgenbottem, 4450 Vista Avenue, a chauffeur.

"Counterfeit Whisky Labels Seized in Raid"
January 2, 1926, *St. Louis Post-Dispatch*

Prohibition agents seized a collection of counterfeit whiskey labels in the home of Frank Langley, 3108 Minnesota Avenue, and found moonshine and other homemade liquor. As the agents waited for Langley, a saloon-keeper, to return home, they answered his phone and received six orders for liquor.

"Another Big Still Raided"
July 1929, *Jefferson County Record*

A four-hundred-gallon still set up in the old shirt factory at Hercula-neum was state of the art, which spelled its downfall. Electrically driven pumps circulated the mash, and an electric ventilating fan carried the fumes outside, where they found their way to the nostrils of a passerby.

ton, Missouri, resident who decided to make his own moonshine in the basement. The still blew up and badly burned him. "There were a lot of accidents," she said. "Especially if they tried to do it in the house."

In rural areas, small-scale bootleggers and sometimes even buyers risked harsh sentences and tarnished reputations. On November 13, 1924, after receiving a deluge of letters from Stoddard County officials, Missouri Governor Arthur M. Hyde ordered Sherman Tippett pardoned and released from the Stoddard County jail. In September 1922, Tippett had been sentenced to one year in jail and fined twelve hundred dollars for a first offense of making and selling whiskey. As a result of the litigation, he lost his farm, said to be one of the best in Stoddard County, and left his wife and family to support themselves. "I know of my own knowledge that this woman is without support for herself and five small children save her labor alone," wrote Dr. J. M. Hindman of Advance, Missouri. "This man has been amply punished, and is thoroughly whipped."

Working-class women often bootlegged to make ends meet. In April 1925, police raided three homes on North Eleventh Street in St. Louis. "At No. 1428, they found a still and two small barrels of mash," a story in the *Star* noted. "They arrested Mrs. Mary Bunshak. At 1432A they found two barrels of mash, but did not take Mrs. Peter Deptula into custody because she has four small children and a husband who is in the workhouse, serving a term for assaulting her. At No. 1418 they found Mrs. Helen Chesendroski pouring whisky into a sink and the police are awaiting her husband's return from Granite City, where he is employed."

Mrs. Anna Kubelka, a widowed mother of six in Madison, Illinois, was "pinched" in January 1933 after she turned to bootlegging with a ten-gallon still to feed her family. She was forced to walk nearly thirty miles of the way to her court date in Springfield, but her case was dismissed and sympathetic authorities drove her home. "The children had been going without underwear, but they needed it for the winter," she explained. "I just made a little beer and whiskey."

Competition usually was keen, and some bootleggers attempted to even the score. While most violence took place between gangs of bootleggers, occasionally it was directed at the general public. At 2:30 a.m. on a Sunday in December 1923, an explosion ripped through the home of Henry G. Peukert and his wife at 4906 Hummelsheim Avenue in the Gardenville neighborhood of south St. Louis County. The blast, believed to be caused by dynamite, also shattered all the windows in an adjoining house, and a neighbor, seventeen-year-old Mildred Kettler, was cut by flying glass. Peukert told Deputy Sheriff John Toman he wrote prohibition authorities about two months earlier, saying he suspected two men on the block of making moonshine whiskey; federal agents later raided the home. Toman questioned the men, but both had satisfactory alibis and no arrests were made.

Albert Winkler of Kirkwood also heard a story of a territorial dispute involving a bootlegger's house on the southwest corner of Dickson Street and Essex Avenue. The bootlegger had invaded another bootlegger's territory, and persons unknown came by during the night and shut off the gas to the home. Two hours later, they returned and turned the gas back on; the occupants were found dead of carbon monoxide poisoning the next morning.

FOR RICHER, FOR POORER

Some died. Some went to jail. And some became rich, or at least that was the story that circulated. The oft-quoted phrase, "Well, so-and-so is sending his son off to be a doctor, and he can well afford it because he's been bootlegging for years," wasn't just a cliché, J. Willard Conlon said. "That's an actual quotation," he said, and chuckled. "I even know the doctor."

Bill Drake, a Negro League baseball player, recalled in 1971 that in the early days, blacks who owned ball clubs were saloonkeepers, gamblers, or bootleggers. "I had a fellow that'd buy seven suits, basketball suits," Drake said. "He was a bootlegger. He had the money, and I gave him the idea. He bought the uniforms, bought an automobile, and I took those seven ball players and jumped in the car and lit out through the South. So that's the way those things in the early days originated. Some man with enough money to buy us some uniforms. . . ."

The liquor business also was good to James K. Johnoff of St. Louis, at least for a time. Johnoff went public in April 1934 with the story of how he made and lost a fortune. He handled $2 million worth of liquor, owned a fleet of one hundred cars and trucks and a yacht, sent by rail carloads of liquor labeled cabbage or shrimp, and had an interest in a schooner that picked up cargoes of whiskey at British Honduras (now Belize). The ship went down, the yacht was confiscated at Cahokia, he paid thousands of dollars in fines imposed on his employees, and he was taken in by double-crossers and "gyps." The final blow was an unsavory element of "hijackers" who entered the business around 1924, literally stole his booze and his profits, and "ruined the game for those who had pursued it in a serious and respectable way," he said.

"Mr. Johnoff says that in 1925 he could have liquidated his enterprise, which was already rather liquid, for $200,000," noted the *St. Louis Globe-Democrat*. "But, alas, in bootlegging as in other lines of business, all is not easy profits. Some of his shipments by river and highway were confiscated. Unkind judges fined some of his employees and he had to pay these fines. He also had to pay a fine for tax evasion, and he says he is now back where he was thirty years ago, trying to recoup his fortunes in the restaurant business."

As $2 million worth of shipments from Canada and Honduras were flooding the land, however, Johnoff was incredibly fortunate. He himself was convicted only twice of liquor law violations and paid a mere one hundred dollars in fines. One of Johnoff's charges stemmed from a New Year's Eve 1925 raid at the St. Louis Elks Club, of which he was a member. He must have enjoyed the hospitality industry. When prohibition ended, Johnoff purchased State Permit No. 1 for the legal sale of liquor by the drink and managed the Bismarck café at 410 N. Twelfth Street.

CHAPTER 7

SOUR GRAPES

PERHAPS NO OTHER TOWN IN THE ST. LOUIS VICINITY WAS AS THOROUGHLY devastated by prohibition as the little German enclave of Hermann, Missouri. Grape culture and wine making had grown the city from a frontier outpost in 1837 to a thriving community that drew a steady stream of immigrants by 1848. Town fathers offered vacant lots to buyers for fifty dollars each, to be paid without interest within five years provided the lots were used for grape cultivation. Later, the payment time was extended to ten years; all together, some six hundred "wine lots" were sold. Farmers relied on the hard-earned wisdom of Hermann-area resident George Husmann and others, who worked tirelessly to develop the best grape varieties for Missouri's steamy summers and harsh winters.

In 1904, Missouri shipped one-twelfth of the wine placed on the market by all of the states, more than 3 million gallons, and of that quantity more than 2.9 million gallons were produced in Gasconade County. The city's Stone Hill Wine Company was the third-largest wine producer in the world and the second largest in the nation, with a capacity of 1.25 million gallons annually. Founded by Michael Poeschel and later owned by George Stark, the winery also operated a brandy distillery in Hermann and a large bottling plant in St. Louis. Its wines captured gold medals in at least eight world's fairs. "The steady increase of the sales of the firm and the universal recognition of the pure and good quality of their wines at the World's Exposition, Vienna, Austria, 1873, at the Centennial Exhibition Philadelphia, 1876, and at the International Exhibition, Paris, France, 1878, are sufficient proofs that their progressive efforts have been successful in every respect," the *Rolla New Era* described Stone Hill Wine Company on December 20, 1884. "If more wine and less whiskey were drunk by our people there would be less drunkenness and its resultant, want. We do not know anything nicer for a Christmas drink than a few bottles of some of their delightful wines, Martha, Herbemont, Riesling, Norton's Virginia, Taylor, Goethe, Catawba or Concord."

Other vintners received plaudits, too, beginning with a Missouri Wine Prize Competition hosted by the German-language *St. Louis Anzeiger* in 1847. George Riefenstahl—whose descendants continue to run the Adam Puchta Winery—took first- and third-place awards.

Hermann, Missouri. Courtesy Library of Congress.

"Missouri produces some of the best claret made in this country, if not quite the best," B. F. Clayton, editor of *The Wine and Fruit Grower* of New York and a representative of the U.S. Department of Agriculture, said on a visit to Missouri in 1888. "The Cynthiana and Norton's Virginia grapes, which are best adapted to the climate and the soil about Hermann, Mo., where most of this wine is made, make very good wines . . . our varieties can stand comparison with the best produced in Europe."

GRAPES GONE BUST

In 1920, the wine-making livelihood was forced to a halt, and Hermann entered the Great Depression a decade ahead of the rest of the country. "Hermann's economy was pretty much based on the wine industry," noted Bruce Ketchum, site administrator of the Deutschheim State Historic Site, 107 W. Second Street in Hermann. "By 1900 there were over sixty wineries producing almost 3 million gallons of wine a year. A lot of other people raised grapes as a cash crop; they were selling grapes to wineries and other places."

The quiet community, which had no jail cell within its limits until 1906, by statute was breaking the federal law. At the outset of prohibition, federal officials came in and destroyed many of the vineyards. "Old-timers mentioned seeing wine and beer flowing down the street when federal officials came in and broke up the wine and beer barrels," he said. Many varieties of grapes disappeared. "On the historic site we have some Norton varieties planted in the 1850s that weren't bothered," Ketchum said. "Every once in while, someone will move into the Hermann area and find ancient grapes back in the woods someplace. I think both Stone Hill and Oak Glen wineries have some really ancient vines back off in the woods."

Federal officials also destroyed much of the equipment, including intricately carved wine casks, Ketchum said. Wine wasn't just a business in Hermann, it was part of the German culture. Stone Hill had boasted the largest series of underground cellars in the world. There, a dozen barrels each engraved with images of the twelve apostles were broken down to ship to Germany to save. Their whereabouts are unknown today, Ketchum noted. Another barrel carving escaped notice because it was stored in a Missouri cave used as a winery during prohibition. It depicts Bacchus, the Roman god of wine, and is available for viewing at the Deutschheim site. "It is one of half a dozen left in North America," Ketchum said. "The rest are in California."

The International Shoe Company factory helped keep the town in existence during these lean years. There had been a shoe manufacturing operation in the city since 1903. In 1911, the factory became part of the International Shoe Company. A three-story addition, built at the original site of Gutenberg and Fourth Streets in 1923, increased the factory's employment to about four hundred workers. Thrifty and proud, none of the town's citizens would ask for or accept government relief. The cellars of Stone Hill were converted to a mushroom farm in 1923, and for years Hermann-grown mushrooms were shipped as

A wine vault in Hermann, Missouri. Courtesy Library of Congress.

An engraving of the Stone Hill winery and vineyards, circa 1888. Courtesy Library of Congress.

far as Florida and Brownsville, Texas. The farm was purchased in the 1940s by an employee, Bill Harrison, and his wife, Mary, said Patty Held-Uthlaut, public relations director for Stone Hill Winery. Many grape farmers turned to general farming for their livelihood, and many continued to produce a small amount of wine each year for their own use. Among them were Riefenstahl's grandson, John Henry Puchta, and Puchta's son, Everett. They converted most of the vineyards to cropland but continued to make wine from the reserved vines and from elderberries, blackberries, and even dandelions, which ensured their place as the oldest continuously owned family farm winery in Missouri.

There was one bright side to prohibition in Hermann, one that wouldn't become obvious until years later, noted Lois Puchta, a member of the Puchta wine-making family and archives director for the Gasconade County Historical Society. "That's probably the reason we have so many of the old buildings here," Puchta said. "The money wasn't there for renovation. It was kind of a 'status quo' period of history."

A Proud Tradition

Years before the Germans settled in Missouri, wild, native grapevines were observed by the French throughout the Missouri River Valley from St. Charles to Boonville, in the Ozarks, and in southern Missouri. The Germans established the viticultural tradition. By 1858, Boonville alone produced about six thousand gallons of wine each year. Before the turn of the twentieth century, the Germans were joined by Italians, who established vineyards in the Ozark highlands of Rosati, St. James, and Rolla. Missouri boasted wineries in forty-eight counties shortly before prohibition.

Some two hundred acres of vineyards filled the Femme Osage township near Augusta, and another two hundred acres stretched from St. Charles to O'Fallon, Wentzville, New Melle, Hamburg, Cottleville, and beyond in 1885. As in Hermann, these areas boasted great numbers of German immigrants, and their products enjoyed commercial success. Among them was the Mount Pleasant Wine Company in Augusta, owned by the Muench family, whose native wines, homemade brandies, and bitters were advertised in the 1909 official souvenir program for the St. Charles centennial. One of the larger wineries in the area, Mount Pleasant produced a superior red wine known as Auslese and won repeated honors, William Baggerman noted in an article in the *St. Charles Heritage.*

Local proprietors received their wine in various sizes of kegs and barrels, which were dispensed into the customers' own bottles or jugs. Transportation could be creative. "Wine was often delivered to Washington, Missouri during the winter in wagons driven over the frozen Missouri River," Baggerman wrote. "Presumably to save the usual charges of the boatmen."

Mount Pleasant cofounder Friedrich Muench of Warren County was a Lutheran minister who, like George Husmann, did much to advance Missouri's wine industry. He made a two-week journey through the Ozarks in search of wild grapes that would grow well and authored a book, *School for American Grape Culture.* Muench considered wine a healthy, enlivening drink.

In the 1945 book *Grapes and Wines from Home Vineyards,* author U. P. Hedrick praises the Missouri River Valley region around Hermann and Boonville. "All growers of American grapes are greatly indebted to this region as can be seen by reading the chapters on varieties, to a dozen or more men, Germans, who, in the last half of the nineteenth century, bred and distributed a hundred or more good grapes, some of them being among our best wine grapes," Hedrick wrote.

In 1917, with the rumblings of prohibition close on the horizon, George and Paul Muench closed the Mount Pleasant Wine Company and sold the entire stock of wine to a jobbing firm in Sandusky, Ohio, Anita M. Mallinckrodt noted in *Augusta's Harmony—The Harmonie-Verein Cultural Society, 1856–1922.* "The Mt. Pleasant closing would, of course, temporarily change the job situation around Augusta, for a number of its employees would have to find new work," Mallinckrodt wrote. Prohibition also closed the Bardenheier Wine Cellars in St. Louis, established in 1873 by John A. Bardenheier, an immigrant from Oberlahnstein, Germany, and one of the largest wineries in Missouri.

The Mount Pleasant wine cellars as they appeared in 1962. Courtesy Library of Congress.

The Mount Pleasant winery in Augusta, Missouri, in 1962. Courtesy Library of Congress.

Ironically, half a century earlier Missouri's vintners had helped save the wine industry in France, where the vines had become infested with the root louse phylloxera. Beginning in 1871, Charles V. Riley, the Missouri state entomologist, worked with root stock at Jefferson County's Bushberg Vineyards and discovered American vines had developed a resistance to the damaging effects of the louse. He recommended that American vines be used to graft roots on European stock. French vineyards used stock donated by Bushberg owner Isidor Bush in a successful trial. Bush, a Jewish immigrant born in the ghetto of Prague, achieved prominence in St. Louis and later established vineyards on 241 acres of land twenty-five miles south of St. Louis. He built his home on a river bluff just east of Pevely, Missouri. He had studied the phylloxera riddle, as did his colleague and friend George Husmann. Bush, Husmann, and Herman Jaeger of Neosho were among the Missouri growers who provided large quantities of native vine cuttings to desperate Europeans as the phylloxera infestation spread.

NUMBER FOUR IN THE NATION

In Illinois, winemaking began with French immigrants, who had learned to make wine from the native grapes. By 1744, these wines were savory and plentiful enough that the mother country of France forbade their export, fearing its own industry would be ruined. By the early 1900s, wine making had spread up and down the Mississippi River Valley and had become a tradition in many areas of central and southern Illinois: Nauvoo, Peoria, Collinsville, Belleville, Mascoutah, St. Elmo, and Randolph County, among others. At the time of prohibition, Illinois was the fourth-largest wine-producing state in the nation.

Italian grapevines were in the hilly areas around the coal mines in Collinsville, Illinois. They had been planted by Italian immigrants, noted Floyd Sperino, curator of the Collinsville Historical Museum. As with the Germans, wine with meals and at gatherings was part of the Italian culture. "Mr. [Louis] Lumaghi from Europe established the coal mines," Sperino said. "They all settled here because of the mines. In those days they would bring the cuttings of the grape in their clothes. They planted them in the hills and made wine. I remember they would stomp the wine—they had rubber boots they would use. All the swinging places were around the mines: outdoor dance floors with beer and wine, lights, concertinas, and accordions.

"I can remember you always had to eat with your window open so you could hear the whistle that signified whether there was work the next day or not," he added. "And, of course, when there was an accident in the mine, the whistle blew, too, and that was frequent. They're not big like they used to be, but there are still some vineyards."

The coal mines didn't last as long as prohibition, Collinsville newspaperman Karl Monroe recalled in 1973. "Well, the coal mines died off in the twenties about the same time prohibition was in power, in effect, and some of these folks who had normally been raising vineyards on their hillsides east of town because that was their way of life in Italy, made more of a business out of it than they had before," Monroe said. "And a lot of them went into making bootleg wine."

Vintning Tradition in Nauvoo

On a horseshoe bend of the Mississippi, the Illinois town of Nauvoo boasted winemakers of three Western European traditions: French, German, and Swiss. John Tanner of Switzerland introduced wine making to the community in the early 1850s, and one of the earliest wineries was operated by a man named Rheinberger, Thomas Pinney noted in *A History of Wine in America*. Nauvoo became known for more than six hundred acres of vineyards and its stone-arched wine cellars, in addition to the commercial success of the finished product. Many cellars still stand today. "I think that there were forty-four wine cellars in and around Nauvoo, arched wine cellars," Nauvoo native Raymond Repplinger recalled in 1972. "And all of them back in the old river packer days were sending wine to St. Paul and St. Louis and just about all around by rail. It seems that many of the Germans had their vineyards and their wine cellars. And my dad

Tropical Wine

Wine of a different sort could be found in the Palm House at Shaw's Garden in March 1927. One could observe a wine or sugar palm known as a "hooch tree," of which the sap, when fermented, "gives an awful kick," in the words of floriculturist Paul A. Kohl. The forty-foot tree, a native of the Molussa and the Philippine Islands, featured a crown of green leaves and sparse flowers. Its wine was known as "toddy" in the South Seas, where the natives fortified themselves with the beverage prior to battle. Large doses of it were said to produce a state that was described as near insanity.

Emile Baxter, founder of the Nauvoo Winery, circa 1880 to 1890. Courtesy of Kim Orth and the Logan family.

was quite a wine drinker and I got to visit quite a few of these wine cellars with him. I remember Hertenstein's best. . . ."

Nauvoo had been settled by Mormons in 1839 and became home ten years later to Etienne Cabet of France and his Icarians, who launched an ill-fated experiment in communal living. But many of the French remained behind with their German and Swiss neighbors and cultivated grapes. Among them was Emile Baxter, who started his winery in 1857. His three sons, Emile, Jr., Tom, and Cecil, joined him in the business, which became known as E. Baxter and Sons, proprietors of the Golden Hills Vineyards. The winery earned awards for best wine and best red wine from the Illinois State Board of Agriculture in the 1870s, and in 1880 the family purchased the Wasserzierher Wine Cellar on East Parley Street. Around this time, wine sold for twenty-five cents a gallon.

With its grape pruners, hoers, cutters, and other employees, wine was the largest industry in Nauvoo prior to prohibition. Some forty family-owned wineries operated there, and Baxter's was one of the three larger operations, according to Mary Baxter Logan, Emile Baxter's great-granddaughter. After the lid came down, the Baxter family produced wine for family use only and shipped more than 120 railroad cars of grapes to northern markets each fall. Later, they shipped apples and pears as well to markets in Minnesota, Wisconsin, and Michigan as the Gem City Vineland Company.

It was never difficult to find bootlegged wine, home brew, and liquor in Nauvoo, Repplinger recalled. One proprietor was Dick Baxter, who used his family's expertise in making wine and brandy to earn some extra money when times were tough. Such enterprise did not come without risk, however. "Now Dick had hidden away a good quantity of wine for future use and being the sort of man who made friends very easily, was contacted by one of his 'friends' who suggested that Dick help out a judge in Des Moines, Iowa who was craving some good brandy," Dick's son, Dan Baxter of Altamont, Illinois, recalled in family correspondence in 2007. "Now the judge's name was a secret as was his address, but if Dick could distill the wine to make the brandy and deliver it to a garage in an alley in Des Moines, Dick could count on a tidy sum of money for his time and trouble."

Because the fragrance of cooking wine is unmistakable, Dick decided to cook it in his cellar, Baxter noted. His wife, Eula, agreed to stomp her foot on the floor above the cellar to warn him if anyone came to the house. Sure enough, someone did. "Of all the days for the local priest to come visiting, he chose the one day that Dick had picked to cook his illegal batch," Baxter noted. Finally, Dick produced fifteen gallons of good brandy and decanted it into a wooden keg that fit in the back of his Model A Ford. He covered the contraband with a blanket and was making good time when catastrophe struck. "The trouble happened with a loud bang and the unmistakable flump-flump-flump of a flat tire," Baxter observed. "After surveying the situation, Dick could see that he would have to uncover the keg of brandy to get to the spare tire in back of the car."

A snowy scene outside the Nauvoo Winery in Nauvoo, Illinois, as it appeared in 1977. Courtesy Library of Congress

An Iowa state trooper putt-putted in on his motorcycle. "It sure looks like you're having bad luck, Mister," he smiled. He asked about the nature of Dick's visit and the weather in Nauvoo, and offered to help him fix the flat. Dick replied he was there to survey the market at grocery stores for apples from his family's orchards and would have no problem changing the tire. The trooper departed. "Dick changed the tire and made his delivery and the judge paid the money for the brandy," Baxter noted. "Best of all, Dick had a great story to tell *after* they repealed prohibition."

To Ferment or Not to Ferment?

In 1921, the Internal Revenue Service declared that heads of families could obtain permits that would allow them to manufacture two hundred gallons a year of "non-intoxicating cider and fruit juices" exclusively for use in the home. Certain types of vintages were considered illegal, including dandelion wine, because the dandelion was not a fruit. Another ruling, however, limited the alcoholic content of fruit juices and cider to no more than 0.5 percent.

In his book *Federal Criminal Law Doctrines: The Forgotten Influence of National Prohibition*, Kenneth Murchison maintains the home use provision was exempt from the 0.5 percent definition of intoxicating liquor. Several newspapers of the time didn't see it that way. They described the law as allowing only 0.5 percent alcohol, regardless of the use. "The effect of this is not to allow the manufacture of 200 gallons of intoxicating wine free from the restrictions of the National Prohibition Act, but merely to allow the manufacture of 200 gallons of non-intoxicating fruit juices free of tax," read a statement from the Internal Revenue Bureau in the September 20, 1921, *New York Times.* "There is no legislative provision anywhere for manufacturing either intoxicating wine, cereal beverages, so-called home brew, or distilled spirits in the home, or elsewhere, for beverage purposes."

It was all a moot point, Louis Geiger noted in "In the Days of Prohibition: Cooper County, 1919–1934." "The one half of 1 percent limitation on homemade wine or cider was utterly unrealistic, for if grape or apple juice were left in the open air they would naturally ferment to an alcoholic content of 10 to 11 percent," Geiger wrote. "The process could only be stopped by heating and sealing, which produced an inferior taste and stopped the production of vinegar as well; many rural households did honestly depend upon the cider laid down in the fall for the year's supply of vinegar. The end result of the ruling in re the production of wine and cider was that local law enforcement officers made no effort to regulate home production as long as the product was not sold and the manufacturer did not become a public nuisance. All through the 1920s it was customary for many households in the Billingsville community to serve a pitcher of cold hard cider with Loepp Kuchen at wintertime neighborhood gatherings. . . ."

In May 1920, the Reverend J. Komara, pastor of St. Joseph's Catholic Church at 1030 Chouteau Avenue, pleaded in federal court for leniency for a wine-making parishioner, Joseph Kofviva, of 910 Carroll Street. The priest told Judge Charles Faris that he, himself, did not know until after reading Faris's opinions from the bench that the law prohibited persons from making wine for their own use. At the time of the offense, both he and Kofviva believed it was permissible. He added that Kofviva could not read or write, and that two of his children had died of influenza during the winter. Faris agreed that the circumstances were in Kofviva's favor. However, he said, it was the duty of people such as the priest and other community leaders to inform others of such laws. He fined Kofviva twenty-five dollars.

Even the National Commission on Law Observance and Enforcement on Prohibition Laws, a.k.a. the Wickersham Commission, was confused over the law when it reported in 1931. "The failure to fix the meaning of 'non-intoxicating' in this connection, leaving it a question of fact to be passed on by the jury in each case, in effect removes wine-making from the field of practicable enforcement," the commission observed. "Why home wine-making should be lawful while home-brewing of beer and home distilling of spirits are not, why home wine-making for home use is less reprehensible than making the same wine outside the home for home use . . . is not apparent."

To Make or To Buy

Boonville, Missouri, was known as the "Vineclad City" for a reason: Nearly every farm in the county had an apple orchard and at least a couple of rows of grapevines. Those who didn't had to rely on those who did, or they tried some imaginative alternative wine ingredients such as elderberries, rhubarb, or dandelions. "Perhaps the most imaginative—one could say desperate—expedient was wine from green tomatoes," Geiger wrote. "Those who tried this evil concoction found it unique, to say the least, the absolutely worst drink they had ever tasted, guaranteed not to lead to alcohol addiction. A good many amateur vintners gave up after a few tries."

Those with no grape skills could buy the finished product, dealcoholized or not, from Garrett & Company, manufacturers of Virginia Dare Wine on Union Avenue at Brown Road. In 1920, the New York–based company invested approximately $700,000 for machinery at its St. Louis plant to dealcoholize the wine and convert the alcohol into flavoring extracts. The company's goal was to develop one of the largest flavoring extract plants in the United States. One of its products, Virginia Dare Wine Tonic, was a medicated tonic that required no prescription and was sold in drugstores. "Medicinal wine tonic became a popular tipple, because buyers soon learned its secret; when refrigerated, the horrible-tasting medicaments settled to the bottom of the bottle, leaving a drinkable wine," Leon D. Adams observed in his book *The Wines of America.*

Bootleggers were everywhere. Among the smaller vendors was sixty-five-year-old Catherine Utry, who pleaded guilty in March 1924 to manufacturing intoxicating liquor. She was fined five hundred dollars. A St. Louis police officer found four hundred gallons of wine, three gallons of alcohol, fifty gallons of grape mash, and a fifty-eight-gallon still at her home at 2344 S. Seventh Street the previous December.

For Health, Wealth, and the Great Beyond

Wine, like whiskey, was an approved medicinal beverage that could be prescribed by doctors and dispensed by pharmacies through a system of government permits (see Chapter 11). Although Prohibition Bureau figures show it was prescribed more than rum, gin, brandy, or grain alcohol, wine took a backseat to whiskey as an oft-prescribed medicinal beverage. For the fiscal year ending June 30, 1923, more than 1.3 million gallons of whiskey were prescribed nationwide, compared to 30,752 gallons of wine. By 1928, those numbers remained roughly the same.

The government allowed state prohibition directors to issue sacramental wine permits to ministers, priests, rabbis, or other church or congregational officials and issued permits to individuals to manufacture wine for sacramental purposes. Clergy could buy from these wine dealers or secure permits to manufacture enough wine to supply the needs of their congregations for one year. "The larger part of ritualistic wine is used, not in church services but in religious rites in the homes of the members," U.S. Prohibition Commissioner Roy A. Haynes explained in 1923. "In the main, these are Jewish homes. Not all Jews, however, observe in their homes rites requiring the use of wine, and those who do not observe such rites clearly are not entitled to take wine into their homes.

The responsibility, therefore, is placed on the rabbi to determine whether or not any particular family actually requires wine for use in religious rites. The largest quantity of ritualistic wine that may go into a home is ten gallons a year."

Not surprisingly, abuses ran rampant. By 1925, permits to manufacture wine were held by the thousands in the "foreign quarters" of larger cities, prohibition officials said, and each was legally allowed to produce two hundred gallons. "General [Lincoln] Andrews believes they are serving as an almost endless supply of the lighter intoxicants," the *New York Times* noted. In 1928, 750,000 gallons of wine were shipped or delivered for sacramental purposes throughout the nation. New rabbis were everywhere, Walter Ehrlich noted in *Zion in the Valley: The Jewish Community of St. Louis, Volume II.* "The Volstead Act permitted families to purchase 'sacramental' wine through their clergymen, who became, in effect, dealers in bottled goods," Ehrlich wrote. "Apparently several Orthodox rabbis headed 'congregations' in which dues-paying members named Sullivan and O'Brien and Caruso (as well as Goldberg and Rubenstein) might purchase 'legal' allotments. Most of this was reputedly overseen in St. Louis by Detroit mobster 'Big Maxie' Greenberg, whose associates in this traffic in other big cities included the notorious Meyer Lansky, Irving 'Waxy' Gordon, and Arnold Rothstein."

Benjamin Victor worked at Ralph's Drugstore in Springfield, Illinois, during his high school years (see Chapter 11). He helped bottle gin, sold under the counter, with an older student whose father was a high-ranking prohibition administrator. Victor himself went on to become chairman of the board of Thrifty Drugs, Inc. "The prohibition administrator, one of the things he did, he read the law over completely, and he found out where sacramental wine could be administered for religious purposes," Victor recalled in 1978. "And now, they could get a barrel a week; one barrel of wine would last all the congregations in the country—a Jewish congregation—for a year, as much as they used in ceremonial things. But he ordained more rabbis . . . by the name of O'Reilly and Vendetti and all . . . they also got a barrel of wine. . . . He became very wealthy out of this."

Some were indicted, including Major Percy B. Owen, federal prohibition director for Illinois, in July 1925. Owen and Ralph W. Stone, his predecessor, were charged in connection with a sacramental wine graft scheme that diverted thousands of gallons of wine into illegal channels. The charges followed a year-long investigation of a sacramental wine scandal in Chicago, in which wine dealers willing to pay the price got permits in the names of non-existent Jewish synagogues, athletic clubs, and Protestant congregations. A jury later found Owen and Stone not guilty of the charges.

By December 1925, Andrews had drafted new guidelines for state prohibition administrators and new regulations for wine withdrawals, designed to tighten the loopholes. "The rabbi will be instructed when he makes application for permit that he must submit a list of the names and addresses of his worshipers, showing family groups where they exist," the letter read. "The Treasury decision prescribes one gallon per year per adult, not to exceed five gallons per family, but also provides that if in your judgment a greater quantity is necessary per family it may be allowed."

Among the producers of sacramental wine was the St. Stanislaus Seminary in Florissant, which was allowed to continue to operate through prohibition. Jesuits produced tons of grapes in the seminary vineyard, most of which were made into Welch's grape juice.

Even when the sacramental wine arrived at its intended destination, there were abuses. On a Monday night in May 1926, twenty-six-year-old John Wright of Freeport, Illinois, developed an irresistible craving for sacramental wine and broke into St. Patrick's Catholic Church in Decatur. He was drunk by the time police arrested him.

Writer Dickson Terry recalled going out with a woman whose father bought grapes by the truckload and made three types of wine. "He always said he made it just for his sick friends, which puzzled me," Terry wrote in 1964. "All his brands packed a wallop, and when I considered the effect they had on me, I wondered what they did to his sick friends. The best of the three was the white wine, which was fine while you were drinking it, but which left you (the next morning) with a sense of impending doom. This was true of most home-made wines."

A LONE HOLDOUT

While most of the vineyards were cleared for farmland during prohibition, a group of Italian immigrants at Knobview in Phelps County, Missouri, kept their vines going. "Though they had arrived in the United States only twenty-five years before national prohibition began, their steadfastness kept viticulture alive in Missouri during the alcohol ban and provided a starting point for the reemergence of winemaking in the state after repeal," Robert F. Scheef observed in the April 1994 *Missouri Historical Review.* They had negotiated with officials of the St. Louis and San Francisco Railway Company, or the Frisco line, for land adjacent to the tracks on the northern border of the Ozarks. The colonists grew other crops as well as grapes, but each farm included at least one acre set aside for grapes. In 1920, the year prohibition went into effect, colonists formed the Knobview Fruit Growers Association. "Unlike many wine-growing regions in the eastern United States, Knobview actually increased its vineyard acreage during the fourteen years of prohibition," Scheef wrote. "After a drastic decline in 1920, Missouri vineyard acreage reached its highest mark in the twentieth century in 1924 with approximately five million vines in place. Concord and Catawba plantings in Phelps, Crawford and Barry counties substantially buoyed this figure from the middle of the prohibition era."

The railroad was a great boon to the settlers, Scheef noted. Refrigerated cars carried the grapes to Denver, Minneapolis, and other locales, as well as the Welch Grape Juice Company processing plant in Springdale, Arkansas. "Grape growers in these areas had a distinct advantage over other viticultural regions in the state: the Frisco line provided a direct connection to Welch's plant in Springdale," he wrote. "Growers in Hermann and Augusta first had to ship their delicate produce to Kansas City or St. Louis to make the connection to the nearest surviving grape buyer."

The Italian Americans renamed their community Rosati after the former St. Louis bishop, and after repeal they formed the Rosati Winery. "Not surprisingly, Prohibition started a seller's market for grapes, and the price of harvested grapes tripled in just a few years," Robert C. Fuller wrote in *Religion and Wine: A Cultural History of Wine Drinking in the United States.* "It is estimated that wine consumption jumped from approximately 0.53 to 0.64 gallons per capita during Prohibition. This wine, however, was poorly made, since it was required to be neither 'wholesome' nor 'good,' but simply cheap and intoxicating."

BRICKS AND BATCHES

One prohibition-era harbinger of this decline in quality was the famous "grape brick," which consisted of dried grapes pressed into two-pound blocks and sold by the Vino Grape Brick Company of California. They caused a flap among prohibition officials, who declared them illegal, but they created an acceptable wine when placed in water with yeast and allowed to ferment. Columnist Stanley Wilke recalled the morning of September 16, 1927, when Vino salesman Charles Hemple arrived in Washington, Missouri, to hawk his product. "It became known that Charlie had once been arrested for placing a label on his product which read, 'Caution, if brick is placed in water it might ferment and become alcoholic,'" Wilke wrote in 1976. "That was against the law! The label on a can of White Banner malt syrup was more discreet; it read, 'Dots the kind Looie uses, and Looie is a baker.' Mr. Hemple could have said about his brick, 'Dots de kind that Heinie uses, and Heinie is a bricklayer.'"

Several companies also sold wine-grape juice, and one manufacturer caused a flap with the federal Prohibition Bureau when it represented the product to be a governmentally backed venture designed to help the struggling grape farmers of California. "The advertisement set out that it could be obtained in such varieties as port, Virginia Dare, Tokay, Muscatel, Burgundy, Claret, Sauterne and Riesling in five or ten gallon kegs, under the 'absolute guarantee that it must *please you,*' the last two words being italicized," the *New York Times* commented.

Curiously, some "grape juice" manufacturers were receiving federal aid when the Wickersham Commission issued its report in 1931. "It appears to be the policy of the government not to interfere with [home winemaking]," the commission concluded. "Indeed the government has gone further. Prepared materials for the purpose of easy home wine making are now manufactured on a large scale with federal aid. Much of home-made wine gets into circulation . . . why it should be penal to make wine commercially for use in homes and not penal to make in huge quantities the material for wine-making and set up an elaborate selling campaign for disposing of them is not apparent."

Thirsty St. Louisans could purchase "do-it-yourself" wine kits from the Taylor Wine Company of Chicago, which had set up a grape juice headquarters in St. Louis's Times Building at Broadway and Chestnut Street. There, district manager John Ickenroth of University City trained representatives to sell the stuff and, for impatient customers, demonstrated methods to speed the fermentation process with sugar and yeast. His office was raided in January 1924 after a prohibition agent answered his advertisement for salesmen to sell juice in Perry

1820 Was a Very Good Year

Presumably, the bottle of "London Dock" sherry presented to the Missouri Historical Society in July 1928 was kept out of the glass-bashing hands of dry agents. Henry Shaw had brought the liquor from Europe in 1820 and bottled it at his country home, Tower Grove, in 1869. A week before his death he gave a case of it to Mark R. Chartrand of Florida, member of an old St. Louis French family and son of a former Carondelet mayor. Chartrand donated one bottle to the Missouri Historical Society at the height of prohibition.

and Ste. Genevieve counties. "A gallon bottle of unfermented juice and two small bottles of fermented wine were introduced at the hearing," the *Post-Dispatch* noted. "The agent said Ickenroth gave him the small bottle and instructed him to circulate around and let the thirsty taste it, and then tell them about the grape juice which, if properly aired, would become like it." Ickenroth was charged with manufacture, possession, and sale of liquor; possession of articles designed and intended for violation of the law; and maintaining a nuisance. He was released on bond.

"Servicing the Grapes"

Another do-it-yourself outfit was the West Coast Vineyards Company of Chicago, whose principals demonstrated amazing moxie when they took the witness stand in St. Louis in July 1929. They attempted to prove—without revealing they were violating the law—that they had been wronged because their product had not been properly fermented by the distributors. The company was suing Colony Vintages Company of St. Louis and Italian-Swiss Products Company of California for one hundred thousand dollars, alleging breach of contract through the shipment of kegs of grape juice that spoiled for lack of "servicing" and turned to vinegar. "The trial has disclosed how grape juice companies have reaped a harvest since prohibition, supplying the thirsty with grape juices which fermented, and when properly 'serviced,' become beverages with a 'kick,' advertised variously as port, sherry, muscatel and champagne types," reported the *Post-Dispatch*.

Mrs. H. T. Myers, secretary and wife of the president of the West Coast Vineyards Company, was asked what would happen to a barrel of grape juice that was handled properly. She spent two hours beating around the bush on the stand in Federal Judge Charles B. Davis's court. "She left the stand without admitting that she had ever suspected that grape juice could be converted into wine," the *Post* declared.

Jack Brandley, an officer of Colony, explained the "servicing" concept. "The service man visits the customer, takes hold of his kegs and places them up on racks so air can circulate beneath the kegs," he said. "Then he opens the patented bung holes, allowing the air to reach the grape juice and start the fermentation. . . . When fermentation has ceased, or when the wine has quit working, he clarifies the liquid by straining it through filter paper. The kegs are cleaned out and the wine put back. Later the customer is shown how to bottle the goods." Judge

Davis found the definition convincing, "so much so that it provoked a secretary of the plaintiff company to admonish the witness to 'temper your testimony or we will all be indicted,'" he observed.

Yet another complaint against the defendants was that the company's "champagne" fizzled. "To remedy this defect, some inventive genius, perhaps a reader of [Rube] Goldberg's cartoons, invented a champagne converter which was brought into court yesterday as an exhibit in the trial," noted the *Post*. "The apparatus included an oblong metal box containing a cylinder, plus faucets, gauges and gadgets. The conversion process, attorneys explained, began with the placing of 10 gallons of grape juice in the cylinder, cooling it with an ice pack, charging it from a tank of carbonic gas, rotating the cylinder so the juice and gas would mix, and then bottling the mixture. The machine, according to attorneys, worked fine on paper, but when tested was unable to cork bottles fast enough to keep the gas from escaping and blowing the 'champagne' all over the basement."

H. T. Myers, president of West Coast Vineyards and whom the defense claimed to have invented the machine, was on the witness stand at the time. "[Myers] looked coldly at the machine and said he had never seen it before," the *Post* reported.* Davis wasted no time dismissing the suit. He found "against the plaintiff," but not for the defendants, maintaining that none of the parties came into court with clean hands.

Three months later, federal prohibition agents raided the headquarters of Colony Vintages at 18 South Broadway and charged its president, William Davis, with sale and possession of intoxicating liquor. Among the items they had purchased three months earlier were samples of Jamaica ginger and well-fermented grape juice. During the raid, they confiscated a high-alcohol-content extract labeled "tutti-frutti" and a quantity of "woodentine," or shavings from the interiors of old whiskey barrels designed to serve as a substitute for the aging process. Davis's lawyer told reporters that he had entered the wholesale drug business three months earlier as a sideline and was distributing Jamaica ginger for medicinal purposes.

Fruit juice salesmen were still around in September 1931, when chief pro-

---

*West Coast Vineyards could have taken some lessons from the Bronx, where a small Italian bakeshop provided much of the "champagne" sold at local nightclubs, the *Post-Dispatch*'s New York bureau reported in 1926. The catch was, the spiked wine had to be sold and consumed within twenty-four hours, or it would fall flat. "The decoction in the Bronx factory is made by a wine master from Bordeaux, who, after the bottles are partly filled, spikes them with some redistilled denatured alcohol, a mixture of flavoring liquors like that made in the Italian section, then pops in a pellet of bicarbonate of soda to give it a fizz," the *Post* reported.

hibition agent James Dillon purchased five gallons of juice and other paraphernalia from Max Rader of St. Louis. Dillon followed the instructions and waited, and when the mixture developed an alcoholic content of 11.8 percent he arrested Rader.

RETURN

When the Eighteenth Amendment finally was repealed in 1933, the table wine industry in Missouri and Illinois largely had been wiped out. A twelve-part series in the November and December 1933 *Post-Dispatch* by Horatio F. Stoll, "noted wine authority," on how to select, judge, keep, and serve American wines hammered home a certain snob factor, and many turned to beer or mixed drinks. "One group of wines sold well—the dessert wines—port, sherry, tokay, and muscatel," Leon D. Adams wrote in *The Wines of America.* "At that time, these dessert wines were classed legally as 'fortified' because they were strengthened with brandy to 20 percent alcoholic content. Because the federal tax on wine was only a fraction of the tax on liquor, 'fortified wine' was the cheapest intoxicant available, and much of it was drunk by the derelicts called 'winos' on the skid rows of the nation." It wasn't until 1961 that Americans drank more table than dessert wine, Fuller noted in *Religion and Wine.*

In 1965, farmers Jim and Betty Held and their family purchased the Stone Hill Winery from Bill and Mary Harrison and revived the wine-making tradition. Lucian and Eva Dressel did the same in 1966 with the Mount Pleasant Winery in Augusta, which in 1980 became the first region in the country to be designated an American Viticultural Area, or grape-growing region. For thirty-eight years, Stone Hill was the largest winery in Missouri, and today it is the second-largest. The largest is St. James Winery, located in the Ozark Highlands, where Italian immigrants had settled more than a century earlier. Its vineyards are adjacent to an old schoolhouse used to educate Italian American children.

In Nauvoo, Cecil Baxter obtained a license in 1936 to manufacture wine as Illinois Bonded Winery #52, which for a time was the only winery in Illinois and became known as the Nauvoo Winery. "Out of the forty wineries in Nauvoo, ours was the only one to re-open after prohibition," said Kim Orth, Emile Baxter's great-great-great-granddaughter. "The other proprietors had all moved on to other occupations or the children didn't want to restart the family business."

Baxter's Vineyards, as it is now known, celebrated its 150th anniversary in 2007 as the oldest surviving family-owned winery in Illinois. Orth's parents, Kelly and Brenda Logan, operate the winery and grow several varieties of apples.

Jim and Betty Held, proprietors of the Stone Hill Winery, in the cellars during the winery's early years. The Helds poured samples for guests in the cellars. Courtesy Held family.

The Missouri and Illinois wine industry has accelerated its pace in recent years and has earned numerous awards and honors. Missouri is the eleventh-largest wine-producing state in the nation with more than 750,000 gallons produced annually by seventy-four wineries, and more than two hundred commercial grape growers with more than 1,400 acres of grapes. The industry in 2007 had a statewide economic impact of $701 million, said Jim Anderson, executive director of the Missouri Wine and Grape Board. "We are a growing industry in the state," Anderson said.

Illinois is the nineteenth-largest wine-producing state with 500,000 gallons produced by seventy-eight wineries, and 450 grape growers with 1,200 acres of grapes. The annual economic impact of the industry is more than $253 million annually, said Megan Pressnall, director of external relations for the Illinois Grape Growers and Vintners Association.

CHAPTER 8
THE BIG GUYS

Money split by the gang did the members little good. We had places to live and drove motor cars—
but that was all. It was come easy, go easy. All mine went for gambling and attorney fees. I've
dropped $1,500 or $2,000 a night shooting craps. I've seen others of the gang do the same thing.
And the next day I had to hunt another chance to commit a robbery to get money to pay a lawyer
to defend me in some case. Believe me, the lawyers got plenty.

Dint was supposed to have put some of his dough into bonds and stashed them away for a rainy
day. I've got exactly forty cents, and my wife has to work for a living.
—Ray Renard, former Egan's Rats gangster, March 1925

A SMALL MAN WITH ROUND, HORN-RIMMED GLASSES AND A NEATLY TRIMMED mustache, Joe Mogler was known by children in the Hyde Park neighborhood for the nickels he handed out on Saturday mornings.

Mogler, a Missouri state senator and the son of German immigrants, also was known to have befriended members of the Hogan and Egan gangs and to have signed bail bonds for them free of charge. That association likely led to his death at the hands of two masked gunmen at 9 a.m. on December 2, 1929, in the foyer of his Mogler Theater, located at 3936 N. Ninth Street. Mogler was one of several St. Louis–area residents who got in the way of local gangsters and paid for the experience with their lives in the most violent decade St. Louis had yet known. It was not uncommon to read in the newspapers about a bullet-riddled body left by the side of a road in St. Louis County. The killings of—and by—gangsters were prevalent enough that St. Louis Archbishop John Glennon forbade priests from giving gangsters last rites. Some, like Father Timothy Dempsey, did so anyway.

The Mound City boasted no less than six major gangs that made big money bootlegging and running gambling rackets when they weren't robbing banks or knocking each other off. They included the Egan's Rats and Hogan gangs and the Cuckoos and Green Ones gangs in St. Louis and metro-east Illinois, and the Birger and Shelton gangs in southern Illinois. "In this area, whiskey was one of the great things that they fought about between the gangs," recalled Rose Marguerite Boehm, a retired St. Louis nurse, in 1972. "Oh, they were killing

Joseph Mogler. Courtesy of St. Louis Post-Dispatch.

each other right and left, but fortunately they killed each other mostly. Although once in a while they'd, if there was a bystander that saw them kill somebody— well, they'd have to kill him so he couldn't be a witness.

"You see, they had these touring cars at that time and had curtains on the side of these touring cars and that's where they'd shoot from, you know, poke those guns out those curtains. And the thing about it was, when they'd kill them they weren't satisfied with killing them, they'd always just keep shooting, you know, so that when they were dead they'd have a half a pound of lead in them or something. We always made a joke [that] they really didn't die from being shot, they died of lead poisoning. It was awful."

No matter how brutal their ends, good gangsters never squealed. This was a cardinal rule, the *St. Louis County Watchman-Advocate* observed after Egan gangster Ben "Cotton" Funke was mortally wounded by the Russo Gang at the Rigoletto Inn in November 1920. "He was sullen and proved to be a true gangster by refusing to name his assailant before he died," the newspaper noted.

The Egans and Hogans

"A Right Guy"

Joe Mogler's murder, which was never solved, was front-page news in local dailies and an oft-discussed topic. "In the neighborhood where the State Senator and movie theater owner was known to virtually every man, woman and child, the favorite topic is 'who killed Joe Mogler?'" the *Post-Dispatch* reported.

This author's father, Bob Courtaway, was one of the kids who received nickels from Mogler. Courtaway lived at 1111A Salisbury Street in the late 1920s, across the street from the McKinley Bridge on what is now the northward path of Interstate 70. He remembered seeing silent films at the Mogler, which featured an orchestra pit with a piano player. Mogler's murder was the talk of the neighborhood, he recalled. "The theater floor slanted, and I vaguely remember [people saying] the blood ran down the aisle," he recalled. "That was something that stuck in my mind."

Hyde Park wasn't the best neighborhood in St. Louis in the 1920s, and it wasn't the worst. Two men had entered the theater early on a Monday morning and taken the building's janitor hostage. When Mogler arrived at 9 a.m., he was murdered almost instantly with a gunshot wound through the head. Police found Mogler's body still wearing heavy fur gloves, a fur cap and overcoat, a diamond ring and diamond tiepin, and a purse containing eight dollars. His derby hat lay a few feet away. "Gangsters spoke of him as a 'right guy,' meaning the sort of man who could be cajoled or bullied into helping a man in trouble," the *Post* reported. "Besides signing bonds he frequently interceded at times for paroles." Three weeks earlier, Mogler told an employee he was "going to quit this business of signing bonds," which he was said to have found distasteful.

St. Louis Circuit Judge John W. Calhoun was among more than four hundred people who attended the wake at the A. Kron Undertaking and Livery Company, 2707 N. Grand Boulevard, along with regular folk, circuit judges and state legislators, and fellow motion picture theater managers including Fred Wehrenberg. Calhoun told a reporter that Mogler had signed a bond for a member of the Edward J. "Jellyroll" Hogan gang eight or nine years earlier as a favor for a politician friend, only to be threatened by their enemies, the Egan mobsters. "From now on, you'll sign bonds for us too, and you won't get a dime of it, either," the Egan gangsters reportedly told Mogler. He signed.

MOTION PICTURE MOGUL

Mogler grew up on a farm near Jackson, Missouri, and was fifty-three by news reports and sixty-one by his death certificate. He tended bar in the late 1890s in a saloon near St. Louis City Hall, where he curried favor with politicians. Eventually, he owned a saloon of his own and became an enthusiastic precinct worker. In 1906, he entered the ground floor of the motion picture industry when he purchased a vacant lot and established one of the first airdome theaters. Seven years later, he married his ticket seller, Miss Adele (Adelaide) Heuer. The two had no children and lived at 4458 Athlone Avenue near O'Fallon Park, not far from Mogler's three movie houses. Mogler, also an attorney, was described as a good fellow who liked everybody and took it in stride even when he was held up. In the state senate he attracted little attention. "On the few occasions that he rose to speak his high piping voice and his extravagant gestures were unimpressive," the *Post* noted. "Occasionally his meager knowledge of English provoked laughter and he joined in the merriment."

From the outset, police were stumped. The theater's janitor, Edward Phinney, had been taken prisoner by one of the gunmen and didn't get a good look at the assailants; Adelaide Mogler did not know of anyone who would want to murder her husband. A witness, Lawrence Frederick, said he saw two men run out of the theater in medium brown coats and caps but didn't have much more to offer. "Almost everyone we talked to seemed to be Mogler's enthusiastic friend," St. Louis Police Detective Sergeant Thomas Moran complained early in the investigation. "I don't see how a man with so many friends could be killed without some of the friends finding out who killed him."

At a memorial service at the Second Ward Regular Republican Club, friends told stories of Mogler providing coal and food to needy families in the neighborhood and other good deeds. For six months in 1928, Mogler purchased a twenty-dollar bag of nickels from Bremen Bank and gave them out to neighborhood children each Saturday morning. During a contentious 1928 campaign for Second District Republican city committeeman, however, "it became common knowledge Mogler was attentive to women, that he frequently entertained women in the rooms above his theater," the *Post* reported. "He acquired a group of hangers-on, known as his '50-cent men' because they would appear in his theaters and mutter threateningly to him until he led them aside and handed over 25 or 50 cents."

Adele Mogler said the stories of her husband with other women were political gossip. "The investigation, however, has made common knowledge of

many other sides of his life—his friendship for gangsters and underworld characters, his activities as bondsman and parole advocate and his associations with
numerous women," the *Post* reported. Mogler went further than any other local
bondsman to bring back bond jumpers, which also concerned police.

Although Adele Mogler and others offered a total of eighteen hundred
dollars for information leading to the arrest of the murderer, a coroner's inquest
was closed December 21 with a verdict of "homicide at the hands of persons
unknown." The reward offer was equivalent to more than twenty thousand
dollars today.

When Mogler was killed, nine members of Egan's Rats were serving sentences in federal prison after being convicted of a $260,000 robbery of an
armored mail truck in downtown St. Louis on April 2, 1923, and a $54,000
mail robbery several weeks later at Staunton, Illinois. Mogler's killers likely were
Egan gangsters Lester Barth and Dewey Goebel, who went on to freelance in
robbery and murder, author Daniel Waugh noted in his book *Egan's Rats: The Untold Story of the Prohibition-Era Gang That Ruled St. Louis.* Barth and Goebel were said
to have been involved in several robberies and murders. In November 1930, they
were machine-gunned to death in a roadster as they pulled away from Oldani's
Grocery on the Hill.

A LEGACY OF LEAD

Headed by William P. "Dinty" Colbeck, the Egan gang controlled a good deal
of the bootleg booze in St. Louis County and City until the gang leaders were
sent away. They paid a couple of Italians by the week to look for moonshine
stills, the owners of which were ordered to pay a weekly fee ranging from $25 to
$125 to Colbeck. The gang operated a saloon at Olive Street Road and Ahern
Lane. "Many a still was blown up because the owner refused to kick in," former
Egan member Ray Renard told reporter Harry Brundidge of the *St. Louis Star*
in 1925. Renard became a heavily guarded prosecution witness against his Egan
gang buddies after he contended they were trying to kill him, and in return he
received a two-year sentence when the rest of the gang was sent away for more
than a decade. The gang specialized in robberies of banks and mail trucks and
collected from crap games and houses of prostitution. Renard estimated the
take from the robberies alone at more than $5 million.

The predecessors of Egan's Rats and the Hogans had been throwing their
weight around the near north side for decades. John Auble, author of *A History
of St. Louis Gangsters,* quoted an 1878 city guidebook that mentioned "poor but
independent folks whose chief amusements consist of punching each other's

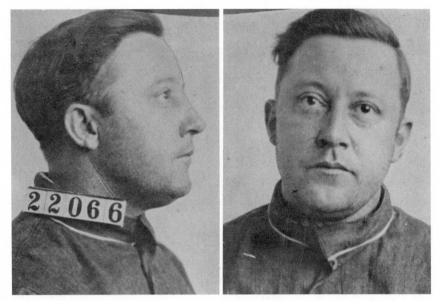

William "Dinty" Colbeck. Courtesy of the St. Louis Globe-Democrat *archives of the St. Louis Mercantile Library at the University of Missouri–St. Louis.*

eyes." Police estimated in 1909 that sixteen violent deaths were the work of Egan's Rats. The situation came to a head in 1911, when Thomas "Skippy" Rohan was murdered in the saloon of the late Thomas Egan, leader of the Rats, at Broadway and Carr Street. A series of shootings followed over the next ten years, culminating with the Halloween night slaying in 1921 of William T. Egan at his saloon at 1400 Franklin Avenue. William Egan, forty-six, was the brother of and successor to Thomas Egan, a Fifth Ward Democratic committeeman and saloonkeeper who had the good fortune to die peacefully in 1919.

ONE HALLOWEEN NIGHT

Nine-year-old Abe Stein saw the whole thing happen. Abe was the son of Mr. and Mrs. Sam Stein of 1428A Biddle Street and a student at Carr School:

> *I was coming home from the Columbia Theater, Sixth and St. Charles streets, and I was walking on the south side of Franklin Avenue between Thirteenth and Fourteenth. I saw Egan coming out of a doorway—I think it was the Palace Theater door. He walked ahead of me. Then I saw a big, black touring car coming east on Franklin Avenue from Sixteenth Street and stop in front of the saloon. It had the (window) curtains up, but they were loose, so you could get in easy.*
>
> *The machine stopped in front of the saloon and two men ran out of the saloon and got in*

it. One of them had a brown suit and was pretty tall and thin. He was carrying a sack over his shoulder. The other one had on a woman's black hat and veil and a white dress, but he had on a man's shoes and walked like a man. There was a man in the back seat already and a dark negro, with a chauffeur's cap in the front seat. They kept the engine running.

The man in the back seat fired a shot from a revolver into the front window of Egan's saloon, and then the man with the sack got a rifle or a shotgun from the car and fired a couple of shots at the wooden stand the newsboys stand in, in front of the saloon. After that I ran over to the corner, and I could see the feet of the man who was in the back seat and he wore blue trousers.

Egan ran to the door of the saloon and looked inside. Then he turned around and all three of the white men began shooting at him with revolvers. Egan fell down and the machine drove a block north on Fourteenth street to Wash street and turned east.

William T. Egan died shortly before 10 p.m. at City Hospital without naming his assailants, at least to police or Father Timothy Dempsey, who administered the last rites. The Egan murder was thought to be in retaliation for the shooting earlier that year of John P. Sweeney, a lawyer who had been a record clerk in the circuit attorney's office. Sweeney was killed instantly by a bullet through the head while he talked at Sixth and Chestnut streets with Max Greenberg, a gangster-gambler and former Egan associate turned bitter enemy. The bullets were intended for Greenberg, who survived with a fractured jaw. He later left town. "Egan sent Greenberg down south to bring a lot of whiskey up the Mississippi on a boat," Renard recalled. "Max came back and said he bought the stuff, but that the boat sank on the way to St. Louis. Egan accused Max of giving him the double cross and their friendship ceased. Soon after this somebody took several shots at Greenberg while he was talking to John P. Sweeney . . . it was just a couple weeks later that an automobile speeded by the Egan saloon at 1400 Franklin, while the occupants in the car pumped lead into him. Colbeck took charge of things the same day and you have to give him credit, he was some organizer."

Organized Murder

Dinty Colbeck's organizational abilities resulted in a full-scale gang war with twenty-three murders. One of the more sensational killings involved Jacob H. Mackler, attorney for the Hogan gang, on February 21, 1923. Mackler was driving south on Twelfth Street about 6:45 p.m. when a coupe pulled up alongside and three men emerged from the floor of the coupe and fired fifteen bullets into his car. Four hit Mackler, one of which severed the spinal cord in his neck and crumpled him over the steering wheel. Mackler was thirty-five years old and lived with his wife and three children at 1119 Clara Avenue. He feared the Egan gang, and shortly before his death he had posted a ten-thousand-dollar reward for his murderers "in the event I am 'bumped off.'" The reward went unclaimed.

A stocky plumber and World War I veteran, Colbeck was an outwardly pleasant man with a pleasant-sounding nickname. "They called him Dinty because when he worked on pipe, his big hands got in the way and he would usually dent the metal," Auble wrote. "'Denty' turned into 'Dinty.'" Colbeck made friends with police officers at every opportunity and kept them happy with whiskey and beer. He would call them by name, flatter them, slap them on the back, and even loan money to them, Renard told the *Star*. "He posed as a man whose closest friends were judges, police officers and big politicians, and he claimed to 'carry the keys' to all the police stations and the St. Louis jail," Renard said. "Many a St. Louis cop I've seen at [the gangsters' clubhouse, the Maxwelton Inn] around Christmas time—coming out for his Christmas whiskey. Lots of times when some policeman would want to question a member of the gang about a robbery the cop would call Dint by telephone. 'I've got to bring in Oliver Dougherty and Steve Ryan,' perhaps the cop would say. 'Where can I get them?' Colbeck would promise to have the men meet the cop and after the men had cleaned up, shaved and put on fresh clothing they would go to the copper, who would make out a report that he had 'picked them up' at such and such a place."

The Egan gangsters were regular customers at the Sutter family's filling station at Olive Street Road and Maple Avenue. Because of this, "mine was the only station that wasn't robbed for miles around," Orval C. Sutter recalled in his memoirs in 1980. Renard often pulled into the station wearing an immaculate tweed suit and a gray Stetson hat, Sutter said. He specialized in stealing high-powered cars to be used in robberies. Later, he moved to California and served as a technical advisor for gangster movies.

"Frequently I stole automobiles of prominent citizens," Renard told the *Star*. "Colbeck would call them up and say, 'I heard you lost your automobile— I'm going to see if I can't find it for you.' After a while he would call them again and say, 'I found that car of yours—I'm sending it in to you.'"

JELLYROLL, DINTY, AND FATHER TIM

The nemesis of the Egan gang, Edward "Jellyroll" Hogan, was among the longest-lived of the gangsters when he died at age seventy-seven in the summer of 1963. His ample size and wide smile made him look more like comic Ed Wynn than a 1920s gangster who never went anywhere without a revolver. His brother,

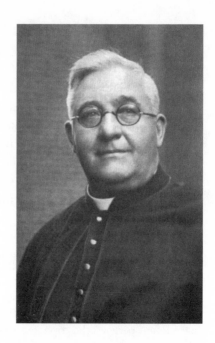

Father (later Monsignor) Timothy Dempsey arranged two truces between "Dint" Colbeck and "Jellyroll" Hogan.

Jimmy, was believed to have been involved in the William Egan shooting. Jelly-roll later became a state senator and sought respectability but could never shed his seamy reputation. A Kerry Patch saloonkeeper who later organized a soft drink bottlers' union, Hogan insisted he packed a pistol for his own protection only. "I never went gunning for anybody," he was quoted as saying.

The Hogan and Egan gangsters were all good guys in the eyes of Timothy Dempsey, pastor of St. Patrick's Catholic Church on Sixth Street, who negotiated an unsuccessful armistice between the gangs in June 1922. "We hear overmuch of the Egans and the Hogans, but it is not all fact," Dempsey told a reporter. "I know all these boys and most of them are excellent fellows. I have known Danny, Jimmy and Eddie Hogan and their friends, the two Burkes and the Flanagans for years, and know them to be decent, likable fellows. I also know their other friends, Cipolla, Marmino, 'Red' Smith, Bommarito, Bass, Greenberg and 'Hitchy Koo' Zorensky. They are not bad; on the contrary, they are honorable boys, at least among one another.

"Of the Egans, I have known Willie Colbeck since he was knee-high to a duck, and I can say for him that he's afraid of no man in shoe leather. And there is Dave Robinson, who has some kind of a savage nickname [Chippy], and he's no savage at all. And Charlie Smith, the two Doughertys, the two Doerings and Isadore Lund [Londe], not bad fellows. But they will be at one another if you don't watch them, and that's the sin of it."

Edward "Jellyroll" Hogan. Courtesy of the St. Louis Globe-Democrat *archives of the St. Louis Mercantile Library at the University of Missouri–St. Louis.*

Drink aggravated the situation, Dempsey explained. "The two greatest curses upon this nation are drink and prohibition, and I don't know which is worse," he said. "The stuff that is being served under prohibition is next to poison and is quite plentiful. It makes you white in the face instead of red, as the real thing used to do, and you can go perfectly crazy for 50 cents."

In retribution for the death of Mackler, the Hogans were said to have shot to death Clarence "Little Red" Powers, on February 25, 1923, at an Olive Street Road nightclub he owned with "Belvedere Joe" Gonella. Powers was asleep in a one-room shack just west of the roadhouse, located about two and a half miles west of the city limits. Powers had been a bartender for Egan, and in 1921 both he and "Whitey" Doering had rushed to the mortally wounded Egan just before police arrived.

The Hogans got a bad rap, Renard later told authorities. A few months earlier, Little Red had broken amicably with Colbeck's mob to go straight. He thought he had their blessing. "He just up and said that he was off the booze and off the rough stuff," Renard said. "He said the cards were stacked against him and that he was sure to be killed if he continued with the mob." But Powers angered an associate of the gang after he made it plain he was no longer running with the mob. The man threatened Powers, who hired a bodyguard. The associate and a friend visited gang leaders and told them they thought Powers had turned stool pigeon. After talking it over, they agreed that they could kill Powers. The associate and his friend arrived at the Olive Street Road nightclub, slipped up to the shack, and announced their plans to the bodyguard, who knew them and did not resist. "To protect the watchman from Powers' friends and to make it look like he had protected 'Little Red' they shot him 'easily' in an arm and leg," Renard recalled. "He died from an infection of his 'easy' wounds."

In March 1923, fifty-five-year-old Father Dempsey announced plans in his thick, Irish brogue to negotiate yet another truce. Soon after the second truce, on March 24, a fusillade of shots was fired at a car in which Jellyroll Hogan was riding on Grand Boulevard between St. Louis Avenue and Montgomery Street. Two days later, a revolver battle between the occupants of two racing automobiles left a trail of broken windows and bullet-scarred buildings along Locust Street. The mayhem prompted one automobile dealer, R. C. Frampton, to offer one thousand dollars to a public fund to hire lawyers and detectives to help rid the city of gangsters. "They will be shooting up our homes next," read a sign painted on Frampton's window. "How long will St. Louisans tolerate these Jesse James tactics?" But the violence didn't stop, and the truce was considered a joke among gang members. "We'll quit looking for Hogan's mob—but if any of you birds see one of them, do your stuff," Colbeck reportedly told his men in April 1923.

TARGET PRACTICE

The Rats had plenty of target practice at their Maxwelton Inn, originally located at St. Charles Road west of Ferguson Avenue at a racetrack that had gone out of business. They spent as much as $50 a day—the equivalent of $570 today—for ammunition. Neighbors who faced the clubhouse, just west of Wellston, kept their kids out of the front yards. "There used to be a plowed field between our house and the club," said Mrs. L. Hubert of 1408 St. Vincent, one of the homes that faced the club. "On the days when they were shooting over there you could see a cloud of dust kicked up by their bullets hitting the clods of earth. When they aimed higher they hit our front porch. Then they started to shoot so high that the bullets went through the roof. I told the children never to play in the front yard. It would have been like walking before a firing squad."

"All the shooting was done in the daytime," Hubert told a reporter for the *St. Louis Star* in 1925. "When the first bullet hit our house my husband got his gun and wanted to go over there and clean them up, but I didn't want to be a widow. I wouldn't let him go."

Another bullet-weary resident, Mrs. P. E. Waller at 1401 Leroy Avenue, thought the *Star* reporter was a police officer when he visited her home while researching a story on the Maxwelton. "Well, it certainly has taken the law a long time to get interested out here," she told him.

In 1923, a bullet that bounced off the Waller home traveled through a large front window at the home of Lieutenant Sigmond McLean at 1400 Leroy. McLean and his family were out, and they returned to find a bullet in the bed of their seven-year-old son, Donald. A neighbor called the sheriff's office that night "but never heard any more about it," the *Star* noted. "On the same night that the bullet smashed the neighbor's window, several people saw a shirtless man running over the hill near the club, in the glare of automobile headlights, his cries punctuated by shots," a *Star* reporter wrote.

Wellston-area neighbors breathed a sigh of relief when the gang moved the Maxwelton in 1923 to 9470 Olive Street Road in Olivette and the old site became part of Valhalla Cemetery. Along Olive, a new crop of neighbors was subjected to flying bullets from target practice. The home the gangsters used for their new clubhouse had once belonged to Judge A. H. Werremeyer, former justice of the peace in St. Louis County, and was furnished with items from the 1904 World's Fair, Barbara Kodner noted in *Olivette: Chronicle of a Country Village*. It was torn down in 1955 for the Eden Rock Apartments.

Yet the gangsters had a lighter side. Kodner related a story by Herb Mooney, operator of the Fourteen-Mile House, about how Colbeck's mob liked pulling pranks. One rainy day they shoved Mooney's car into a sinkhole on Olive Street Road. "Mooney, who was big and had a quick temper . . . marched to the Maxwelton Club and hammered on the door," she wrote. "There was no answer at first, but finally Colbeck opened up and faced the fuming roadhouse keeper. 'If the blankety-blank hoodlum that shoved my car in that sinkhole doesn't get it out fast, I'm going to kill the so-and-so,' Mooney yelled. Having made himself clear, Herb marched back to his tavern. The car was pulled from the hole, cleaned and returned to Mooney."

Retired journalist and public servant George Schuppe of Springfield, Illinois, was threatened by the Egan gang after federal agents arrested them in a raid in East St. Louis. "And for safe-keeping—they thought there would be trouble down there from rival gangs who'd try to come into jail and knock off the Egan gang, so they moved them to Springfield, and then on up to Sterling, Illinois," he recalled in the mid-1970s. "I was working for United Press at the time. I remember I went down to the police station to see the gangsters and they threatened to get me if they ever got out. They said I wasn't giving them a fair

Orval C. Sutter. Courtesy of the Historical Society of
University City.

shake. . . . I wasn't exactly frightened. I mentioned to my boss, Don Chamberlain,
I said, 'What do I get if I get killed for this?' and he said, 'You'll be a hero.' And
I said, 'I don't want to be a hero at these prices.' He said, 'Why don't you quit?'
And I said, 'I do. I quit now.' And he said, 'Well, you can work until three o'clock
when the wire closes.'"

Last Ride

One night in a blizzard, an Essex sedan driven by Egan gang member Cotton
Eppelsheimer pulled into the Sutter filling station with a geyser of steam spout-
ing from the radiator. "I told him, 'You have to get into a heated garage, to thaw
it out,'" Orval Sutter wrote in his memoirs. "He threw his car in gear and as he
passed me I looked into the back seat of the sedan. I noticed an army blanket
wrapped around something. Next morning the newspaper reported that a body
was found on Natural Bridge Road. It was wrapped in an army blanket and was
identified as Ed Lanahan [sic], a member of the Hogan Gang."

Eddie Linehan, a member of the Egan gang, was found murdered on Goodfellow Boulevard, about three hundred yards north of Natural Bridge, at 2:45
a.m., February 13, 1924. The still-warm body had been wrapped carefully in a
tan blanket "and apparently had been taken from an automobile and deposited
there," the *St. Louis Star* reported. "At the morgue, it was found he had been shot

nineteen times." Police speculated that Linehan had been knocked off by his own gang because he was a "copper-hater," in the words of the press, and had been involved in the fatal shooting of a respected police officer named William Anderson only days before. Police arrested both Colbeck and Robinson but later released them. The gangsters denied knowing who shot Linehan, but the late William T. Egan's edict had been "shoot no policeman."

"The fact that the body was so wrapped, and that it had not been dumped roughly into the ditch beside the road, lends color to the theory that Linehan was slain by gang friends who, exacting the toll demanded by their warped code, still had been unwilling to subject him to the additional indignity of being pitched into the mud," the *Star* explained.

It was all bunk, Renard said. "When Colbeck told the police 'his boys' wouldn't shoot a policeman he was feeding them a lot of salve," Renard later told the *Star.* "I was at the Inn the night that Linehan's murder was plotted. Indirectly I helped in the assassination." Renard's job was to round up Eddie for his final encounter with the gang. He knew the gangster could be found with a certain woman near Page and Hamilton avenues. He told Linehan one of the gang leaders wanted to see him and drove him back to the Maxwelton. "The mob was afraid of Linehan," Renard recalled. "He talked when he pleased and said what he liked to anyone. . . . When he'd get drunk at Maxwelton Inn he'd pull his gun out and announce that he didn't care for anyone in the place and that he'd shoot it out with anybody if they had the nerve to take him on. A score of times I saw him look around from one to the other and shout: 'You can all go to hell!'"

Linehan was separated from his wife and had two children, ages one and three. He had been arrested thirty-five times. Gang members believed he wanted to displace Colbeck as leader and saw him as a liability.

Back at the Maxwelton, Linehan, Renard, and another man had a few drinks, then Linehan retired to a room opposite the bar. There, three men were playing cards. Four men came over to watch the game. They were the firing squad. "Oh, Eddie, you lousy ____" were the last words Linehan heard. The four emptied their pistols into Linehan and, unsatisfied, reloaded with fresh clips and emptied their guns again, this time at close range to where the body lay in a pool of blood. "He'd have killed two or three around here if we hadn't gotten the louse," one of the gangsters was said to have replied. "Well, let's get him out of here," said another.

Linehan had been killed in much the same way he offed Patrolman William Anderson days earlier, Renard said. Linehan had been drinking heavily in the joint of Edward "Putty Nose" Brady at Vandeventer Avenue and Natural Bridge Road. About 5 a.m., Anderson came in for the second time and told everyone to go home. Linehan challenged him and got cocky. Anderson confiscated Linehan's weapon, arrested him, and began to lead him through the bar. Linehan grabbed a bottle and cracked it over Anderson's eye. He groaned and fell to the ground. "Gimme my gat!" Linehan said to the bartender, Jimmie Miles. Miles handed him the holster, and Linehan emptied it into Anderson's body.

Only one other gang member was more cold-blooded than Linehan, Renard noted. The *Star* series doesn't name him other than as "a lieutenant of Dint Colbeck who regarded murder as an art and a pastime," but author Daniel Waugh identifies him as David "Chippy" Robinson. "Eddie didn't have the love for murder that _____ had, but if there was a reason for emptying a gat into a guy, or if Eddie was drunk, he was just as dangerous as _____," Renard recalled. "Time after time I have seen him gloat over a dying victim. He got a big kick out of watching them pass out. . . . His idols were gunmen and killers. . . . I have seen him fire at a tree for hours. The tree, to his mind, was a human being. He was the most dangerous man in the mob because when he felt the urge to kill, he would just as soon shoot a friend as an enemy."

LIQUOR CAPERS

Liquor provided a lucrative sideline to murder and robbery, before the Rats were sent away to prison. Edward "Red" Powers, brother of the slain "Little Red," was sentenced to six months in jail in March 1925 for operating a still in St. Charles County. At that time, he was identified as a "former" Egan gangster. Ed Powers ran a garage in St. Louis where he would take stolen automobiles used by the Egan gang and file off the identification numbers so authorities couldn't trace them, Rose Boehm recalled in 1972. She was told the story by Ed's wife, Florence, who visited the doctors' offices at Mullanphy Hospital where Boehm worked as a nurse. Mullanphy was located on Montgomery Street east of Grand, and later on Kingshighway Boulevard, during the 1920s. "Yes, oh, yes, they stole cars right and left," Boehm recalled. "And they had those cars for their liquor business, I guess, because they were always changing cars all the time.

"Florence, his wife, oh, she was the nicest person, but she always had a roll of bills," Boehm added. "Oh, big denomination bills [that she] carried around with her. She was a lovely person as far as we knew."

Jellyroll Hogan also dealt in liquor and operated an establishment known as the Blue Front Cafe at 9025 South Broadway. Deputy sheriffs in St. Louis County had frequently asked Hogan to move his business elsewhere. Just three days after eight deputy sheriffs raided the place, a high-powered explosive de-

David "Chippy" Robinson and Steve Ryan, 1940s. Courtesy of the St. Louis Globe-Democrat *archives of the St. Louis Mercantile Library at the University of Missouri–St. Louis.*

stroyed the building, on August 19, 1924. Two men sleeping in the rear of the building were thrown from their beds but were not injured. Patients at the Mount St. Rose Sanitarium across the street suffered nervous shock. Broken windows and other damage at the tuberculosis sanitarium were estimated at fifteen hundred dollars.

Apparently Hogan re-established his saloon at 9025 South Broadway, because in January 1928 the bullet-riddled body of his former bartender, twenty-two-year-old James Haley, was found near the intersection of Green Park and Reavis Barracks roads. Haley had tended bar and served as a porter at the establishment until a month before the murder, newspaper accounts said. The body had been wrapped in an automobile lap robe and trussed with a rope; Haley's left arm was hanging out of the bundle. He had been shot seven times. Hogan himself was indicted by a federal grand jury in 1925 for violating prohibition laws by shipping "real" beer to Jefferson City (see Chapter 4).

RETRIBUTION

By this time Colbeck, Robinson, and their associates had been sent to the pen on mail robbery charges, their fate assured by the prosecution-friendly testimony of Renard. Renard maintained he had never planned to snitch—he and his wife had fled to Tijuana, Mexico, briefly to escape the charges—but the gang had put a price on his head and tried to kill him. He went to Leavenworth after filing a not-guilty plea on the mail robbery charges, wrote to Colbeck and Dougherty but did not receive a response, and grew bitter.

In April 1925, as the *Star* closed its series of Egan gang disclosures by Renard, reporter Harry Brundidge visited Leavenworth to talk to Colbeck, who had little to say. He would make a statement later, he told Brundidge. That didn't mean he was accepting Renard's stories as true. "Colbeck stood there, with his little prison cap in his hand," Brundidge wrote. "Outwardly, at least, he was unruffled. His smile was the smile of old, but the man-about-town appearance was gone—probably forever. Blue denim overalls and a wrinkled jumper have replaced the tailored suit. Across the front of the jumper was stenciled the number 22066. . . .

"A few minutes later the writer, with Warden Biddle, visited the great kitchen, where 10,000 meals are prepared each day. Here was found David (Chippy) Robinson, the 'bad man' of the Egan gang, at work among the pots and pans . . . he seemed to have been in a stupor and gave the impression of a man who did not know what it was all about; he seemed unaware of his surroundings. Prison life has not agreed with him. He smiled, finally, and shook hands with the writer. He had no comment to make, other than to ask that his regards be conveyed to his friends in St. Louis."

Other gangsters were there as well: Gus Dietmeyer, washing dishes in the kitchen; Steve Ryan, working with a hammer and chisel in the stone yard; Louis "Red" Smith, covered with perspiration and coal dust and working in the boiler room; Charles "Red" Lanham, cobbling shoes; and Oliver Dougherty, learning to sew in the tailor shop.

Brundidge stayed for the noonday meal, which he pronounced as good: stewed heart of beef, gravy, mashed potatoes, bread, coffee, and apple cobbler. "What a change for those members of the Egan gang, some of whom, in the old days, were not averse to firing bullets at the feet of waiters who displeased them," Brundidge wrote. "What a contrast, too, in the menu—stewed heart of beef versus lobster Newburg. In those old days the gangsters looked about them at the dinner hour and nodded smilingly to business men and politicians; today as they gaze about at meal time they see Indians and Orientals, Hindoos [*sic*] and negroes."

OUTSIDE INFLUENCE

Even from the pen, the gangsters managed to exert some control. On a frigid day in November 1926, twenty-seven-year-old Mabel Robinson was found weeping in the snow at Jennings Road and Melrose Avenue. In her lap she cradled the head of a twenty-two-year-old laborer named Jack Barrett, Jr., his bullet-riddled body motionless by her side. Barrett had been murdered at the Blue Front Cafe, 6121 Natural Bridge Road. Mrs. Robinson was said by a reporter to be "nearly out of her mind with grief."

Police found in Mabel Robinson's Easton Avenue apartment items belonging to Barrett, photographs of both of them, and letters from her husband Chippy, the latest of which took her to task for being lax in her correspondence and hinting that something was wrong. Police believed Barrett was murdered by friends of Chippy on his behalf. Barrett worked as a steamfitter's helper at a local heating company and lived with his parents on North Market Street. He did not drink, was even-tempered, and had no enemies, his father told authorities.

A few Egan gangsters became notorious. One, Fred Burke, was among the gunmen in the infamous St. Valentine's Day massacre in Chicago. He also shot down a Michigan policeman in cold blood. Federal investigators called him "the most dangerous man alive" until March 1931 when they arrested him, sleeping, in a farmhouse near Milan, Missouri. Another, Leo Vincent Brothers, was convicted in 1930 of the murder of *Chicago Tribune* reporter Jake Lingle. Brothers served an eight-year sentence and died of natural causes in 1951. Isadore Londe, serving a twenty- to forty-year sentence for a Detroit jewelry store robbery, escaped from Marquette Prison in Michigan in 1925 and fueled a posse search. Later, he was sentenced to twenty-five years in the Missouri State Penitentiary for the 1938 bombing of a St. Louis cleaning shop.

Himself a Kerry Patch native, the Reverend Monsignor Joseph M. O'Toole visited Colbeck and Robinson in prison. He urged Colbeck to go straight when he was released in 1941. But some say Colbeck reverted to his old ways when he got back in society and became involved with gambling interests in East St. Louis. He was shot to death as he returned home from East St. Louis on February 17, 1943. East St. Louis gangsters likely were responsible: Depending on the source, it could have been the Shelton Brothers or Frank "Buster" Wortman. "A year after Dinty's release, he and his wife were playing cards, one evening at home," O'Toole wrote. "It was about 9 p.m., when the phone rang. A voice asked—ordered?—Dinty to come across the Mississippi to East St. Louis at once. At 11 p.m. that same night, the police found Dinty's body in his car— both [he and the car] had been riddled with machine gun bullets. Only seven dollars were found in his pocket."

THE GREEN ONES AND CUCKOOS

GUNS, GRAFT, AND GORE

Aloys Frank Beelmann chose the wrong restaurant on an otherwise uneventful summer night in 1927. After a long Wednesday spent practicing law, Beelmann was unwinding with his newspaper at the Lyric Coffee Pot at 116 N. Sixth Street. Unfortunately for Beelmann, Benny "Melonhead" Giamanco also had stopped by the Lyric on August 24. Giamanco was an enemy of the Green Ones gang, which was looking to pick him off before he could avenge the deaths of his two friends the gang had murdered. A lookout was waiting outside the restaurant when Giamanco emerged just before 11 p.m., picking his teeth. The lookout signaled, a car drove down the street, and five shots were fired, killing Giamanco. Passers-by screamed and ran for cover as the car drove away rapidly in second gear.

A moment or two later restaurant patrons noticed the man reading the newspaper had slumped over the counter. "He's dead," said one of the surprised patrons. Beelmann was unconscious from a bullet wound through the right temple and died an hour later at City Hospital. He was thirty years old, single, and lived with his parents, Frank and Margaret Beelmann, at 2314 N. Fourteenth Street. He was among the innocent victims of the Green Ones or Green Onion(s) gang, a savage group of Sicilian bootleggers and extortionists that grew out of the old "Black Hand" crime organization in the Little Italy neighborhood near downtown St. Louis.

It had begun in 1910 when three young Sicilians—James Cipolla, Vito Giannola, and Alphonse Palazzolo—heard of opportunities in St. Louis and financed their trip to America by holding up a local theater owner, author Gary R. Mormino noted in *Immigrants on the Hill*. Once in America, the three went their separate ways to set up shop in St. Louis; Springfield, Illinois; and Chicago; but later reunited in St. Louis to bring Little Italy under their control through extortions, taxes, and other rackets. They also bootlegged and demanded a cut of the proceeds from stills operated by other bootleggers. Those who didn't comply faced dire consequences:

Tony Riggio, owner of a grocery store at 1018 N. Ninth Street, was shot three times and seriously injured on August 31, 1922, as he carried vegetables from an outside display into his store. He told police he did not see his assailants, but his wife, Antonia, told a reporter he had received a letter demanding one thousand dollars about two months earlier, with threats to end his life and blow up his store if the money was not paid.

Angelo Pastori, a cook at Garavelli's Restaurant, was stabbed in the heart and beaten with baseball bats on September 16, 1923, as he screamed in pain and begged for mercy. His battered body was dumped from the Kingshighway viaduct sixty feet onto the pavement in front of Sala's Restaurant. He had refused to buy meat from a gang-affiliated company and laughed at their threats.

Sam Palazzolo, a bootlegger who lived on Odell Street, refused to pay a tribute to the gang for the still he operated. On September 12, 1924, he was lured to Fifty-Ninth Street and Columbia Avenue, beaten into unconsciousness, and dragged by rope behind an automobile to a local dump. The official cause of death was strangulation.

From time to time there were incidents in the Hill neighborhood of south St. Louis, but most of the violence occurred in the Little Italy neighborhood near downtown St. Louis. John Favignano, who was born at Lexington Avenue and Biddle Street in 1917, recalled being watched by a bodyguard hired by his father, who owned a grocery store. "I've seen a lot of killing in my day," Favignano told an interviewer in 1973. "When we heard a lot of shooting we'd hit the curb and the gutter until everything was done and over with, see, we'd get the hell away from there."

The gangsters also were active in Springfield, Illinois, where twice they blew up the grocery store owned by Samuel Sgro's grandfather on the southwest corner of Ninth and Washington streets. "My grandfather's store was blown up because he wouldn't submit to extortion, or 'protection' as it was called," Sgro told an interviewer in 1972. "So he rebuilt the store and it was blown up a second time. Finally peace was made, and they allowed us to continue business as usual."

Women, as well as money, were on the gangsters' lists. The *St. Louis Star* told the story of the unmarried daughter of a bootlegger who made payments to the Green Ones. One day she caught the eye of a leader who came to collect a payment. Alone at home, she attempted to fight him off but he put a gun to her head. He began to visit frequently. "Another of the gang leaders accompanied him on one of these visits, and after seeing the girl, told his companion: 'I want her,'" the *Star* wrote. "'You may have her,' said the first gunman. This barter, conducted in the girl's presence, was too much. She told her father and he, unable to fight the powerful gang, sent her to another city, where she still lives."

BOOTLEG BOOTY

Extortion and bootlegging brought the Green Ones large and powerful automobiles, silk shirts, jewelry, and real estate, the *Star* noted. Because the Egan gangsters controlled the St. Louis liquor operations, the Green Ones found greener pastures in Madison County, Illinois, and expanded into St. Louis County after many of the Egan leaders went to prison. "By the spring of 1925, the gang's liquor operations in Madison County had assumed gigantic proportions," the *Star* wrote. "The liquor output had trebled; by threats and occasional shootings a regular market had been secured for the product and Madison County boot-leggers not in the gang were paying tribute regularly. . . . The $7,500 a month [in liquor income] represented clear profit."

Some 150 St. Louis bootleg establishments, masked as soft drink bars, sold the Madison County whiskey, gin, and brandies, the *Star* noted. This was in spite of the fact that the gang charged sixteen dollars per gallon when the market price was twelve dollars per gallon. "Alphonse [Palazzolo] solved the transporta-tion problem by forcing legitimate Italian American merchants who were above suspicion by the police, to loan their trucks to the gang on penalty of death or destruction of their property," the *Star* wrote. "Each night these trucks, bearing the name of well-known and respectable fruit and vegetable merchants, rumbled across the Mississippi River bridges with scores of five-gallon alcohol cans un-derneath a thin camouflage of vegetable crates."

The Green Ones took charge of Italian men smuggled illegally into St. Louis by the Black Hand organization and put them to work tending stills, or "cooking." Later, as they became accustomed to the new country, these men were promoted to gunmen.

In 1927, John and Vito Giannola were among more than 110 people in-dicted by a federal grand jury in Quincy, Illinois, for conspiracy to violate the Volstead Act in Madison County.

ENTER THE CUCKOOS

A gang known as the Cuckoos took over the holdups that formerly had been committed by Colbeck's gang before its leaders went to prison. But the Cuckoos were making headlines well before that time: Humbert Costello and Sam Bo-guslaw were questioned in September 1920 in the fatal beating of men's store owner Jacob Krause with an iron bolt. "Costello and Boguslaw are ex-convicts and are associates of the 'Cuckoos,' a gang infesting lower Chouteau Avenue," explained the *Post-Dispatch*.

Like the Egan gangsters, they enjoyed the lucrative proceeds of mail, payroll, and bank robberies and dabbled in extortion and murder. To their chagrin, how-ever, the St. Louis Police Department was cracking down on robbers. So they turned to bootlegging on the East Side and for a few short months ran stills and sold alcohol in peaceful competition with the Green Ones. They made their headquarters at Eagle Park near Collinsville, a resort run by John and Catherine Gray. John Gray purchased his liquor from his friends the Cuckoos until one day in 1925 when four Green Ones called at Eagle Park. They told him in no uncertain terms he would buy his liquor from them. He agreed, fearing he would be killed, but openly complained about the situation. "The 'Green Ones' heard of this and decided such talk must stop," the *Star* reported. "For ten nights in succession they drove to Eagle Park to find Gray. Each time he saw them coming and hid in an alcove in the kitchen. Then he bought a fast, powerful automobile in place of the light coupe he had owned, and thinking the Italians would not know his new car, took Mrs. Gray out for a ride. As he drove back to the resort on the evening of September 14, 1925, he found an auto parked across the road, blocking his path." Four men approached the car and shot the Grays to death. The killers drove the car to an isolated spot five miles away, poured gasoline over the bodies and saturated the upholstery, then dropped a lit match inside. The bodies were burned almost beyond recognition.

When the Cuckoos found out a few days later, they were enraged. After dark one evening the occupants of two Cuckoo automobiles sprayed dozens of bullets into the Green Ones' farmhouse headquarters near Horseshoe Lake, six miles from East St. Louis. The Green Ones were not injured, the attack was not repeated because Gray had not been a Cuckoo, and a temporary state of armed neutrality settled in after the Cuckoos decided they could not compete with "the Italian mob," as they called them.

The Cuckoos were proficient with firearms, in contrast to the Green Ones, knife wielders who shot at close range to make their mark. Known as a Syrian American gang, the Cuckoos had Irish American members as well. For much of the 1920s they were led by the Tipton brothers, Roy, Ray, and Herman. Roy later went to prison with the Egan gang for a mail truck robbery, and Herman, arrested more than one hundred times, was implicated in an extortion plot against the wholesale cleaning and dyeing business in St. Louis. Cuckoo gangster Sylvester Baldwin, proprietor of the Plantation Inn in Wellston, received five years in prison for the 1924 holdup of a laundry wagon driver and was implicated in other robberies and the shooting death of an Overland State Bank cashier. John Joyce, the twenty-three-year-old pal of Roy Tipton, was arrested 102 times from 1916 until 1923, when he was shot to death by a watchman as he tried to break into a gambling house in Venice, Illinois. In 1923 and 1924, Cuckoo gangsters Oliver Hamilton and Clarence "Dizzy" Daniels received life sentences for the murders of St. Louis Police Officer William E. Griffin and Luxemburg (Lemay) merchant John L. Surgant. Fellow gangster August Webbe was sentenced to ten years.

Brutal Tactics

During Hamilton's trial, a grisly story unfolded of how Hamilton and his Cuckoo pals held up the Spider Web dance hall at Telegraph and Sappington roads in south St. Louis County on June 10, 1923, and robbed several men and women. They moved on to the Telegraph Inn, farther south on Telegraph Road. There they killed Griffin as he sat with friends. They held up Surgant and forced him to drive them into the city. Fearing he might "squeal," they shot him down in cold blood and threw his body out of the automobile. The *St. Louis County Watchman-Advocate* described the crime as "one of the most brutal and cold-blooded in the history of the county."

Through the trial, Hamilton, sporting a fashionable brown suit and a fresh haircut, twirled his thumbs and seemed "absolutely unconcerned," noted the *Post-Dispatch*. "He smoked cigarettes, chewed gum, whistled and sang in the prisoner's cage when the jury later deliberated on the evidence."

Five years after Hamilton's trial, Cuckoo gangsters Henry Etzel and Carl Fiorita were sentenced to fifty years each in the penitentiary for killing Elmer Baltz, a Madison, Illinois, bank cashier, in a $23,500 holdup in March 1928.

Not surprisingly, members of all the gangs often needed medical attention. Some of them patronized Mullanphy Hospital, where Rose Boehm worked. "They were an odd bunch of people," Boehm recalled. "I mean, they always carried a bankroll and when they'd come up for treatment, maybe one or two of them would have something wrong. So they'd just take out this bankroll and peel off whatever it was the doctor asked them for. Pay for each other's treatments, you know, just like they were buying a cup of coffee or something.

"And doctor was nervous a lot of times for fear they'd get mad at him and do something to get even because they did do things like that . . . see, they'd have gunshot wounds and if they'd take one of their members to a doctor's office he had to take care of them. That was all; of course, they never wanted that reported. They killed this one doctor because he wouldn't take care of them. Just killed him. That's right. His name was Dr. Sante and his office was down around Grand and Chouteau."

In February 1927, Dr. August H. Sante had practiced medicine for thirty-five years, and the sixty-one-year-old practitioner was trying to avoid making night calls. One evening he declined a call to the dying mother of a man police

Oliver Hamilton. Courtesy of St. Louis Post-Dispatch.

believed to be a Cuckoo gangster. The woman died the next morning, and the gangster vowed revenge. After sitting up with her body late into the night at an undertaking establishment at 917 Chouteau Avenue, the man and an accomplice drove to Sante's home at 1115 S. Grand Boulevard shortly before 2 a.m. on February 6 and rang the bell to his first-floor office. A third man waited in the car. "The doctor is believed to have known his slayers, otherwise he would not have admitted them," the *Star* reported. "He did not go out on night calls unless there was a grave emergency and when he answered the door bell at night he always carried the automatic pistol with him."

The men emptied several shots into Sante's back as he led them into his office, and after he fell face down on the floor they fired several more shots into his body, for a total of fourteen wounds. He was dead by the time his wife, Laura, and daughter, Norma, rushed downstairs. A neighbor saw two men jump into an automobile in front of the house, and the vehicle turned around and sped away to the north. Police took into custody five suspects, four of them Cuckoo gangsters. One, Louis Mandel, was tried for and acquitted of the murder.

SHAKEDOWN TURNED SOUR

The Green Ones' bootlegging activities were interrupted briefly on January 29, 1926, by Madison County Constable Ohmer Hockett and his buddy John Balke of Edwardsville. Hockett, thirty-eight, was a member of the Ku Klux Klan, his wife said, and Balke, twenty-three, had served a term for robbery in the state reformatory at Pontiac. On a cold afternoon, Hockett and Balke drove out to Horseshoe Lake and announced a raid. A worker cried a warning in Sicilian, and a superior came out. He spoke English and said he might pay them two hundred dollars each to go away. He drove off to find a telephone, came back twenty minutes later, and said his boss was coming over from St. Louis. Hockett and Balke became nervous as they waited and no boss showed. Finally, at dusk, automobile lights appeared down the road. The leader emerged, and Hockett and Balke followed him. As he stopped at the door, gang members slipped up behind the constable and his friend and struck each on the head with the butts of heavy pistols.

When they regained consciousness, their arms and legs had been tied with baling wire. They were held hostage overnight and tortured. The gangsters shot off bullets painfully close to their heads. Finally they took Hockett and Balke outside and made them watch as the laborers retrieved spades and began digging what appeared to be a large grave. The leader then told them he was only joking, and that they could walk away. The laborers loosened the baling wire, and the two captives struggled to their feet. As they started to step away they were shot point-blank, shoved into the hole, and covered with dirt.

The Green Ones packed up operations and abandoned Horseshoe Lake. John Giannola had the men's vehicle towed to a Venice garage, ostensibly for repairs. Giannola, who identified himself as a candy store owner, was questioned but not charged with the murders.

After the Hockett–Balke murders, Green Ones recruit Caesar Cipriano was arrested as a suspect in a robbery committed by the gang months earlier. The police told him they had strong evidence against him, and Cipriano and his higher-ups decided to frame one of the Cuckoo gangsters by breaking into his home, hiding some of the robbery money under his mattress, and telephoning police.

The ruse worked, and when the Cuckoo gangster was released on bond his henchmen exacted revenge. They robbed bootleggers working for the Green Ones, then held five Green Ones hostage and demanded a fifteen-hundred-dollar ransom. The Green Ones attempted their own revenge, and an all-out war ensued; among those killed were Green Ones gangsters Joe Manzella, Cipriano, and Joe Bommarito (a former Egan gangster), and Cuckoo associate Pete Webbe. The injured included "Long Nose Jimmy" Capasso, a bystander who had shown a preference for the Green Ones.

"A distinctive pattern emerged from the violence of 1920–30," Mormino wrote. "First, none of the murderers were ever brought to trial. Italians continued to obey the ancient law of *omerta*, that of complete silence. Second, there is strong evidence that the motivation as well as the muscle behind the killing originated in Little Italy, not on the Hill."

WORSE THAN SNAKES

"They ought to take the snakes out of the zoo and put the gangsters in instead," Josephine Palazzolo declared from her home at 785A Aubert Avenue. "They're a whole lot more poisonous."

It was 1927 and the gang war was at its peak, a war that in one month's time had killed a person a day. Thirty-one-year-old Josephine had just been left a widow with five young children. Her husband, Nick, had done some work for William Russo, owner of a service station at Seventh and O'Fallon streets, who was paying him back in gasoline and automotive services. Russo was said by author Gary Mormino to be the leader of the Cuckoos, though newspaper accounts of the day described him as leader with his brothers of a rival group of the Green Ones called the Russo gang or the American Boys. Either way, the Green Ones hated him.

At 4:55 p.m. on a balmy Sunday in November 1927, a gray Chrysler sedan pulled up to Nick Palazzolo's fruit store at 1015 Pendleton Avenue. Palazzolo came to the doorway, guessed the occupants' intentions, and tried to flee, but it was no use. The gangsters fired three shots into his head, two at such close range that they caused powder burns. Nick Palazzolo was forty-seven years old and, like his assassins, a native of Sicily. Like many of his fellow immigrants, he was no lawbreaker. Two days before Palazzolo's murder, St. Louis Police Chief Joseph Gerk appealed to Italian Americans to report to police any extortion attempts against them. He promised the reports would be confidential. After Palazzolo was killed, Gerk said the week before he had placed the police force on twelve-hour shifts with orders to arrest all gangsters on sight. Had those orders been followed, Nick Palazzolo might not have been killed, he said. "The fear of vengeance is deep-seated with Italians," Gerk said. "But if an intelligent Italian-American business man knew how quickly we would handle the men who may be robbing him, there would be little hesitancy to tell us. . . ."

Josephine Palazzolo took Gerk up on his offer, although her husband's killer was never brought to justice. In an interview with a *Star* reporter after his death, she said she feared for her life. "We have known the Russos for years, and are friends of his family," she said. "Russo owed Nick $187. Frequently Nick went by the Russo home to collect it. Russo told him he was unable to pay it at the moment. At that time one of my youngest children was very sick and we needed the money. Russo told Nick to go by his gasoline station every time he needed gas and oil and he would fill the tank on my husband's automobile and subtract that amount from what Russo owed him. . . . Oh, those dirty, murdering curs—to shoot down a man for no real reason!" His coffin buried under a heap of floral offerings at the Church of Our Lady Help of Christians, 1010 Wash Street (now Cole), Nick Palazzolo was laid to rest in Calvary Cemetery. Father Caesar Spigardi, who officiated, made a second appeal for peace.

It was not to be—yet. On September 23, 1926, eight men in the Submarine Bar were discussing the Dempsey–Tunney fight that had ended two hours earlier. Glasses clinked as they refought it verbally blow by blow, when the two doors to the place swung open. There at the entrance to the bar, at Fourteenth and Locust streets, were three masked Cuckoo gunmen with blue steel automatics. Without a word they opened fire, killing Frank Christian, a cook; Anthony Dattalo, the proprietor; and Joseph Rubino, a customer from N. Twenty-Second Street. Three other men were wounded. All were innocent bystanders. The Green Ones were not in the bar that night.

The violence continued, and the Green Ones began to purchase bulletproof vests and armor plates for their cars. But police soon learned of the plans to plate the cars and informed the mechanics they would be held as accessories to any crime in which the cars were used. Mechanics refused to proceed with the work. Then the police raided an office the Cuckoos had been using as a hangout, arrested nine gangsters, and seized a number of weapons. The raid revealed that the Cuckoos were planning a new offensive against the Green Ones, who quickly arranged for a truce. It was negotiated by Benedetto Amato, a Sicilian who formerly lived in Brooklyn, New York, and who had brought with him some New York Italians who were friends of the Cuckoos.

In November 1926, representatives of both gangs worked out a truce that clearly favored the Cuckoos. It gave each of the Cuckoos a new, high-powered automobile and a suit of clothes and allowed Cuckoos who were operating East Side stills to avoid paying tribute to the Green Ones. In addition, wealthy Sicilians would sign bonds for any Cuckoo arrested on any charge and the Cuckoo would not, under any circumstances, jump the bond.

GETTING THEIR REVENGE

The Green Ones had their hands full with the Russo gang or the American Boys, so named because their members were native-born Italian Americans. They also were fighting a group of disgruntled Green Ones known as the Santino gang.

Early on, Anthony "Shorty" Russo had been deemed a troublemaker by the Green Ones. Russo, arrested 146 times by the police, refused to extort money from certain merchants and once slapped Green Ones leader Alphonse Palazzolo in the face. Palazzolo never forgot this. According to the *Star's* account, he lured Russo and his friend, Vincent Spicuzza, to Chicago, ostensibly to establish connections for liquor running. There, while visiting cafes and roadhouses in the countryside, the Green Ones enlisted the aid of two Cicero gangsters who shot Russo and Spicuzza to death in a new, four-thousand-dollar touring car on August 9, 1927. They dumped the bodies into a ditch and the car into a water-filled quarry. They later returned to Chicago, visited an exclusive store, and purchased white felt hats in imitation of a Black Hand leader they admired. "Now," Palazzolo said, "We'll go back and run St. Louis."

In *Capone*, author John Kobler said Russo and Spicuzza went to Chicago to execute Al Capone at the request of his rival, Joseph Aiello. In any case, the dead gangsters had a nickel clutched in each hand, the signature of Capone gunman Jack McGurn.

That's where Benny "Melonhead" Giamanco, a friend of Russo and Spicuzza, came in. He vowed to avenge the murder and announced plans to take Russo's place as a protector of Italian merchants. Before he got the chance, the Green Ones mowed him down at the Lyric Coffee Pot in August 1927, along with innocent bystander Aloys Beelmann. Five months earlier, Giamanco had been sentenced to six months in jail and a five-hundred-dollar fine for carrying a concealed weapon. A veteran of fifty-one arrests, Giamanco said—prophetically—he carried a revolver because he feared for his life.

Pasquale Santino, a former associate of the Green Ones who had fallen out of favor, set up Alphonse Palazzolo for his final encounter with hired gunmen. He was standing on Tenth Street, less than a block away from the Carr Street police station, when Santino approached and shook his hand. "Good-bye, Mister Alphonse," Santino said. Santino took two steps back, and three gunmen discharged their pistols into Palazzolo's back. His white hat, spattered with blood, fell beside his body.

The shooting also injured a ten-year-old boy, Emanuel Caprano, who eventually recovered. At the time, however, angry observers assumed the boy had been killed, and told police everything they knew of the Green Ones. Prosecutors made twelve indictments, one of which was later dropped.

By this time, many former Green Ones had allied with Santino. The Green Ones, seeking revenge for the Palazzolo killing, headed to Springfield, Illinois. There, at midnight on November 10, 1927, brothers Frank and Robert Aiello were playing cards at the Bluebird Cafe, when two masked men entered. One of them pointed a sawed-off, pump-action shotgun at the brothers and fired four times, killing them instantly. Two others at the table were wounded and later recovered. The Aiellos' brother, Tony, was said to be related by marriage to William Russo.

Two more killings followed in St. Louis in rapid succession: the murder of peacemaker Benedetto Amato by the Santino gang on November 15, and that of Santino himself by the Green Ones on November 17, in much the same manner as the man he had set up, Alphonse Palazzolo. Santino gang member Carmelo Fresina succeeded Santino as the new leader.

Then, in late December 1927, the Russos knocked off Vito Giannola, leader and a founder of the Green Ones. A brief truce between the Green Ones and American Boys fizzled after the Green Ones added a new member, Vincent "Bananas" Barbera, who had forged alliances with both the Cuckoos and Black Hand and planned to launch a new gang of extortionists and racketeers. Russoites James Russo and Mike Longo considered the action treachery, and Barbera was murdered on June 25, 1928, as he approached his automobile after a wedding.

Evil Alliance

Formerly bitter enemies, the Green Ones and Cuckoos came together in the summer of 1928 to fight off the Russo gang. Their goal was to reactivate the Green Ones' extortion racket, which St. Louis police had broken up in the winter of 1927. Cuckoo gangster Tommy Hayes likely was responsible for the demise of the Russos. A perpetrator of many murders in the late 1920s, Hayes was said to have come from a respectable family, neither drank nor smoked, worked out regularly, and by most accounts was known as "an efficient killer."

On the evening of July 25, 1928, Hayes told his former landlady, Dorothy Wood, to get out of the house she owned at 1219 Sutter Avenue in University City because the area would be swarming with police. "We're going to kill a couple of Dagoes," Hayes told her.

That day, just across the street, James Russo and Mike Longo had been invited to a baseball game at the Cuckoo gang headquarters at Plymouth and Sutter avenues. There, the Cuckoos grilled them about the Barbera murder, then ambushed them with machine gunfire. Russo was shot twenty-eight times, and both his shoulders had been broken, the coroner reported. Longo had been shot eight times. A third Russo gang member, Jack Griffin, was seriously injured. The Green Ones were said by authorities to have paid $5,000 for the murders, or the equivalent of $56,000 today. Among those arrested in connection with the murders was future Cuckoo gangleader James Michaels, Sr.

On a hot Saturday, July 28, 1928, Longo and Russo were buried side by side in Calvary Cemetery. Two thousand dollars' worth of flowers were heaped on the sidewalk as James Russo's casket was carried from his tenement at 1218 N. Sixth Street. Longo's funeral, at 1017 N. Eighth Street, was less extravagant. Throughout it all, police cruised the district in automobiles equipped with submachine guns, and officers walked through the crowds with revolvers ready. Two hundred and fifty people attended Russo's funeral alone.

American Boys Take Off

The evening after the funeral, William Russo had had enough. He asked police for, and received, an escort for his family to Union Station. He had always insisted that he had never been a gangster and that his business pursuits included only the service station and a produce stand at Union Market. "Leaving for good?" asked Captain Francis Nally. "Yes, for good," answered Russo. So Russo, his wife, and two children boarded a train at Union Station along with Russo's brothers, Lawrence and Francis. Russo offered to tell police the destination, but detectives told him it would be safer to keep it a secret. He was said to be next in line for assassination by friends of Vito Giannola and Alphonse Palazzolo. The 1930 census lists a Missouri-born William Russo as living in Tarrant, Texas, with his wife, Annie, and two daughters.

Some on the other side of the war had had enough, too. John Giannola, once a business associate of his slain brother Vito, announced in late July 1928 that he was withdrawing permanently from all gang activities. Giannola said he would focus his energy on his wholesale fruit business at Fourth and Piasa streets in Alton, Illinois. He lived on Princeton Avenue in University City with his wife and one child. "Vito's wife and four kids live out there with us," he told the *Star.* Two years earlier, Giannola had threatened to kill reporters who followed him. This time he was friendly and answered questions readily. "I've got no guards," he told the *Star.* "I'm through with all that stuff. That stuff is wrong. If you want to keep your face then you've got to work for a living." As the reporter watched, Giannola sorted out a box of apples, placed the best ones on top, and surveyed his handiwork. "One time, armed men rode by his side, and Sicilian folk trembled at the mention of his name or the sight of his expensive automobile in the narrow downtown streets," the reporter observed. "Now he sorts apples for a profit of a dollar and fifty cents."

The same summer Giannola ended his life of crime, a north St. Louis laborer was an apparent victim of mistaken identity in the gang wars. Sweltering heat had enveloped the city on July 5, 1928, and Valentine Gross sought cooler quarters on the locked screened porch of his home at 4911 Alcott Avenue. He was asleep on a pallet about 1:45 a.m., when someone slunk up to the house and shot Gross through the top of the head. His wife was awakened by an explosion. "Daddy, did you hear that torpedo some boy threw on the front porch?" she asked. There was no response. She saw the bloodstained pillow and cried, "What's the matter, papa?" Gross, fifty-eight, raised himself from the floor but slumped back against the door frame, moaning. A grandfather and employee of the Maloney Electric Company, he died four hours later at City Hospital.

The assassin had fired at close range: both Gross's head and the screen door were powder-burned. His son, Delmore Gross, observed a young man running away from the house wearing a dark suit and cap. Family members said the cottage had previously been owned by a neighboring Italian family, who moved to Chicago just two days earlier.

CUCKOOS CLOCK OUT

The Cuckoos eventually joined forces with the Sheltons to fight the Birger gang in East St. Louis. After the demise of the Birger gang, the Sheltons ordered the Cuckoos out of their territory, but Herman Tipton enjoyed the money he earned bootlegging and reportedly refused. Carl Shelton then convinced Hayes to split from the gang and fight Tipton, journalists Mario Machi, Allan May, and Charlie Molino wrote in an online article. A faction war resulted that killed about a dozen gangsters.

Among them were Peter McTigue, twenty-three, and William E. Boody, thirty-four. Both were Cuckoos, and Boody was a former business agent of the East St. Louis Plumbers' Unions. They were killed during a machine-gun attack at dawn on October 2, 1930, on a still operated by the Cuckoos near Valmeyer, Illinois. Another two were injured: Sam Therina, twenty-four, a twice-convicted bootlegger, and Joe Moceri, twenty-eight. Renegade Cuckoo gangster Tommy Hayes and former Eganites Lester Barth and Dewey Goebel were said to be responsible.

Barth and Goebel were shot to death a month later and, at 1 a.m. on April 15, 1932, Hayes and two bodyguards—William Conrad "Willie G." Wilbert and "Pretty Boy" Lechler—were gunned down. Hayes's body was found at 1:50 a.m. beside his armored sedan in a vacant lot in Madison. The car had crashed through a high board fence into an enclosure. Wilbert was found dead an hour later in a bullet-riddled roadster on a back road northeast of Granite City, a loaded submachine gun still clasped in his hands. Lechler, gravely ill, lay beside him. A bill of sale in the roadster showed it had been purchased the previous day in Chicago.

The *New York Times* advanced a couple of theories:

> One was that they were murdered by followers of the Shelton brothers, Hayes having probably ignored an order from the Sheltons to get out of East St. Louis, because his activities were "putting too much heat on the mob." Another was that the Cuckoo gang, of which Hayes had been leader, had included in its activities the bombing of a race track news service, a later attempt to bomb the new St. Louis mart building, to which the news service had moved, an unsuccessful pistol attack on "Crying Dave" Klegman and "Spooky Joe" Lander in front of the American Hotel, the bombing of a handbook partly owned by Herman Tipton, and the murders of Eddie Menken and Milton Rost.
>
> Such extensive operations, the police were informed, caused the break with the Sheltons, who were trying to conduct their bootlegging and gambling "rackets" as inconspicuously as possible. The Sheltons, with whom Hayes had been cooperating, are understood to have ordered him out of their "quiet area" and his defiance of them is believed to have led to his "elimination."

Hayes had spearheaded an attack on an East Side roadhouse in 1931 that killed three people and was interpreted as an attempt to kill Earl Shelton, according to author John Auble. He maintains Hayes's death was a classic double cross arranged by Shelton and carried out by two "friends" from Chicago who were riding in the backseat.

Although some of their legendary members bit the dust, other Cuckoos lived on to fight other gang wars, Auble noted. The last of the Cuckoos, James "Jimmy" Michaels, Sr., was blown up in his car in 1980 while driving south of St. Louis on Interstate 55.

CHARLIE BIRGER AND THE SHELTON BROTHERS

COCKTAILS, MOLOTOV AND OTHERWISE, IN LITTLE EGYPT

Life is awfully sweet. You never know how much you want to live until you come to a fix like this. I've shot men in my time, but I never shot one that didn't deserve it. I was always lucky, too. Always the other fellow got the first shot at me, but I didn't get hit or if I did I got over it.
—Gangster Charlie Birger on the last night of his life, April 18, 1928

Deep southern Illinois was no stranger to violence in the early 1920s. A 1922 massacre of twenty strikebreakers by coal miners in Herrin, Illinois, brought the region national attention. Then a self-styled vigilante named S. Glenn Young, crusading for the Ku Klux Klan after he was kicked off the federal prohibition forces, busted up bootleggers near and far and prompted bloodshed between Klan and anti-Klan forces. He was eventually killed in a January 1925 gunfight with a Herrin deputy sheriff named Ora Thomas, who also was killed (see Chapter 15).

Two groups of bootleggers—Charlie Birger and the Shelton brothers, Carl, Earl, and Bernie—had operated rather quietly up to this time, though Birger made headlines in 1923 after he shot and killed two people in one week at Halfway, a Williamson County bootlegging and gambling parlor he co-owned. The first was a young bartender named Cecil Knighton; the second was "Whitey" Doering, an Egan gangster who was appealing a federal sentence for a mail truck robbery. Birger, who was seriously wounded by Doering, claimed self-defense in both cases.

Birger and the Sheltons joined forces against S. Glenn Young and the Klan, who occasionally ensnared them in liquor raids. The Sheltons dealt in local booze and earned one thousand to fifteen hundred dollars in profits from each four- or five-day rum-running trip to a Florida inlet about ten miles south of

Daytona. So said one of their gang members, identified only by the pseudonym "Ralph Johnson" in a *St. Louis Star* series. Johnson later decided to go straight at the urging of his wife, and he told his story to the *Star*.

For a time, the gang used a grimy oil tank wagon that masqueraded as a gasoline truck. The tanker was retrofitted with a compartment that held seventy-five cases of liquor. The 110-gallon gas tank and pump worked, and to avoid suspicion the truck frequently stopped to help stalled motorists. Also in the fleet were regular trucks, sedans, and coupes, in which cavities were created under the seat and beneath the floor of the rear compartment to hold between 350 and 400 quart bottles. They hauled exported American whiskey until it ran out in May 1925, and from then on handled Canadian and foreign brands.

The route was first surveyed shortly before Christmas in 1924, and it avoided most of the big cities. Well-armed escorts or "tails" followed the cars closely to guard against hijackers and prohibition agents. Near Smyrna, Tennessee, the first day's five-hundred-mile run ended at a plantation, where the rum cars were driven into the barn and the runners literally "hit the hay" in the loft. The second day's run ended at a garage about twenty miles south of Henderson, Kentucky, where tires and spare parts were changed and the mechanics helped themselves to a case once in a while. "Indiana is a 'hot' state—liquor law violators got stiff sentences—so the run across it is made as short as possible," Johnson wrote. "In the spring of 1925, however, Georgia got to be a 'hot' state and protection was shut off for everybody except one big bootlegger. So the southern part of the route was altered to keep clear of Georgia.

"The purchase money was always sent to Florida by telegraph, to avoid the possibility of robbery en route. Carl Shelton generally handled the selling end up north, Earl handled the money in Florida and Bernie and Charlie Briggs did most of the hauling."

SHADY REST

In the spring of 1925, the Sheltons shifted the base of operations from Florida to New Orleans. One of their best wholesale liquor customers was Charlie Birger, who would become their bitter enemy one year later. "Clever fellows, those Sheltons," author Gary DeNeal wrote in his book, *A Knight of Another Sort: Prohibition Days and Charlie Birger*. "They even showed Charlie how to convert [his wife] Beatrice's new washing machine—one of the first in town—into a device for mixing distilled water and 190 proof alcohol. The proper ratio of water and alcohol along with a certain amount of burned brown sugar was poured into a small wooden barrel. This barrel was then placed into the oblong tub with corrugated sides, there to shake for a day and a night. During the interval, Birger and his new friends could be found playing cards in the garage."

In the spring of 1925 Birger established his Shady Rest tourist camp and barbecue stand about twelve miles west of Harrisburg, Illinois. He was now in the "case lot class" in the booze business and was wholesaling to various roadhouses in Williamson County, Johnson said. "Birger invested about $10,000 in Shady Rest, where in addition to the other attractions he had a small menagerie, a dog and chicken fighting pit, a bar, a bottling establishment and gambling tables," Johnson wrote. "Meanwhile, Birger continued to prosper in the booze business, getting much of his better stuff through the Sheltons. He followed a policy of cutting this before wholesaling it, so that by the time it reached the consumer only about one-fifth of the original contents of a quart bottle remained—a proportion which holds good in practically every quart of 'good imported stuff' sold today. Such cutting was skillfully done. A St. Louis house supplied bottles (both of the 'non-refillable' and other types), caps and labels at $3 a case, though $5 was the usual price to the trade. Counterfeit seals were readily obtained." The gangs also patronized World War I veteran John H. Mayes, a student of photo engraving who started a successful business in counterfeit bills in Murphysboro, Illinois. Secret Service agents ended Mayes's career in 1927.

Soon, however, the Shelton–Birger alliance turned sour. The two factions teamed up to gain control of the slot machine rights in Williamson County and install the machines in some of the roadhouses there. Birger, the treasurer for the operation, was found to have stiffed the Sheltons for $550 in March 1926, Johnson claimed. The Sheltons didn't call Birger on it immediately, but in May they refused to sell him any more of the liquor they had run. In July, they broke with him for good, Johnson recalled:

> *Birger, with four or five men at his heels, walked up to Carl, who was surrounded by an equal force of his own men.*
>
> *"Carl, what have you got against me?" Birger demanded.*
>
> *Shelton whipped out his pistol.*
>
> *"Charlie, you _____ _____, I ought to kill you," he said. But after a few more hot words, Carl withdrew with his men.*

The Birger gang at their southern Illinois clubhouse, Shady Rest, in 1927. Charlie Birger is at center, sitting on top of the car.

Charming and Cold-Blooded

The son of Russian Jewish immigrants, Shachna Itzik Birger sold newspapers in St. Louis as a boy and grew up to serve a stint in the U.S. Cavalry early on, during which he developed a fondness for riding breeches. A handsome and charming man with penetrating, steely eyes, he would throw coins to neighborhood children, give bags of groceries to families in need, and with equal ease, murder in cold blood those who displeased him. "Visitors meeting Birger for the first time were invariably impressed by his attractive appearance and pleasant greeting," author Paul Angle wrote in *Bloody Williamson*. "Dark skin, prominent cheekbones, and heavy black hair suggested his Russian Jewish parentage, but he spoke with no trace of accent. His handshake was hearty, his smile quick. The riding-breeches, puttees, and leather jacket that he customarily wore were neat and clean. Just under six feet tall, he carried himself with military erectness, and looked younger than his forty-four years. He usually wore two guns in holsters, and often cradled a sub-machine gun in one arm as he sat and talked."

Birger was seen as a Robin Hood type of guy, said Tom English, a banker from Hamilton and Saline counties who stopped in for a Coke from time to time at Birger's roadhouse near Crab Orchard. "He had a lot of friends," English recalled in 1979. "You know, people he'd helped. So if his life had been channeled for good instead of being illegal, why think what it would have been."

Even when he was on Death Row for murder, Birger never failed to fascinate. His rapt audiences included Billy Sunday, a popular evangelist of the day. "At the time Birger was in jail waiting to be hanged, we had in West Frankfort a giant crusade—a Billy Sunday crusade," journalist Henson Purcell recalled in 1972. "I was probably more interested or more concerned about what I thought would make a good story than I was in Charlie Birger's soul. But somewhere along the line I decided it would be a good deal to see if I could take Billy Sunday up and let him talk to Charlie Birger while he was in jail waiting to be hanged. . . . Oh, he just warmed up to it quickly, and said, 'Why, yes,' he'd be glad to go. . . . I could hardly wait because I could just imagine how a guy like Billy Sunday was going to preach to Charlie about how he had wasted his life, and all this stuff. To my great amazement, Billy Sunday hung on the bars of the jail outside the cell, and Charlie did all the talking about his escapades and his run-ins with these gangsters and all this kind of thing. And Sunday was the audience."

WAR IN WILLIAMSON COUNTY

By November 1926 bodies of gang members were turning up all over the place. Among them were William B. "High Pockets" McQuay, a Birger bartender whose body was found riddled with bullets near Herrin, Illinois, and Ward "Casey" Jones, another bartender whose body was found the same day in a creek near Equality, Illinois. *Time* magazine reported the scene:

> *The first mute witness to law and order in Herrin was a human hand which reached stiffly for the sky, emerging from the shallows of the Big Saline river near Equality, Ill. A Negro boy saw it. He had been playing on the bridge. He looked down, and there was the hand. It did not move. The Negro did. A sheriff who discerned something more than fantasy behind his terrified eyes and whirling words, followed the boy back to the river and found, under the hand, the body of a onetime bartender for Mr. Birger, wrapped in a horse-blanket and riddled with bullets.*

The *Time* reporter went to see Birger and found him in the cellar of his roadhouse, Shady Rest, playing with a white dog. Shady Rest was located off Route 13, between Harrisburg and Marion, Illinois.

He had on a bullet-proof jacket. Six men sat around, spitting and smoking and laughing at the puppy. They all had rifles. Outside in the shed was an armored touring car that Charles Birger used when he drove abroad on his affairs. The roadhouse was barricaded. Machine guns looked out between the shutters. Mr. Birger said he would get Carl Shelton.

But Carl Shelton wasn't to blame. McQuay and Jones were done in by Birger's own men because they were suspected of giving information to the Sheltons, author Bill Nunes reported in his book *Southern Illinois: An Illustrated History*. So was Lyle "Shag" Worsham, another Birger gangster suspected of providing information to the Sheltons. He was shot, and his body was doused with gasoline and set on fire. "His charred body was burned so badly that his own mother couldn't identify him," Nunes wrote.

By 1928, the gangs had racked up a total of fourteen murders, including two mayors, Joe Adams of West City and Jeff Stone of the village of Colp, and a state highway patrolman and his wife, Lory and Ethel Price.

Dr. C. H. Williams of Orient, Illinois, was called on at times to treat the "war wounded." "I often had to get up [at night] and pump out some poor guy's stomach who had drunk some of that bootleg whiskey," Williams recalled in 1978. "I remember a man came to my office with his foot shot by a friend who was in the Birger gang. I told him to come back after dark. He came back, and I fixed up his foot. Another time, a machine gun was stuck against my stomach, but the man backed off when he recognized me. He said, 'Sorry, Doc,' and left."

The stories that circulated about the gangs in the local papers were enough to make anyone skittish. The Sheltons modified a gasoline tank truck to a rolling shooting gallery with a machine gun mounted at the back, Taylor Pensoneau wrote in *Brothers Notorious: The Sheltons*. Birger's gang responded by sheathing the sides of a Reo truck in sheet metal. "If the two ponderous vehicles ever met in a clash like the Monitor and the Merrimack, there was no record of it," Pensoneau wrote.

Between assorted murders and shootings and the conviction of Carl, Earl, and Bernie Shelton in 1927 for a Collinsville mail robbery, Birger's Shady Rest was bombed twice in two months. The first attempt, from a stunt plane, may have been the first civilian bombing raid in the country. It wasn't very successful, although it did kill one of Birger's bulldogs and one of his pet eagles. The second time, four people were killed after the roadhouse was dynamited from the road and burned. Sightseers swarmed the ruins and picked up souvenirs. "Birger's dogs were carried away in automobiles to become pets under more peaceful surroundings," reported the *New York Times*. "When he visited the place today he found that his pet eagle, pet monkey and the squirrels, rabbits, ducks, geese and goats, which made up the remainder of his small zoo had been carried away by sightseers."

GRISLY MURDER AND THE GALLOWS

In sheer brutality nothing compared to the murders of Illinois State Police Patrolman Lory Price and his pregnant wife, Ethel, on a cold night in January 1927. Price, an easygoing, well-liked man, was a frequent visitor to Birger's Shady Rest. "Rumor had it that he worked with Birger in the stolen-car racket—Birger's men would steal a car, hold it until a reward was posted, then park it in some out-of-the-way spot and tip off the officer," Angle wrote. "Price would 'find' the automobile and divide the reward with the gangsters. Whether that was true or not, it is certain that Price was on intimate terms with Birger and several of his men."

Arlie O. Boswell, state's attorney of Williamson County and a Birger ally, tipped the gang that Price knew about their six-thousand-dollar holdup of the Bank of Pocahontas in November 1926 and was planning to turn them in. So they abducted Price and his wife from their Marion home on January 17, 1927, and killed them. Price's body was found in February 1927 in a farmer's field, his hands gnawed away by animals. His wife's body was found after Art Newman, already convicted of the murder of West City Mayor Joe Adams, told the sordid story to investigators the following summer. Newman had been Birger's former chief lieutenant.

Price, he said, was subjected to more than an hour of recrimination and then taken to the barbecue stand on the site of Shady Rest and shot several times. In another car, the gangsters took Ethel Price to an abandoned mine shaft north of Marion, shot her seven times in the back and threw her body into the shaft, along with a large concrete block and a mass of debris. Her battered watch stopped at 1:19 a.m.

Still alive after the shooting at the barbecue stand, Price was loaded into a sedan for his last ride. The gangsters took turns sitting on his body, and even they were sickened as he spit blood and drifted in and out of consciousness. Birger ordered the car stopped at one point and vomited violently at the roadside. "Every time I kill a man it makes me sick afterwards," he observed. "I guess it's my stomach." The gangsters had planned to dump Price's body in a coal mine, but a watchman was there. They proceeded to a schoolhouse where they planned to burn both body and building, but it was raining hard. Finally they reached a farmer's field near Dubois. "There he was taken out, laid on the ground, and while he groaned for mercy was put to death in a fusillade of revolver shots," a *Post-Dispatch* reporter wrote. "His body, horribly mutilated, was found there February 5, 1927."

Newman and former Birger gangsters Freddie Wooten, Leslie Simpson, and Riley Simmons pleaded guilty in 1929 to the murder of Mrs. Price and two charges of conspiracy to murder the Prices, and they were each sentenced to life imprisonment and 114 years on the conspiracy charges. They said Ethel Price was murdered only because the gangsters saw fit to murder her husband, and she would have been a witness to his abduction. Connie Ritter, on the run, was captured later that year for the murders.

By the time of the sentencing, Charlie Birger had been dead for well over a year. He had been hanged in April 1928 for the murder of Joe Adams, a Shelton ally. At the outset he never expected the Adams charges to stick, since he was nowhere near the murder scene. "Arrested? Me? Oh, no!" Birger joked cheerfully with a reporter from the telephone of his Harrisburg home, when officials announced plans to arrest him for the Adams murder. He had paid two young brothers, Harry and Elmo Thomasson, fifty dollars each to do the deed. Elmo, in the meantime, was one of four who died in the bombing and burning of Shady Rest. Harry became convinced Birger set the fire that killed his brother, so he pleaded guilty to Adams's murder and became the state's star witness against Birger and gang members Newman and Ray Hyland. Newman, Hyland, and later Connie Ritter received life imprisonment; Birger was sentenced to hang.

Birger received a shave on the morning of April 19, 1928, and a breakfast of eggs and toast, then proceeded in handcuffs to the gallows. On the way, he stopped to see the jailer's wife to thank her for the treatment he received while in jail, Henson Purcell noted. Then he went out and climbed the thirteen steps to the scaffold. Among the five hundred or so gathered outside was Joe Adams's wife, Beulah, who had watched her husband shot to death in his own home by Birger's men.

"Though his face was white and his hands trembled so that his manacles clinked together, Birger smiled on his executioners," *Post-Dispatch* correspondent Roy Alexander reported. "There was nothing of bravado, nothing of the old swaggering pose in his last minutes. The trap was sprung at 9:52 o'clock and 15 minutes later he was dead."

"Beautiful world," were Birger's last words as he took note of a tree near the Benton jail.

Last Night

On April 18, 1928, the last evening of his life, gangster Charlie Birger stayed up and talked with guards and visiting reporters, including *Post-Dispatch* correspondent Roy Alexander. Earlier that day, he had watched intently from the Benton jail as curious spectators milled around the scaffold where Birger would be hanged the next day, Alexander observed.

"Never did see so many ugly people in my life," he said, once, grinning at the guards. "They're no better looking than you fellows. . . ."

Later, when the writer returned to sit with him, the condemned man had decked himself in a suit of silk underclothing given him by Jailer Millard Lovan and he was half sitting, half lying on his cot, which illuminated every corner of the bare cell with garish distinctness. "Glad you came back," the gangster said. "I need company tonight. . . ."

As the evening wore on, an odd change came over him. His voice lost its flatness and rose and fell with a more pronounced inflection. The old hates, gathering through the years, seemed to fall away from him, and he spoke even of his enemies, impersonally without rancor. . . .

He told, too, of many wild incidents of his life—how he shot out the lights on the Harrisburg town square on the day the armistice was signed and how on another occasion he went into his own grocery store and "shot up the canned goods."

"I'll never forget," he said, "how a policeman stood at the other end of the store waiting until I'd empty the pistol so he could disarm me. I always fooled him by keeping one cartridge in the chamber while I reloaded the piece and he never did get a hold of me. . . ."

"The gangsters ran the country down here, just like they have for years. Sometimes I think they ought to give the country back to the Indians. Anyhow, here I was, making $100 a day [$1,124 today] and more, selling whisky, running gambling games and collecting from our slot machines. The Sheltons were making lots too. But we got too strong against the law and the law broke it all up. The law organized just like the gangs were organized, and whipped us."

Only once during the long hours before the dawn, did he show any real sign of emotion. That was when he talked of his daughters, Minnie, 10 years old, and Charline, 6.

"The poor little kids," he said, his eyes filling, "they don't know what it is all about now. But what will they think when they see me in that casket? I must not think of that, must I?"

When the sun came up, the last time for him, he was still talking, a little more haggard than before, but still calm. Only the tensing muscles in his neck, and the nervous movement of his feet, betrayed agitation. His voice was still even, his manner oddly gentle.

QUIETLY BLOODY

While the Birger gangsters faded into the sunset, the Shelton brothers stayed busy. Taylor Pensoneau quoted one reporter as saying Carl Shelton "had the softest tongue and the bloodiest hands of any gangster who ever operated on the East Side."

As a young night manager at an Illinois telegraph office, Vera Niemann used to serve two of the Shelton brothers, who dressed conservatively in business suits. "My silent prayer was Please keep me from saying, 'How's business today?'" Niemann wrote in 1984. "Good customers, they were always polite and quietly friendly. Sometimes one man's wife came in to transact their business. She was also pleasant and likeable. . . . I began to wonder how they could be part of the press stories.

"The older brother brought us handsome boxes of candy for Christmas. Even though I felt neutral, I wanted no presents. He was in great, jovial holiday spirits, reminding me of a big, happy Teddy Bear so I could not refuse the gifts. My solution was accept them with thanks, later giving them to the messenger boys."

Their bootlegging operation flourished: Earl Shelton supervised the transport of liquor from places such as Florida and the Bahamas, according to Pensoneau. "They became big wholesalers, middlemen acquiring a boatload of booze and reselling it a case at a time for a terrific profit," Pensoneau wrote. "The business required a payroll of drivers and persons to guard the trucks and the secret warehouses. Old Shelton standbys, such as Blackie Armes and Ray Walker, were still on board, along with newcomers—young thugs like Frank [Buster] Wortman, a son of an East St. Louis fire captain."

On August 10, 1932, the gang's high-profile victim was Alden Oliver Moore, president of the East St. Louis Central Trades and Labor Union and business agent of Boilermakers' Union No. 363. Moore was shot down on the street near the union office by a carload of gangsters with machine guns and sawed-off shotguns. His murder followed a labor dispute between union workmen and officials of the Phillips Petroleum Company, which had hired non-union workmen to build eight tanks at the company's plant on Highway 3. Union leaders claimed the company hired Carl Shelton and his men as guards. Questioned by authorities, Shelton would only say that he was hired by the company as an "arbitrator." He also had an alibi for the murder.

"My brother . . . said that Shelton asked him, 'How would you like to make some money [$30,000] by letting non-union men go ahead with the building of those tanks at the Phillips plant?'" Moore's sister, Cleta, told a reporter the day after the murder. "My brother told him that he would not have any dealings with him. Shelton met him later and said, 'I know where you live.' All day yesterday, strange men were driving around our house in automobiles, and my brother told me that five or six carloads of gunmen had come down from Peoria to take a hand in the labor dispute. When my brother left home last night, he said that he was going to have the police arrest these gunmen and drive them out of town."

Company officials said they had found it necessary to hire guards to protect company property but had not authorized violence. St. Clair County Sheriff Jerome Munie said he had not furnished guards for the Phillips Company because he didn't want his deputies associated with the Sheltons.

The murder was never solved. Moore was thirty-seven years old and lived in East St. Louis with his wife, Edna, and sons James, eleven, and Richard, seven.

The Sheltons expanded into other vices, including prostitution, but held their grip on illegal liquor until the bitter end. In June 1934, gang members Monroe "Blackie" Armes and Frank "Buster" Wortman were convicted of resisting and interfering with federal agents who raided a still in Collinsville in September 1933. Armes, it was noted, "had so steady a hand on a Tommy gun even in a moving automobile that the close grouping of bullet holes in a victim became for the police a trade-mark of his jobs." The Sheltons moved their operation to Peoria after Sheriff Jerome Munie ran them out of East St. Louis and St. Clair County, according to author Gary DeNeal, and Buster Wortman took over their old turf. Carl and Bernie and another brother, Roy, were picked off by their enemies in the late 1940s. "Crime paid handsomely for the Sheltons," wrote Andrew Theising, author of *Made in USA: East St. Louis.* "Their empire stretched from Cairo in the south to Peoria in the north, which became the dividing line between Chicago and East St. Louis syndicates. The Shelton organization grossed $4.75 million in 1930 alone, and $1.9 million of that was pure profit."

Miscellaneous Gangsters

East Side Operatives

Elsewhere in Illinois, an Italian American known as Dominic Tarro controlled a bootlegging ring beyond his hometown of Benld. Described as an alcohol "broker" and liquor kingpin of Macoupin County, Tarro was indicted in October 1929 on three counts of violation of the liquor laws and conspiracy. He was said to be a "go-between" for corn sugar and yeast manufacturers in Macoupin and Montgomery counties and illegal still operators in southern Illinois. He planned to turn state's witness for the government in its prosecution of the still owners but never got the chance. Tarro disappeared in January 1930, and weeks later his body was found in the Sangamon River north of Springfield. His arms and feet had been tied together with wire, and one of the strands had been drawn around the neck to pull his head to his knees. Nearly all of his clothes had been stripped from his body. "There are an increasing number of Dominics throughout the nation," eulogized the *Edwardsville Intelligencer.* "There may be bootleggers who have made money and then retired into peace and security, but we doubt it. It's hard to get out of a racket like that. Too many persons fear the retired bootlegger may sometime forget himself and talk."

Federal authorities had larger conspirators to convict. Among them were the Corn Products Refining Company and Fleischmann Yeast Company, charged in Chicago along with 31 other corporate and 156 individual defendants with conspiracy to violate the prohibition law. The Corn Products Refining Company allegedly sold large shipments of sugar to illicit distillers from its plants at Chicago, Pekin, and Peoria, Illinois, and Kansas City, Missouri. Fleischmann, headquartered in New York, provided the yeast. Officials of Corn Products pleaded nolo contendere, and the company was fined five thousand dollars by federal judge Louis Fitzhenry in July 1931. Two months later, Fleischmann—which also pleaded nolo contendere—was fined three thousand dollars. In a nolo contendere plea, the defendant admits the facts that are charged but denies criminal intent.

Northwest of Springfield, the struggling coal town of Colchester, Illinois, was home to a bootlegger named Henry "Kelly" Wagle. Considered a "Robin Hood" of sorts, Wagle earned a reputation as "most notorious man in McDonough County" before he was shot dead on the street in April 1929, author John E. Hallwas noted in his book *The Bootlegger.*

Another Dominic, Dominic Italiano, worked in Collinsville, Illinois, and was said to be one of the biggest East Side dealers in bootleg alcohol. He fared a little better than Tarro: He was sentenced in 1929 to three years at Leavenworth Penitentiary for transportation of liquor. His reputed business associate, Joseph Buzamatto, was deported to his native Italy. Three other Collinsville men were murdered in separate gang war activities within four blocks of the West Clay Street home of Karl Monroe. "One of them was the father of the now retired city librarian, a fellow named Bowers," Monroe, a retired newspaperman, recalled in 1973. "Another one was a fellow named Colone. And the third one was Snipe Maddelino. Snipe was the manager of the Collinsville Park Ballroom."

Lou Colone, a brother of the murdered Colone, was a deputy sheriff and tended bar at a tavern in town. One evening, a younger employee named "Boom" Ciallala went outside to provide curb service, Monroe said. The people inside the car were armed, told Ciallala to get out of the way, and riddled the tavern with machine-gun fire. The bullets missed Colone and hit the adding machine. Colone deputized several people, headed to Snipe Maddelino's house, and shot Maddelino dead. "He was acquitted by a jury," Monroe recalled. "He said it was self-defense. The man was in bed with no weapon, but I guess Lou was in mortal fear of life at that point. He was in mortal fear later because he disappeared from town for about two years. Subsequently [he] came back and was a deputy sheriff for many, many years."

The Oakland Court Gang

A ragtag group of eight men and one woman played havoc with businesses and passing motorists in central Illinois in a series of armed robberies and holdups. They were led by a scary-looking fellow named Monte Crist, a.k.a. Edward Miller, twenty-six, an ex-convict from St. Louis who had served a robbery sentence in the Missouri State Penitentiary. They became known as the Oakland Court Gang for their last hideout in April 1930: a quiet community of little frame cottages in Decatur, Illinois.

They loved to terrorize their victims and had a flair for spectacular holdups, noted Janet Janes in the *Decatur Herald and Review*. "A favorite trick was patrolling country roads and robbing motorists," she wrote. "The bandits always topped off their road blockade escapades by disassembling the victims' cars." They also held up various banks and local businesses, and they got in a shootout with Mattoon police during a robbery of the Humboldt State Bank. In one raid on a bookie joint they wore green goggles; another time they bound a night watchman and ransacked the town of Strasburg. Irate businessmen hired a private attorney, George Geer, who traced the gang through their landlady to 709 and 717 Oakland Court and posed as a liquor buyer. He told police of the gang's whereabouts, but they had been tipped. At 1:30 a.m. on Saturday, April 19, thirteen officers surrounded the cottages and arrested the gangsters. Miller, considered to be one of the most dangerous members of the gang, made a dash for the gang's arsenal but stopped when he was warned by police.

"You're ——— lucky," Miller told Deputy Sheriff Virgil Belcher at the county jail. "If that buddy of mine hadn't moved the shot gun, you would be stretched out on a cooling board by now. Maybe both of us would." Miller told Belcher he would rather be dead than locked up. "Yes, I am a tough guy," he said, "and I wouldn't hesitate a second to kill you. You took me by surprise, in fact, not a soul knew or had the least suspicion that the officers were near."

Because they did not expect anything, the men were unarmed when police burst into the rear doors of the cottages. At 709 Oakland Court, the men had been playing cards at a kitchen table outfitted with several beer and whiskey bottles and cherry, chocolate, and custard pies. The living room was cramped with mattresses used for sleeping and housed an aquarium with a dozen goldfish, a radio that concealed two pistols and ammunition, and a rocking chair. The kitchen and back porch were crammed with bottles of hard liquor and home brew. The bedroom was filled with suitcases, a trunk, and two vacuum cleaners believed to have been used by gang members when posing as salesmen. The bedroom also contained "enough guns to equip a small army," the *Decatur Review* reported, including four rifles, three sawed-off shotguns, ten pistols and revolvers, "jimmy bars," hacksaws, keys of all makes, hunting knives, and more.

In addition to Miller, those arrested included Charles M. Wilson, twenty-five, a taxi driver who rented 709 Oakland Court; his wife, no first name given, twenty-three; John A. Fleming, a truck driver who rented the other Oakland Court cottage; Lionel Glenn Rommel, twenty-six, of 717 Oakland Court; Joseph G. Hartman, twenty-four, a millwright from Casey, Illinois; Carl Sanders, thirty-four, a resident of Marblehead; and Robert Raymond, twenty-five, of Cleveland, Ohio. Two gang members, Cecil "Tuck" Wright and Marion "Smiles" Bowles, escaped in a stolen automobile the night that the Oakland Court cottages were raided. Police later arrested them in Chicago following the robbery of the Guards Armory in East Chicago, Indiana. All of the gang members were sentenced to fifteen years in federal prison.

They were an interesting bunch. One of the gang members, Carl Sanders, claimed to be an experienced knife thrower who could split a peanut at thirty yards. Two others were physically challenged. "Rommel, a former railroader, lost both legs in a yard accident in Indiana several years ago, and Miller, who admits that he is a desperate character, has lost two fingers," noted the *Decatur Review*. Three children, offspring of the Wilsons, also were part of the group. They were turned over temporarily to Lionel Rommel's wife, who was pregnant and living with her parents on North Church Street. "The Wilsons were as good neighbors as you could find," Mrs. A. J. Jessee of 735 Oakland Court told a reporter. "They would talk to us from the back porch when we would be out in the garden. The children came over all the time to play with our little boy, and I took them to Sunday school at the Westside Nazarene church each Sunday morning."

THE Big Guys

The Oakland Court Gang was a bunch of choirboys compared to Chicago's Al Capone and his henchmen, whose bloodthirsty tactics and illustrious stories remain fascinating to this day. Although based in Chicago, the gang was said to have dealings in downstate Illinois and the St. Louis area. Rural Illinois and Missouri were considered safe havens from high-pressure gang life, and rivers were said to hold a special appeal for them, including the Meramec River southwest of St. Louis and the Illinois River in Beardstown, Illinois. In Beardstown, gangsters lived on houseboats with built-in burglar alarms: frogs that stopped croaking when a stranger came near.

Born in Beardstown in 1898, May Carr McNeil recalled how the Chicago gangsters would come to town for a little duck hunting, and they bought their liquor at a home that doubled as a bootleg joint called Pharr's. Though she stayed away from bootlegging joints, McNeil was compelled to go inside Pharr's one day when two men fighting outside threatened her safety. "So I went inside and there was a studio couch pulled out in the middle of the living room," McNeil said in a 1987 interview. "There was a swell-looking young guy laying on the couch and he was all beat up and the next day they found a man in the junk yard right across the alley. They said he had a heart attack and bruised up on the junk. But he didn't, he died there at that bootlegging joint because I saw him. I was going to tell it. My husband told me to keep still because those gangsters from Chicago would come down here duckhunting and they always bought their liquor at Pharr's. My husband said if I told and it happened to be one of them that killed this guy, that they would kill me to keep me from telling. So I didn't tell it."

ABDUCTIONS 'R US

Seven gangsters—described by police as associates of the Fred Burke, Cuckoo, and Shelton gangs—were arrested in East St. Louis in May 1931 in connection with bank robberies totaling more than $5 million, kidnappings that brought $1 million in ransom, and a 1922 robbery of the Denver Mint that netted $200,000. The abductions included Cora Garrison, wife of Peoria gambler Clyde Garrison, and Fred J. Blumer, a Monroe, Wisconsin, brewer. Those arrested were Cuckoo gangsters Tommy Hayes, Thomas O'Connor, Jack Britt, Howard Lee, E. Hawks, William McQuillan, and Dewey Sullivan.

Cuckoo leader Herman Tipton was arrested in the February 1930 kidnapping of Charles W. Pershall of Granite City, Illinois, a banker and operator of several grocery stores, for a forty-thousand-dollar ransom. At the time, Tipton lived at 3401 Magnolia Avenue in St. Louis and gave his age as twenty-eight. Tipton also was among seven suspects interviewed the following November in connection with the kidnapping of Alexander Berg, a wealthy St. Louis fur dealer, for a $100,000 ransom. Both victims were released unharmed.

Kidnappings were big business in St. Louis in the early 1930s, and one of the biggest was the abduction of Dr. Isaac D. Kelley, a prominent physician who lived at 53 Westmoreland Place. On the rainy evening of April 20, 1931, the eye, ear, nose, and throat specialist answered a sick call that turned out to be fake. He was taken to a shack on a farm four miles southwest of St. Charles and held there, and four other places, for eight days until the ransom was paid. Nellie Tipton Muench, a society matron in St. Louis, was charged with masterminding the kidnapping; four years later she was acquitted by a jury in Audrain County Circuit Court. Among others indicted was Shelton gangster Tommy Wilders. Three former gangsters also were implicated, all of whom had been killed by the time of the trial. They were "Pretty Boy" Lechler, "Willie Gee" Wilbert, and Tommy Hayes.

The Golfing Gangster and Other Stories

A smiling, dapper fellow, Jack Wilson of Alton, Illinois, donned his fashionable golf togs each morning and played eighteen holes with the "nice people" at the Rock Springs Country Club in Madison County. Authorities didn't know Wilson headed one of the most clever automobile theft rings in the country and was wanted in Detroit, Michigan, for the theft of fourteen cars and in Philadelphia for additional thefts. He played golf not because he loved the sport but because it helped him meet potential customers for his stolen "machines," including respectable car dealers. Wilson's body was found on a lonely road near Chouteau Slough on Saturday, September 21, 1929. He had been murdered gangster-style, and police soon arrested Wilson's golfing buddy and another companion.

Another minor-league mob was the Shenandoah gang of St. Louis, said to be composed of a group of troublemakers from South Broadway. The gang was credited by police with the shooting of Charles Amsler in his automobile in the 6400 block of Gravois Avenue on February 26, 1923. Amsler, thirty-eight, was the proprietor of the Tesson Family Club on Tesson Road near Gravois Road, and was shot while driving to his home at 2286 South Broadway. At least fourteen shots lodged in his car, but Amsler was able to sit up the day after the shooting. Amsler himself had been arrested sixteen times for various offenses, including several liquor charges, police said. He was a former associate of the gang but was unable to identify his assailants.

CHAPTER 9

DRY AND DRIPPING

THESE DAYS GLENN HENSLEY CAN BE FOUND BUILDING INTRICATE SHIP REPLICAS for area museums and serving as a volunteer at the Kirkwood Train Station. But in his younger days, armed with his Daisy BB gun, he was a paid foot soldier in small-town Missouri's war against liquor. "At the time my parents and I were living with my grandfather, I. J. Holt, in Stanberry," recalled Hensley, who lives in Kirkwood. "Granddad Holt had some brush-filled pastureland out at the south edge of town. It was a favorite place for St. Joseph bootleggers to drop off the 'stock' for the pool halls of Stanberry. They'd half-hide the glass jugs in a gooseberry thicket, to be picked up by the recipient when such action would be less apparent.

"Granddad would pay me a penny a bottle to find the 'stock,' lay a well-aimed shot into its side, gather up the bottle's neck and turn it in to him. For that I'd get my penny. WOW, what pay, and for taking a real chance that some of the 'suppliers' might be watching for just such a terrible fate to befall their carefully distilled 'corn likker.' I guarantee you I steered clear of those pool hall operators because somebody just might have seen me having fun with my BB gun.

"But the thrill of 'enforcing the law' at nine or 10 years of age—and using my own, trusty, Daisy BB gun—was something I wasn't going to miss," he added. "Sneaking like a super G-Man, peering over my shoulder, I'd locate a stash of booze, belt it with a six-foot shot, and watch the glass fly and the grass wither as the contents trickled merrily down the hillside. How many kids today have such a fabulous opportunity to aid the 'law'?"

"A RIP-ROARER OF AN EXPOUNDER"

Prohibition was the law, and Hensley's family figured prominently. His dad's aunt, Roena E. Shaner, was a national organizer and lecturer for the Women's Christian Temperance Union (WCTU). In 1926, she trimmed her schedule to cope with her mother's ill health and the sudden death of her beloved foster sister, giving only about four and a half months of field work. Still, the dedicated volunteer visited twenty-four counties, delivered ninety-seven addresses at venues from women's club luncheons to schools and colleges, recruited eighty-four members, and organized four unions, according to a report she made at the forty-fourth annual state convention in 1926. And there were probably more. "The misfortune of having lost one of my notebooks leaves me with statistics for less than one-half of the time," she apologized.

The Jackson, Missouri, resident celebrated her twentieth anniversary with the organization in 1929 as its national vice president. She was described by the *Columbia Missourian* as "indefatigably zealous." "The ballot is the most effective way of enforcing the law," Shaner told a crowd at the Baptist Students' Center in Columbia that year. "Women should vote. Nothing less than one's own funeral should prevent one from going to the polls. Prayer is our chief weapon against the liquorite. It is the only one he cannot touch. The value of total abstinence must always be impressed on everyone."

Hensley remembers her as a large and dedicated woman, and not his favorite family relative. "Aunt Roena was a buxom 'maiden lady' woman," he said. "Naturally, she wore her hair up in a bun on the back. She always brought, for her lectures, some of the most gory scenes of diseased livers and rotted teeth you could imagine. Typical WCTU lecturer, I'd imagine. She always wore dark clothes of some kind, certainly no fashion plate. She was a rip-roarer of an expounder. The town would dry up like the Sonoran Desert for twenty minutes after she left the city limits."

PART 1: DRYS

THE WHITE RIBBON LADIES

Two major organizations played a critical role in making the cause of prohibition a constitutional amendment. One, the Anti-Saloon League, was a political action group against saloons that represented Protestant churches, enjoyed big-business backing and lush budgets, and was rocked by scandals as the 1920s progressed.

The other, the WCTU, was a different animal. Composed largely of volunteers and run mostly by women, it preached not only prohibition but also many progressive reforms of the day, such as improved working conditions, women's suffrage, child welfare, and fair labor laws. Auxiliaries were located in more than fifty countries worldwide, and members were known for the little white ribbons they wore. "We believe that God created both man and woman in His own image, and therefore we believe in one standard of purity for both men and women, and in the equal right of all to hold opinions, and to express the same with equal freedom," read a portion of their creed. Millions took "The Pledge":

I hereby solemnly promise, God helping me, to abstain from all distilled, fermented, and malt liquors, including wine, beer, and cider, and to employ all proper means to discourage the use of and traffic in the same.

The WCTU "Americanization Center" in St. Louis taught English, sewing, and crochet lessons to immigrants at 1012 N. Seventeenth Street, called on the sick in hospitals and homes, visited with new mothers to get their citizen papers, and made home visits. "We took a group of these Mothers to the Lafayette Union, where they represented our Americanization Work on the programme," one member reported in 1926. "They sang our songs. One Mother repeated the 18th Amendment. The best part of it, she knew the meaning of every word. Two of these Mothers joined our Union, paying their dues, making four who have signed pledge. This means much when these Mothers will pledge to not take wine, which has been . . . handed down to them for generations. One of my Mothers said she made no man wine. When her friends came, she gave them tea and soda pop.

"We had our Annual Picnic in July where Mothers and Children went to Forest Park in a chartered car, paid for by the Mothers' Club and obtained through Mrs. Wheeler. Games were played and prizes given, over 75 being present."

Missouri alone boasted active chapters in eighty-seven counties in 1926, the largest in St. Louis City with 791 members and an annual budget of $748. St. Louis County came in second with 455 members and a $360 budget. Deep-rooted chapters could be found in such enclaves as Webster Groves and Kirkwood and outstate dry communities including Hannibal and New Franklin, Missouri: Even the largely wet bastions of Boonville and St. Charles received chapters in September 1924 and June 1925, respectively. A special group for children, the Loyal Temperance Legion, was organized in Columbia, Missouri, in February 1929.

UNWAVERING COMMITMENT

"Their consecration is sincere, unwavering and utterly unselfish," Mabel Walker Willebrandt, former assistant U.S. attorney general in charge of prohibition cases, said of the WCTU in 1929. "You seldom find them voting for a carousing public official solely because he voted for a dry law." And if he happened to be representing a convicted bootlegger, they were demanding, as Kirkwood City Attorney Robert Powell learned in 1924. In addition to his duties for Kirkwood, he had represented Peter Gounis, proprietor of the Eden Park roadhouse in Meramec Highlands, who had been sentenced to six months in jail for violating an injunction proceeding to close establishments where liquor was sold. Gounis also had been named one of four notorious liquor violators in a recent St. Louis County Grand Jury report. On the grounds that "no man can serve two masters," the Kirkwood WCTU in February 1924 demanded the dismissal of Powell, who also served as attorney for the Kirkwood Board of Education. Apparently that effort was not successful; the city's minutes through October 18, 1926, continued to list Powell as city attorney, current Kirkwood City Clerk Betty Montano noted.

One of their most extensive campaigns, in 1928, sought to prevent the election of New York Governor Alfred E. Smith as president. Smith, known as a "wet" and a Catholic to boot, came from a background in the Tammany Hall political machine, where liquor was plentiful. "Prohibition obeyed and enforced will result in a healthy people, in happy homes, in well-born children and a continuance of economic prosperity," national president Ella A. Boole told members at the October 1928 state convention of the Illinois WCTU in Evanston, Illinois. "Give it a chance by voting for Herbert Hoover." Smith was soundly defeated (see Chapter 16). The following January, the St. Louis County WCTU chapter held a ninth-birthday celebration for prohibition at the Maplewood Methodist Episcopal Church. Mrs. Jasper Blackburn, president of the group, presided over the program of lecture and song. "Give Prohibition Its Chance; the Liquor Traffic Has Had Its Day" and "Youth's Problems" were the lectures.

COMMUNITY BETTERMENT

The WCTU's service extended to the community. Miss Irene McGinitie of 1313 North Clara Avenue was director of the West End WCTU's Flower Mission. In September 1924, she held the state record for relief and mercy work:

She had spent twenty years taking flowers to the sick and to shut-ins, bringing jams and jellies for "bedside picnics," and shopping for those who could not get out. "As I go from the prisons to the home and to the hospitals, I always have a little music service and then offer a short prayer," McGinitie told the *St. Louis Star*. "Kind people have furnished me with chairs for invalids, mechanical drawing tools for a boy in prison, clothes for needy girls and other things."

Anna Sneed Cairns also left behind years of accomplishments in 1931 when she died at the family home at 5720 Cates Avenue in St. Louis. Cairns had served for seven years as legislative superintendent of the Missouri WCTU and was active in the woman's suffrage movement. In 1861, she founded the Kirkwood Seminary with little money, no ground, and no building. The girls' seminary grew from seven students to a thriving institution with boarding and day pupils alike by 1889, when philanthropist Henry Shaw offered Cairns a four-acre site in what is now Tower Grove Park. His death later that year quashed the deal. Cairns found a site on Oakland Avenue south of Forest Park, and her husband, John Cairns, designed a stone building that would be known as Forest Park University. "Debts on the Kirkwood plant and on the newer building burdened Mrs. Cairns for years and she took no salary from the proceeds of the

KICKLESS COCKTAIL

Officials of the Anti-Saloon League in December 1929 endorsed a new "1930 cocktail" concocted by Mrs. James M. Doran, wife of the U.S. prohibition commissioner, for a dinner party. Though it was served in frosted glasses and garnished attractively, it failed to impress the *St. Louis Post-Dispatch*. "Under its spell, no romantic Romeo will defy death for a Juliet," observed an editorial writer. "For the sad it will not represent nepenthe, nor for the gay, elixir. It will build no bridges, fling no architectural masterpieces toward the sky. Though the golfer, after 36 weary holes, toss a dozen Doran cocktails into his gullet, those missed putts and hooked drives will remain sharp and clear in the memory like so many wounds.

"Here is the insipid recipe: Take a pound of seedless grapes chopped very fine and a quart of grape juice. Stir thoroughly and serve very cold.

"May we suggest the last line be changed to read: Stir thoroughly and throw into the sink."

school," read an obituary in the *Post-Dispatch*. "Mrs. Cairns made a special effort to offer superior courses in music and decorative art. . . . Mrs. Cairns also made religious teaching an essential part of the curriculum. 'The Bible shall be a daily textbook' was stipulated in the charter of the school."

When the Municipal Assembly in St. Louis was considering a bill for a streetcar line on the south side of Forest Park, Cairns was one of the advocates. Promoters had planned a wine supper for the House of Delegates, "but Mrs. Cairns persuaded them to let her give the delegates dinner at Forest Park University, where she served them coffee and ice cream," the *Post* noted.

The House of God

Several other groups supported prohibition, among them the seventy-five-thousand-member Women's Missionary Federation of Greater St. Louis, the International Order of Good Templars, and the Metropolitan Church Federation of St. Louis, an organization of Protestant churches that sought greater democracy and goodwill. Prohibition, Church Federation members believed, reduced pauperism, increased savings accounts, and resulted in better-fed children and more orderly neighborhoods. Another organization that preached abstinence, the Irish American group Knights of Father Matthew, met with some resistance in dripping-wet St. Louis and eventually folded.

One's religious affiliation usually was a reliable indicator of one's stand on prohibition, and evangelical Protestants ranked high on the dry scale.. The *St. Louis Christian Advocate*, the newspaper of Southern Methodism, viewed the amendment as a remarkable achievement in 1923. "Where once were saloons, now there are clothing stores, drug shops, men's furnishing establishments, ladies' notion houses and other lines of legitimate trade," the *Advocate* noted in an editorial.

Most Catholics were opposed to the dry law, and St. Louis Archbishop John Glennon was no exception. "The Constitution has been considerably weakened by the addition of the Eighteenth Amendment," Glennon said during a visit to Atlantic City, New Jersey, in August 1922, "for the prohibition clause limits rights while the rest of the Constitution grants rights."

The Reverend Linus A. Lilly, regent of the Saint Louis University Law School, maintained during a talk in December 1932 that a glass of 4 percent beer was no more intoxicating than a glass of water. Lilly, an authority on U.S. constitutional law, said prohibition bred profound disrespect for the Constitution. "If I were to learn respect of the Constitution from prohibition, I would learn kindness from Nero, truth from Ananias and loyalty from Judas Iscariot!" Lilly declared.

Many Lutherans weren't much different from the Catholics in their views on prohibition. It is unrighteous, but it is the law and should be obeyed, said Professor Theodore Graebner, a member of the faculty of Concordia Lutheran Seminary in Clayton and editor of the *Lutheran Witness*, the periodical of the Missouri Synod of the Lutheran Church. He argued that Martin Luther, John Calvin, John Knox, and even John Wesley, founder of the Methodist Church, drank wine and beer. "But while solidly ranked on the side of law enforcement the Lutheran Church is out of sympathy with the prohibition act and with the entire type of legislation which it represents," Graebner said in February 1926. "The Lutheran Church holds that everything not forbidden in Scripture is permitted.

"The churches which have put over prohibition through their political organ, the Anti-Saloon League, hold that nothing is permitted unless specially authorized in the Bible. . . . But the greatest leaders of Protestantism have not only approved the use of wine and beer, but have themselves used these beverages."

"THE CHURCH IN ACTION"

By far the largest organization that supported prohibition was the Anti-Saloon League, a political action group that fought the liquor traffic for its member churches. "The Anti-Saloon League, however, differs from other pressure groups in that it is an organization of Protestant churches," Peter H. Odegard noted in his book, *Pressure Politics: The Story of the Anti-Saloon League*, originally published in 1928. "This fact worries some people considerably, for if there are those who fear that the election of a Catholic President will put us under the iron rule of Rome, there are others no less fearful lest we be governed by a narrow and bigoted group whose ideas find their historic source in Geneva."

The Anti-Saloon League was omni-partisan in its selection of candidates and never insisted that a candidate abstain from liquor, a policy criticized by many. Better to have a drunkard who would vote dry than a teetotaler who would vote wet, its members reasoned. League officials would question candidates at length on their views and, if they were not satisfied, would put up a candidate of their own or abandon the race. Despite the recent victory of nationwide prohibition, the league bailed out of St. Louis in the August 1920 primaries and confined its activities to nominating dry candidates for Congress in the thirteen other districts outside the area. "We built a dike around St. Louis," said the Reverend W. C. Shupp, superintendent of the Missouri Anti-Saloon League, "and let the city drown in its own beer."

JANITORS AND JUGS

No matter how dry the destination, wetness had a tendency to creep in. Virginia Hyndman, a longtime volunteer at First Congregational Church in Springfield, Illinois, recalled in 1980 that spirits, holy and otherwise, could be found at the church. "By the way, we even had some enterprisingly talented janitors," Hyndman said. "During prohibition, one of them did a little moonlighting in moonshine. And the church alley door was frequently opened to the signal knock and the presentation of the jug."

UNSAVORY ALLEGATIONS

In 1924, State Representative Leonidas C. Dyer of Missouri repeated charges from the American Federation of Labor that the Anti-Saloon League spent $2.5 million to lobby each year, and that the big businesses who contributed were the real power behind the league. Among them was merchandising magnate S. S. Kresge, who signed his name to a solicitation letter sent to a St. Louis business-man, Charles L. Knower. "Besides the state organization the national division of the Anti-Saloon League under separate budget, has 200 employees who keep the organization everywhere strong and by voice and print do tremendous educational service," Kresge wrote. "In its legal, legislative and law enforcement departments it stimulates and backs up enforcement of the law throughout the nation. Additional contributions are urgently required for current expenses and for special work for 1924 now begun, including the big convention at Washington in January, for publicity and public sentiment. . . . I have personally given during the past year $10,000 to the National League as a 'good business investment.'"

National league revenues, apart from each state's chapter, averaged $574,104 per year from 1920 to 1925, or $6.5 million per year in today's dollars. State league revenues averaged $228,203 per year in Illinois during the same period, and $44,998 per year in Missouri. "The Anti-Saloon League is now building the strongest organization it has ever had in Missouri. . . ." Reverend Shupp wrote in 1922. "We should have for the work mapped out $60,000 or more. We expended $49,000 in the last prohibition campaign and then we ran short about $5,000.

The board of directors of the Anti-Saloon League of America, shown in 1924 at the organization's headquarters in Indianapolis. Courtesy Library of Congress.

"Our organization will fight [Missouri] Senator James A. Reed and other candidates who have furnished wet leadership. . . ." Reed headed an investigation that revealed the league's graft, Ernest Kirschten noted in his history of St. Louis, *Catfish and Crystal.* "Under Wayne B. Wheeler [the league's general counsel, who died in 1927], this organization was no more than a self-perpetuating board and a gang of moneyraisers who exploited church people," Kirschten wrote. "The Reed Committee showed, for example, that . . . William Jennings Bryan got $700,000 [$7.9 million today] for a four-month speaking tour. Wheeler told the Reed Committee that up to the end of 1925 the League had spent $67,565,312.72."

Missouri's Own Scandal

Anti-Saloon League officials and Shupp worked closely, and enjoyed great influence, with prohibition enforcement officials. Periodically Shupp accompanied agents on raids. Abuses in that area began to surface after papers were stolen from Shupp's offices in the Victoria Building, 819 Locust Street, during a burglary in January 1923. Two days later police announced the arrest of Roy Edgerly, twenty-two, of the 300 block of Chouteau Avenue, and Charles Beecher, forty-five, a boarder at 3 S. Twenty-first Street. Shupp said nothing of importance had been stolen, but he had a pretty good idea of the culprit, either a prominent organization or liquor interest.

On January 27, 1923, the Missouri Branch of the Association Against the Prohibition Amendment (AAPA) released to reporters affidavits that charged that Shupp accepted a five-hundred-dollar bribe to write a letter to the state prohibition director, W. H. Allen, endorsing an application for an alcohol permit by Dr. B. J. Ludwig of the Ludwig Remedy Company at 1939 Franklin Avenue. During prohibition, companies could handle and dispense alcohol for legal purposes, such as production of extracts, provided they secured a permit from prohibition authorities. Shupp acknowledged that he had written the letter but denied accepting any money in the Ludwig case. He said in all his years of fighting the liquor traffic, he had never seen "such a vile, dirty, filthy display of determination to get revenge." Ludwig, an acquaintance of Shupp, agreed. He told a reporter he was "played for the goat" by Charles F. Smith and Arthur U. Wigand, investigators hired by the AAPA, and said he never saw Shupp accept any money. He said he had been in the retail drug and patent medicine business for thirty years and had no intention of doing anything illegal with the alcohol he withdrew.

Smith and Wigand, who posed as would-be investors in Ludwig's small drug business, told a different story. They reported that Shupp asked, "How much is it worth to me?" of Ludwig's permit request, and said, "I'll guarantee to get you boys that permit" when they met for lunch in December 1922. He then accepted a roll of ten fifty-dollar bills as they ascended the stairs leading to a Washington Avenue restaurant, and polished off a $3.05 turkey dinner (worth

$35 today) purchased by Wigand. After leaving the restaurant, Smith walked with Shupp to Third Street. "For God's sake, don't tell anything that I'm doing for you boys," Smith quoted Shupp as saying.

Shupp endorsed a similar application for the Druggists' Co-Operative Drug Company, a downtown St. Louis venture in which he and his son, Homer Shupp, were involved. Investigators of the AAPA claimed to have purchased eleven bottles of bonded whiskey, two gallons of alcohol, two gallons of moonshine whiskey, one ounce of Mexican morphine, and one ounce of domestic morphine from Druggists' Co-Op. Shupp said his son planned to use the alcohol to manufacture bay rum, iodine, and glycerine but never used the permit. Homer entered Mount St. Rose Hospital in August 1922 with advanced tuberculosis and was recuperating in the country near Manchester, Shupp tearfully told a reporter on January 27, 1923. "I am afraid that he will see these accounts and that he will suffer," Shupp said. "I would rather go to jail than that he should be subjected to this because these men are going after me on account of my fight against the liquor traffic." Federal investigators looked into the charges and, on January 29, filed charges of "facilitating and aiding and abetting the sale of narcotics" against an officer of the Druggists' Co-Operative Company, chemist Harold W. Trippett.

THE PLOT THICKENS

Shupp's influence on the "untimely transfers" of St. Louis prohibition agents McCampbell and Louis Gualdoni also was questioned in February 1923. The transfers followed a raid on a large chemical company in January 1923. Druggists' Co-Op, the agents had learned, appeared to have connections with the old Missouri Chemical Company. "It seemed that the way was open to discover what connection, if any, existed between that company [Missouri Chemical] and the Co-operative Drug Company," Missouri Attorney General Jesse Barrett wrote in a public statement. "Almost immediately McCampbell and Gualdoni were ordered transferred to Pittsburgh. I am advised that Gualdoni (whose whole experience has been in St. Louis and who cannot be nearly so useful elsewhere) refused to accept transfer to Pittsburgh and was then ordered to Omaha. I am further advised that he likewise declined to go to Omaha, and was then given leave of absence for fifteen days.

"This in spite of the fact that the St. Louis district is in great need of a larger force. . . . Prohibition Agent [Gus] Nations tells me he has only five or

The Victoria Building, which housed the headquarters of the Missouri Anti-Saloon League, was at Eighth and Locust streets downtown. *Courtesy Library of Congress.*

six men for the entire eastern half of Missouri. In this situation the Gualdoni incident seems to warrant at least my informal inquiry.

"Prohibition enforcement is a most difficult task and should be kept free from even suspicion. I am transmitting to the federal authorities all the information that I have been able to gather and I am satisfied that they will take appropriate action."

Gualdoni resigned from the prohibition forces in August 1923, after he received a transfer to Minneapolis, Minnesota.

There were other incidents, Barrett wrote in a letter to James C. Espy, editor of AAPA's *Minute Man* publication. In 1921, agents had arrested some bootleggers in St. Louis County who said they paid "protection" fees to a deputy sheriff and constable. They arrested the officials and began an investigation into the higher-ups. But John C. Dyott, assistant to the U.S. attorney general, was asked by Shupp to "hold off that county matter." Dyott also was summoned to the Department of Justice in Washington and was told persons of political prominence should not be prosecuted unless conviction was sure, or the result would be unfavorable to law enforcement (see Chapter 14). "His [Dyott's] personal desire was to prosecute, but he feared conflict with superior officers," Barrett wrote.

On March 17, 1923, Shupp announced his resignation from the Anti-Saloon League, citing health concerns. He said he and his family would be moving from St. Louis to a new home in the country.* Shupp himself was never charged with anything, and his supporters condemned the allegations against him. He was fifty-five years old, of slight build, thin-voiced, and nervous, and planned to head south to regain his health. Shupp had been a minister at a church in Ohio when he came to Missouri in 1909. At one time he accepted the spoils of a liquor raid from Gus Nations, several large vats that he planned to use to build a garage, but ended up selling to a vinegar company. "On just what terms has never appeared," sniped the *Post-Dispatch.*

The *Post* conceded it took a lot of guts to be a dry in dripping wet St. Louis, where the headquarters of the state Anti-Saloon League was located. "Preaching vegetarianism at a stockyards or predicting blizzards at winter resorts would be a task for a popularity seeker, in preference to the work of official dry-law advocate and unofficial aid in dry law enforcement in St. Louis," the *Post* noted.

"Dangerous Shoals"

One person who kept a discreet distance from the Anti-Saloon forces was Mabel Walker Willebrandt, former assistant U.S. attorney general in charge of prohibition cases. "Wayne Wheeler was an able lawyer," Willebrandt wrote in 1929. "He was a determined, politically astute man. I always believe he guided the league into dangerous shoals by too much political activity. Early in my tenure he offered to help me if I wanted to secure appointments and if for the 'good of the cause' I would let him know of matters officially under consideration here. The latter, of course, I could never do—consequently my relations with the Washington office of the Anti-Saloon League remained distant, but they were always cordial."

The Missouri office of the league was another matter after State Labor Commissioner Heber Nations, a dry leader, was charged in connection with a beer protection scheme involving the Griesedieck Brewery (see Chapter 5). Immediately, league officials jumped to the defense of Nations, demanded the

---

*Shupp's problems were financial as well as medical. In December 1926, he filed for bankruptcy in U.S. District Court in St. Louis, listing liabilities of $77,497.56 and assets of $300. Losses in land deals in southeastern Missouri several years earlier were to blame, the *Jefferson City Tribune* reported.

Missouri Attorney General Jesse Barrett. Courtesy Library of Congress.

charges dismissed, and urged its members to take action:

> *Write to President Coolidge TODAY, demanding an investigation and protesting against the trial of Nations, a well-known editor, dry leader and law-enforcement advocate in wet St. Louis, on the testimony of interested bootleggers and brewers seeking immunity, whom Nations has raided.*

Willebrandt, who prosecuted the case, said she had never seen a more flagrant example of misuse of influence and power by an organization than used by the Anti-Saloon League in the Heber Nations trial. "It seems unbelievable that an organization pledged to secure and obey the law would resort to such tactics to prevent one of their members from facing trial," Willebrandt wrote in one of a series of articles on prohibition enforcement, "The Inside of Prohibition." "It was obstruction of justice, bordering closely on contempt of court, and I condemn it as quickly and resist it as vigorously as when bootleggers' friends attempt the same interference with trials by different means."

Illinois State Representative Truman A. Snell had harsher words for the league in Illinois, after he helped pass the O'Grady repeal bill in 1931 that sought to end the Illinois prohibition law and the state search and seizure act. Snell, a former state director of the league and a dry floor leader in previous sessions, called the league "the most intolerant, bigoted, inconsistent, repugnant organization in Illinois."

Chances are, many local members were more like J. Elmer Ball, who moved his family to Webster Groves in 1920 from Moberly, Missouri, and joined the Tuxedo Park Christian Church. Ball, who had been educated as an attorney, was the special agent for the Home Insurance Company in St. Louis. He was a Bible scholar, a lecturer on the Circuit Chautauqua (touring assemblies featuring lectures and cultural offerings), and the teacher of an adult bible class at the church until his death in 1942. He also penned a book, *A Laymen's Handbook on the Kingdom of Heaven.*

DRY AND DIVIDED

The crux of the debate between the drys and wets was summed up in May 1925, when *The Christian Evangelist* of St. Louis commented on a recent exposé of the rum-running industry by the *St. Louis Star.* "This is the kind of people and the kind of conduct the liquor traffic has made," the *Evangelist* wrote. "This is the spawn it has been, and is, spewing out of its mouth in defiance of, and in the hope of, destroying the Eighteenth Amendment."

The *Star* drew the opposite conclusion. "The liquor traffic has not made that kind of people and conduct," it replied. "They have always been here, but the impracticable Volstead Act has given them opportunity to do just what they are doing—make millions . . . out of an unregulated opportunity to supply the demand for liquors from a large proportion of people. That demand has never ceased to exist, and it will not, until Christian churches and leaders like our contemporary quit trusting to statutes to change men's appetites and hearts."

In 1929, the dry forces were confident of a dry future, but their influence had begun to wane. "At the end of the decade, supporters of prohibition viewed the Eighteenth Amendment as impregnable," Kenneth M. Murchison wrote in *Federal Criminal Law Doctrines: The Forgotten Influence of National Prohibition.* "The political effectiveness of the Anti-Saloon League declined appreciably after the death in 1927 of Wayne Wheeler, its longtime general counsel, and groups opposing prohibition were much better organized by the late 1920s."

Mabel Walker Willebrandt.
Courtesy Library of Congress.

PART 2: WETS

THE OPPOSING FORCES

Throughout the 1920s, organizations such as the Association Against the Prohibition Amendment (AAPA) and the Missouri Beverage Dealers' Association
lobbied for modification of the law to legalize beer and light wines. Invariably,
legislation introduced as a result of those efforts failed or was vetoed. By the
second half of the decade, however, the wets strengthened their efforts as liquor
violations, scandals, gang bootlegging activities, and problems with enforcement
dampened the enthusiasm of all but the most ardent prohibition supporters.
The Missouri Association Against Prohibition, the Association Opposed to
Prohibition, the Illinois Association Opposed to Prohibition, the Crusaders, the
American Women's Council of Justice, and the Women's Organization for National Prohibition Reform (WONPR), among others, stepped in as the years
progressed and began to chip away at the Eighteenth Amendment. The most
popular arguments were that it could not be enforced and that it had led to an
increase in graft and crime.

Nicholas Murray Butler, renowned anti-prohibitionist and president of Columbia University, opened a campaign by the Missouri Association Against Prohibition in December 1927 at the Odeon Theater at Grand Boulevard and Finney Avenue. He characterized the terms "wet" and "dry" as vulgar and meaningless. "I shall not call those dry who defend a fallacy that has flooded the country with illegal liquor," Butler said. "Nor would I describe as wet the many total abstainers who are earnestly opposed to this revolution in our form of government.

"The eighteenth amendment affronts our form of government, and opens the way as completely to its destruction as did secession. It would consolidate us into an imperial bureaucracy at Washington."

Conscientious Objector

In the early years the wet groups made headlines but little headway, such as in May 1924 when Edgar R. Rombauer, a prominent Republican attorney in St. Louis, resigned from the board of curators of Lincoln University in Jefferson City. Rombauer, a member of the executive committee of the Association Opposed to Prohibition, had been appointed to the Lincoln University board in 1923 by Missouri Governor Arthur M. Hyde, who supported prohibition. A year later, Hyde announced his candidacy for the national vice presidency. "The reason I have resigned is because it is my intention to actively oppose your nomination as vice president of the United States, and that I hold it unfitting that I should do this while holding office as an appointee of yours," Rombauer wrote to Hyde. "The reason I shall oppose you is because I differ with you radically on the liquor question, which will be the question that will control my political action in the coming campaign."

At the time, Rombauer lived on Flad Avenue in the Shaw neighborhood with his wife, Irma Rombauer, who went on to create the bible of cookbooks, *The Joy of Cooking*. His late father-in-law, the esteemed physician Dr. Max von Starkloff, had been active in the St. Louis meetings of the National German-American Alliance, which fought Sunday liquor sales restrictions and later prohibition. The alliance eventually was beaten down by World War I, anti-German fervor, the Anti-Saloon League, and the WCTU.

Rombauer himself was described as bright, clever, practical, strong-minded, conscientious, and concerned with public issues, author Anne Mendelson wrote in *Stand Facing the Stove: The Story of the Women Who Gave America the Joy of Cooking.* More than a decade earlier he had served a two-year term as speaker of the city's old House of Delegates, and he was asked by Mayor Frederick Kreismann to revise the city's code of ordinances. He suffered from disabling bouts of depression, however, and died in February 1930 from a self-inflicted gunshot wound. "The letter that arrived several days later from U.S. Senator Harry Hawes, a Democrat who had no special reason to remember Edgar as a political soul mate, surely expressed the opinion of many: 'He was a very remarkable man, so straightforward, courageous, and patriotic, that I always felt that some day he would be able to serve his country or State with distinction in a political capacity,'" Mendelson wrote.

Under Fire

Officials of the WCTU criticized the WONPR and the AAPA as organizations funded by millionaires who sought to reduce their taxes by creating federal liquor revenue for the government. Well-heeled business magnates did pour funds into the AAPA. "None provided the [AAPA] with anything like the $350,000 which John D. Rockefeller gave the Anti-Saloon League between 1900 and 1919," David E. Kyvig wrote in *Repealing National Prohibition.* "Nor did they represent the sole backing for the AAPA, any more than Rockefeller, Henry Ford, and S.S. Kresge did for the Anti-Saloon League. In fact, for the principal organization of both wets and drys, well over 90 percent of all donations were under $100."

WONPR was founded by Pauline Morton Smith Sabin, a cultured and sophisticated Republican volunteer from New York who became concerned about children growing up amid a growing defiance of the law and ineffectiveness of law enforcement, and an increasing abuse of drinking and prestige of bootleggers. In 1928, she founded WONPR after hearing national WCTU president Ella Boole tell a congressional committee, "I represent the women of America." Sabin decided Boole did not represent her. Neither did Boole represent about 1 million others, who joined WONPR and helped it turn the tide by electing candidates who would repeal the law, including President Franklin Delano Roosevelt.

By 1930, WONPR had reached a membership of sixteen thousand women in Illinois, which organizers boasted was equal to the membership of the state's WCTU. "By energetic work we have acquired that membership within the last four months," a spokeswoman said.

The Illinois WONPR membership climbed to 214,000 by 1933, or 13 times that of the state WCTU.

The Missouri branch of the WONPR grew to be one of the largest chapters in the country, with fifty-two thousand members in 1933. Though its headquarters was located at the Park Plaza Hotel, members of the executive committee hailed from cities across the state, including Jefferson City, Sedalia, Kansas City, and St. Joseph, along with suburbs such as Webster Groves and Kirkwood. Like many organizations in February 1933, it was desperate for cash and sold tickets to the Fox Theatre to raise funds. "For three years we have put forth every effort for the cause of repealing the Eighteenth Amendment and restoring the liquor traffic to the legal orbit of taxation and revenue," Missouri branch president Mrs. Howard Benoist wrote in a letter that month to Joseph Hahn, secretary of Local 6 of the Brewers and Maltsters Union. "We no longer have the money to carry forward our work. We believe the reopening of this industry with its attendant employment will stimulate many lines of business, therefore it behooves you to support us at this critical time."

The Illinois Association Opposed to Prohibition, in 1929, also tried a new tactic: challenging the law in court to recover state jurisdiction over medicinal liquors, sacramental wines, industrial alcohol, and non-intoxicating beverages that the association said the Volstead law had no legal right to regulate in the first place. And the Missouri Association Against Prohibition offered a proposal in 1930 for complete regulation of the liquor traffic, in the event of repeal. James W. Byrnes, president of the association, suggested state boards be created to control liquor sales, grant and revoke permits, and control establishments. The state also would run the liquor stores, and only approved hotels and licensed grocers would be able to sell beer and wine.

Repeal and Law and Order

As a deepening depression furthered its cause, the Missouri Association Against Prohibition offered some heartening news in a March 1931 letter to Local 6 secretary Joseph Hahn. "The vote on March 5th in the Missouri Legislature is very encouraging," Byrnes wrote. "George B. Calvin, Representative of Franklin County, presented a resolution proposing a referendum in Missouri to test the sentiment of the voters for repeal or modification of the prohibition laws at the next General Election. Four years ago we could not have gotten a bill about prohibition out of the Committee.

"The Anti-Saloon League and the WCTU fought and defeated the measure, but the vote on this made a public record which heretofore we had been unable to get. . . . Our educational campaign and state-wide organization is bearing fruit."

The next year, the Missouri Association Against Prohibition distributed some 300,000 pieces of literature and 100,000 sample ballots and made 40,000 county election endorsements. Petitions were sent on behalf of the group from eighty outstate counties, asking the legislators to vote favorably on modification and repeal. Despite twelve years of enforcement, there were three speakeasies for every pre-prohibition saloon, a nationwide drink bill of more than $1 billion, arrests for drunkenness three times the 1920 number, deaths from alcoholism four times the 1920 figure, and three times as many prisoners as in 1920, WONPR claimed. "Prohibition was repealed for a variety of reasons and with the participation of a number of groups," Kenneth Rose wrote in his book, *American Women and the Repeal of Prohibition*. "For a number of reasons, however, it was the feminine influence on repeal that was decisive." There was considerable surprise when women spoke out for repeal, Rose said, because they had long been associated with prohibition.

The momentum of the wets was clinched by the formation of the United Repeal Council of Missouri in 1933, an umbrella organization chaired by lawyer Joseph T. Davis. It represented WONPR and the Crusaders; the Association for Repeal of the Eighteenth Amendment; the Voluntary Committee of Lawyers, headed by state bar association members; the Missouri Division of the American Hotel Association, with approximately 250 hotel members; and the Missouri Federation of Labor.

"In a talk in St. Louis in early 1932, Dr. Alva W. Taylor of Vanderbilt University blamed Prohibition's failure on the lack of temperance education in the schools," Elizabeth Detweiler Burnett wrote in a 1984 dissertation, "Thy Kingdom Come: The History of the Church Federation in St. Louis, 1909–1969." "A whole generation of Americans had grown up thinking alcohol was exciting and had not learned its dangers."

Mrs. Clifford Gaylord, president of Missouri WONPR in August 1933, also expressed concern for the younger generation in an interview with the *Globe-Democrat*. She said the cause of temperance had been retarded fifty years. "There is an old saying, you can't teach an old dog new tricks, but I believe this generation is sufficiently young and flexible that it can be taught the wisdom of temperance as an attribute of character," Gaylord said.

Chapter 10
Toasts of the Town

IT APPEARED TO BE AN ORDINARY REAL ESTATE OFFICE ON THE SECOND FLOOR OF the Gamble Building at 620 Chestnut Street. The office vault, once a repository for property sale documents, was stocked with six and a half cases of beer and a quart and two one-gallon jugs of whiskey. When police raided the place on a sultry Friday afternoon in July 1929, they found three men seated around a table with two glasses of beer. They arrested the man in charge, fifty-five-year-old William Carey of 517 Walnut Street.

The Gamble office was a garden-variety speakeasy, one of thousands of establishments that served illegal liquor throughout the area. Depending on the digs and/or the location, they were called speaks and beer flats, roadhouses and blind pigs, "joints" and saloons, and soft drink parlors. Some, like the real estate office, operated behind a "front" while others dispensed brazenly. For many it was a fleeting existence. Others remained in business for years and operated through the end of prohibition.

By 1931, conservative estimates put the number of speaks at three thousand in Missouri and forty thousand in Illinois, according to Maurice Campbell, former New York City prohibition administrator and editor of *Repeal* magazine. Closer to home, prohibition agents estimated St. Louis alone boasted fourteen thousand "beer flats" that served home brew and other drinks, and one thousand hard-liquor speakeasies.

Roadhouses offered music, dancing, drinking, and gambling and could be found in rural areas, and one at 816 South Florissant Road in St. Louis County so flagrantly violated the law that the drinks were printed on the menu:

Drinks—Beer, gin, wine, whisky, creme de menthe, apricot brandy. Sandwiches—Fried chicken, baked ham. . . .

In plain sight of patrons, a long bar in the roadhouse was lined with liquors from pre-Volstead days. No prices were given. On May 29, 1928, prohibition agents arrested the owners, James and Exie Walsh, and destroyed more than nine hundred quarts of home brew, twenty-seven pints of whiskey, twelve quarts of gin, and a small quantity of wine.

Many of the places that served liquor were restaurants, noted Earl Maschmeier, a resident of Kirkwood, Missouri, for more than eighty years. "I won't name the places, because they're still popular eating places," Maschmeier said. "They would always serve it in coffee cups or tea cups. One place, when I went to Washington University, I used to go there and get a big ham sandwich for 15 cents and a glass of beer for a nickel. If you were well-known, you could get a highball in a tea cup."

A Tale of Two Establishments

Maschmeier himself was privy to an upscale source of liquor at the Kirkwood Country Club, later known as Woodlawn, where he worked his way up to caddy master and assistant golf professional by the time the country club closed during the Depression. A social hub during the 1920s, it hosted the likes of Babe Ruth and Lou Gehrig, who visited with their teammates from the New York Yankees on Mondays. They teed off on a round of golf with members of the St. Louis Browns baseball team. "They usually had five caddies: four caddies for carrying clubs and the like and usually one caddy to carry a gallon or so of gin rickeys," Maschmeier recalled. "That was par for the course in those days." The refreshments were stored in a cool area underground, he said. "There was not a basement under the club house: in those days, it was hacked out of the clay and back of what we used to call caddy shacks," he said. "In those days there was sort of a shelf carved out of that clay; one portion was where we had the machinery to clean and polish the clubs . . . in back of that machinery there was a shelf that was always cool the year round and deep enough—you could always stack beer a couple of cases high. On Fridays they [the management] would bring in a truckload of what was classified as home brew . . . they would put it into the iceboxes, wooden boxes where the lids slid in horizontally. And of course, they always brought in their bathtub gin."

More plebeian but equally enjoyable for its patrons was the speakeasy run by Josephine Sperino in her Collinsville, Illinois, home. She was divorced and had to make ends meet, and she cared for her young grandson, Floyd, for a short time when his parents were separated. "She had a juke box in the dining room, and they'd sit there and drink their white mule [whiskey]," recalled Floyd Sperino at age eighty-two, a lifelong Collinsville resident. "I was about four years old: she would dress me in a red cotton dress and black cotton hose and I would dance to the tune of 'Tiger Rag' for a nickel. She was very, very respectable and didn't mess around with anybody getting inebriated. A lot of the World War I veterans would come and one, named Fitzpatrick, would stay until she grabbed him by the seat of the pants and threw him out. She would say, 'Fitz, it's time to leave.' From the front yard he would say, 'I love you, Mom.'"

Floyd Sperino wasn't thrilled about dancing or his costume, so anyone who tried to put on his stockings risked a bite to the fingers. The liquor was delivered by a bootlegger in five-gallon cans to Sperino's grandmother, who would store it secretly behind panels in the home. To color the white mule she'd cook it on the stove with burnt sugar. When she wasn't working she read about Hollywood stars Charles Fay and Janet Gaynor in the movie magazines, and she went to the Miners Theatre every night, even if it was the same movie. "She was a character, but she had a heart of gold," Sperino recalled. "She was a very heavy woman who weighed well over 300 pounds, and it was hard for her to buy clothes. She wore a size 52, so she'd go in the store and they'd say, 'Oh, we've got a new supply in of dresses: we've got six colors.' She'd take all six." Once, when grandson Floyd became scared while watching a Tom Sawyer movie, Grandma Sperino put her arm around him, pulled him to her ample breast, and nearly smothered him. "My grandma, she was a wonderful woman," said Sperino. "Rough as a cob, but she was a wonderful woman."

Soft Drinks and More

On October 29, 1929, Famous-Barr Company opened a soda fountain at 404 S. Seventh Street in St. Louis, said to be the largest in the world at the time by its builder, Liquid Carbonic Company. Built luxuriously with air-conditioning, electric conveyor belts, and marble walls, ceilings, and counters, it seated five hundred and featured lunchroom service from 7 a.m. to 7 p.m. The irony here was that Famous-Barr actually sold carbonated soda products, while numerous other businesses advertised as "soft drink parlors" specialized in drinks with more kick, sometimes with a little gambling thrown in. The City of Maplewood closed six such stands, all glorified saloons, in December 1923 for violating the prohibition laws. They included Bartold Grove, established in 1857 and operated by Herman Bartold at 7900 Manchester Avenue; Henry Craemer, Jr., 7343 Manchester Avenue; Ernest Strassner, 7501 Manchester Avenue; Sidney Steffe, Oxford Avenue and Big Bend Boulevard; Achilles Fratini, 7228 Manchester Avenue; and Max O. Pfitzer, 3528 Greenwood Boulevard.

The Famous-Barr Building,
downtown St. Louis.

Earlier that year police had raided another soft drink parlor operated by Pfitzer, the Maplewood Inn on Big Bend, where Maplewood Police Chief Thomas J. Caldwell and City Attorney Merrill Vincent, aided by three officers, found an icebox full of unlabeled bottled goods believed to be home brew. "According to the chief of police, when they entered the place, there were between 20 and 30 patrons," the *St. Louis County Watchman-Advocate* reported. "The bar was lined with drinks which were swept from the surface when the raiders entered."

In August 1923, the Maplewood City Council revoked the inn's beverage license and ordered it closed for a year, after reading an affidavit by J. D. Hodges that "on August 16 and on many previous occasions he bought and was given whiskey to drink by the owners and proprietors of the soft-drink parlor. ...."

Albert Wilmas was a Republican candidate for St. Louis County sheriff in October 1924, when authorities arrested his brother, Fred, for running a soft drink bar at Manchester Road and Woodlawn Avenue. Fred Wilmas was behind the bar when prohibition agents arrived and was so determined to destroy the evidence that the agents had to strike him to subdue him. The incident didn't

Nightspots in the News

Liquor-related arrests were made at the following watering holes during prohibition. Some were repeat offenders. This list names only a few of the establishments that operated in St. Louis and beyond.

St. Louis City
Theodore Albes Saloon and Grocery, 2361 Adams Street
John Shea Saloon, 1200 N. High Street (now Twenty-Third Street)
Charles Albrecht Saloon, 108 N. Fourteenth Street
Riviera Nightclub, 4400 block of Delmar Boulevard
West End Waiters Club, Vandeventer Avenue between Enright Avenue
    and West Belle Place
Harry Burns Bar, 1801 Lucas Avenue
Vito Velandi Fruit Store, 722 N. Vandeventer Avenue
Charles Maynard Saloon, 3232 S. Grand Boulevard
Cocoanut Grove Nightclub, Kingshighway and Delmar boulevards
Jazzland, Easton Avenue (now Martin Luther King Drive) and Grand Boulevard
Cafferata Cafe, Delmar Boulevard and Hamilton Avenue
Belvedere Cafe, Euclid Avenue and Delmar Boulevard
William Schollmeyer Bar, Odeon Building, 1046 N. Grand Boulevard
Joseph M. Cody Saloon, 1321 N. Grand Boulevard
Andrew Manestar Saloon, 2700 Market Street
John Barry Saloon, 800 Market Street
Joseph Weinhardt Saloon, 100 S. Ninth Street
National Cafe, 117 N. Sixth Street
"Turtles" Reardon Saloon, 4137 Olive Street
Dennis Tuohy Bar in the Fullerton Building, Seventh and Pine streets
Charles Hutton Saloon in West End Hotel, 927 North Vandeventer Avenue
Josephine Bolanovich Saloon, 801 South Vandeventer Avenue
Walter Brady Saloon, 6786 Manchester Road
Francis Dougherty Saloon, 1159 South Kingshighway Boulevard
Fred Kaiser Saloon, 2859 S. Broadway
Arthur Weaver Saloon, 2525 S. Eighteenth Street
George Mesler Saloon, 1116 Carr Street
Orpheum Bar, 725 St. Charles Street
Richard Winklemann Saloon, 2034 Olive Street

North

Edrus Club, St. Charles and Natural Bridge roads

Charles Rodenberg Saloon, 6212 N. Broadway

Alamo Nightclub, Maple Avenue just west of the city limits

P. F. Walsh Saloon, Maryland Heights

James Kane Saloon, 8605 Florissant Avenue

Tony Originale's Saloon, St. Charles Rock Road and Edmonson Avenue

Gus Harris Pool Room, 2550 Woodson Road

William P. Colbeck's Maxwelton Inn, St. Charles Road west of Ferguson Avenue

John Pelligrini, Charles and Clara Palmissano Soft Drink Parlor, Wellston

Tony Foley's Gambling House, 6128A Easton Avenue

William Meyer, West End Buffet, 571 Clay Street, St. Charles

William Artkrass Saloon/Soft Drink Parlor, Main and Adams
     streets, St. Charles

Eugene Reed Saloon/Soft Drink Parlor, Halls Ferry Road near Parker Road

South

John Butyenek's Lakewood Inn, Heege Road and Fleta Street, Gardenville (Affton)

Rock Saloon, Crystal City

Cottage Inn, Lemay Ferry Road

Sharpshooters' Park, Lemay Ferry Road

Leonard Nottebrock's Dime Joint, 400 Vulcan Avenue, Luxemburg (Lemay)

Al Singer establishment, 9960 S. Broadway

Charles Amsler's Tesson Family Club, Tesson Road near Gravois

John Rittmeyer's Schmierkase Garden or Bear Pit, 8917 S. Broadway

Thomas Hearty and John Surgant's Telegraph Inn, Oakville

Jellyroll Hogan Saloon, 9025 S. Broadway

Raymond Thomas and Ike Carrow Saloon/Soft Drink Parlor, Festus

Mrs. Otto Hamel's Saloon/Soft Drink Parlor, DeSoto

East

Clubhouse at Stolberg's Lake, west of 159 near Belleville, Illinois

Mike Murgic Saloon, East St. Louis

Pat Rochelle's Cache Inn near Cairo, Illinois

Georgeoplis Saloon, East St. Louis

Tiefon Siampos and Gus Giatras, Unique Pool Room, 130 Illinois Street, Alton

Travelers Inn, Peoria Road north of Springfield, Illinois

West

Walter Niehaus's Rose Inn, North and South Road

Henry and Josephine Sanzoterra (Sommers) Saloon/Soft Drink Parlor,
    North and South Road in Brentwood

Jerry Moreland Saloon, North and South Road and Missouri Pacific tracks
    in Brentwood

Herman Bartold Saloon/Soft Drink Parlor, 7900 Manchester Avenue

Henry Craemer Jr. Saloon/Soft Drink Parlor, 7343 Manchester Avenue

Ernest Strassner Saloon/Soft Drink Parlor, 7501 Manchester Avenue

Max O. Pfitzer Saloon/Soft Drink Parlor, 3528 Greenwood Boulevard

Sidney Steffe Saloon/Soft Drink Parlor, Oxford Avenue and Big
    Bend Boulevard

Achilles Fratini Saloon/Soft Drink Parlor, 7228 Manchester Avenue

Gingham Inn, Manchester Road one mile east of Barrett Station Road

Busch's Grove, St. Louis County

"Belvedere" Joe Gonella's Blarney Castle, Manchester Road east
    of Kirkwood

Walter F. Niehaus, Cretonne Inn, Manchester Road one mile west of
    Geyer Road

The Maples, Manchester Road near Brentwood

Beccard's Grove, Meramec Highlands

Peter and Harry Gounis, Eden Park, Meramec Highlands

"Belvedere" Joe Gonnella's Roadhouse, Olive Street Road

Louis Colombine Saloon, Big Bend Boulevard and Woodbine Avenue

"Spots" Reagan's Olive Inn, Olive Street Road in University City

Rigoletto Inn, North and South Road south of Clayton

Mark Gumperts and James McGhee, Fauna Flora, Manchester Road one
    half mile west of North and South Road

Tony Foley's Los Angeles Club, 9008 Manchester Road

Claymo Hotel Bar, formerly the Autenreith Hotel, run by Joseph Parks
    and located across the street from the county courthouse in Clayton

Betty's, Osage County on the Gasconade River east of Rich
    Fountain, Missouri

The following locales were said to dispense liquor during prohibition:
Barrel Bar, Hermann, Missouri
Riverside Inn, Lake of the Ozarks
Dance Studio in Bohm Building, Main and Vandalia Streets in
 Edwardsville, Illinois
Spanish Inn, 1200 E. Cantrell Street, Decatur, Illinois
Lone Wolf Lodge, Castlewood
Barroni Restaurant and Saloon (now Al's Steak House), First and
 Biddle streets
Big Chief Restaurant/Filling Station, Wildwood
Soulard Dance Hall, 1730 S. Eighth Street, now Phelan's Pub and Grill
Cave in Richland, Missouri, now Caveman Bar-BQ
Candy shop at 10 N. Newstead Avenue
Drugstore at 2028 S. Ninth Street, now Hammerstone's
Louis Boehm's Ice Cream Parlor, Hermann, Missouri, now the Concert Hall
 and Barrel Bar
Moonlight Gardens, Chatham Road and Wabash (later a Kroger store)
 Springfield, Illinois
No Coat George's Lemay Club, Lemay Ferry Road just across the
 Jefferson County line

hurt Al Wilmas, who was elected sheriff by a six-thousand-vote margin over his Democratic opponent, Wilfred Jones.

In the Italian American Hill neighborhood of south St. Louis, many taverns continued to sell liquor under the fronts of soft drink parlors or candy stores, Gary R. Mormino noted in *Immigrants on the Hill: Italian-Americans in St. Louis, 1882–1982.* "The case of Cesare Regna typifies this delicate transition," Mormino wrote. "Born in Lombardy, Regna labored at the brickyards until he had saved enough money to purchase a small saloon in 1917. Quicker than one could say 'Volstead Act,' Regna discreetly rearranged the fixtures to resemble a respectable soft drink parlor all the while quietly serving adult customers in the rear of the store. . . . By 1931, seventeen soft drink parlors and eighteen confectioneries operated on the Hill. Before Prohibition there had been only a handful of such establishments."

The abuses became so widespread that a new Missouri prohibition law took effect on June 24, 1923, which required all screens, curtains, or other blinds to

Isidore Oldani, Sr., co-founder of the Blue Ridge Bottling Co., stands with one of the soda company's first trucks in 1916. The company originally was located in St. Louis' Blue Ridge subdivision, which extended from Southwest and Hampton avenues to Arsenal Street. Courtesy of the late Isidore Oldani, Jr.

be removed from the doors and windows of soft drink establishments, subject to arrest of the proprietor. St. Louis County Sheriff John F. Willmann announced his intentions to enforce it. But, as with many laws, a loophole excluded restaurants. "Proprietors of soft drink bars . . . are rushing to the office of License Collector [Oliver] Chapman and taking out restaurant licenses," noted the *St. Louis County Watchman-Advocate.*

ROTGUT RELIEF

Soda figured into the equation not just as a front, but also as a flavoring. With prohibition, the demand for flavorful soft drinks increased, in part because drinkers wanted to cover up the taste of the rotgut hitting the streets. Highballs and sweet mixed drinks came into vogue out of necessity.

Blue Ridge Bottling Company, 1827 S. Kingshighway Boulevard on the Hill, came up with a popular solution. Special High-Ball Lemon was made from oil of lemon imported from Messina in the native Italy of its founders, Isidore Oldani Sr. and Louis Venegoni. Of all the drinks the company offered, High-Ball Lemon was extremely popular during prohibition, the late Isidore "Tiny"

Oldani, Jr., recalled in 1988. "We made a good lemon soda that would make any moonshine taste good," Oldani said.

Some companies took a bolder route. Both Blue Ridge and the New Empire Bottling Company on Gravois Avenue experimented with bottling lemon-lime soda together with alcohol. Federal agents soon stopped the practice, Oldani said.

Those who wanted to flavor their booze had yet another option: cut-alcohol stores. One, at 1017 N. Eighth Street in downtown St. Louis, offered it for "10 cents a half pint and bring your own bottle." Whites and blacks alike brought their bottles to be filled from a pitcher handed through a window. In 1928, an estimated 150 "cutting plants" in St. Louis turned cases of good whiskey into three to five times that amount in bootleg booze, noted Beulah Schacht of the *Globe-Democrat*. Larry Mantowich of Springfield, Illinois, said he relied on the stuff during prohibition. "You'd buy a half of a pint of cut alcohol and mix it half and half with water," he said. "Well, a half of a pint of alcohol, during them days, we paid 25 cents for it. Mix it with another half a pint of water, so you had a pint of whiskey for 25 cents. Then we used to go to Nugrape Bottling Company and buy the peach and apricot coloring or whatever it was, a sweetener. . . . And we used to make peach brandy or apricot brandy or anything out of that."

Hip Flasks A-Go-Go

For its portability and potency, hard liquor became the drink of choice during prohibition, William Grimes observed in *Straight Up or On the Rocks: A Cultural History of American Drink*. "Prohibition not only changed what Americans drank; it also changed the way they drank," Grimes wrote. "It put a nudge and a wink into the experience. It encouraged the massive binge, the hangover worn as a badge of honor, the hip flask displayed as a naughty signal that the bearer belonged to a rather daring fraternity."

Sterling-silver flasks were popular Christmas gifts in the 1920s, said Frank R. Sullivan, a Springfield, Illinois, attorney born in 1908 and a founder of the Sangamon County Historical Society. "The sale of intoxicating liquor was unconstitutional," Sullivan recalled in the late 1970s. "But it seemed that an awful lot of drinking was going on. And the type of liquor they were drinking was not very good. At various parties, dances, people would drink. They'd carry their flask."

People prized their flasks. George Lurie asked for his to be returned after it was confiscated by a prohibition agent who spotted Lurie transferring the flask from one pocket to another during a December 1922 raid at Cafferata's Café at Delmar Boulevard and Hamilton Avenue. Lurie, president of the Missouri Glove Company, 6299 Maple Avenue, was turned away empty-handed by Judge Charles Faris during a hearing in February 1923. "A flask can be used for only one thing—that is, to carry liquor in violation of law," Faris declared. "Therefore, it is contraband and an outlaw."

If hip flasks were outlaws, nightspots were their hideouts. Flasks and plain old pint bottles went everywhere, from hotels and clubs that served set-ups to riverboats on the Mississippi. "They wouldn't let you on the *JS* or the *St. Paul* [riverboats] if they saw your bottle," said one reveler of the time, "but if you hid it, nobody bothered you once the boat left."

Raymond F. "Peg" Meyer, leader of a Cape Girardeau–based jazz band known as Peg Meyer's Original Melody Kings, said excursion boat officers would frisk male patrons coming up the gangplank for bottles or flasks. After women began to hide bottles in their clothing, they, too, were frisked. "Although the officers were not 100 percent efficient in keeping liquor off the boat, they certainly destroyed a lot of it," Meyer recalled in his book, *Backwoods Jazz in the Twenties.* "Once I saw a fellow on the wharf toss up a fifth of *Four Roses* to another on the second deck. During prohibition this would have been valued about the same as gold. As the man on the second deck caught it he turned around into the arms of the boat officer who politely took the whiskey from the fellow, pulled the cork and gently poured it into the Father of Waters."

Flat pint bottles were the choice of Springfield, Illinois, resident Howard Souther and his friends at dances or parties. "They'd sell setups then at a lot of the places," Souther recalled in 1972. "You could go in and order a glass of ginger ale and ice. It only cost you ten or fifteen cents and then you poured your own gin, whiskey, or whatever you were drinking into it."

Bubbling Bellhops

"Whiskey, usually diluted, can be obtained through bellboys at most of the hotels at $20 to $25 a quart," the *Post-Dispatch* reported in August 1920. "Stories are told of prodigious profits made by persons who laid in a supply of whiskey before Constitutional prohibition went into effect and have been selling it since . . . one enterprising bellboy at a large downtown hotel invested $450 in four barrels of whiskey which he proceeded to increase to eight barrels by adding Mississippi River water, which mixture he has since been selling at $20 a quart.

At another downtown hotel the price is $25 a quart with the degree of dilution conjectural." At the outset of prohibition, prices were exorbitant. In 1923, a male stenographer-clerk earned only a little more than one hundred dollars per month.

Shortly before Christmas in 1924, prohibition agents hauled in one Harry Deigman, bell captain at Hotel Jefferson, on a charge of selling liquor. Agents had registered at the hotel seven times and each time had purchased whiskey through the bellboys, said W. C. Goshorn, chief of the St. Louis group of prohibition agents.

In May 1925, two detectives visited "the new negro West End Hotel" at 927 N. Vandeventer Avenue and West Belle Place. Their suspicion was aroused when James Wilson, the bartender, began whispering excitedly to others around the bar as they entered. When he left the bar and headed to Room 219, they followed. In a closet of the room they found fifty-two pints of moonshine, which they took with Wilson to the station.

In April 1926, the dealer turned out to be a seventy-five-year-old coat-check operator at the upscale Maryland Hotel. William Rannells, an eleven-year employee, was approached by strangers who asked for liquor. He retrieved a pint bottle and a small glass from a locker. "Sample this stuff," he is said to have told the prohibition agents. "If it's not good you needn't buy." They liked it, said it tasted like moonshine with a little real whiskey mixed in. Then they arrested him and found three more pints and two half-pints of liquor in the locker. Rannells told authorities he had bought the liquor "at a place on Cass Avenue." He earned thirty dollars a month and tips at the check room. Hotel managers said they knew nothing about his bootlegging activities. "The check room is to the right of the clerk's desk and in plain view from the lobby," observed the *Post-Dispatch*.

Dancing the Night Away

Liquor could be brought to dances or obtained from bootleggers lurking around a dance hall or outdoor platform. This at times resulted in a windfall for the neighbors, Meyer recalled in *Backwoods Jazz*. "Stikes Hall in New Hamburg [in southeast Missouri] was always one of our best locations," he wrote. "Some of the county law officers were always present and saw that no liquor was taken into the hall, so the drinkers would go across the street to a cemetery where they hid their bottles in the grass around the monuments. Local residents soon picked up on this, and, instead of buying their bootleg, they could go over there on dance nights, pick up a handful of fine gravel and toss it into the grass around the monuments. When they heard the gravel hit a bottle they knew they had hit the spirits jackpot."

Litchfield, Illinois, resident Harley Edgar Logsdon danced to five- or six-piece bands at halls in Carlinville and Hillsboro, Illinois, and at Tarro's, a ballroom near Benld, Illinois. "Tarro's was just a great big building with an upper deck around for viewing the dance hall," Logsdon, a retired employee of Brown Shoe Company, recalled in 1973. "It was a nice place, very nice compared to the other places you might want to go, and it had a good dance floor." Logsdon learned to dance from his younger sister, who gave him a half-hour's worth of lessons for a two-dollar pair of silk stockings. Popular dances at the time were the Chicago Hop or the Southside, and the Dago Walk, the forerunner of the Breakaway, he said. "The Breakaway is the basic step of all your modern jitterbugging and rock; all that came from the original step of the Breakaway," Logsdon said. "We had waltz contests, we had Kangaroo Hop, we had a Dago Walk contest; we had all those. Those were all entertainments. The difference in those days was the fact that dances were given for dancing's sake alone, not like the modern taverns. . . ."

The other difference was the onlookers, Logsdon noted. "During prohibition at dances I remember on occasions seeing two nattily dressed men accompanied by a tall, beautiful, platinum-blond-haired woman stroll in leisurely and sit back at a table drinking and watching the dancers," he said. "It was rumored that the men were head men dealing in liquor running."

Meramec Highlands Park and Eden Park were popular dance spots in Meramec Highlands, then west of Kirkwood, James F. Baker noted in his book, *Glimpses of Meramec Highlands*. To gain an edge over its competition, Eden Park frequently offered giveaways and contests, such as a ten-dollar prize for the best fox-trot couple, ten dollars for the best waltz couple, and five dollars for the best two-step couple at a dance in March 1923. Plenty of proprietors stood ready to sell high-spirited concoctions, Baker noted, and in 1926 Eden Park reopened under new management as Meramec-Arcadia Park and remained in business until at least 1932. It offered a first-class orchestra, chicken dinners, picnic grounds, "girl singers," and good dance floors.

Howard Souther recalled attending a dance at the Jefferson Hotel in St. Louis with a friend who was a dental student at Saint Louis University. "And every table had their bottle," he said. "And they'd just take the bottle and put it under the tablecloth. Of course, it made a hump in the tablecloth, but they [hotel owners] didn't want you sitting it up in the middle of the table because there might be a raid or something and then it might be difficult for them to prove they hadn't sold you the liquor as well as the setup. Some people set it down under the table against the table leg or something. This is what one of the fellows in our crowd did, and somebody getting up from the table kicked that pint of whiskey right out in the middle of the dance floor and it busted all over the dance floor." Souther laughed. "We thought it was real funny except that it cut the hell out of your liquor supply at a time when none of us were very wealthy," he told an interviewer. "I was maybe making as much as twelve or fifteen dollars a week and liquor [was] a dollar or so a pint; a buck was a big part of your week's wages. And then we probably paid a dollar and a half or two dollars to go into the dance. Luckily that wasn't mine that got busted, but the guy that did bust it started helping me to drink mine, so it didn't help me."

One never knew who might show at the dances to sell their wares. Lincoln County Sheriff Wilson arrested well-known Flint Hill blacksmith Henry Bross in April 1925 at Moscow Mills and charged him with selling booze at a local dance. Bross pleaded guilty and was fined five hundred dollars by Justice J. T. Gilmore in Troy, Missouri. And the proprietor in a January 1929 bust at Gambrinus Hall, 3631 Salena Street in south St. Louis, was William Schwartz, a state legislator from the First District in St. Louis. Federal prohibition agents didn't bother the three hundred people attending a dance at the hall but went straight to anterooms where a bar had been set up. They consumed several glasses of alleged home brew and arrested Schwartz and his sixty-one-year-old bartender, Frank Brueggeman, for possession of intoxicating liquor.

VARIETY AND ACCENTS

Many people at dances and nightclubs enjoyed the lively new jazz music, transported upriver to St. Louis by the likes of King Oliver and Louis Armstrong. It was interpreted by black performers, mostly, and a few whites, and was popular on the pleasure boats that plied the Mississippi. "These were paddle boats," Logsdon explained. "They weren't like the *Admiral* [a riverboat that is now a St. Louis casino] now; they weren't as modern and they had a sloping deck toward the inside and just a little railing that held a top. They were steam-powered and had a big paddle wheel in the back. And dancing—boy, they had the hottest bands on there you ever heard, all jazz bands. Cecil Scott, and that was when Louis Armstrong played in that band although I don't recollect—all I knew, they were good. He wasn't a name then. . . . The best little band around here was Roley Fenton. He would do a lot of solos on the clarinet. Oh, he was just a jumper in those days."

Streckfus steamer J.S Deluxe
*on St. Louis riverfront, early
1920s.*

A successor to the ragtime that once reigned supreme, jazz made names for St. Louis bandleaders including Fate Marable, Charlie Creath, Dewey Jackson, Frankie Trumbauer, Reuben Reeves, Oliver Cobb, and Cab and Blanche Calloway.

Whites also made names for themselves on the jazz circuit, though segregation ruled and the white and black musicians' unions battled frequently. In the mid-1920s, cornet player Bix Beiderbecke and clarinet/alto sax player Pee Wee Russell were members of the all-white Frankie Trumbauer Band, which played, among other venues, at the Arcadia Ballroom and later the Racquet Club near Forest Park, and Elks Club dances in Carbondale, Illinois, author Dennis Owsley wrote in *City of Gabriels: The History of Jazz in St. Louis, 1895–1973.* Although the black musicians couldn't play in public with them, after-hours they shared their common interest in jazz and hung out together. The musicians all had Mondays off and used to visit Beiderbecke's and Russell's apartment in Granite City. "We got together just for kicks," black bassist Pops Foster recalled in *City of Gabriels.* "The colored and white musicians were just one. We'd stay all night, drink out of the same bottle, and go out with the same girls. We used to all pile in Bix's car and go over to Kattie Red's in East St. Louis and drink a lot of bad whiskey. It was green whiskey, man, they sure had bad stuff, but none of us ever got sick on it."

Many parents and pastors considered jazz immoral. Dr. Arnold Sach of the University of Heidelberg went so far as to blame the hectic pace of the modern jazz age for a host of bodily ailments including tooth decay, the *St. Louis Globe-Democrat* reported in March 1927. Even the staid Business Men of North Broadway, however, enlisted the services of a local jazz band to liven up its Shop-in-Baden-Week promotion from December 5 to 10, 1921. And one St. Louis County social group called itself the Jazz Lizards.

Gangsters owned many of the nightclubs in those days, and musicians didn't have written contracts, St. Louis jazz musician Martin Luther Mackay recalled in 1971. He played in the early days with six- to eight-piece bands led by Hot Lips Page, Count Basie, Clarence Love, and Coleman Hawkins in all-black venues. Along with the music, the clubs or roadhouses served bootleg liquor, frog legs, and fried chicken. "Your contract in those days was a gangster's pistol," Mackay said. "We played in little clubs for as little as 85 cents a night. A dollar and a half was tops at one time. But you were dependent for the most part on tips, which were pretty good. I remember in 1928, I played at the White House Tavern, and it was during an election year. It was nothing for us to make a hundred dollars apiece on Saturday in tips."

Gus Perryman, a St. Louis piano player and jazz musician, played all over the country. In 1922, he got a job playing at the old Maples roadhouse, which he said was in Webster Groves. At one time it had been owned by Egan gangster William "Dinty" Colbeck, Perryman said. "They called [jazz] variety and accents . . . that's a good definition for it," Perryman said in 1972. "Take the strains of the melody instead of playing the straight melody, we'd add on a couple of notes, you know."

Peg Meyer spent Labor Day 1921 in St. Louis, where he took in an excursion that featured a musical competition by Charlie Creath's and Dewey Jackson's orchestras. "It was tough choosing between the two, as they were both tremendous," Meyer recalled. "After listening to these two groups we then decided to go over to the *St. Paul* to hear a new and young cornet player with the Fate Marable orchestra. It turned out to be a night I will never forget. Louis Armstrong was the young musician. He could only have been about twenty years old at the time, and I don't see how he could have possibly improved with age over that night's performance."

BACKWOODS JAZZ

A graduate of Cape Girardeau Central High School, Peg Meyer loved jazz music and the greats who played it. He and his Melody Kings band members performed at dances and boat excursions in southeast Missouri, southern Illinois, and St. Louis. Their trusty Model T roadster frequently fell prey to muddy roads and radiator cap thieves. Meyer was one of the first professional saxophone players in the country and earned about fifty dollars a week, roughly the same as his professors at the Southeast Missouri State Normal School, of which he later dropped out. "There were no books on Jazz or any special arrangements available for musical lads in the backwoods in the Twenties," Meyer explained in 1989. "We had only a few arranged numbers, such as *Fidgety Feet, Clarinet Marmalade,* and *Tiger Rag.* So we spent a lot of time in the record shops, listening to all of the new releases hoping to find some new pattern or style developed by some jazz great that we could imitate. Radio was just appearing, and one of the early features was live broadcasts of big bands from famous hotels and ballrooms. On nights when we were not playing somewhere we would sit for hours with our headphones listening to these broadcasts, stopping only when the pressure on our ears cut off the blood circulation."

Despite the rudimentary education, there were some fine performers, he said. "Some of the backwoods jazz greats were terrific performers but were never 'discovered' or known outside their own isolated area," Meyer wrote. "Many simply never had the desire to leave home. One trumpet player I knew carried a telegram around with him for years until it literally fell apart. It was from Paul Whiteman offering him a job in his world famous orchestra. The fellow never even answered the telegram."

Previously, orchestras played in a very sedate and sophisticated manner, Meyer noted. "Musicians in the Twenties practically became contortionists playing their musical instruments in any unconventional manner, standing on chairs, swaying in unison to the rhythms, wearing crazy hats (our drummer, Berg Snider, must have had 30 hats and donned a different one for each number) and clowning in general," Meyer wrote.

The Melody Kings didn't drink on the job. Often, however, they would stop at a little tavern in Old Appleton, Missouri, for a cheese sandwich. "As we approached the village from the south we would turn the motor off at the top of a hill and coast quietly down to the front of the tavern where we would then, in unison, count to three and yell, 'Cheese Landing,'" Meyer wrote. "The operator

The Melody Kings in costume, 1919: Berg Snider, Peg Meyer, Jess Stacy, Bill Gadbois, and Martell Lovell.
From Backwoods Jazz in the Twenties, *courtesy Center for Regional History, Southeast Missouri State University.*

of the tavern, a jovial fellow with a distinctive German brogue, would say, 'Gott! It's dem crazy Pack Mars Musicioneers. Look hout.'"

While some jazz greats succumbed to heavy drinking and hard living— Beiderbecke, for instance, died of an alcoholic seizure at age twenty-eight in 1931—not everyone did. Peg Meyer started a successful music store and repaired instruments until a year before his death in 1995, noted Frank Nickell, editor of *Backwoods Jazz in the Twenties* and director of the Center for Regional History at Southeast Missouri State University. Meyer's fellow band member Jess Stacy went on to become a successful jazz pianist who played with a number of the great jazz bands, including Benny Goodman. He also provided the piano background for the dancing of Fred Astaire. "Jess Stacy's two-minute impromptu solo on 'Sing, Sing, Sing,' is one of the great moments in twentieth-century music," Nickell noted. "Peg Meyer started most of the high school bands in southern Illinois and southeast Missouri, a legacy that is significantly overlooked today. Peg and Jess remained good friends to the end of their lives."

Be It Ever So Humble...

Prohibition brought the drinks "home" in more ways than one. Until prohibition, most drinkers were men in saloons. "The traditional home of good beer, it might be expected that its reaction against any restriction would be emphatic and definite," Louis LaCoss of the *New York Times* wrote in 1930. "But again there is the strange paradox that St. Louis probably has fewer speakeasies than any other city of its class. This may be due, as has been explained, to the fact that St. Louisans are beer drinkers and home brew is a staple commodity in many homes."

Home cocktail parties were popular. Those in need of cash often held "Saturday night rent parties," Doris Wesley noted in *Lift Every Voice and Sing: St. Louis African Americans in the Twentieth Century.* "The host charged admission to collect money to pay his rent, and he served bootleg whiskey and invited someone to play the piano or the guitar and sing the blues," she wrote.

The 1931 debut of *The Joy of Cooking* by St. Louisan Irma Rombauer featured all sorts of snappy hors d'oeuvres and other appetizers designed to sop up booze at home parties, author Anne Mendelson noted in *Stand Facing the Stove.* Prior to that time, fussy little tea sandwiches and other items—no liquor-absorbing qualities needed—had been the vogue. "By the end of Prohibition in 1933, instant substitutes for the fussy underpinnings were widely available in the form of packaged potato chips, thin crackers, Melba toast rounds, and small pretzels," Mendelson wrote. "Cream cheese—virtually unknown for such purposes thirty years earlier—had become a quick all-purpose binder for 'spreads' (also a new word in this context), while commercial mixtures like deviled ham helped anyone throw together ballast for an alcohol-fueled event by simply opening a jar or can."

Deputy Sheriff William Perkins expected a quiet celebration in his home when he celebrated his forty-fifth birthday on January 23, 1923. The resulting brouhaha ended in a court battle. Perkins's half-sister, Mamie Hauser of St. Louis, called Perkins's wife, Margaret, that day and offered to bring some friends over to their Clayton home. "Nine men and five women came with Mrs. Hauser," the *Post-Dispatch* reported. "Besides the jug [of whiskey] they had flasks. Mrs. Perkins stood for things, she testified yesterday, until a girl in a red and black dress, smoking a cigarette, started a shimmy dance right in front of the Perkinses' 9-year-old daughter.

"When the hostess protested, the dancing girl exclaimed, 'What the hell kind of party is this, anyway? A Sunday school?'"

Margaret Perkins said she had given her guests glasses after they began sloshing liquor from the jug over the dining room buffet. William Perkins asked his guests to leave at midnight, and Margaret soon learned her three-hundred-dollar fur coat was missing and had her sister-in-law arrested. Mamie Hauser then filed an affidavit accusing the Perkinses of possession and sale of liquor, saying that the guests paid $3.50 each for liquor supplied by the Perkinses. A year later, on February 19, 1924, a jury acquitted the Perkinses.

"Home" Is Where the Bottle Is

Other "private home" destinations were not private parties at all, but booze parlors and nightspots. Beer flats and booze joints, home-brew joints, and some roadhouses and speakeasies were located in private homes or multifamily flats. "Right there at Fenton a fellow who had a cabin, he sold beer," Joe Phelan of Murphysboro, Illinois, recalled in *Drinking the Dipper Dry: Nine Plain-Spoken Lives.* "You ought to see the crowd. A lot of prominent people, too. He had a big place. We used to go down there. They'd take three pints of beer and throw it into a bucket. That cost you 50 cents. They'd pass the can around. You'd buy it and the next guy would buy it and that's the way they did it. You'd get a boot out of it. He made good home brew."

In St. Louis, police raided a beer joint at 1401 Louisville Avenue during the wee hours of July 11, 1929. They were admitted by a Mrs. Florence Pappas, who invited them to search the place. They found four men seated at a table in the basement. Fifty-five quarts and two buckets of beer were chilling in an icebox nearby. They arrested the men and Mrs. Pappas.

At the ripe old age of seventy-five, Mrs. Susie Kassabaum operated a rooming house at 713 S. Broadway where ninety bottles of beer were confiscated in July 1929. Mrs. Kassabaum and two others were arrested for violation of the prohibition laws. One popular place in Springfield, noted by Frank R. Sullivan and others, was a little house owned by a woman named Gretchen Grossmutter. "People would drive out in cars and sit in her yard, her backyard, and sideyard, and drink home brew," Sullivan said. "That was more of a beer place. That seemed to be quite popular. . . . One of the very popular places was on South First Street, on the east side of the street. People'd be sitting around the kitchen drinking gin bucks and the like."

Howard Souther said he couldn't recall buying liquor anywhere except in a private home or apartment. Because the business was fleeting, proprietors might rent a house for only a couple of months and then move to another location several blocks away. Beer joints tended to be rough places, he said. Anthony Massaro said he remembered some homes—or what appeared to be homes—that were securely monitored and had peepholes or glass in the door to identify callers, just like in the movies.

In St. Louis and other older cities such as Springfield, Illinois, "beer flats" were in vogue in urban areas. Beer flats were generally upstairs over businesses, Massaro said. Most "blind pigs" were beer flats. "Generally what you found up there was a—today we call them an apartment," he said. "They would come in and give us a bottle, and we'd pay them. Or we would be sitting at a table somewhere—and generally every room had a table—and the party that you were with would try to sit at a table. It might be two or three parties in one room—sometimes just one.

"Now most of these homes, a lot of these homes, the family lived there. The children thought nothing of it—it was part of the family life, and that was it."

Some were a little tonier, such as the Silver Slipper Club on Clayton Road in St. Louis. When police raided the place in July 1932 they found four couples, a seven-piece orchestra, and a group of ballet dancers. Six people were arrested and taken to the mounted police station in nearby Forest Park. "Sleepy neighbors reported the rendezvous at 6821A Clayton Road was the source of some music, considerable shouting, and miscellaneous noises they suspected to be crooning," the *St. Louis Star* reported.

WIDE OPEN

Other commercial establishments openly flouted the law. Physician Emmet Pearson recalled a bar directly across the street from St. Louis City Hall. "Everybody knew it was a bar," Pearson noted in 1983; "you could walk right in."

There were plenty more, J. Kirk observed in a letter to the *Post-Dispatch*. Now demolished, the Title Guaranty Building was located at Seventh and Chestnut streets. "Within two blocks of the Title Guaranty Building on the twelfth floor of which is located the office of the Prohibition Administrator, there is by actual count 14 wide open saloons and bootlegging joints which openly and unafraid of the law, sell booze every day in the week to anybody, man woman or boy, if they have the necessary lucre or price thereof," Kirk wrote in October 1928. "Should one or two policemen be present and witness the sale it makes not the slightest bit of difference."

CLOSED

FOR VIOLATION OF

NATIONAL PROHIBITION ACT

BY ORDER OF

UNITED STATES DISTRICT COURT

_____ DISTRICT OF _____

All persons are forbidden to enter premises without order from the UNITED STATES MARSHAL

U. S. MARSHAL

This sign was posted when an establishment was shut down by enforcement agents for liquor violations. Courtesy Donald Roussin and Kevin Kious

The roadhouses of Brentwood apparently were equally accessible. In July 1921, the Brentwood board of trustees passed an ordinance imposing a three-hundred-dollar licensing tax on "road houses, refreshment parlors and pleasure-seekers' resorts operating within the limits of the town."

"Brentwood has more resorts than any municipality in the county," the *Watchman-Advocate* declared. "One place in particular, and there may be others, has been running on a wide-open basis since the lid 'went on,' and it is rumored you can get something far stronger than water when you visit the place. A jazz band and ragtime dancers are some of the drawing cards, but there are others that it would not be well to dwell on here. It is rumored that the proprietors have cleaned up a bunch of coin and some of them who a few years ago could not get credit for five cents' worth of dog meat can now write their checks in five figures. They have been getting the cream of the coin and it is no more than right that they should pay the fiddler." Brentwood city leaders should have set the licensing fee at five hundred dollars, due to the thick auto traffic, the *Watchman-Advocate* opined.

Another wide-open bootlegging place was located near Barrett Station Road and Big Bend Road, Orville and Clinton Bopp recalled in a 2006 interview with the Kirkwood Historical Society. Jefferson City had its share as well: Prohibition agents found seven bars stocked with liquor and arrested fourteen people during a raid at the capital on June 19, 1924. The arrests included one woman, Mrs. Alice Thorpe.

Bereaved patrons frequented a speakeasy saloon on the corner of Bates Avenue and Morganford Road in south St. Louis, recalled Fritz Zenthoefer of Chesterfield, who grew up in the Bevo neighborhood. With one cemetery just across the street and one a short distance east on Bates, the speakeasy—known as Beckes—became a post-funeral gathering place for families, he said.

BLACK AND WHITE

In the African American community, residents could catch a movie at the Criterion Theater on Franklin Avenue and then repair to a small place operated by Jesse Johnson on Franklin east of Jefferson for a sandwich, nickel beer, or 25-cent cocktail, Julius Hunter noted in his book *Honey Island.* "Many cops who looked the other way while taking payoffs during the Volstead Act's enforcement noted that it was against the law to *sell* alcohol, not to *drink* it," Hunter wrote. "And so, Willetta [Hunter's aunt] remembers that some of the speakeasies she visited dispensed their bootlegged booze in coffee cups and had their patrons pay for it at another time."

The Rosebud Bar or Cafe at 2220–2222 Market Street, originally operated by ragtime composer Tom Turpin, no longer was a first-class establishment by prohibition days, Hunter noted. A popular drink there was sloe gin.

Although the nightclubs were segregated, the speakeasies weren't, Robert H. Goins told an interviewer in 1970. "All right, the speakeasy was illegal in the first place and you know people love to do things that are illegal anyway and they don't care who they do it with," said Goins, a St. Louis resident and retired civilian employee of the U.S. Army. "That's the only thing that I could say would account for it. Another thing different between now and then, people acted like decent folks. . . . I'm drinking out of my bottle and you're drinking out of yours, you're not bothering me and I'm not bothering you, and the man behind the counter didn't care who those bottles belonged to, they could belong to a purple man.

"That's the way it was, it wasn't all that bad, of course there were certain things we couldn't go to," Goins added. "Turn right around, the same person that wouldn't let us go to their dance halls, would come in the speakeasies and we would dance together."

BAKER, BANKER, AND BOOTLEGGER

On a visit to a bakery at 1405 Chouteau Avenue in April 1925, a St. Louis police officer noticed a small hole in the floor. He peeled up the boards with a crowbar, excavated two feet of dirt, and uncovered two barrels of whiskey. "A suction pump and a rubber tube brought the liquor into the bakery," the *St. Louis Star* noted. "Pat Coironei, the proprietor, was arrested."

Liquor establishments masqueraded during prohibition as office buildings, bakeries, confectioneries, florists' shops, and more. The tradition had been common at the turn of the twentieth century, when many drugstores operated a service called a "blind tiger," author Mahlon N. White noted in *Farmin' in the Woods During Prohibition Days.* "Well known customers, who didn't want to be seen going into a saloon, could wander into the drug store and be served a drink from under the counter," White wrote. "Bill Salley's drug store [in Fairfield, Missouri] was no exception and the Saturday Special was three shots for a quarter."

Liquor-dispensing fruit markets were located in the 2900 block of Chouteau Avenue and the 4300 block of Labadie Avenue in St. Louis. Offices also were popular. One repeat offender, a bar in the Central National Bank Building at Seventh and Olive streets, was characterized by federal prohibition agents as a favorite spot to raid when they had the time.

In April 1925, St. Louis police tore up the floor of a washhouse adjoining a saloon at 1026 Geyer Avenue and found thirty bottles of beer underneath. They arrested the proprietor, John Suchsman. The same day, they passed the poolroom and barber shop of Annanias Cade at 938 Hodiamont Avenue and observed barber William Lee pouring whiskey from a big bottle into a little one.

TAKING A GAMBLE

Many drinking establishments offered gambling as well. As soon as police cleaned up one area, the action would move to another. "Two hundred yards from the city hall at Venice, Illinois, is a wide-open crap game which has been doing a rushing business since the drive began in St. Louis County to run the gamblers out of that territory," the *St. Louis Star* announced on March 3, 1924. "The game is in a saloon at Broadway and Main streets and was found Saturday by a reporter for *The Star.* The proprietor serves drinks in one room, lunch in another and, in a third room, the crap tables are located."

The reporter was unable to learn who was running the game, but he noted some of the players were drunk and were encouraged by the gamekeepers, who always found a place for them when they returned from the bar with another drink. "The place was crowded Saturday with workingmen from the steel mills and other industries of Venice, Granite City and East St. Louis," the story read. "Several machines bearing Missouri license tags were parked outside."

The Business Men's Club, 4251 Lindell Boulevard in St. Louis, filed suit in March 1929 to enjoin police from further raids after they invaded the gambling resort four times in a three-week period. The club, formerly known as the Progressive Realty Club, changed its name following earlier raids in its former quarters in the Missouri and Laclede hotels. It was incorporated in 1927 as a "benevolent and social enterprise." "The only reason police have not caught the members in [the] act of gambling is that the police are not admitted until the members have put a safe distance between themselves and the gambling paraphernalia," the *Post* reported. "Capt. [Charles] Maupin has instructed patrolmen on the beat to make nightly calls at the three-story residence, known as 'the 14-room house without a bed.' The repeated raids by police have caused a falling off of business at the club, it is said, which is financially embarrassing as the club is paying $250 a month rent for the building. The owner is Charles Geraghty, an undertaker next door."

Horse racing was illegal when the Fairmount Race Track opened in September 1925. However, the racketeers paid off political officials, Collinsville newspaperman Karl Monroe noted. Pari-mutuel betting was legalized in 1927, and tracks were placed under the supervision of a racing commission. Dog racing was a flourishing, if illegal, enterprise on both sides of the river, Monroe told an interviewer in 1973.

In the African American community, candy stores and confectioneries were used as fronts for gambling joints, not speakeasies or booze joints, Goins recalled. One was run by his wife's cousin. "On Vandeventer, between Winter and West Belle, he had an ice cream place, I don't know if it was a Velvet Freeze or what, well, they put ice cream in the front and in the back they had a gambling joint," Goins said. "And right around the corner on Delmar, they had a House of Custard."

THE BILTMORE

Located a stone's throw from the St. Louis County line on Gravois Road just south of Fenton, the $200,000 Biltmore nightclub (equivalent to $2.3 million today) celebrated its opening on August 31, 1929, with "all the glitter of a Hollywood premiere," the *St. Louis Post-Dispatch* reported. By comparison, a similar new resort, the Mounds Country Club in Madison County, Illinois, had cost $90,000.

Patrons arrived in chauffeured limousines and presented membership cards and invitations, then headed inside to dine, dance, and play dice, roulette, and other games. Membership was offered only to those whose names already appeared on the rosters of country clubs and similar organizations. A *Post* reporter called it

The most elaborate combination night club and gambling establishment around St. Louis. . . . Behind luxurious leather easy chairs and divans hung tapestries [in the lounge]. A table-size equestrian bronze of Joan of Arc raised a sword from the other side of the room and ornate mirrors hung every few feet. Passing from here to the cloak room, the visitor almost stumbled against a marble fountain, from which Cupid himself poured a never-ending stream of water from the tip of his finger.

The one-story building overlooked the Meramec Valley and was surrounded by woods of tall oaks, elms, and hickories. Armed guards watched over the Biltmore at the gate and in lookout towers on the roof. Legends surrounded the place, with its luxurious red carpets and indoor fishpond. "One legend concerns the police raids on the establishment," Della Lang wrote in *River City: The Story of Fenton, Missouri.* "When the Jefferson County sheriff arrived on the scene, the owners showed a deed claiming the building was in St. Louis County. If the St. Louis County police arrived, they showed a deed proving they were located in Jefferson County."

Everything was on wheels, brewery historian Donald Roussin said. This worked well until 1927, when officials of both counties made a joint raid. "They were paying off both groups, and they got a little cocky—they stopped paying," he said. The joint raid closed the Biltmore, but only for a few months, according to Lang. "Some people claim the judges were paid off," she wrote. "If that was true, the payoffs continued for the next ten years. But in 1939, a new Jefferson County prosecuting attorney, who had promised to close the Biltmore if elected, kept his campaign promise. The club closed that year, and the building sat idle for eleven years. It was reopened as a supper club in 1951."

Author and radio/television personality Ron "Johnny Rabbitt" Elz visited the vacant club in 1948 with his grandfather, who worked in real estate. "It was like something you'd see in a George Raft movie," Elz recalled. "It was a first-class place. All the tables and chairs were set up, the bandstand was still set up, the kitchen was fully supplied." Today the buildings and trees are gone, replaced by an office park.

RED LIGHT DISTRICT

In Madison, Illinois, and some other areas, the oldest profession was practiced. Some thirty women were jailed in June 1923 following a raid on Madison's joints and resorts, Ron Stern wrote in *A Centennial History of Madison, Illinois, 1891–1991*. Most of the Madison resorts were located in the back room of some so-called soft drink parlor, he noted.

Beardstown, Illinois, had two red-light houses that weren't affiliated with bootlegging joints, and each of the city's six bootleg joints had two or three "girls" who offered their services, resident May Carr McNeil noted in 1987. Houses of ill repute also were a problem in Hannibal, Missouri. In one case in 1924, thirteen women appeared in police court following raids at "resorts" on Bird and Center streets, author Gregg Andrews wrote in his book, *City of Dust: A Cement Company Town in the Land of Tom Sawyer*.

An equally lively destination was the Sprague Hotel at 920 N. Taylor Avenue in St. Louis, where an intoxicated policeman was said by owner William A. Sprague to have participated in one raid on the establishment in 1924. Sprague sought, but was denied, an injunction in St. Louis Circuit Court against further police raids on the hotel, which didn't seem to be doing much good anyway. Nude patrons, drunkenness, and general debauchery were said to be the order of the day. At a hearing in March 1924, Detective Sergeant Robert H. Stuart described that some of the patrons were in "nude attire."

"What do you mean by that?" asked Sprague's attorney, Albert Johnson.

"Well, they didn't have any clothes on," Stuart replied.

"Were they ashamed?"

"Nope."

Most of the raid cases against the hotel, including one not long before the hearing, had been dismissed by a Provisional Judge Gallant, Stuart said. "Did anybody escape in this raid?" Johnson asked. "Some jumped out the windows," Stuart noted. "One woman left her wig behind and we found a piece of a teddy bear or whatever you want to call it hooked on a window sill." Most of the women were about twenty years old and had bobbed hair, Detective Sergeant Thomas J. Lynch estimated. "And most of 'em run around with a lot of red-hots [known gang associates]," Lynch said. "One of them said she didn't give a damn if she was arrested, so we accommodated her."

Patrolman Charles Brockhausen said he was stationed in front of the hotel to warn unmarried couples to stay away, but he was unsure how to determine if the couples were married. "I guess I had to take their word for it," he said.

THE OLD GRIND

May Carr McNeil had no desire to hang out in a bootlegging joint operated by an acquaintance, Hob Rohn. But her husband, Emmet, was sick and she needed a job. "I'd scrub the floor where they danced and then wash and rinse a tub of beer bottles and then I would come home before anybody stopped to come to drink," she recalled in 1987. "They would always come in the afternoon. I know I used to be ashamed for people to see me go in that bootlegging joint. I'd go all the way around the block if I'd see anybody that I knew before I would go in."

Besides the bootlegging joints in Beardstown, Illinois, which included Rohn's establishment on Seventh Street, there were saloons or taverns that sold liquor. Except for one woman, the female residents of Beardstown wouldn't go to the bootlegging joints, although they patronized the taverns. "They always treated us with respect and tavern owners would say, 'Lady in the house,' and everybody knew not to swear or talk dirty or anything," McNeil noted. "I can remember there was only one woman in Beardstown that drank and her name was Kate Steen. She'd take a bucket and go to the back end of the tavern on Fourth Street and stand at the back door. They'd take her bucket in and fill it full of beer and she'd take it home."

At the bootleg joint, Rohn would allow McNeil to go home if anyone came in to drink. One time, she noticed Rohn put some lye in the booze to give it bite. "I told him at the time, I said, 'Hob, that will kill people.' He said, 'Oh, it won't hurt them, just clean them out.'"

McNeil also made and sold crepe paper pillows that male patrons won for their girlfriends at the bootlegging joints. "You take crepe paper and you paint a gold edge on it, then you got a way of making scallops with your fingers and then you'd gather that on a piece of cloth, go round and round," she said. "Then put a rose in the center that you'd make and then you'd stuff it with newspaper and you'd get two dollars a piece for them. Sometimes a dollar."

A ROUGH LIVING

Proprietors were easy targets. John Kiel was bending to pick up a bottle in his saloon at 2301 Warren Street in St. Louis when someone reached over the bar and shot him behind the left ear in July 1928. All of the men in the saloon had fled, so he staggered to the house of a friend, who had him taken to Mullanphy Hospital on Kingshighway Boulevard. Police believe the shooting was a grudge affair and took into custody one of the customers, whom Kiel was unable to identify.

Walter D. LeVey, operator of a roulette wheel at the Mounds Country Club, died of a bullet wound through the heart on December 19, 1929. He had reportedly been snowbound at the gambling house, on Illinois Route 11 between East St. Louis and Collinsville, and was still wearing his hat, overcoat, and scarf when he walked into St. Mary's Hospital in East St. Louis, supported by two men who quickly left the hospital. Attendants reported that LeVey murmured something about being shot in an automobile and thrown out. His last words on the operating table were, "Whoever got my money shot me." He was forty-nine and lived at 5126 Delmar Boulevard with his wife, Belle, who told police he was carrying about $225 in cash when he left for work the day before.

The two men who accompanied LeVey were later identified as James Noonan, a floorman at the Mounds Club, and Harry Wolf, a customer. Noonan told a reporter he was driving into East St. Louis when he found LaVey leaning against a pole. On the way to the hospital, Noonan said, LeVey said he had been robbed.

Charles Connors escaped with a fractured skull and a badly lacerated head after two burglars entered his apartment over his roadhouse, the Maples, on Manchester Road in St. Louis County, the *St. Louis Star* reported in March 1923. Connors formerly owned the National Cafe, 117 N. Sixth Street, where he was arrested several times for liquor law violations, police said.

Walter Nichols, proprietor of a saloon in Granite City, Illinois, owed his life to his 105-pound wife, Julia. Nichols narrowly escaped death on his twenty-eighth birthday after robbers entered his bar at 2400 Edwards Street. Nichols, said to be an expert marksman, turned his own gun on two would-be bandits about 11:30 p.m. on a Tuesday night in March 1923. He wounded one of the bandits and killed the other following a revolver duel. The wounded man then sprang to the attack, revolver in hand, and a struggle ensued behind the bar for possession of the weapon. Five customers had been forced by the robbers to face the wall.

"The bandit slowly but surely was getting his revolver into a position to fire at her husband," the *St. Louis Star* reported. "Mrs. Nichols attacked with a scream. She fastened her fingers in the robber's hair and put her whole weight upon him, breaking his hold upon her husband." Nichols then struck the man with all his force, knocking the revolver from his hand. As the robber fled toward the door, Nichols picked up the weapon and fatally shot him. The robbers were identified as William Emerson, of Madison, Illinois, and William Peck, of Granite City, Illinois.

Side Effects

Sometimes it didn't pay to go out. In July 1932, ten dancers were injured—seven seriously—when hoodlums broke up a dance at the Jungle Club on Arsenal Island in the Mississippi River. The injured were brought ashore on a gasoline barge and taken to City Hospital for treatment. "The police believe the attack may have been made by bootleggers," the *Naborhood Link News* reported. "They say the five youths who operate the club had been warned to get off the island."

The hoodlums, some armed with revolvers that they used as clubs, approached the dancers and threw rocks and pop bottles. The injured included John Derns, Jr., twenty-one, a jeweler, possible skull fracture; Russell Elliston, twenty-one, a laborer, skull and jaw fracture; Norma Sifverson, seventeen, cuts and bruises; Joseph Vores, twenty, a musician, skull fracture and cuts and bruises; James O'Dell, nineteen, a jeweler, cuts and bruises; John Putz, Jr., nineteen, scalp wounds and fractured right wrist; and Nolley Byrd, a laborer, skull fracture.

Some would-be home party guests caused trouble in 1928 for Conrad Tappeiner, a carpenter. Early in the morning of April 16, six strangers drove up to a party at Tappeiner's home at Grant and Rock Hill roads. Four men and two women demanded admission and drinks and became enraged when Tappeiner slammed the door in their faces. "We'll fix you," one shouted as they drove away.

An hour later an automobile stopped outside, and Tappeiner and a guest, George Michael of 5109 Dresden Avenue, went out to investigate. Someone in the auto fired a shotgun, which hit Tappeiner in the right shoulder and arm and Michaels in the right arm. Fourteen slugs were removed from Tappeiner's body at St. Anthony's Hospital at Grand Boulevard and Chippewa Street.

A quarrel over a 10-cent difference in the price of a can of beer resulted in the fatal shooting of Donald Gray in a basement saloon at 1801 Wash (now Cole) Street. Gray, a railroad switchman, had entered the saloon in October 1928, paid 45 cents for his can, and passed it around a table he shared with three other men and and his twenty-year-old wife, Goldie. When a fourth man sat down, ordered a can of beer, and laid down only 35 cents, Gray demanded

A group of unidentified partygoers, 1925. Courtesy the Missouri History Museum.

to know why. The newcomer reacted with profanity. Both rose to their feet. The bartender threw an empty bottle to stop them. "Mrs. Gray stepped between her husband and his antagonist to make peace, she said, but the newcomer drew a revolver from his waistband and began firing," the *Post-Dispatch* reported. "His first shot at her missed, she told police, and he then fired two shots at Gray, one taking effect in his left side."

The man, described as thin with a red face and bug eyes, ran out. So did the others at the table. Bartender Frank Sams, known as "Dubie," turned out the lights and locked up the place. Gray collapsed on the floor and was taken to City Hospital by his wife and a friend, John Gregori, who had been waiting outside the saloon. Gray died two hours later. He was twenty-eight years old.

Michael Herbst's trip to City Hospital in July 1928 cost him his life. Herbst, a thirty-nine-year-old railroad foreman, was riding in a car with friend John Gallagher at Ninth and Destrehan streets when they were arrested by police. "They had been drinking and when they arrived at City Hospital were taken in hand by Dr. Abraham Bouhasin, physician in charge of the receiving room," the *Post-Dispatch* reported. "After a stomach pump had been used, Dr. Bouhasin gave Gallagher a cup of salt solution and ordered an attendant to get another dose for Herbst." Instead of the epsom salts, the attendant took by accident a similar bottle that contained formaldehyde and gave Herbst a cupful. When hospital staffers discovered the error, they retrieved the stomach pump, but the damage had been done. Herbst died soon after, his stomach badly burned.

CHAPTER 11
THE MEDICINE SHOW

ON A COLD MONDAY NIGHT IN JANUARY 1926 A CROWD OF FOUR THOUSAND DELUGED St. Louis's Union Station, an assemblage unrivaled since American troops arrived home at the end of World War I. The spectators included prominent St. Louis politician Louis P. Aloe, an unsuccessful candidate for the Republican nomination for mayor not long before, and former state beverage inspector and gang leader Edward J. "Jellyroll" Hogan. As a train hauling the chartered Pullman car "Palfrey" pulled in at 8:30 p.m. on Track 7, the crowd poured down to the gate "like a heavy fluid," *Post-Dispatch* correspondent William P. Allen reported. They greeted the occupants with smiles, shouts, hugs, and tearful wishes, along with enough candy, flowers, cigars, and baskets of food for a cross-country journey.

But these guests of honor weren't headed across the country. En route from the jail in Marion, Indiana, within hours they would be changing their civvies for brass-trimmed blue woolen prison uniforms at Kansas's Leavenworth Federal Prison. They all had been convicted in Indianapolis, Indiana, days earlier of a scheme to siphon whiskey from the Jack Daniel Distillery in St. Louis.

In the car were eleven St. Louisans, including Nat Goldstein, former St. Louis circuit clerk and a twenty-year Nineteenth Ward Republican committeeman; Arnold J. Hellmich, collector of internal revenue of the eastern district of Missouri, appointed by President Warren Harding in 1922; William J. Kinney, a former deputy collector under Hellmich and the brother of Democratic State Senator Michael Kinney; Robert E. Walker, a former St. Louis deputy sheriff; Edward J. O'Hare, a lawyer and Democratic ward politician; Daniel O'Neil, former deputy constable in St. Louis; Mike Whalen, a member of the Democratic City Central Committee; Anthony (Tony) Foley, a gambler and resort keeper in St. Louis County; Harry Levin, a former deputy constable; Morris Multin, a whiskey dealer; and five Cincinnatians including John "Jew John" Marcus, one of the first whiskey runners in the nation.

Their terms ranged from a year and a day to two years, although many were released early on appeal. Except for Marcus, who also was a pickpocket and accused murderer, the prisoners were allowed to leave the car. The crowd called Nat Goldstein to the steps, and a woman threw her arms around him. "Dear,

St. Louis Union Station.

dear Mr. Goldstein, you never forget a friend in need," she told him. "Attaboy!" "You tell 'em!" came the shouts from the crowd. "Goldstein seemed more deeply affected by the greeting than any of the prisoners," Allen observed. "There was an obvious repression beneath his old jaunty manner and one felt that when he smiled he was fighting back the tears."

Fellow prisoner Harry Stratton of Cincinnati was amazed. "This must be a good town to come from, even when you're going to the penitentiary," Stratton told Allen. Whalen comforted his sobbing wife as his daughter clung to him. Hellmich's son, who had boarded the train at East St. Louis, talked cheerfully until the car was pulled out into the yards. "There was an odd quiet in the crowd as the locomotive bell began to ring and a trainman swung his lantern slowly," Allen wrote. "The car began to move. The prisoners pressed their faces to the windows for a last glimpse of their friends.

"There was a sudden brief cheer, so spontaneous that as it died away each man looked at his neighbor in wonderment at their unanimity of thought. The car slid out through the darkened train shed, its red lights growing dimmer and dimmer until they disappeared in the murky yards."

The homecoming celebration was on the prisoners' minds as the train neared Kansas City. "If I ever get blue," noted Goldstein, now prisoner number 24525, "I will remember that night. I know now that I can come back and find my friends waiting for me. It makes it wonderfully easy."

"About cuts the time in half," added Hellmich.

"I've got enough votes to elect me Justice of the Peace in St. Louis County," joked Foley.

REMUS AND THE BIG DISTILLERY HEIST

The men might have gotten away with their whiskey caper had they followed the advice of its primary bankroller and would-be ringleader, George Remus of Cincinnati. Remus, an attorney, entered the lucrative medicinal whiskey trade after he represented several not-so-bright bootleggers who became rich.

Although medicinal whiskey was legal during prohibition under certain conditions, Remus took the process to illegal ends. "To call George Remus a bootlegger is like saying John D. Rockefeller owned a filling station," *Post-Dispatch* reporter Dickson Terry observed in an article on Remus's death in 1952. "Remus wasn't a gangster or racketeer like Capone or others whose names we associate with the evils of prohibition. He wasn't even a toughie. He was an ex-lawyer who turned business man. His business was liquor, and he set out to become the Napoleon of the business."

During prohibition days, the whiskey stored in a distillery or warehouse might belong to the distiller or to those who purchased whiskey certificates, which anyone could purchase on the market. Many people bought them as investments, Terry noted, and Remus made his millions by buying up all the whiskey certificates at his various distilleries and becoming the sole owner of the whiskey. At one point Remus owned nine distilleries or warehouses and their contents. He withdrew and sold nearly one-seventh of the bonded whiskey in the United States. He operated several complete drug companies that purchased whiskey from these distilleries, in effect buying whiskey from himself. He ran a network of rumrunners and surmounted many obstacles by paying off prohibition officials, from beat cops to Jess Smith, the companion of U.S. Attorney General Harry Daugherty of the Harding administration.

Bonded whiskey is stored in a federally bonded warehouse, in which taxes are not paid until it is bottled and removed for sale. Certain requirements accompany bonding, including the need for it to be aged for four years before bottling. Said whiskey was guarded by a government-employed "gauger," whose job before prohibition was to see that the whiskey had aged properly before it was sold. During prohibition, however, the gauger made certain that no liquor was withdrawn without proper permits from the local liquor control director.

Bootlegger John Marcus hatched a scheme to milk the Jack Daniel Distillery, 3960 Duncan Avenue, with Morris Multin and the late Jack Kratz, a Republican politician and former café owner in St. Louis. Marcus concluded that only Remus could pull off a job of that size. Initially Remus refused, saying he had enough distilleries, but after several conversations with Kratz and Goldstein he agreed. "What about this collector, Hellmich?" Remus recalled asking Goldstein in 1923. "Are you sure he can be handled?"

"Certainly," Goldstein was said to have replied. "I 'made' the Dutch boob for a purpose and now is the time to use him. He'll be right, and he'll see that the gauger is right." After several negotiations, Remus agreed to pay distillery owner Lem Motlow and his two partners $125,000 for the whiskey, along with a bond of $90,000 to indemnify him if the operation should result in the confiscation of the property by the government.

Kinney was set up as the gauger and was to receive one dollar per gallon as his cut. Kratz, in charge of protection, said twelve dollars a case would take care of the revenue collector's office, including Goldstein. The distillery contained 896 barrels, each with a little less than 40 gallons. Because they had no permits to legally withdraw whiskey, Remus proposed to take about six gallons of whiskey from each barrel and then substitute water and alcohol to keep the proof up.

PENITENTIARY PRACTICE

"This would have given us about 5,000 gallons of whiskey, and as we expected to get $30 a gallon for it, the proceeds would be in the neighborhood of $150,000," Remus told *Post-Dispatch* correspondent Paul Y. Anderson in 1926. "In other words, with the protection subtracted, it would just about give us our investment back. At the end of a year, after the liquor had been regauged, I would take out another 5,000 gallons, and the $150,000 from that sale would be nearly velvet, and the danger of discovery would be negligible. My share would have been slightly less than $75,000, and I was perfectly willing to wait a year.

"But this St. Louis crowd was determined to get rich off of one deal," he continued. "They objected to my plan. Kratz said it was too slow, and besides he didn't know where they would get the alcohol to substitute for the whiskey. He said it was uncertain how long they could [maintain the protection agreement] and therefore the thing to do was clean out the place while we had a Collector and a gauger who were right. Then we could sell it immediately, get our money back and take our profit."

Remus protested vigorously, then returned with his wife to his quarters at Hotel Chase to "sit tight and trust in the Providence that looks after fools and children."

"I know this business thoroughly, and you fellows are simply trying to break into the penitentiary," Remus said he told them. He left on a business trip and when he returned, found his cohorts were pumping the barrels dry and sending

MAGICAL MOTLOW

The nephew of legendary whiskey maker Jack Daniel, Lem Motlow lived a strangely charmed life: He bounced back from two felony indictments to become a magistrate judge.

Just six months after the milking of the Jack Daniel warehouse, Motlow was charged with the murder of a Kirkwood, Missouri, resident, Pullman car conductor C. T. Pullis, as the train headed through the Eads Bridge tunnel out of St. Louis in March 1924. Police said Motlow was drunk when arrested and admitted to the shooting. He had been asked to be quiet by a porter, Ed Wallis. "No nigger can keep me quiet," Motlow replied. Pullis attempted to quiet Motlow and finally pushed him into a seat. Motlow drew a revolver and fired two shots, one of which struck Pullis. The conductor died at St. Mary's Hospital later that evening. Pullis was mourned by his wife, mother, and sister and was buried in Kirkwood's Oak Hill Cemetery. Motlow was acquitted by a St. Louis jury on the murder charge.

Motlow had been indicted but managed to avoid trial in the Jack Daniel siphoning, and in 1928 the Vicksburg, Tennessee, resident was regarded so highly by residents of that state that they elected him county magistrate.

In July 1928, Judge Motlow and partner Harry Dahlman appeared in St. Louis to oppose the government's effort to confiscate their warehouse at 3960 Duncan Avenue. "Testimony of Motlow and Dahlman was that, when they sold the whiskey in the Jack Daniel warehouse to a group of men, they did not know the whiskey was to be illegally removed," reported the *Post-Dispatch*. "Therefore, they contended, they should not be punished by having their building taken away.

"In the event, however, that the Government does take the building, Motlow and Dahlman will buy it back for $20,000."

By 1929, Motlow had reacquired the property from government seizure by paying penalties totaling twenty thousand dollars. He received an unexpected bonus: forty thousand gallons worth of vinegar that fermented from the leftover alcohol in the barrels since they had been milked more than five years earlier. The vinegar sold for about three cents a gallon, or about twelve hundred dollars.

the contents to Tony Foley's farm. They refilled the barrels with water and left only one barrel filled with whiskey for the gauger to sample.

In the meantime, Egan gangster William "Dinty" Colbeck learned of the operation and demanded a cut of 5 percent of the gross proceeds. Egan gangsters guarded the liquor with riot guns as trucks were loaded with the whiskey and headed out Olive Street Road. "Just as quick as the out-of-town men made deals, whiskey was taken from the place where we had carried it and shipped," Egan gangster Ray Renard told *St. Louis Star* reporter Harry Brundidge. "Some went out on trucks, some went down the Mississippi in boats and some was shipped in freight cars. There were almost 1,000 barrels and Dint told me later that it had been sold for almost $2,000,000."

The Multin family's Rex Realty Company in the Arcade Building at 800 Olive Street was set up as the sales headquarters, and small quantities of the whiskey were transported from Foley's farm to the Walker-White Bill Posting Company on Chestnut Street. Remus wasn't getting the share of the profits he had been promised, and was told sales were sluggish. Later it was learned that the bootleggers were "cutting" the product in such generous proportions that the doctored stuff made three gallons out of every one. "As I understand it, this whiskey was being bought by the best people in St. Louis," Remus recalled. "Some of them had it analyzed and sent it back."

"I Should Never Have Consented to Go to St. Louis"

By this time, Remus had been convicted in federal court following a raid on his Cincinnati-based distribution center, Death Valley Farm. He appealed the conviction, but Treasury Department investigators kept a close watch on him.

Only one month after the milking, on September 15, 1923, prohibition enforcement agents inspected the Jack Daniel Distillery and found the depleted goods. Treasury officials surreptitiously installed a dictaphone in the offices of the Rex Realty Company, and one Treasury employee kept watch with opera glasses. The agents heard transactions being made as well as mundane conversations—Morris Multin, for instance, bet one thousand dollars on two consecutive days on the 1923 World Series in progress. As suspicion grew that a listening device was present, some of the office regulars decided to play it to the hilt. They announced in loud voices orders for a case of whiskey from the likes of President Calvin Coolidge, Wayne Wheeler of the Anti-Saloon League, and a leading clergyman in town.

Remus, who knew the conspirators were headed for trouble and sensed a double-cross, tried to get out with as much whiskey as he could. He received five hundred gallons of undiluted stock that he sent to Cincinnati, but a second batch of five hundred gallons was hopelessly diluted. Remus was beside himself. "I should never have consented to go to St. Louis," he said later.

Remus was in federal prison in Atlanta, ordered there after his appeal failed on the Death Valley case, when about twenty federal grand jury indictments in the Jack Daniel siphoning first rolled out in May 1924. Remus received immunity after he agreed to testify for the prosecution. The federal investigation continued for more than a year, and in November 1925, twenty-two additional St. Louisans were indicted, including Goldstein, Hellmich, William Kinney, Multin, Michael Kinney, and St. Louis County Republican leader Fred Essen. In press interviews, Hellmich and Goldstein said they knew nothing about the scandal. Eventually fifteen St. Louisans were convicted in 1925, eleven of whom were sent to Leavenworth. Another four served out their sentences in the Marion County (Indiana) Jail.

The convictions of Goldstein, Whalen, O'Neil, Multin, Levin, and Stratton were upheld in an appeals process, and they were ordered back to Leavenworth in March 1927. Goldstein was pardoned by President Herbert Hoover in March 1929 after serving eight months of a two-year sentence. State Senator Michael Kinney had been convicted with the others, but the judge set his conviction aside and ordered a new trial due to a lack of evidence against Kinney. Motlow and his associates were never tried. The convictions of O'Hare, Foley, Walker, and John Connors were later set aside. The indictment against Fred Essen was dropped in March 1928 because the government's star witness, George Remus, no longer was considered competent. Remus was confined in a hospital for the criminally insane for the murder of his wife, Imogene. She had promised to meet him at the gate when he was released from prison in Atlanta but enraged him by running off with a Department of Justice agent while Remus was still serving time. He returned home to find cash and securities missing, and many valuable items stripped from his palatial mansion in Cincinnati. In 1927, he chased down Imogene and shot her to death on a Cincinnati street. Remus used the insanity defense when he represented himself in a trial later that year. "Remus's brain exploded when he shot her," said Remus, who usually referred to himself in the third person. "He was momentarily out of his mind." While in Ohio's state hospital for the criminally insane, Remus proved he was sane, and later was set free.

FOR WHAT "ALES" YOU

From ancient times, whiskey and wine and other liquors were used as home remedies: hot toddies with whiskey to soothe aching throats, heated wine with black pepper to produce a sweat, and many others. Liquor also was a reliable drink in areas where the purity of local water was in question.

In Collinsville, Illinois, Gilbert Killinger's father would mix a quart of whiskey with cherries from a wild cherry tree. He'd shake it up and let it sit for three or four months and use it for any kind of ailment. He'd also infuse whiskey with balsam. "He'd plant a balsam vine," Killinger, a journalist and former Collinsville mayor, told an interviewer in 1976. "When the thing was small enough to get in the neck of the bottle, he put it inside the bottle and wrapped the bottle around the limb. This balsam would grow till it almost filled the bottle. Then he'd fill that with whiskey till he got balsam whiskey. And that was good for any kind of a stomachache."

In Decatur, Illinois, Herbert Sullivan's family would make cough medicine out of whiskey and rock candy. "Seems to me it was on a string like beads and you could take it off the string and put it in the bottle and it would dissolve, and shake it [to make] kind of a cough syrup," Sullivan, a retired truck driver and mechanic, told an interviewer in 1984. "Kids would like to get a cough then."

When prohibition was enacted there were more ailing people than ever, and a system was set up whereby medicinal liquor could be prescribed by doctors with permits and filled by druggists with permits. Meticulous record-keeping and government reporting was required, only a pint of liquor could be prescribed for use by the same person every ten days, and no prescription could be filled more than once. Doctors received a set of prescription blanks, the stubs of which were to be filled out and returned to the internal revenue collector. Physicians were limited to one hundred liquor prescriptions every three months and were allowed to purchase an additional six quarts of whiskey and five gallons of grain alcohol annually for office or surgical use.

Dentists who took out permits were allowed two gallons of alcohol a year in general practice, and specialists—both doctors and dentists—were allowed additional quantities. Veterinary surgeons with permits also were allowed two gallons of alcohol a year.

"Never had I known so many diseases could be cured by one remedy—whiskey," St. Charles historian Edna McElhiney Olson wrote after reading a prohibition-era medical record. "Nor had I known the inventiveness of the medical mind. At the risk of being too long-winded, I list some of the epidemic of small diseases: flu, fever, senility, debility, drug addiction (withdrawal), heart block, tuberculosis, fatigue, dyspepsia, post-measles, symptoms of ptomaine poisoning, insomnia, exposure, flatulency, exhaustion, shock, asthma, malaria, baldness, gall stone pain, chronic bronchitis, epileptic attack, neurasthemia, whooping cough, scarlitina, cerebral anemia, mitral insufficiency, acute indigestion, confinement (?), dropsy, valvular lesion, pernicious anemia, post-operative pain, and broken arm. . . . The medication was to be taken in ice water, cod liver oil, hot mik, with egg nog, sweetened water, or straight."

Due to the burdensome regulations and a revenue tax of $2.40 a gallon on the bonded liquor, druggists interviewed by the *Post-Dispatch* in January 1920 doubted that many pharmacists would take out permits to sell liquor. "Another reason for this decision, they said, was that they did not believe reputable physicians would prescribe whiskey as a beverage," the *Post* noted.

They were wrong. Reputable and unreputable physicians alike prescribed the stuff, and a bevy of St. Louis politicians secured permits to wholesale whiskey for medicinal purposes. In 1922, Gus Nations, chief prohibition enforcement agent for the St. Louis district, estimated two of his six agents—responsible for thirty-five counties—spent nearly all of their time investigating applications by physicians and drugstores for permits to prescribe and handle whiskey. This involved looking into the character of the applicant and his moral and professional standing, and making a recommendation to Missouri's prohibition director, W. H. Allen, who made his own recommendation to prohibition authorities in Washington, D.C. The federal agency granted or denied the prescription privilege.

Of 11,268,469 liquor prescriptions made nationwide for the fiscal year ending June 30, 1923, Illinois was second in the country with 2,168,788. An estimated fifty thousand physicians nationwide, or one-third of all doctors, used the liquor prescription privileges.

And as a flu epidemic raged in January 1923, Acting Prohibition Commissioner J. E. Jones issued an emergency order that allowed physicians whose liquor prescription quotas had been exhausted to continue to prescribe liquor for their patients. "While the order was issued to meet an emergency, we feel confident the privilege we have extended to the medical profession will not be abused," Jones said.

In 1929, an estimated 8 million gallons of privately owned whiskey was held in bond in warehouses throughout the country, with an estimated 1.5 million gallons of whiskey used for medicinal purposes each year. In 1928 alone, 30,973 gallons of whiskey were removed from bonded warehouses in Illinois, and 32,013 gallons were withdrawn in Missouri, according to the *New York Times*.

Amazing Recovery

The St. Louis Zoo's Reptile House in the 1920s.

Medicinal alcohol helped R. Marlin Perkins recover from a serious snake bite in 1929. Perkins, curator of reptiles at the Saint Louis Zoo, became the first person in the history of medical science to live after being bitten by a Gaboon viper. Years later, he hosted the popular *Wild Kingdom* wildlife television series beginning in the 1960s.

Perkins and an assistant had been washing mites off of the African snake on New Year's Eve 1928 when it lunged and sank a two-inch-long fang into his index finger. Almost immediately, Perkins became dizzy. Dr. Forest Staley, the zoo's medical consultant on poisonous snakebites, rushed over and loaded Perkins in his Hudson Super Six automobile for the trip to St. Mary's Hospital. No Gaboon antivenin was available, so antivenin from the cobra and other snakes was used. Perkins lost consciousness and nearly stopped breathing due to paralysis, and his arm swelled to twice its normal size. He was in the hospital for three weeks and required nearly six months to recuperate.

"George Deickman, president of the Zoology Board of Control, brought me a whole case of port wine, which was put into the closet of my hospital room," Perkins recalled in *My Wild Kingdom: An Autobiography.* "This was pre-World War I vintage, rare in those dry Prohibition days, and he wanted me to take a sip every day to help build up my blood. By the time I felt well enough to take sips of port wine, most of it had already been consumed by my well-wishing friends who had learned about this good supply. Dr. Staley also believed a little alcohol might help my appetite, so he provided me with prescriptions for pint bottles of whisky. This made my apartment a popular meeting place for my friends and in part made up for the fact that I had spoiled their New Year's Eve parties."

STICKY FINGERS

Wherever liquor was stored, it was a tempting target for pilferers. Prohibition had given liquor the appeal of gold. Even the Le Gear Stock and Poultry Remedies Company, 1531 N. Broadway in St. Louis, was a target in June 1920 when burglars carried off four metal drums full of alcohol worth $875. The burglars must have been well acquainted with the place, company officials said, because a vicious bulldog kept on the first floor for protection had not been disturbed.

On Saturday, March 10, 1923, three bandits entered the government hospital at 5300 Arsenal Street shortly before midnight, slugged and bound a private watchman, and escaped with three barrels of whiskey that were to be used for medicine.

On November 20, 1922, a major plot to rob the American Distilling Company warehouse at Pekin, Illinois, was frustrated by police and deputy sheriffs following a gun battle in which at least twenty shots were exchanged. The attackers attempted to enter the distillery by boat; between four thousand and five thousand barrels were inside.

On January 25 and 26, 1923, two trains were held up near Peoria, Illinois, and alcohol stolen. In the first instance, one hundred cases of alcohol were taken; the next day ten barrels of alcohol valued at ten thousand dollars were taken. They were being shipped from the American Distilling Company at Pekin.

Drugstores were convenient targets. On November 5, 1924, robbers broke open the safe in the drug store of C. J. Deckmeyer on Florissant Road in Jennings, Missouri, and removed more than three hundred dollars in cash, three hundred dollars in narcotics, and sixteen pints of whiskey.

Two armed men entered a drugstore at 2858 St. Louis Avenue in March 1927 and held up proprietor Fred Buescher, a clerk, and several customers. They led Buescher to the store safe, forced him to open it, and took thirty-six pints of Kentucky Dew whiskey valued at $198 at prescription rates, along with $10 worth of narcotics.

Short of the aforementioned Jack Daniel caper, one of the biggest heists in St. Louis was the Egan gang's holdup of the same distillery eight months earlier, on December 8, 1922. This was a robbery, not a milking, Egan gangster Ray Renard told Harry Brundidge of the *St. Louis Star.* "I guess we better pull it," Renard recalled Dinty Colbeck as saying. "The mob can use a little real whiskey for the holidays, and a lot of the guys downtown have been asking for some pre-war stuff. Ray, you go borrow a couple of trucks. [Joe] Powderly, you'd better take a final look and see that the lay is o.k. If you give us the go-go, we'll make it tomorrow night."

They began by sneaking up on, and subduing, four watchmen at the distillery, Renard recalled:

"We're going to work now," Chippy [Robinson] told the four cops. "Get me right: if any of
you guys do any funny stuff you'll have a funeral at your house day after tomorrow. And if any
of you ever identify one of us for this job you'll get a big dose of lead. See?"

One of the watchmen said they were cold, could they have their coats. Funny how guys get
cold when they get scared. Chippy, who would just as soon have killed one as to have looked at him,
got their overcoats and then got them whiskey kegs to sit down on. He even let one of the watchmen
smoke a pipe.

"Now, if you guys are good maybe we'll give you a good drink before we leave," Chippy told
them.

Then we went to work. We got a cro-bar and forced a door in the room where the case liquor
was kept. Everybody lent a hand and passed out the cases. Barrels were rolled out and lowered with
the elevator. We put a good load on both trucks.

The gang had a great time. Every once in a while one would take a cro-bar and smash in the
head of a barrel and then sip a drink. Chippy rubbed a lot of it in his hair—said it made him
smell good.

We made enough noise to arouse the whole city. In the midst of our work a bell rang and we
all jumped.

"Burglar alarm?" demanded Chippy, aiming his gun at the watchmen.

"No—telephone," said one of the watchmen. We marched him to the phone and made him
answer it. It was his wife calling, I think.

"Tell 'em you're busy, to call later," I said. The man made that statement and hung up.

After cutting the telephone wires and giving the four watchmen some advice about keeping still, we
made our getaway and took the liquor to the [Maxwelton] Inn. We had sixteen barrels and 120 cases.
I got a barrel and seven cases for my share. I didn't doctor it, but sold it to some friends for $2,200.

For weeks, every bootlegger in town had Jack Daniel whiskey. Some of it was the real stuff;
most of it was doctored hooch."

Several days after the robbery, police questioned the Egan gangsters. They
were forced to release them after the four watchmen told police they could not
identify the gang members as the robbers.

Bootleg Drugstores

There were easier ways to steal and sell medicinal liquor than by highway robbery. Theoretically, a patient in need of medicinal fortification took the doctor's

liquor prescription to the druggist, where it was filled and recorded. The druggist, in turn, purchased his allotment of thirty, forty, fifty, or ninety gallons—all to be dispensed in pint bottles, eight to every gallon—from a whiskey salesman representing the bonded distillery.

Even on the up-and-up, the profits were good. "Doctors write whiskey prescriptions for $3 a pint and druggists fill them for $3 a pint," the *Post-Dispatch* noted in 1920. "It costs them $25 for a case of 24 pints."

The potential for abuse was enormous, and some druggists became "bootleg drugstores." Unscrupulous salesmen would buy from unscrupulous physicians whole books of liquor prescriptions, signed and sometimes with a fictitious patient's name added, and sell them to druggists with thirsty customers. Many druggists did not destroy the canceled liquor prescriptions but gave them to the whiskey salesmen, who would "wash" out all the writing except the doctor's signature and sell them back to the druggist for 75 cents apiece. Some druggists also sent cases of good, legally purchased liquor to local cutting plants, which would add water, alcohol, and flavoring and return the product. Ten cases of alcohol could wind up as many as fifty this way. Druggists could sell the extra product under the counter without a prescription.

Much of the whiskey sold in drugstores throughout the country was not pure but "split whiskey," Lincoln C. Andrews, assistant secretary of the Treasury, told a Senate investigating committee in April 1926. Senator James A. Reed of Missouri explained the concept: "They take a gallon of approximately 100 proof whiskey, make it about half water, reducing it to about 50; then take a gallon of 100 or 110 proof alcohol and make that half water, so they have four gallons, and mix the whole together, so that the purchaser gets in the end 25 per cent alcohol, 25 per cent whiskey and 50 per cent water."

Liquor profits in part helped Benjamin Victor buy a coveted Pierce-Arrow bicycle from Mussillons in Springfield, Illinois. In high school, he was earning five dollars a week as a clerk at Ralph's Drugstore; the bicycle cost forty-five dollars. He purchased it in nine weeks and had spending money besides. He earned tips off the prescription whiskey sales and helped make bootleg gin that was sold in a back room, Victor told an interviewer in 1978. "Well, you take a gallon of grain alcohol, forty percent alcohol balanced with water," said Victor, who went on to found the Thrifty Drugs chain and become chairman of the board. "Before you put the water into it, you put glycerine, four ounces of glycerine to a gallon of gin, then we had the various drops for flavor, you know, and we used to put those together and then we added water to it after those things were dissolved. . . . We sold it for two dollars a [pint] bottle."

In St. Charles, Missouri., Dr. Otto B. Ilch served as St. Charles county coroner and health commissioner for many years. His city practice was located at 102 S. Main St. Shown here is his prescription book, which listed the patients' names and addresses, ailments, liquor prescribed, and serial numbers of the prescription stubs. A filled-out prescription is beneath the book. Courtesy St. Charles County Historical Society.

When the state legislature was in session, Victor also made money selling to his cousin, Bernard Dworwaski, who was chief lobbyist for the sanitary district in Chicago. "Every day when he was in town, I would pick up a standing order— three bottles of whiskey from the drugstore, and I delivered them to him at the St. Nicholas Hotel right at six o'clock, and I was there right on the dot, and he would take the three bottles of whiskey, give me a twenty dollar bill. Now I had to turn in eighteen dollars for the three bottles of whiskey or three liquor prescriptions; it didn't make any difference which, and nine dollars. In the meantime, I had a doctor friend that would sell me three prescriptions with some phony names on them for two dollars apiece, so I made five dollars to start out with."

Jacob L. Babler, a Republican national committeeman from Missouri, also benefited from whiskey prescriptions, former Prohibition Agent Charles D. Tamme alleged in February 1923. Tamme maintained Babler, vice president of the International Life Insurance Company, asked doctors to take out policies with his firm in return for an extension of physicians' whiskey prescription privileges. Babler denied the allegations.

The St. Charles Drug Company in downtown St. Louis was another happening place. A clerk, Joseph M. Hobbs, was convicted in November 1927 of possessing and selling liquor at the pharmacy, on the southwest corner of Ninth and St. Charles streets. The conviction later was overturned and a new trial ordered by Judge Charles Faris because Hobbs had been convicted of another Volstead Act violation in a similar case just days before, and Faris said jurors in the second case may have read news articles on the first. The arrest of Hobbs and his boss, drugstore president John Jackson, followed a visit by a prohibition agent to the store on July 8. The agent struck up a friendship with Jackson after he pretended he was a tourist and mentioned the name of a mutual friend. Jackson gave him a card on which he had written, "Joe, O.K., Jackson" which enabled him to buy liquor from the store on two occasions. The agent said the liquor was stamped with bogus Canadian revenue stamps. A subsequent search of the store turned up fifty-five bottles of prescription whiskey that the drugstore was entitled to keep in stock, because it had a permit to dispense medicinal liquor.

In Peoria, Illinois, in April 1922, six physicians and two druggists were indicted for conspiracy to violate the prohibition law after a local pharmacy bought whole books of liquor prescriptions for an average of three dollars apiece and waited for the "right" customer. When he approached, he was sold liquor and one of the prescriptions was canceled and placed on file.

At the Traveler's Inn restaurant and nightclub in Springfield, Illinois, proprietor Nick Campo kept under the bar pints of bonded whiskey obtained from Springfield drugstores, among other suppliers. "You know, the drugstores were supposed to have been for medicinal purposes," Campo recalled in 1974. "And they sell you a little bit, too. They were doing a little cheating, too. So that's the way we were getting it."

Among the biggest offenders were the proprietors of Albrecht Wholesale Drug Company at 328 E. Broadway in East St. Louis, operated by wealthy St. Louis café owners Henry Albrecht and Henry Albrecht, Jr. Some 195 gallons of illegal liquor were confiscated in a raid in March 1924; the next month, the Albrechts were sentenced to a year in jail, fined $3,500 each for multiple liquor law infractions, and branded "undesirable citizens" by Federal Judge Walter C. Lindley at Danville, Illinois. The Albrechts, who made their previous court appearance in September 1923, offered no defense.

The lure of liquor profits was hard to resist. Writing about prohibition in Cooper County, Missouri, Louis G. Geiger recalled a druggist in Clark, Missouri, who reportedly made enough money selling prescription liquor to retire early. At the state pharmacists' convention in Columbia, Missouri, in 1929, Dr. Charles E. Caspari, dean of the St. Louis College of Pharmacy, called it a mistake to give druggists the role of distribution of prescription whiskey. In outlining the abuses of the prescription privilege by pharmacies, members of the Wickersham Commission observed in 1931 that the number of drugstores had increased out of proportion to the increase in population.

UNSCRUPULOUS DOCS

In Decatur, Illinois, the city council unanimously passed a law in 1925 that abolished liquor permits in the city. "The cause back of the act was the suspected violation of the privilege by certain physicians," noted the *Decatur Review*. "In order to remedy the situation, apparently caused by a few physicians, the entire medical profession in the city suffers."

In September 1929, prohibition agents charged Dr. Clarence M. Westerman with improperly issuing whiskey permits, after they allegedly purchased eight prescriptions for three dollars each from Westerman at his office in the Arcade Building in downtown St. Louis. Westerman also failed to give them a medical examination, as was required by law, the agents said. Westerman was well known in the American Legion and in boxing and wrestling circles, the *St. Louis Star* noted.

Once in a while doctors sold their own. In November 1927, Dr. Paul R. Nemours was arrested by prohibition agents for illegally selling booze. Nemours, whose office was in the 417 Wall Building downtown, reportedly sold two prohibition agents a pint of whiskey for $5.50. He was released on $1,000 bond. "This is the first instance in St. Louis in which a doctor is accused of bootlegging," observed the *St. Louis Star*.

Dickson Terry said he was one of the lucky ones who had a doctor for a friend. "When we wanted to entertain, he would write a prescription and then we would make something which he called rectified whiskey," Terry wrote in 1964. "He combined the pint of fine, old whiskey with a pint of grain alcohol, two quarts of distilled water and a few drops of glycerin, to make it smooth. It was to be several years before I heard of blended whiskey, but that was what we had and it was quite an improvement over what the bootlegger—by this time— was delivering to our front door when we called him on the telephone."

OLD AS THE HILLS

Residents of counties that voted themselves dry prior to nationwide prohibition knew all about liquor prescription abuse. In Howard County, Missouri, in

May 1913, prosecuting attorney David Bagby took steps to revoke the licenses of some of the county's doctors, who he said had been writing such prescriptions indiscriminately during the previous few months. Some of the fifteen area drugstores failed to file a monthly list of prescriptions with the county clerk, as was required with the local option law, and a few drugstores were selling liquor on any kind of prescription, Bagby said. One drugstore alone reported 2,947 whiskey prescriptions during the period from December 1912 to April 1913.

Even those who obtained prescription booze legally had to mind their p's and q's, as Gus Nations explained in 1922. "Recently, one of our agents discovered a man standing in front of a bar in a saloon, with a prescription bottle ten days old in his pocket," Nations told a reporter. "When a person entered the saloon for a drink, the bartender set a glass in front of him, and the man with the prescription poured the whiskey, and then put the bottle back in his pocket, the bartender collecting for the drink. We considered that an illegal use of prescription whiskey, and arrested the man."

The Fenton Drug Store and Friedewald Pharmacy in Fenton, Mo., handled medicinal whiskey or "Spiritus Frumenti." A few of the prescriptions handled by the Fenton Drug Store are shown here. Courtesy Fenton Historical Society.

CHAPTER 12

THE ARM OF THE LAW

ST. LOUIS POLICE WERE HOT ON THE TRAIL OF A COUPLE OF WHISKEY-RUNNERS they had chased from Twelfth and O'Fallon streets to Eighteenth and Biddle streets. Suddenly, a women intervened. With her baby in her arms, she flung herself at the muzzle of a riot gun that Detective Sergeant Thomas Sheller was aiming at the fugitives. "Shoot, you coward!" she cried, attempting to defend the fleeing suspects. "Kill me and my baby if you want to."

"Lady, you don't understand," Sheller replied, trying to sidestep the woman, but she nimbly managed to remain in the line of fire. Finally, Lieutenant James Vasey and two other officers caught up with the suspects, Floyd Felts and Jerry R. Horner, both of St. Joseph, Missouri. Their car, filled with 126 bottles of liquor, had just rammed a sedan and seriously injured two occupants inside.

It was April 1922, two years after prohibition had taken effect. Few people were quite as militant as that mother, but police and prohibition agents found themselves in a losing battle. The majority of St. Louis residents—and many in other communities—did not support the prohibition law, and that feeling extended to those who enforced it. The prohibition enforcement ranks were always shorthanded, while the violations increased each year along with criticism for not making more arrests. Many police officers liked to drink and didn't cotton to the idea of arresting their friends and neighbors. All took exception to being shot at by gangs and bootleggers. "But even if larger appropriations were available and the prohibition force were increased, I don't think the Volstead act and the eighteenth amendment could be enforced effectively," retiring prohibition administrator Jefferson Davis Taylor, a thirty-three-year government employee, told a *Post-Dispatch* reporter in 1928. "The co-operation of at least three-fourths of the population is necessary to enforcement of prohibition in any locality. And I don't believe there is such a place in the United States."

Although local police officers, sheriffs, and deputies were expected to enforce federal and state prohibition laws, they had other duties as well. The St. Louis Metropolitan Police Department had approximately 1,800 officers for a population of about 1 million in 1924. St. Louis County, with ten times the territory and a population of about 140,000, had twenty regular deputy sheriffs

Prohibition agents pour bottles of whiskey down a sewer. Courtesy Library of Congress

that same year. Outstate communities were in much the same boat.

At the outset of prohibition, a dedicated enforcement agency was established through a branch of the Bureau of Internal Revenue first known as the Prohibition Unit, and later moved to the Treasury Department as the Bureau of Prohibition. In 1920, the unit received $2.2 million in funding and, overseen by state prohibition directors, employed fifteen hundred agents nationwide.

"The creators of national prohibition anticipated only a modest increase in the task facing law enforcement officials," David E. Kyvig observed in his book, *Repealing National Prohibition*.

By 1927, the agency's appropriation had increased to $11.9 million, and it had been placed under the leadership of an appointed prohibition commissioner and divided into twenty-four field districts that followed the boundaries of United States judicial districts. Criticized in the past as a political patronage vehicle, the bureau now required employees to pass civil service merit exams. At the national level, a field enforcement division and special investigation division handled major conspiracies, serious charges against prohibition agents, and cases in more than one district. The headquarters in Washington also oversaw various permits, legal matters, warehouse watchmen, reports and statistics, mails and files, and narcotics enforcement. It also housed a laboratory that approved plans for alcohol denaturing plants and authorized formulas to denature alcohol.

Field District 13—headquartered in Chicago—covered all of Illinois, Iowa, and one judicial district in Wisconsin; deputy administrators were located in Springfield and East St. Louis, Illinois, Des Moines and Fort Dodge, Iowa, and Milwaukee, Wisconsin. In March 1929, it employed 175 civil service employees, including 153 agents, inspectors, and chemists, its numbers woefully inadequate for a two-plus-state area that included Chicago. Most agents received a salary of $2,300, or $27,700 in today's dollars. The office spent $864,052 in fiscal year 1928 and arrested 2,780 violators, according to a report published by the Brookings Institution in 1929.

Field District 16—headquartered in St. Louis—covered Missouri and Arkansas and featured deputy administrators in Fort Smith and Little Rock, Arkansas, and Kansas City, Missouri. It employed 121 employees including seventy-three inspectors, chemists, and agents, many of the latter also earning $2,300. The office spent $304,473 in fiscal year 1928 and arrested 2,703 violators.

UNDERSTAFFED AND OVERWHELMED

Grand juries regularly investigated crime conditions in St. Louis and Jefferson counties, and the prognosis was not good. "In DeSoto and in Crystal City, the fact was brought out conclusively that many dives of every nature, and operated wide open seemingly without fear of the law, were doing business," read a January 1925 grand jury report. "Existing conditions, particularly in Valle and Joachim Townships, are so extremely bad that the Jury feels the constables in both these townships have thrown themselves open to most severe criticism on account of their laxity in the performance of their sworn duties."

The same was true in southern Illinois, a federal grand jury in Springfield reported in 1925: "From our investigation we find that in this district there are apparently two classes of violators: one class deliberately and apparently for profit, violates the law and defies its enforcement. There appears also to be another class of what may be termed negative violators. This latter class includes public officers who either connive with the violators of the law, or do not take the duties of law enforcement seriously."

"The prohibition law has not received much cognizance from the officials and citizens of Monroe County," U.S. District Judge Fred L. Wham noted dryly in October 1929, after he sentenced the mayor of Valmeyer, Illinois, and several others on liquor offenses.

A St. Louis County grand jury estimated in 1924 that the area within a twenty-mile radius of the St. Louis City courthouse furnished two-thirds of

St. Charles County Sheriff John Grothe, right, and Deputy Sheriff James Morton pose with a confiscated still. Courtesy John J. Buse, Jr., Collection, 1860–1931, Western Historical Manuscript Collection– Columbia, Missouri.

all the illegal liquor in the state. One road, North and South, earned the name "whiskey chute" for all of the liquor carried over its pavement. "Sales are made through meat markets, grocery stores, garages, soft drink parlors and by peddlers," the jury wrote. "In many cases school children of tender age are permitted to buy this poison. . . . Notorious law violators like Tony Foley, Mark Gumperts, Peter Gounis, Joe Gonella, etc., are numbered among the successes of the Federal officers, but in the reports submitted to us by Sheriff [John] Willmann they are invariably marked 'no evidence.'"

In St. Charles, local enforcement was halfhearted, and many of the prosecutions were made in federal court, Steve Ehlmann noted in *Crossroads: A History of St. Charles County, Missouri*. On at least two occasions when arrests were made, the evidence was stolen before a grand jury could convict anyone. "A former citizen of St. Charles who was recently visiting the old town informed a newspaper reporter that he received an invitation to see the still located not far from this city which has a sufficient capacity to supply the local demand," the *Daily St. Charles Cosmos-Monitor* reported in June 1925. "It has been suggested that not one but several could be found if a close search was made for stills in this county. If these reports are true somebody is certainly neglecting their duty."

LACKLUSTER IN EVERY WAY

Missouri Governor Arthur M. Hyde, attending a "prohibition luncheon" hosted by President Warren Harding at the White House in 1922, criticized the work of federal prohibition agents. Despite pledges of assistance from local law enforcement agencies, they had not brought the proper zeal or enthusiasm to their work in the state, he believed. The letters he received, from residents across the state, must have been a factor. "There must be several places here where they buy their home made brew and also where it is made," Mrs. William Schmiederkamp of Union, Missouri, wrote in 1922. "I have a brother that drinks most ever day. P.S. Names of some that my brother said he got drink from here in Union. Geo. Vossbrink. The Plumer [*sic*] Geo. Stolz. A garage man Hy Peters. A shoe repairing man. . . ." By return mail Hyde suggested she contact the state prohibition director, W. H. Allen, in Kansas City.

Ste. Genevieve was a veritable "bootleggers' paradise," Mrs. A. Rutledge wrote in 1921. "This is a town of about 2,300 inhabitants," Rutledge wrote to Hyde. "We have seven saloons, now called 'soft drink parlors,' where all kinds of intoxicants are to be had and every kind of slot machine . . . these places run all the time. . . . I am making this appeal to you in behalf of a very dear member of my family who is a victim of the habit. It is useless to refer me to our prosecuting attorney for he is 'one of the boys.' I am not a prohibitionist but favor government control of intoxicants. I am also a good republican and an ardent admirer of our President." By return mail, Hyde promised to discuss the matter with the state's attorney general.

The problems didn't go away as the years progressed. On February 6, 1931, a federal grand jury charged inefficiency in the St. Louis unit of the Prohibition Bureau. Federal Prohibition Commissioner Colonel Amos W. W. Woodcock arrived in March to investigate the jury's complaint that local units concentrated on petty cases to the exclusion of larger violators.

"The situation in St. Louis is one where there is not much activity on the part of the city and county authorities to close up speak-easies," a Prohibition Bureau official reported in 1929, "and hence we are working on the distilling and alley [bootleg] brewing end, and are unable to give very much time to the speak-easy condition; that is, the retail sales end."

A revolving-door agency, the bureau's turnover of enforcement officers ranged from a low of 15.9 percent in 1920 to highs of 50 and even 96 percent as the years progressed. By 1930, it had "moderated" to 22.7 percent.

Members of the National Commission on Law Observance and Enforcement on Prohibition Laws (a.k.a. the Wickersham Commission) concluded in 1931, "There is yet no adequate observance or enforcement." They recommended a 60 percent increase in the number of agents and a pay increase for the agents.

ON THE JOB

The continual regressions weren't always due to lack of effort. Prohibition forces scheduled frequent cleanups, but the violators returned and their numbers multiplied. During a one-month period in spring 1923, St. Louis County deputy sheriffs confiscated 75,500 gallons of booze, conducted 39 raids, and made 48 arrests. Federal agents made 114 arrests in a three-day "dry Thanksgiving" drive in November 1929 in Jefferson City, Columbia, Sedalia, Marshall, and various counties. A countywide raid netted 18 arrests in November 1932 in St. Charles, Boschertown, Orchard Farm, Harvester, O'Fallon, Flint Hill, and other areas. In East St. Louis, three weeks of "snooping" culminated in raids by 40 prohibition agents that resulted in 36 arrests in an hour and a half shortly before Christmas, 1926. In the three counties of "Little Egypt" in southern Illinois, about 150 prohibition agents were brought in from other states in July 1931 to raid 11 cities and towns in an area once dominated by Klan members and bootlegging gangs. They arrested more than 100 people, who were jammed into the Franklin County Jail at Benton.

Kirkwood, Missouri, police brought in two bloodhounds from Lexington, Kentucky, in July 1923 to help them with their captures. They arrested twenty-four alleged bootleggers and home-brew dispensers, with a few intoxicated souls thrown in for good measure, in a series of raids in April 1925. In Springfield, Illinois, in the spring of 1931, federal agents arrested nine bottleggers believed to be responsible for most of the city's supply of illegal booze. They also charged the bootleggers' supplier of corn sugar, the Hubinger Company of Keokuk, Iowa. All were convicted by a federal grand jury. Police in St. Louis made nightly raids in February 1924 on the haunts of "red-hots," or known gang associates, and pledged to continue until the crime was curbed, which never happened. On one day in February 1924 they arrested 321 people; in May 1925 they made 157 arrests in one day in liquor and gambling raids throughout the city.

Prohibition agents launched a "sniff" squad, posed as decoys, and disguised themselves as bartenders. They even set up a ruse called "home brew hound from the hills," in which a country bumpkin in a Ford touring car sought malt extract, a recipe, and other items used to make home brew. This he did at the Premiere Supply Company, at Commercial and Walnut streets in St. Louis, in

February 1923. Two hours later, two federal agents arrived with a search warrant charging that the business manufactured and sold malt extracts and syrups, compounds, and utensils for the manufacture of illicit liquor. "We do not manufacture anything, and the extract we sell contains less than one-half of 1 percent of alcohol," company vice president John J. Miravalle told a reporter. "We do not and never did give any recipes for making beer or anything else. The charges in the search warrant are ridiculous." Miravalle said he asked about the "yap" who bought the extract and was told by one of the agents the young man was as advertised. He came from a town in the hills, eighteen miles from a railroad, and never saw a tall building until he came to St. Louis a few days earlier. The country boy was proving quite successful as a decoy, the agent said.

The agents also posed as bartenders in saloons where they had arrested the owners for liquor sales. Agents took over in February 1920 at the saloon of Joseph Haderlein at 1427 South Broadway. Reported the *Post:*

> Soon a telephone call came from a man, speaking with a German accent, who asked what was the matter with the front door of the saloon. The front door bore a sign, placed there by Haderlein, which read "Closed by John Barleycorn." The inquirer was told to come in by the side door.
>
> Soon the man appeared. He carried a wicker-covered demijohn, and he asked where Haderlein was. "He's sick," said the man behind the bar.
>
> "Well," said the visitor. "I want a gallon of that $30 stuff. If you don't know which it is, I will show you the barrel. I've been getting it every day."
>
> He pointed out the barrel, and paid $30 for a gallon of the contents. Then the hidden members of the squad popped out and arrested him.

LOOKING FOR THE BOYS

A wayward pen helped demonstrate the futility of the exercise known as a raid. In November 1927, St. Louis Police Captain George Tabb of the Laclede Avenue station raided a soft drink bar at 1408 North Grand Boulevard at lunchtime, confiscated sixty-five bottles of home brew, and arrested and released on bond the bartender, Larry Brown. Tabb then discovered his pen was missing. He sent two patrolmen back to the saloon for it, but they returned empty-handed an hour and a half later. So Tabb went back himself. "He did not find the pen," the *Star* noted. "But he reported that he did find Brown again leaning languidly on the bar and sixty more bottles of home brew reposing in the icebox. Brown made another trip to the station, and the beer was confiscated."

THE THIRD TIME'S A CHARM

A few minutes after an unsuccessful raid on Charles "Buck" Keenan's bar in the Pontiac Building in February 1924, St. Louis Police Sergeant William Holtman walked down the alley in the rear of the building. There, plain as day, was a barrel of beer. He went for a patrol wagon to haul away the beer, but it had disappeared by the time the wagon arrived. So he raided the bar again, and this time there was beer in the icebox.

Attracted by the odor of mash, St. Louis police in September 1924 found a three-story-high still and portable vats containing more than twenty thousand gallons of mash in a brick warehouse at 316 S. Main Street in a block occupied by warehouses. They waited unsuccessfully for the proprietors to arrive and answered the phone when it rang. A voice on the other end wanted to know if "any of the boys had been around."

In March 1932, Jefferson City police raided the largest liquor plant ever found in the city. The four-hundred-gallon-capacity still was run by three men and a woman and located in a house in a hollow between Jefferson Street and Broadway, barely visible from Jefferson. A still was in one of the rooms; the kitchen housed a container of two thousand gallons of mash. Another room was used as living quarters for Arthur Surface, his bride of three weeks, and her brothers, Robert and Edward Wren. In the basement was yet another still, and their car held three empty ten-gallon barrels. The bootleggers operated a twenty-four-hour, two-shift business and owned a .32 caliber pistol and a billy club.

Having two sons employed as St. Louis policemen didn't save Theodore Albes, a grocer and saloonkeeper at 2361 Adams Street, from being arrested with 104 cases of 2.75 percent beer, 45 gallons of whiskey, and 10 gallons of wine by prohibition agents in February 1920. Agents said they purchased liquor from Albes for two days prior to the raid. Albes pleaded guilty and was fined three hundred dollars on each of the two counts by Federal Judge Charles Faris.

Especially outstate, agents and deputies could work long hours for a small arrest. Raids could be strenuous, dangerous, and just plain difficult. "On one steamy Missouri summer day the officers waded a swollen stream, stealthily worked through brush, then lay in wait for hours, only to discover when they pounced that the moonshiners had decamped," Louis Geiger wrote in "In the

Days of Prohibition: Cooper County, 1919–1934." "The raid turned out all right; the operators were found farther on in the woods dead drunk on their own product."

St. Louis prohibition agents spent three long hours hiding in bushes and trees on a farm near Festus, Missouri, in July 1928 as they waited for a driver to haul away 275 gallons of moonshine manufactured the previous night. Finally, a truck bearing the name Konrad Service, 2423 S. Thirteenth Street, drove up to the plant, and agents arrested the occupants, Fred Koetter and Albert Zinbel. They also arrested the still operators, Carlo Deliberto and Frank Castillone. All of the men said they were merely hired hands and received twenty-five dollars a day for their work. They declined to give their employer's name.

The government men were out of breath in April 1925, after six of them had to pull a tree down to get through a narrow place in the woods. The journey was worth the effort. A reporter from the *St. Louis Star* told of a moonshiner's last moments of freedom:

The strains of the 'Alcoholic Blues' floated softly over the Big River last night from William Price Carrow's new phonograph, neatly placed beside the big, shining still in his little brown cabin near Ware, Mo. William Price Carrow is 63 years old. He sat on a new davenette surrounded by an array of new furniture. For four months he had been a moonshiner on a consignment basis, with pleasing financial results. . . . Little did Carrow know that his red-haired hired man, Chris Johnston, out for a drive, a few miles away with a lady friend, was heading his rattling good car along the road behind other automobiles, filled with an even dozen prohibition agents from St. Louis. And neither knew that these same prohibition agents were looking for a "red-haired hired man who knows where the big still is."

Thus it was fatal to the peace and quiet of William Price Carrow and his still when Chris tried to pass the agents and they noticed his auburn locks.

"Where's old man Carrow's place?" one of the agents called.

"Right this way," said Chris over his shoulder, giving his puddle jumper the gas.

But the agents' cars had two more cylinders apiece than the one Chris drove and they pulled in ahead of him again. They stopped him and asked him if he worked for Carrow. He countered: "What do you want to know for?"

Just then one of the agents noticed a bottle in his hip pocket and removed it, diagnosing it on the spot as whiskey. The agent got in the front seat with Chris, while the lady friend moved to the rear . . . they got into the cabin in time to find the still yet warm.

It was the cleanest still the agents had ever seen, with all its copper joints polished like a ship's boiler room. The 63-year-old moonshiner told them that he got $5 a gallon for his product, and said that he sold it to St. Louis men who called for it at the cabin door some sixty miles from St.

RADIO BUST

Crawford County Sheriff Raymond Donahoe caught the news on the radio in the Schwider family garage: Al Capone had escaped from the Atlanta penitentiary in a trimotor plane, headed toward Missouri. "The plane is believed to have landed between Salem and Cuba, Missouri," the announcer's voice continued, in February 1933. A reward of twenty thousand dollars was offered, and Donahoe wasted no time making one dollar in phone calls, one to the Dent County sheriff in Salem. He dispatched automobile loads of officers.

"Donahoe was in the thick of the search when a friend informed him that the big news had been faked by Latham Schwider with the aid of an accomplice and an attachment on the garage radio," the *Naborhood Link News* noted. Schwider agreed to pay the expenses of the search, including the telephone calls. "Everyone but Donahoe enjoyed the joke," the *News* commented.

Louis. *The shining still had a capacity of 200 gallons a day.*

Clyde Williams, Carrow's stepson, was also in the cabin, and although the step-father protested that Clyde was just visiting and listening to the phonograph, both of them were given a free ride to the St. Louis jail.

Carrow pleaded guilty to operating a still in January 1926 and was sentenced by Judge Charles Faris to six months in jail and a $1,500 fine.

REPEAT OFFENDERS

To take a bite out of crime, police agencies experimented with illegal raids, or raids without search warrants, on repeat offenders. By the late 1920s, both prohibition agents and police in St. Louis made numerous raids on home-brew joints and other establishments, ostensibly to harass them. In July 1928, police from the Magnolia Avenue District showed up at the door of Louis Amberg, suspected of making and selling home brew at his home at 4337 Fyler Avenue. His wife invited police in, and Amberg helped police carry the 2,016 pints of home brew in his basement out to their truck. "I guess you've got me," he said, "but I don't want any trouble." A short time earlier, the prosecutor's office had refused police a warrant to search the home. "We didn't have a search warrant and I don't believe we can make a case without it," Captain T. George Dineen told a reporter.

In January 1929, Prohibition Administrator Sam Haley pledged to investigate raids by agents without search warrants that had resulted in the cases being discharged by U. S. Commissioner William E. Atkins because the searches were "obviously illegal." In July 1929, St. Louis Police Chief Joseph Gerk defended his policy of warrantless liquor raids, saying he hoped to break up criminal gathering places. Police made five to twenty raids nightly at home-brew joints, stores, and saloons in an effort to "mop up" the city.

Finally, in September 1929, the St. Louis Board of Police Commissioners put a stop to raids without warrants and instructed police to concentrate on more productive areas of law enforcement. "The wholesale raiding has got nowhere," said Board President Lon O. Hocker. "The same places have been raided again and again without putting them out of business."

Amos Woodcock, the federal prohibition commissioner, was fuming in 1931 over a report by Illinois State Representative Charles Adam Karch, D-St. Clair County, that prohibition agents in East St. Louis were associating with lewd women, using them as "decoys" to gather evidence and conducting raids without search warrants 50 percent of the time. In January 1931, federal prohibition enforcement policy discontinued active prosecution of private violators in favor of commercial liquor dealers.

A SOCIETY ON THE MOVE

The 45-mile trip from St. Louis to Foristell, Mo. on the western edge of St. Charles County,
which consumed two days by wagon before the coming of the automobile, was made in one hour
and thirty minutes of moderate driving yesterday by persons who attended the dedication at Wentz-
ville of the 26.5 mile strip of 18-foot concrete roadway entirely across St. Charles County.
—St. Louis Post-Dispatch, September 14, 1924

Times were changing. Cars and trucks increasingly were filling the roadways: The number of automobiles on the streets of St. Louis increased from 26,731 in 1917 to 82,045 in 1922. The same year, 392,969 automobiles and trucks were licensed in Missouri and 782,126 cars, trucks, and buses were licensed in Illinois. By 1926, there were 643,591 licensed vehicles in Missouri and 1,370,500 in Illinois. To get motorists out of the mud, road construction projects and bond issues resulted in 7,640 miles of paved roadway in Missouri by the early 1930s. Illinois by 1930 paved 9,843 miles and earned the distinction of the largest and best system of hard-surfaced roads in the country. By 1932, it boasted 12,812 miles of hard roads. "The new roads and automobiles complicated the task of law enforcement, weakening the state's ability to enforce Prohibition and other laws," Richard S. Kirkendall explained in *History of Missouri, Volume V: 1919–1953.* "Only slightly more than 11 percent of the state government's expenditures went for 'protection' from 1923 to 1928, a lower percentage than was devoted to this purpose by most of Missouri's neighbors. . . . Missourians relied mainly on the local authorities for police action, with the four largest cities devoting nearly 20 percent of their expenditures to this category."

"Machines," as they were called, were the choice of holdup men, bootleggers, and gangsters, who used them for a speedy getaway. By necessity, decentralized law enforcement became a thing of the past: Missouri and Illinois set up state highway patrols, Illinois in 1922 and Missouri in 1931.

The Illinois State Police used World War I surplus puttees, breeches, belts, caps, and even motorcycles, their acetylene headlights lit by matches. Missouri's patrols, set up nearly a decade later, had patrol cars with headlamps on the right front fenders that displayed the word "STOP" when turned on at night. Troopers investigated offenses ranging from bank robberies to chicken thefts. "This was the Prohibition era and frequently motorists stopped by patrolmen carried bootleg liquor," noted a 1981 history of the Missouri State Highway Patrol published by the Missouri Department of Public Safety. "In fear of being arrested, a driver often poured his corn liquor over the floor boards if he thought he was about to be pulled over. Such action was unnecessary if the stop was by a trooper, as he was strictly forbidden from seizing this evidence. When the strong odor of whiskey was detected, patrolmen could seldom refrain from telling the motorist of his error."

Many municipal departments added motor power to their ranks during the 1920s. In 1922, Webster Groves's new motor cop, Robert M. Turner, was "knocking 'em cold" on his new Indian motorcycle. The "Police Department, City of Jefferson" was first emblazoned on a 1925 Dodge touring car purchased by the department. In part because of bootleg whiskey raids at local roadhouses, the Kirkwood Police Department sold its motorcycle in December 1928 to purchase a Ford coach. St. Louis police had cars since 1904 and beginning in 1908 had squads to catch speeders, said Barbara Miksicek, librarian of the St. Louis Police Library. From 1921 to 1922, the police motorcycle squad tripled its arrests, from 3,514 to 11,119 for offenses ranging from careless driving to suspected burglary. In 1928, they began conducting tests of truck and bus chassis for a *super* car—a bandit-chasing armored car with bulletproof glass, able to attain a speed of fifty-

A St. Louis Police Department patrol car from November 1926. Courtesy St. Louis Metropolitan Police Department.

five to sixty miles per hour, to be built by the St. Louis Car Company.

They also obtained a ready-made armored car, a Cadillac sedan that had been purchased for about $7,000 (nearly $83,000 today) by gangster William Russo. A week after Russo bought it, St. Louis Police Lieutenant John Carroll confiscated the car and refused to give it back. Russo sued, and after much litigation the department gave him $1,700 for it.

As usual, sheriff's deputies in St. Louis County ran a poor second to the other departments. In 1924, they were expected to furnish their own automobiles and gas, oil, and tires on their salaries of $1,200 to $1,500 per year. Cars were needed not only to catch criminals, but also to transport witnesses to court. Largely unincorporated at this time, the county did not have its own police department until 1955. By contrast, the average patrolman in St. Louis earned $1,680 per year during the early 1920s and was expected to provide his uniforms and guns, Miksicek noted.

St. Charles police were in much the same boat in May 1925, when Officer Joseph Olendorff told the *Daily St. Charles Cosmos-Monitor* of missed opportunities and humiliation. "Mr. Olendorff says there were several out both Saturday night and Sunday night driving cars while drunk, and if the City would only furnish the police officers with an automobile the car would soon pay for itself in fines, but as the matter now stands the officers can only stand on the sidewalks and see the drunks and speeders go by and they give the officers the 'high ball' and 'laugh' as they go along the streets disregarding all traffic laws," the *Cosmos-Monitor* commented.

St. Louis joined the ranks of only two other cities in the country—Detroit and New York—on March 13, 1928, when a microphone for radio broadcasts was installed at the desk of the chief of police. It connected with radio station WIL at the Missouri Hotel. "The principal purpose of the microphone will be to broadcast news instantly of any major crime, so that both public and police can be simultaneously informed and lend their co-operation," noted the *Carondelet News.* The system paid off later that year in the robbery of insurance agent William Morris, held at gunpoint on Gravois Avenue by two men. The suspects ordered him to drive his Chevrolet sedan to Lemay Ferry Road and forced him out of the car near Point Breeze. Morris flagged down a passing motorist, caught a ride back to the city, and told police, who broadcast the robbery over the radio and gave the license number. "A lady living in Luxemburg [Lemay], listening in on the radio, made a note of the license number and found that the stolen auto had been abandoned near her home," the *Carondelet News* reported on December 21. "The police were notified, and the auto was restored to Morris. Morris has identified Charles Connor and Mark Miller, who are under arrest, as the men who robbed him."

HOOCH HAULERS

Liquor-fueled crimes involving automobiles kept police busy everywhere, from soused rabble-rousers to bootleggers and holdup men. In late August 1920, St. Louis County Sheriff Louis Bopp and his assistants thought they were on the trail of an auto bandit but later discovered their suspect was a private broker from 5418 Cabanne Avenue who had consumed large quantities of raisin mash. William H. Murray, escorted by a chauffeur, was headed north on McKnight Road near Ladue Road at 2 a.m. on September 1, 1920, when he decided to fire a shot from his revolver at a telephone pole. The bullet narrowly missed resident F. B. Williams, continued into the Williams's home, and hit the ceiling, dropping on the floor. The car proceeded to Busch's Grove, where employees called the sheriff about a man in an automobile brandishing a pistol. Police caught up with the car in St. Louis, at a Vandeventer Avenue saloon. Murray was arrested and held in the county jail until bond was provided the next day.

A rattled bootlegger, chased for speeding by traffic officer William Terry of Ferguson, began throwing bottles of hooch from the side of a car in December 1924. "As the chase proceeded the bottles continued to fall and by the time Terry reached the limits of his territory, according to an inventory made later, the motorist had thrown away in the neighborhood of $500 worth of 'hooch,'" the *Watchman-Advocate* reported.

In Festus, Missouri, deputy sheriffs Pete Pappas and Luther McCarty sighted a truck they suspected of running liquor in September 1929. The payload included 505 one-gallon cans of 180-proof alcohol. Truck operators John Bush and George Bowers were placed in jail at Hillsboro, pleaded guilty, and received a five-hundred-dollar fine each. One received ten days in jail, the other sixty days.

And in Paris, Illinois, St. Louis liquor-runner Floyd Washburn, alias Haverstick, was arrested in September 1925 for driving through a funeral procession in his vehicle, which contained one hundred gallons of moonshine whiskey in bottles with bonded whiskey labels. Paris police arrested him and confiscated the goods.

As more vehicles crowded the roadways, the death toll climbed from motor vehicle accidents—St. Louis had 122 fatal accidents in 1922, up from 97 in 1921—and so did the number of arrests for reckless driving and driving while intoxicated. In 1924, the St. Louis Board of Police Commissioners began including arrests for "driving auto while intoxicated" in its annual report. Some 206 incidents were reported that year, all male drivers. The next year, Municipal Judge Harry Rosecan slapped St. Louis's drunken drivers with a fine of $250 ($3,000 today), but it didn't seem to matter. By the late 1920s, the number of drunk-driving arrests in St. Louis climbed to more than six hundred per year.

Injuries from drunk and youthful drivers were taking their toll at St. Louis's City Hospital, Hospital Commissioner Dr. G. A. Jordan told the *St. Louis Globe-Democrat* in May 1924. "The demands upon the surgical wards have been particularly heavy," Jordan noted. "Skull fractures are particularly common in these cases. . . . Alcohol, in my opinion, is responsible for much of the reckless driving, while youthful drivers contribute in carelessness."

Eighteen-year-old Edward R. Daughtry blamed too much moonshine on his murder of fourteen-year-old Ethel Baxter in September 1924. Baxter died from a bullet wound to the head. Ethel, her brother Ralph, half-brother William Baxter, Elsie Patton, and Albert Glank were riding in an automobile in the 300 block of Lemay Ferry Road when Daughtry hopped on the running board and asked for a ride. He drew his revolver and told the driver to stop. "After robbing the men of some small change he attempted to embrace the girls and when one of the men struck him in the face the young bandit fired the fatal shot," the *Watchman-Advocate* reported. "Daughtry, who is a slight youth, of pleasing appearance, said in his confession that he did not know what made him kill the girl except the liquor."

Drinking While Policing

In May 1925, the St. Louis Board of Police Commissioners ruled that officers could not drink intoxicating liquor even when off duty. Previously, they had been forbidden from drinking intoxicating liquor while on duty or entering any place where intoxicating liquor was furnished except in the performance of their duty. "We are trying to give the city an efficient police force," said Allen C. Orrick, president of the board. "Theoretically a policeman is on duty all the time. When off duty he may be called upon at any time. If he has been drinking he is not in condition to work."

The policy change included the immediate firing of two probationary officers, John J. Thierry and Walter J. Wilmas, for drinking. In 1924, the board heard cases against nine officers relating to intoxication and drinking on duty. In 1925, eight such charges were heard. The number was nineteen in 1926, fifteen in 1927, twenty in 1928, nine in 1929, and seven in 1930.

Drinking, arresting, and shooting didn't mix, Deputy Constable James Shea of St. Louis County's Central Township learned in 1923. He had arrested two women on a speeding charge one evening, then accepted their invitation to join them for a drink at "Belvedere Joe" Gonella's Capri Inn on Olive Street Road near Woodson Road. While drinking at the inn, Shea allegedly became angered and fired a shot at his riding partner, Joseph Sherman, who had been tampering with Shea's automobile. Shea, who was dismissed from his duties by Constable E. L. Stanton, said the shooting was only a joke.

Pitching In

Sometimes the public helped out with anonymous tips. A marked-up cartoon mailed to St. Louis Police Chief Joseph Gerk served to quash the Memorial Day 1925 festivities at a saloon at 3232 South Grand Boulevard. The cartoon depicted swinging saloon doors, and someone inscribed the words "Graft Beer" and "Grand and Humphrey." Gerk dispatched Detective Sergeant John P. Coakley of the rum squad to the scene. "Forty thirsty celebrators of Memorial day were lined up at the bar," the *Post-Dispatch* noted. "One of them who gave his name as Peter Leilich of 3331 Gravois Avenue, a dry goods merchant, was near a highball and he was arrested, as was Charles Maynard, the proprietor.

"The raiders found a half barrel of beer on tap and two more half barrels cooling in the icebox. In a rear room they found 25 pints of whisky, two bottles of gin and some sherry wine. After the celebrators had unscrambled themselves and departed, Coakley seized the beer and liquor in the place and Maynard locked his doors."

Municipal departments and vigilante teams frequently pitched in to help local law enforcement teams with their overwhelming duties. In October 1923, for example, a team of seventeen Webster Groves businessmen named them-selves the Webster Vigilantes and pledged to assist the local police department in the prevention of traffic violations and law enforcement in general. "Owing to the low percentage of law violations it is scarcely possible that the Vigilantes will ever be called upon to act in any other way than as informants on isolated and infrequent infractions," the *Watchman-Advocate* surmised. The Madison County Vigilante Society, formed after the kidnapping of wealthy Granite City banker and store operator Charles Pershall, pledged in 1930 to rid the county of crime, gangsters, and racketeers.

Some were more political action committees than vigilante societies. In the wake of a scathing report on crime conditions by a St. Louis County grand jury, citizens formed the Law Enforcement Committee of St. Louis County in early 1924. The organization was said to represent about twenty-five thousand voters and included delegates from the Clean Election League, Church Federation, Mis-souri Pacific Suburbanites (Webster Groves, Maplewood, Kirkwood, and other lo-calities), the Improvement Association of St. Louis County, the League of Women Voters, and the Women's Christian Temperance Union. Members in March grilled Sheriff Willmann on his cleanup efforts. "Anyone but a halfwit could tell that gambling was going on inside," said Charles F. Leonard, a delegate from the Im-provement Association of St. Louis County, who had passed Tony Foley's estab-lishment at 6128 Easton Avenue (now Dr. Martin Luther King Drive) the previ-ous Sunday. "Your deputy says the place was closed that night. I say it was open, and I know. Why? If you wanted the place to be closed, it would be closed. Why don't you want the gamblers to go? Why don't you stop the killings?"

Willmann, according to the *Watchman-Advocate*, skipped the first question. He didn't know how to stop the killings, he said. "I wish, I heartily wish, that I did know," Willmann said.

Dodd W. Gibson, of the Missouri Pacific Suburbanites, told a tale of a touring car from Foley's place that drove up to a Webster Groves church on a recent Sunday, and its occupants enticed four boys to go to Foley's, offering a free ride. "What have you done to stop the operation of Foley's place?" Gibson asked. "What will you do in the future?" Willmann said he could not stop the bootleggers, because they "were out and at it again after every arrest. . . . Do you think I could be crooked when my old mother came to me and said, 'Jack, I know you are straight'?" he asked. "Do you think I would defame my children's name?" Three years earlier Willmann had been acquitted by a St. Louis County Circuit Court jury on charges of neglect of duty and failing to enforce the laws against liquor violators (see Chapter 14).

A change of sheriff failed to correct the problems, and finally in July 1925 Missouri Attorney General Robert William Otto closed Foley's place and another notorious gambling room, Fauna Flora, operated by "Markie" Gumperts.

The same criticism of law enforcers prevailed in many areas, including mid-Missouri. "Strict enforcement of the liquor laws was a regular issue in county elections," noted Louis Geiger of Boonville. "They [sheriffs] started with a great show of activity, but anyone who wanted a drink could still get it with little trouble or risk. . . ."

HOT AND COLD

Between temperance advocates on the one end and bootlegging cops on the other, law enforcement officers covered many shades of gray in the war on booze. "They felt that the enforcement of the prohibition law, itself, was really not their first responsibility," J. Willard Conlon of Springfield, Illinois, said of the local police in 1972. "In an advisory or other capacity, they would help [prohibition agents] where necessary, but in ferreting out or trying to collect evidence, I don't believe they spent much time on it at all . . . it was not really uncommon to run across an off-duty policeman either in a place of that kind or attending a social function where a good deal of liquor was served."

The law was not enforced stringently in St. Louis, Croatian American Cecilia Knez told an interviewer in 1972. "Yes, my husband, one time, came home with some . . . moonshine . . . and he bought a little pint and put it in his pocket, and the policeman came and said, 'Who gave you this one?'" Knez recalled. "He said, 'I don't know who' (he didn't want to say who) . . . and the policeman told him in Croatian, 'Well, that's all right. You go home.'"

Some of the arrests were for show, at least in St. Louis County, Roger W. Taylor noted in his book *Born in the County.* "In general, the local authorities

A prohibition agent smashes a barrel of liquor.
Courtesy Library of Congress.

looked the other way—it was the Feds you had to watch out for," Taylor wrote.
"According to the stories my uncles told me, the local sheriff would ride out on
his motorcycle to warn the brewmasters of any planned bust. Occasionally, for
PR purposes, a bust was staged. An old still no longer in use would be set up.
The next day the papers would have a photo of a beat-up still and some down-
on-his-luck local who was paid to take the rap. By the time the papers had been
circulated the next day, the local was out of jail, and the smell of fresh brew was
once again rising from the creek bottoms."

In Madison, Illinois, police interfered little in the escapades of soft drink
proprietors and prostitutes, although blacks in the community were more likely
to be arrested for possession and fined, Ron Stern noted in *A Centennial History
of Madison, Illinois, 1891–1991.*

Those who did their jobs often were harassed. In July 1923, prohibition
agents George Bausewein, Louis "Jean" Gualdoni, Albert Burrows, and Special
Deputy P. E. Toelle raided the Florissant farm of John H. Toebben after watching for several weeks. It was their second raid on the farm, and they found three
vats of thirty thousand gallons each and four stills with a capacity of one thousand gallons each. Left to guard the contraband from early morning to late night

on July 23, Toelle and Burrows faced a dry duty in more ways than one. "The agents said whenever they tried to obtain a drink of fresh water, the farmers denied there was any water on the place, in order to emphasize the unpopularity of prohibition agents in St. Louis County," the *Watchman-Advocate* reported.

Although raids were said to be a weekly occurrence in the Italian American Hill neighborhood, in some cases residents and St. Louis's law enforcement cooperated, Gary R. Mormino noted in *Immigrants on the Hill*. Prohibition Agent Gualdoni, a Hill resident, on occasion received advance notice of a raid and warned his still-operating friends to be careful.

"I'd go out on a job with a search warrant, and the first thing you know, I'd run across one of my friends operating a still," Gualdoni told Mormino in 1982. "What could I do?"

Others in public service took bribes, Roland DeGregorio told Mormino in 1973: "My father was connected with the biggest whiskey-making group that there was here. On the Hill, I was probably in the fourth grade and he told me, 'Don't let no kids in this house!' So what did I do? I let a couple of kids in . . . they got in the shed and turned on the spigot and started drinkin' the moonshine. Ohhh, they got plowed. In fact, they got sick . . . the mother of one of the kids called the fire department. They came down and pumped the kid out. My dad, I remember he told me in later life that it cost him two five-gallon cans as a hush. Now you talk about moonshine—I know!"

WHISKEY, EASTERN STYLE

The Italians often took the rap for making hooch, and plenty of German Americans and native-born Americans were arrested as well. But it was news when police arrested their first Chinese American moonshiner in September 1922 on the farm of George Lee on Hall's Ferry Road in St. Louis County, according to a reporter for the *St. Louis County Watchman-Advocate:*

> *"George protested in pidgin English that the still 'no belong to him; that it belong to his father who had used it for long time make medicine. Poor father die year ago. No think he die from moonshine medicine. Just die, and leave George still to make more medicine so George no die.'*

Lee was arrested for violating the Volstead Act and released on $1,000 bond.

In the Line of Duty

Police and law enforcement officers paid for some liquor-related crimes with their lives. "The 1920s were the most devastating years for the St. Louis Metropolitan Police Department," noted Barbara Miksicek. "Forty-six officers lost their lives in the line of duty during the 'Roaring Twenties.' While not necessarily connected directly to Prohibition, the number of police officer deaths indicates how dangerous the streets of St. Louis were during that period of our history."

The first officer to be killed was George E. Geisler, who had entered the soft drink bar of William English at 2100 Clark Avenue on Halloween night of 1920. Gangsters Robert and Thomas Creed shot him to death following an argument. The brothers had sought revenge on Geisler after he had arrested another Creed brother.

On June 23, 1922, Prohibition Agent Charles O. Sterner was shot and killed while searching for liquor at an undisclosed location in St. Louis. He was followed by St. Louis Police Officer William H. Anderson on February 11, 1924, in Edward M. (Putty Nose) Brady's bar at Vandeventer Avenue and Natural Bridge Road. Anderson was reportedly shot by Egan gangster Eddie Linehan (see Chapter 8). The bar was described as a tough, boisterous joint by neighbors, and its lease later was revoked by the building's owner, Anheuser-Busch.

Later that year, on July 26, St. Louis Police Officer Bernard "Smiling Barney" Early was shot to death in Michael Wood's saloon at 3880 Easton Avenue (now Dr. Martin Luther King Drive) by a robber.

St. Louis Patrolman Frank H. Kohring died on February 17, 1926, of leg injuries that worsened after he was kicked in the leg by John Maloney, whom he had arrested for public drunkenness near Cass Avenue and Eighteenth Street. A drunk driver killed Patrolman Joseph P. McGovern on November 11, 1928, at Arsenal Street and Iowa Avenue. He was crushed against a brick wall by a car driven by Herman Williams, who was charged with manslaughter. McGovern left behind a wife and nine children.

Others were near-misses. "Constable Kleeschulte reported that he had been warned [in 1927] by armed men not to interfere with the sale of 'hooch' to the patrons of a dance in O'Fallon," Steve Ehlmann wrote. "Another police officer had a bomb thrown on the front porch of his home. These incidents led some citizens, including Robert Langenbacher, Guy Motley, and Dr. J. L. Roemer, president of Lindenwood College, to call a 'law and order' meeting where a resolution was passed calling on law enforcement officers to enforce the law." Prohibition Agent Gualdoni narrowly escaped a barrage of gunfire one time after his wife opened the front door to their home on Reber Place in St. Louis. A dynamite blast damaged the home of Marshall B. Peterson, a reform candidate for St. Louis County sheriff, at 437 Foote Avenue in Webster Groves in July 1928.

Sometimes it was difficult to tell who was worse, the scofflaw or the law. Prohibition Agent Carrol T. Byrd was severely beaten by Maxville (Arnold) saloonkeeper Peter Frederitzi in November 1930. Byrd, whose head required twenty-two stitches, said Frederitzi was running his place "wide open" and said Frederitzi knocked him down when he attempted to grab a bottle of whiskey for evidence, then struck Byrd in the head with a lead-loaded billy club he retrieved from under the bar.

Frederitzi gave a different account of the incident. "Byrd and two deputy sheriffs came rushing into my place wild-eyed," he said in a statement. "Byrd tried to get behind the bar. He almost knocked me down in the rush so I punched him on the jaw and when he went down I gave him a good beating with my fists.

"When the deputies pulled me off, Byrd drew his revolver and invited me to come outside. I told him I'd do it if he'd throw the revolver down but he refused the invitation."

Byrd, who did not have a search warrant, "has a reputation for being handy with his fists during liquor raids," commented a reporter for the *Naborhood Link News*. Frederitzi was arrested and charged with violating the prohibition law, and U.S. Attorney Louis H. Breuer ordered an investigation of the incident.

In February 1922, Prohibition Agent Douglas Baker was charged with assault with intent to kill Henry Kraemer, Sr., proprietor of a soft drink parlor at 7343 Manchester Avenue in Maplewood. Kraemer's son, Henry Kraemer, Jr., said three men came in, and two of them ordered beer, the other water. He told them he didn't have beer. The men did not announce themselves as prohibition officers, and he said he did not know who they were. At one point the bartender broke a bottle that the officers believed contained whiskey, and a free-for-all fight started. Young Kraemer, an athlete, floored agent Gus Nations with a blow to the back of the ear, and the men hopped on Kraemer and fought their way out of the front part of the saloon. Young Kraemer's father came to the rescue of his son and was shot in the left leg between the ankle and the knee. After firing the shot, the men jumped in an automobile and drove away, leaving Kraemer prostrate on the sidewalk. At the time of the charges, the elder Kraemer was still in the hospital.

THAT'S IT, I QUIT

Not surprisingly, many in the prohibition enforcement business became weary. Among them were W. H. Allen, Missouri's dry chief, who decided to retire after he became ill with pneumonia in 1923. A former country banker, Allen was said to have found the prohibition work distasteful and was depressed by the "snooping" that the job required. Allen had been criticized by federal prohibition administrators as not being sufficiently aggressive in his post and by prohibition opponents as having authorized the infamous raid on the Chase Hotel (see Chapter 1). Illinois's federal prohibition director, John Kjellander, also announced his resignation in 1923 and expressed doubt that the law could be enforced in Illinois.

Former Assistant Prosecuting Attorney Lena Frank made a new name for herself in St. Louis Court of Criminal Correction in 1923 when she began representing defendants in liquor cases. Prospective clients seemed impressed that Frank had enjoyed success for two years as a prosecutor.

Though it was usually the other way around, once in a while a defector would join the prohibition forces. Merritt D. Padfield, former salesman for Plymouth Paper Company, turned prohibition detective in July 1928 and secretly began collecting evidence on the bartenders to whom he had sold paper supplies for nine years. When he came to federal court in January 1929 to testify, about seventy bartenders jammed the corridors to have a look at him. "So that's him," muttered one as he took his seat.

Asked about a given saloon, Padfield would search through his index cards for the name: in this case, Julius Heinrichs, owner of a saloon on the northwest corner of Second and Pine streets. He told prohibition administrators he purchased beer, whiskey by the glass, or whiskey in bottles from Heinrichs on fourteen occasions, eight times alone and six with colleagues from the prohibition enforcement unit. "Padfield also testified against Frank Renje, whose saloon is on the southeast corner of Second and Pine streets, facing Heinrich's place, and against other bartenders figuring in 51 pre-Christmas raids precipitated by Padfield when he decided to take up detective work as a side line to the selling of paper," a *Post-Dispatch* reporter wrote. Padfield was fired by Plymouth Paper when his prohibition activities became known, in response to complaints by irate customers.

Both Padfield and Carrol T. Byrd were later transferred out of the St. Louis prohibition district by Commissioner Woodcock, due to complaints made against them.

CHAPTER 13

SEE YOU IN COURT

THE CASE SEEMED IRONCLAD AGAINST SALOON PROPRIETOR RICHARD WINKLEMANN of St. Louis, who in October 1920 became the first defendant in U.S. District Court to be tried by a jury for violation of the Volstead Act. Prohibition Agent Louis Gualdoni testified that he purchased two drinks of raisin whiskey from Winklemann at his saloon at 2034 Olive Street the previous March 22. He returned the following day and purchased a forty-cent drink from Winklemann's bartender, after prohibition officials recorded the serial number of the one dollar bill he used. The bill was found in Winklemann's till.

A jury did convict Winklemann on October 27, but without the help of prominent businessman Louis Idler. Idler, vice president of the A. Moll Grocer Company in St. Louis, was on the jury panel selected to try Winklemann. Idler was excused from service after he expressed his prejudice against the Volstead Act. "Are you so prejudiced that you would not convict a person shown to have violated that act?" asked Vance J. Higgs, special assistant attorney general. "The government would have to make a mighty strong case," replied Idler.

Idler wasn't alone. The same attitude prevailed in the jury panel on a federal case in February 1923 that involved a local firm charged with the sale of home-brew paraphernalia. "If you can prove that the home brew is being made for sale, I'd be in favor of a conviction," J. F. Kemp of St. Louis told prosecutors. "But if a man is making it for his own use I don't agree with the law. I believe that a man who comes home from a hard day's work ought to have his home brew if he wants it. The only reason I don't make it is because I don't know how."

A. C. Valle of DeSoto, Missouri, said if anyone wanted to make home brew, it was "all right with me." Although he didn't like the law, he "guessed" he would uphold it as a juror and was tentatively retained on the panel. Kemp also was retained. "Juries in the Courts of Criminal Correction have almost unanimously refused to convict defendants put on trial by the Prosecuting Attorney's office," the *Post-Dispatch* reported in September 1929.

NO RESPECT

Few in St. Louis respected the Volstead Act, and that held true with juries, prosecutors, and some judges. A Clayton jury in October 1929 acquitted Henry Kuhn of Luxemburg (Lemay) on a charge of illegal possession of liquor. St. Louis County deputy sheriffs testified they found more than one hundred bottles of beer and a quantity of wine at Kuhn's home, and they entered with a search warrant. Attorneys for Kuhn, however, argued that there were no labels on the bottles of beer placed in evidence to show Kuhn had made it.

There is no prohibition in St. Louis, former U. S. Senator George Williams, R-Missouri, told the U.S. House Judiciary Committee in February 1930, during a hearing on bills to modify the prohibition law. Grand juries refuse to indict liquor law offenders and state prosecutors run for office on non-enforcement platforms, he said. "The prosecuting attorney and the Circuit Attorney in his section of the State of Missouri, Mr. Williams said, are elected with the tacit understanding that prohibition violations will be overlooked," the *New York Times* reported. "He recited two cases from his personal knowledge, in which he said poor men had been hired to serve jail sentences for wealthy persons who had run afoul of the Federal law."

Some judges were openly sympathetic toward the little guy, and openly critical of prohibition enforcement. In the fiscal year ending in 1928, 548 police liquor cases were presented in state courts in St. Louis, with $300 in fines collected from 5 defendants and $68,600 in fines against 338 defendants stayed on payment of costs or on good behavior. The remainder of the cases were otherwise disposed of by Judges Edward E. Butler and Paul A. Gayer. "Every liquor case that has come into my court has been a police case without complaining citizens," Butler explained to a reporter in 1928. "The thief injures another citizen, but his minimum fine is less as fixed by law than that of the man against whom no complaint other than by police is made."

Gayer saw things the same way. "The defendant in a liquor case is usually some poor devil working for the higher-ups," Gayer said. "If the police want to enforce prohibition let them get some of the big fellows. They find a bottle in a man's pocket and can make a case against him, but I am not going to fine him $200 or send him to jail. Let the police get the bootlegger who sold him the liquor and who is making the money."

LIQUOR LOGJAM

The wheels of justice were slowed to a grind by a jam of liquor cases the first year out of the prohibition starting gate. On January 10, 1921, St. Louis County Circuit Court opened with 294 cases, the largest docket in the history of the court. "Liquor cases, almost extinct since the war placed a ban on the liquor traffic and later by the Volstead Act, are now coming back in a new form, under the title of "unlawful use of intoxicating liquors," reported the *St. Louis County Watchman-Advocate.*

In Danville, Illinois, 226 defendants crowded into the U.S. District Courtroom on March 3, 1924, to answer charges made in Williamson County dry raids over the previous five months. With wives, children, and bondsmen figured in, the crowd swelled to five hundred, the *St. Louis Star* reported. Fewer than twenty-five pleaded guilty, and the rest were given trial dates.

The September 1927 liquor cases in U.S. District Court in St. Louis ended with 76 of 110 defendants sent to jail for terms of thirty or sixty days. Thirty-four defendants paid a total of $12,870 in fines.

During the first six years of prohibition enforcement, beginning in January 1920 and ending in December 1925, the number of cases on federal court dockets in Missouri's Eastern District were ten times the number before prohibition, with numbers increasing annually. The courts processed 2,191 convictions over the six-year period and assessed $888,751 in fines, a majority from cases in the city of St. Louis.

Federal Judge Charles Faris of St. Louis modified his fine and sentencing policies over the years in attempts to increase the number of guilty pleas, to reduce the numbers of cases on the docket, and to reduce the numbers of repeat offenders. Nothing seemed to work. In May 1924, Faris sent bootlegger Mike Bartcheller to jail for six months and fined him five hundred dollars. Bartcheller, of Affton, was suffering from gout and hobbled into court on crutches to answer a charge of operating a still. The sentence was the minimum allowed under the Willis-Campbell Act, which revived the still and mash sections of an old revenue law. "I sympathize with your condition but the situation in St. Louis County is so big a stench in the nostrils of decency that something must be done to stamp out the illicit liquor traffic there," Faris told Bartcheller. "I am beginning to believe there is a still behind every bush."

Judge Charles B. Davis was appointed to assist Faris the following year, but the cases kept coming. In 1929, Faris passed sentence on Rosie Cohen, who said she turned to selling liquor as a livelihood after her laborer husband was out of

A view of downtown St. Louis and the government buildings in the 1920s. From left are the Civil Courts Building, the Federal Building, City Hall, the Municipal Courts, and the Municipal Auditorium.

work and her daughter was ill in a hospital. She pleaded guilty to selling a drink of whiskey to a prohibition officer in her kitchen at 2906 Sheridan Avenue. "I don't know what to do with you," Faris told Cohen. "This is one of the troubles with this law—it corrupts men, women and children. I will fine you $1,000 and upon the payment of $200 I will parole you for two years. I will try to make you law-abiding in that way."

In East St. Louis, Federal Judge George English was observed by a *Post-Dispatch* reporter as being particularly lenient with violators who had large families to support. He assessed the heaviest fines against those who told the court they had not done anything since they quit the saloon business. In September 1924, to clear a burgeoning docket of liquor cases, English instituted a policy of allowing defendants with guilty pleas to pay only fines and collected $50,000 in a three-week period. On September 20, 1924, alone, fifty-one St. Clair County saloon and roadhouse proprietors were assessed $19,500 in fines, or from $100 to $1,025 per individual. Many of the charges had been made the previous spring in a liquor cleanup by the Ku Klux Klan. The fine-only policy for guilty pleas was used by other judges on certain days, known as "bargain days" in United States courts. In fiscal year 1928, federal courts in Missouri collected fines of $238,709, and in Illinois $421,761, from prohibition act violators. The average fine nationwide was $103 ($1,220 today) and in southern Illinois $309.

THE FOURTH AMENDMENT

Most judges required police or prohibition agents to obtain search warrants for any liquor-related charges to stick. In March 1921, U.S. District Attorney James E. Carroll in St. Louis dropped prosecution of three hundred cases of alleged violation of the Volstead law. This followed a decision by Judge Faris that liquor or stills obtained by prohibition agents or policemen without search warrants could not legally be used as evidence in the prosecution of alleged prohibition law violations. The dropped cases left five hundred legally sound dry law cases on the court docket.

Among the cases thrown out was one against John Acinnelli and Joe Orlando, who had had raisin mash seized from their homes the previous summer. Acinnelli and Orlando asked the court to have the raisin mash removed as evidence against them. Police officers testified they had raided the home after they smelled the odor of raisin mash inside. They did not have a search warrant but acted on information contained in an anonymous letter.

Faris said the Volstead Act specifically provided that no private dwellings could be searched without a search warrant, and that no search warrant could be issued unless the evidence showed that the liquor was being made for sale. He called the actions of search-warrantless officials an obstruction of justice and a waste of time.

Not all judges agreed. In 1929, in Jefferson City, Federal Judge Albert E. Reeves maintained that a dry agent with a good nose needs no warrant. If the agent smells the odor of what he believes is mash used for making liquor, he has a right to search the premises without a search warrant, Reeves said.

During thirteen years of nationwide prohibition, the St. Louis County prosecuting attorney's office obtained 584 search warrants for the purpose of enforcing the National Prohibition Act, or slightly more than 44 legally authorized searches per year. Often, however, police and prohibition agents searched private dwellings and homes regardless of whether they had warrants. Irving Mitchell, a St. Louis church elder and U.S. commissioner, resigned in 1922 after criticizing the overzealous manner in which the agents and police raided private dwellings and homes in search of liquor law violations. Mitchell, who called himself a "sane dry," drew criticism from some circles when he refused to issue search warrants in a number of prohibition cases.

And in 1924, U.S. Senator James Reed said break-ins by prohibition enforcement agents to homes and businesses without search warrants had caused great resentment, and in many instances property damage as well. A case against

A sampling of confiscated liquor during prohibition days. Courtesy Library of Congress.

proprietor Christina Cafferata and eleven waiters of the Cafferata Cafe, Delmar Boulevard and Hamilton Avenue, was dismissed for lack of evidence by U.S. Commissioner George V. Berry in January 1923. Berry also ruled that a restaurant is a public place and a prohibition enforcement officer does not need a search warrant to raid it. However, there was no evidence to show that liquor found by agents belonged to any of the defendants, Berry said. This included four ounces in a tumbler in the linen cabinet and a quart bottle found behind a soiled apron in what appeared to be a storage room.

In 1929, two police officers raided the home of Eli Smith, an African American living at 2225 Lucas Avenue, without a search warrant and seized a half-pint of whiskey from him. Smith, they testified, told them he had been selling whiskey. Faris would have none of it and acquitted Smith because there was no evidence of a sale having been made from the home. "It is true the officers testified that this man admitted he had been selling whiskey," Faris said. "But there is no corpus. One of you gentlemen might admit that you killed John Smith but you couldn't be convicted unless it was shown by competent evidence that John Smith had been killed."

While reiterating to police in 1923 that homes are inviolate, St. Louis Prosecuting Attorney Albert L. Schweitzer mentioned some exceptions. "The sanctity of the home should ever be preserved," Schweitzer said. "It is of course understood that the police can follow a felon into a home, and having knowledge of his hiding in a particular home, can enter that home and search for that guilty party, and this can be done without a search warrant. In all other instances where the police are legally in a home and discover violations of the liquor law, arrests can be made for that violation."

The U.S. Supreme Court refused to review the conviction of Tony Milyonico and Phillip Abbacco for violating the prohibition law at the Milyonico home in Collinsville. Prohibition agents in December 1928 detected the odor of mash as they passed the home. The defendants said the search was illegal because agents had no search warrant. The government alleged the defendants waived the right to a search warrant by inviting the agents to enter, and lower federal courts upheld that position. Milyonico was sentenced to a year in jail and a one-thousand-dollar fine. Abbacco was sentenced to six months in jail and fined five hundred dollars.

DRASTIC MEASURES

At the outset, sentences for violating the Volstead Act were not severe on first offenders, with a maximum fine of one thousand dollars or six months in jail. Second offenders were subject to a two hundred to two-thousand-dollar fine, or one month to five years in prison, or both. Over the years, however, stringent legislation was added in an unsuccessful attempt by authorities to get a handle on rampant abuses. The Missouri legislature passed its "McCawley Bone Dry" law in April 1923, one of the most stringent state prohibition acts in the nation. It divided offenses into misdemeanors and felonies; those guilty of a misdemeanor could be fined five hundred to one thousand dollars and/or given a sentence of six months to a year in jail. Those guilty of felony offenses—to give away or sell intoxicating liquor that killed others or caused them to become blind, insane, paralyzed, or violently mad—were subject to a term of at least two years in the state penitentiary or a fine of one thousand dollars and imprisonment in the county jail for one year. Manufacturers or transporters of moonshine and corn whiskey also fell under the felony provision.

Nationwide, the Jones Act of March 1929 stiffened maximum penalties for transportation or sale of intoxicating liquor to five years' imprisonment and a $10,000 fine. On the plus side for small dealers, it instructed judges to distinguish between commercialized operations and minor violations, Kenneth M. Murchison noted in *Federal Criminal Law Doctrines: The Forgotten Influence of National Prohibition.*

Reaction to the law was immediate and drastic. Within two weeks, 195 saloons in St. Louis alone closed their doors, including four adjacent to the Municipal Courts, City Hall, and police headquarters. The number of acute alcoholic cases treated at City Hospital dropped by ninety-four in an eighteen-day period. Many soft drink bars that continued to operate did so by delivery only. The price of bootleg whiskey rose from fifteen to twenty-five dollars for a five-gallon can and fifty to seventy-five cents by the drink, and bartenders hired by bootleggers began demanding one hundred dollars a week. "It had been the custom, more or less, for the proprietors to remain in seclusion, and let the bartender pose as the owner," a professional bondsman explained to the *Star.* "If the place was raided, or prohibition agents made a buy, the bartender took the charge and if he got a sentence, the owner paid him so much for every day he spent in jail.

"Now, there are going to be few bartenders who will take the chance of getting five years in prison for a little money, and it's a cinch that the proprietors won't take the chance."

Those who remained in business began carrying weapons and added equipment such as smoke screens, with which they could "fog" pursuers from their vehicles and make a quick getaway. Many went to jail under the new law, which took effect immediately. "Liquor law violators who pleaded guilty before Federal Judge Faris today found that the Court's usual leniency to bartenders, as distinguished from saloon proprietors, was missing," the *Post-Dispatch* reported on March 15, 1929. "Both classes of offenders drew three months in jail for a sale, whereas bartenders formerly got only two months. Twenty-four bootleggers pleaded guilty; 14 received jail terms, the rest were fined."

On March 21, Federal Judge Charles B. Davis sent fifteen of twenty-four liquor law violators to jail, including two women. The next day Faris saddled twenty-two-year-old Elvin Drumm with a $440 fine and two months in jail for sale and possession of liquor in a saloon at 714 N. Eighth Street. Faris was not swayed when Drumm's attorney noted his client had married two weeks before and had forsaken bootlegging to become a drug clerk. "The Court is sorry to have to disturb his honeymoon, but the young man should have had in mind that little game of our childhood: 'Heavy, heavy, hangs over your head,'" Faris said.

In 1931, Missouri legislators repealed the punishment section of the state "Bone Dry" law and substituted jail sentences and fines for penitentiary sentences. It also allowed the trial judge to set the minimum fine for first offenders from one to one thousand dollars and/or not more than one year in jail.

Tell It To the Jury

There was no shortage of intriguing liquor cases. In Boone County in May 1929, a jury deliberated for more than twenty-four hours but failed to return a verdict in the case of Lou Golden, a seamstress from Rocheport who hobbled from rheumatism into the courtroom. "I use that liquor to take the swelling out of my knees, and anybody who wants to can try it and find out that it'll do it," Golden told the jury. She said she used the bottle, one-third filled with corn whiskey when it was confiscated, for external purposes only. Officers came across the bottle after they searched her home, unsuccessfully, for stolen items. With other cases to try, Judge H. A. Collier dismissed the jury. "This is perhaps the first time in several years that a jury has pondered at such length without reaching a decision, in the matter of the possession of intoxicating liquor," the *Columbia Missourian* noted.

It was not unusual for evidence to shrink, or disappear altogether, as Mae Tuttle of Springfield, Illinois, recalled in 1985. "Old Ira Dudley, when they raided his place, they took this wine and had it in a big tank like a water tank, like what they sprinkle the roads with," she said. "They took one of them big water tanks out to his place. They put that wine in one of them big water tanks, and they hauled it to town. They put in there on the corner of Seventh and Jefferson where us kids used to play.

"They had a policeman watch that wine day and night until the day of the trial. The day of the trial they had the jurors go over there to get the wine for evidence that Ira Dudley was a bootlegger. When they poured it out, they had nothing but water."

Dudley had pulled a fast one on authorities, it seemed. "I heard Ira Dudley laugh about them having a policeman sitting there watching all that water," Tuttle said. "He never was convicted of nothing."

"I Order You..."

Just about everybody had an excuse for their liquor infractions, and sometimes the judges bought them. While standing trial at U.S. District Court in Danville, Illinois, in April 1924, Oscar Greathouse told Judge Walter C. Lindley he used mash he had found by the side of the road to feed the hogs at his Marion, Illinois, farm. Lindley found Greathouse not guilty.

What might be termed the most gutsy excuse ever used for a charge of drunkenness and violating parole was made by Herbert Taylor of Taylorville, Illinois, in May 1924. Taylor testified under oath before County Judge C. J. Vogelsang in Pana that four unknown men had grabbed him and poured the whiskey down his throat. "You get another chance to make good," said the judge. "Discharged."

Nick Campo, who ran the Traveler's Inn in Springfield, Illinois, asked for parole and got it from Federal Judge Louis Fitzhenry, at a time everyone else was getting six months in jail. His benefactor was a prohibition agent named Brice Armstrong who was a "freelance" agent in that he was not confined to a single geographic area, Campo told an interviewer in 1974. Armstrong was a trusted man who couldn't be bought, he said. "He used to come in my place all the time," Campo said. "I didn't know who he was."

Armstrong raided the place one night. Campo told him he didn't want to go to jail. "'Well,' he says, 'I'll tell you. . . . You tell your lawyer that when the judge . . . he's going to say, "Six months and five hundred dollars, for everybody this morning." Tell your lawyer to apply for probation.'"

Police officers from the Carr Street Station supervising the draining of a mash vat in an illicit Franklin Avenue distillery, 1920s. Courtesy the Missouri History Museum.

After some debate the incredulous lawyer did that, and Campo got probation. He thanked Armstrong. "You run a nightclub," Campo quoted Armstrong as saying. "You serve a lot of good food. You didn't cheat anybody—I was there many times. These other nightclubs, every time we go in there—my partner and I—we have three or four girls come and sit at the table, mooch drinks from us. At your place, nobody ever mooches any drinks. I know you cheated a little bit, but you run a good, decent place."

Because immigrants were involved in many cases, deportation at times was part of the sentence. In November 1921, twenty-three-year-old Tropea Giuseppe was fined one thousand dollars in St. Louis County Circuit Court and sentenced to a year in jail after he pleaded guilty to manufacturing intoxicating liquor. Giuseppe had only been in the country four months and recently was arrested a second time for tending a still, so Prosecuting Attorney Fred Mueller said he believed Giuseppe came to America for the express purpose of manufacturing moonshine. He offered the suspect parole if his friends would buy him a ticket to Italy and give bond for his prompt departure. If Giuseppe returned or did not leave, Mueller said he would declare the bond forfeited and have the suspect arrested to serve out his term.

Draconian Measures

When judges did the sentencing, some of the rural fellows were a bit on the harsh side. County Judge D. I. Kirkham of Cairo was credited with the record for a first offender in the local court in November 1924, when he sentenced Ernest Fries of Dogtooth Bend to sixty days in jail and a five-hundred-dollar fine for possessing and transporting liquor.

Big-city municipal judges tended to be more lenient, and in February 1929 the *Columbia Missourian* took them to task for not sending any violators of the state "Bone Dry" law to the Missouri Penitentiary. "It appears that in certain sections of the state where feeling is strongly in favor of prohibition offenders have received from two to five years' imprisonment in the penitentiary, and that in other sections where prohibition is unpopular nobody has been sent to prison," the *Missourian* complained. "More than 600 have been sent to prison from the smaller districts, while in larger places few have been indicted for liquor violations. For instance, St. Louis has not sent anybody to prison, and Kansas City has sent only one. Jefferson City is another town which has convicted no one. . . . If it is fair for one to spend five years in prison it is fair for all."

Perhaps the *Missourian* spoke too soon. In June 1924, St. Louis's Federal Judge Faris sentenced August Clausen to eighteen months in the federal penitentiary in Leavenworth, Kansas. Clausen, a farmer at Weber and Union Roads in south St. Louis County, pleaded guilty of failing to register a still, a felony offense under an old revenue law that was revived by the federal Willis-Campbell prohibition law. Agents found the still in his barn. "This is believed to be the most severe sentence ever meted out here on a plea of guilty to violation of the dry laws," noted the *St. Louis Star.*

In December 1926, the Missouri Supreme Court reversed the liquor conviction of James Stratton. In northeast Missouri, a Marion County jury had sentenced Stratton to two years in the state penitentiary for passing around a bottle of whiskey to his co-workers while baling hay in July 1923. The court reversed the sentence and ordered a new trial, saying the state charged but failed to prove that the whiskey he distributed was "moonshine." One witness at the trial testified the stuff was "as good as bottled in bond," but no one said it was "moonshine."

PEN PALS

From the St. Charles County jail to the Missouri State Penitentiary, holdovers and jails were stuffed beyond capacity with liquor cases. By the time of the Jones Act in 1929, St. Louis judges were farming out prisoners to jails in Huntsville, Palmyra, New London, and Troy, Missouri. "Sheriff Grothe went to St. Louis yesterday and brought nine more Federal prisoners to the St. Charles jail, to serve terms of from thirty days to six months," reported the *Daily St. Charles Cosmos-*

Monitor on June 7, 1925. "Two women were among the prisoners brought out yesterday. Mr. Grothe now has fifty-eight Federal prisoners in the county jail."

Time Magazine called it "cattle-herding" in 1929 and said the situation was the same at prisons all over the country. The Missouri Penitentiary was 42 percent over capacity. Nationwide, one in every five prisoners was in for violating the Volstead Act, the Department of Justice estimated in 1927; federal penitentiary populations had doubled from 1919 to 1926.

By April 1930, officials at the Jefferson City pen feared a riot. Not long before, four hundred prisoners refused to leave the main dining room and protested against food and living conditions. The prison's normal capacity of 2,661 had been stretched to 4,052 inmates. Two years later, it reached a population of 4,577 inmates.

Most of the prisoners did not come from St. Louis, members of the Wickersham Commission concluded after reviewing a study of state criminal cases in St. Louis courts made for the Missouri Association for Criminal Justice. Ninety-six percent of convictions in 1928 resulted in little or no penalty: Of 487 defendants who pleaded guilty or were convicted, only four were imprisoned, and none for more than sixty days.

Insufficient evidence and a distrust of the overzealous tactics of prohibition agents was a factor in the leniency, the commission concluded. "In many instances, the character and appearance of the prohibition agents were such that the United States attorney had no confidence in the case and juries paid little attention to the witnesses," the commission wrote. "On the other hand, the prohibition agents were more concerned to secure a large number of arrests or seizures than to bring to the District Attorneys carefully prepared cases of actual importance. It is safe to say that the first seven years' experience in enforcing the law resulted in distrust of the prohibition forces by many of the United States attorneys and judges."

JAILBIRDS WE HAVE KNOWN

Some convicted of liquor crimes served their sentences quietly and fully; many others were released early from the overcrowded jails and prisons. And some served creative sentences—or none at all. The *Columbia Missourian* couldn't resist commenting in March 1929 on the fate of two St. Louis café managers, Hugo Babler and Henry J. Stalker, who were convicted of violating the prohibition law. Both had been sentenced to six months in jail and a four-hundred-dollar fine, but Federal Judge Davis allowed Stalker to run the café while Babler served his sen-

This former general store in Meramec Highlands housed second-floor living quarters that were rented in 1925 by Charles Arthur "Pretty Boy" Floyd. It now serves as home to author and historian James F. Baker and his family.

tence, and vice versa. "People say that anticipation is greater than realization," the *Missourian* opined. "With six months in which to anticipate, Stalker will be serving a double sentence, but in the meantime, the business will be open to the public."

Former St. Louis Police Officer William Probst, sentenced to eighteen months at Leavenworth Penitentiary for operating a still in Jennings, paid four hundred dollars to an illiterate alien named Andy Homoky to serve his prison time. The ruse worked until authorities noticed the parole petition had been signed with a cross mark, indicating that the prisoner could not write. At the time, federal prisoners were not photographed at the time of their arrest. "I was in Chicago last month when I read in *The Star* about my substitution being discovered," the prison-bound Probst told a reporter in October 1929. "When I found the plan was discovered, I came back to St. Louis. Yesterday, I telephoned my bondsman, State Senator Joseph Mogler, and told him I was ready to surrender."

Sam Morfia also disappeared on the way to jail. Morfia, a former bartender in a saloon at 204 1/2 N. Seventh Street, had departed from Union Station with nineteen other prisoners headed to the Audrain County Jail on October 21, 1929. When they arrived in Mexico, Missouri, deputies realized Morfia had escaped from the train. His sentence of six months in jail had been the heaviest assessed by Judge Faris to the twenty-eight defendants who pleaded guilty of liquor violations that day. "Ordinarily deputies do not watch liquor law violators as closely as other offenders, because it has been their experience that the prisoners, anxious to complete the sentences and return to their homes, accept a jail term philosophically," the *Post* reported.

Others were given plenty of "wiggle room" during their incarceration after the local prohibition officers, Notley Shoulders and Arthur Whittaker, made periodic raids, noted Gilbert W. Killinger, a Collinsville journalist and public servant. "They'd be tried and sentenced to Springfield, the federal jail in Springfield," Killinger recalled in 1976. "I didn't see this, but I know that the people talked about it . . . it was the truth because one of them was a man who served. He said they served in the jail but they just slept there at night. In the daytime they would walk around any place they wanted to go." Killinger laughed. "Nobody, even law enforcing officers, was in favor of the Prohibition Act."

THE BIG KAHUNA

Charles "Pretty Boy" Floyd used his moonshine-making skills to manufacture a potent potato-water concoction after he arrived at the Missouri Penitentiary on December 18, 1925. He had pleaded guilty to a $12,000 St. Louis payroll robbery, listed in penitentiary records as his first offense. Before he landed in the slammer, he used to make extra money selling bootleg whiskey with his brother, Bradley. "Floyd used to come after ice and he would take advantage of the opportunity to steal potatoes which the convicts used in making whiskey," Harvey Hayes, former manager of the penitentiary cold-storage plant, recalled in an undated story in *Somewhere in Time: 170 Year History of Missouri Corrections.* "The potato room was not visible from my office and while I was sure he was stealing potatoes, I couldn't catch him at it. I tried to be out in the hall when he came but he was smart and came at a different time every day. Finally I saw him pick up a bag of potatoes, carry them out and throw them in a wheelbarrow with a block of ice. Floyd saw me coming after him, dropped the wheelbarrow and started running. He was rounded up in the yard. He acted insolent and I batted his ears a few times."

Floyd was released from the penitentiary in March 1929; within four years he was wanted for three murders in Missouri alone and was known to police as "the most dangerous man alive." He rode the freights from Oklahoma to St. Louis in the summer of 1925 with Fred "Sheik" Hildebrand, who helped Floyd sharpen his criminal teeth robbing area Kroger stores. This was a popular pursuit among criminals of the day. The *Post-Dispatch* observed in 1923:

"Stick 'em up" has become almost as familiar a request to Kroger grocery managers as "give me a cake of soap." During the last 3 1/2 years the former command has fallen upon the ears

Charles Arthur "Pretty Boy" Floyd. Courtesy FBI.

Floyd's accomplice, Adam Ricchetti. Courtesy FBI.

of Kroger employees 190 times and resulted in a loss of $21,901 to the company's coffers. All of which was accompanied by some slight inconvenience to those robbed, such as being placed in the ice-box, tied in the rear or being forced to lie prostrate on the floor while the armed intruders looted the cash register.

Luckily for the store managers, the Kroger company is well patronized, as shown by an increase of from 200 to 280 stores in St. Louis in the last two years, so captive employees are usually liberated in a few moments by a customer.

The cloth caps worn by criminals in the holdups even earned the slang nickname "Krogers," Harper Barnes noted in a 1992 article in the *Post-Dispatch*.

Floyd and Hildebrand moved out to Meramec Highlands, where they found lodging over a run-down grocery operated by Joseph Hlavaty and a younger brother. Their digs and the store, featured in 2007 on the HGTV series *If Walls Could Talk*, are now the home of author and historian James F. Baker and his family in Kirkwood. "In '25 it was probably real rough living quarters," Baker said. "They had a stairway up the back. Later on it was rented out to families who used it as inexpensive housing. I doubt they even had bathrooms up there at that point. Meramec Highlands was still fairly wide open in 1925."

The two decided a Kroger payroll robbery would net them good profits, and they brought Joe Hlavaty on board as a driver and backup gunman, Baker noted in his book, *Glimpses of Meramec Highlands*. Hlavaty would later insist he was coerced into the robbery.

In a stolen Cadillac they held up Kroger headquarters at 1311 Tiffany Street on September 11, 1925. They returned to the store, split the proceeds of

$11,984, and helped Hlavaty bury his share in the woods behind the store, then Floyd and Hildebrand caught the train at Union Station to Tulsa, Oklahoma. Hlavaty was the first to be arrested, but all were convicted of the crime.

Floyd, known previously as "Charley" or "Choc," acquired the Pretty Boy moniker from Beulah Baird, his girlfriend in Kansas City, biographer Michael Wallis wrote in *Pretty Boy: The Life and Times of Charles Arthur Floyd*. There were, however, two stories suggesting that the name came from St. Louis, Wallis noted. A paymaster from the Kroger heist had described Floyd as "a mere boy, a pretty boy with apple cheeks," and St. Louis Police Detective Sergeant John Carroll also was said to have mentioned him as being "a pretty boy."

One year before he was fatally shot by FBI agents on a farm near East Liverpool, Ohio, Floyd pulled one last big crime in Missouri. He and a companion, Adam Ricchetti, kidnapped Sheriff Jack Killingsworth of Bolivar and took off in a stolen automobile on June 16, 1933. They later released him near Lee's Summit after a five-hundred-mile ride over the roads of central and western Missouri. "I was in the back seat with Floyd," Killingsworth recalled later. "Ricchetti drove for about 35 miles and I was afraid because he was drinking. Then Floyd took the wheel. He sure is a good driver. What worried me from the start was that the boys [other officers] would try to help me out. Floyd, I saw right away, would kill a man, but not unless he had to.

"They told me I would be safe if I would direct them to safety. We wandered over roads I knew would be hard to follow. Then the highway patrol got right behind us. They stuck a gun in my side and told me to wave them back. I was more than willing."

BOOTLEGGERS 'R US

When 195 saloons in St. Louis shut their doors after the Jones law was enacted in 1929, the *St. Louis County Watchman-Advocate* took time out to gloat. The paper's editors were still smarting over Judge Charles Faris's remark five years back that there was "a still behind every bush" in St. Louis County. In St. Louis, it remarked, the situation seemed to be a "saloon" behind every lamp post.

"More stills and illicit liquor joints have flourished in the City of St. Louis than on this side of the city limits line," the *Watchman-Advocate* commented. "Doubtless, stills and saloons have operated in the county as well as in the city, but in all fairness the pot ought to quit calling the kettle black."

CHAPTER 14

ULTERIOR MOTIVES

As justice of the peace for Central Township, with offices in Clayton, Missouri, A. H. Werremeyer made it his custom to consume part of the evidence confiscated in liquor raids. Nearly every official in the St. Louis County Courthouse consumed it as well, after a still on the Lay Road was raided in the summer of 1920, Werremeyer testified.

"Yes, Senator, you got a bottle, too," Werremeyer jabbed at former State Senator A. E. L. Gardner on November 23, 1921. Gardner was serving as counsel for St. Louis County Sheriff John F. Willmann, who was being tried on neglect of duty and failing to enforce the laws against liquor violators.

"What moonshine are you talking about?" Gardner asked.

"I'm talking about the liquor taken in the Lay County affair," Werremeyer replied.

"Well, I didn't know there was that much moonshine around," said Gardner. "But tell me more about my getting this moonshine. I'd like to know about it."

"All right, then," said the justice, "I remember well when you dropped a quart in front of the City Bank right here in Clayton."

The courtroom went into an uproar. Judge John W. McElhinney rapped for order.

"Do you know that that bottle contained moonshine?" Gardner finally asked.

"It was something white, Senator, and it fell out of your coat pocket."

Willmann was acquitted of the charges. He and his successors, however, would be called to task again in future years for their failure to enforce a law in which the corruption increased as the years progressed.

More than a few police officers, deputies, and public officials were on the take during this time. Law enforcement work was tough, the hours long, and the pay low. "If you would pay the deputy sheriff a living wage you could expect better results and the question of honesty among the deputies may sort of disappear," Willmann told a grand jury shortly before his retirement in 1924.

Bootleggers' profits were a constant temptation, future U.S. Senator Bennett "Champ" Clark of Missouri said in a speech in 1931. "These profits, largely made up of revenues, which in former days would have gone for federal, state and local taxes, has permitted the bootleggers to set aside vast sums as slush funds for the corruption of public officials, including those whose duty it is to enforce the law," Clark said.

JOIN THE CLUB

Along with Werremeyer, St. Louis County Deputy Sheriff A. J. Shores told the court of receiving whiskey from former Deputy Sheriff Albert Stuckman, who Shores said resold whiskey obtained in raids and on one occasion boasted of receiving $520 for forty gallons. Three Italian still owners also testified they had paid Stuckman and William A. Rosenthal $300 for protection, and both were indicted by a St. Louis County grand jury. Stuckman denied the allegations and resigned in July 1921 after a disagreement with Willmann. Investigators, including assistant to the U.S. Attorney General John C. Dyott, hoped to track the case to higher-ups. However, Dyott was asked by Missouri Anti-Saloon League Superintendent W. C. Shupp to "hold off that county matter" and was advised by the federal Justice Department not to prosecute persons of political prominence unless conviction was sure. Dyott, fearing conflict with his superiors, held off. The indictments against Stuckman and Rosenthal were dropped in January 1923: By this time the witnesses in the case had left the country.

Prohibition was barely through its second year in November 1921, when Missouri Attorney General Jesse Barrett was swamped with anonymous letters telling of the crooked local officials who permitted the manufacture and sale of moonshine whiskey, from sheriffs to the courts. Barrett estimated 250,000 agents were needed to enforce prohibition in Missouri, and another 125,000 agents were needed to watch the 250,000 enforcement agents. Both Missouri and Illinois received a fraction of that number, and no watchdogs.

Testifying before the House Committee on the Alcoholic Liquor Traffic in June 1928, federal witness William S. Davidson said bribes received by agents of the Prohibition Unit ran as high as one thousand dollars and "if the one down below isn't crooked, the one up above is sure to be." The problem didn't stop there: Davidson told of "exclusive society folk" in western cities who had been protected by government agents, and of banks in St. Louis and other cities financing bootleg gangs.

Connections were everything, as retired federal employee J. Willard Conlon of Springfield, Illinois, recalled in 1972. "Then it was also said that if one was arrested for transporting alcohol, that it was possible to get out without much trouble by simply mentioning the name of some well-known local politicians and underworld characters who would immediately get you out on bail," Conlon said. "In many cases, that seemed to be the last one ever heard of it."

Between January 1920 and February 1, 1926, 752 prohibition enforcement officers, agents, and inspectors nationwide were relieved of duty: 121 of those

for extortion, bribery, or soliciting money, and 187 for intoxication and mis-
conduct. That number included only those resignations accepted with prejudice.
Some supervising field officers requested resignations without prejudice, and the
behaviors leading to the resignations were not recorded.

"Prohibition, as at present operative, is a party-spoils system," Chester Mills
wrote in a September 1927 article in *Collier's*. "Three-quarters of the twenty-
five hundred dry agents are ward heelers and sycophants named by the politicians. And the politicians, whether professionally wet or professionally dry, want
prohibition because they regard prohibition as they regard post-masterships—a
reservoir of jobs for henchmen and of favors for friends."

THAT ENTREPRENEURIAL SPIRIT

"If you're going to keep your promise to rid the city of law violators, why don't
you arrest that 'bootlegging' cop at 5205 Enright Avenue?" a building contractor
asked his friend, Philip H. Brockman, president of the St. Louis Police Board.
The contractor said his laborers had been getting drunk on moonshine they
had purchased from the cop, and it was interfering with their work. So a rookie
from the Police School of Instruction was given two marked one-dollar bills,
told to dress like a laborer, and dispatched to the location in February 1924. He
returned an hour later with a half-pint of moonshine in his pocket and the odor
of hooch on his breath.

"Patrolman Lawrence Doran sold me the stuff," the rookie reported. Doran,
a twenty-six-year department veteran, surrendered the marked one-dollar bill
and refused to resign or make a written report. He was suspended and released
on bond pending a charge of unbecoming conduct before the police board.
Doran resigned from the force while under charges, said Barbara Miksicek, librarian of the St. Louis Police Library.

Across the river in Chester, Illinois, Randolph County Sheriff J. W. Heine
was elected in 1923 on a strict law enforcement platform. For two years he
conducted wholesale liquor raids, even in homes, and one time placed a confiscated still on the courthouse lawn for everyone to see. Suddenly, in 1925, the
activity subsided. Heine explained that State's Attorney William H. Schuwerk
had refused to issue search warrants and dismissed some old cases, but the
excuse didn't work. Charges were filed late that year that Heine took money
from liquor law violators to "protect" them from arrest, and Heine resigned.
He moved to 8301A Gravois Road in St. Louis County and pleaded guilty on

January 4, 1927, of conspiracy to violate the state liquor law. Heine was sentenced by Circuit Judge J. F. Gilham to five months on the Illinois state penal farm at Vandalia. Two others who pleaded guilty were fined: Samuel J. Peters of South Kingshighway Boulevard in St. Louis, who was said to have collected protection money for Heine, two thousand dollars; and Clark Maxwell, a barber and bootlegger from Chester, five hundred dollars. Heine had been a successful contractor before he became sheriff.

One year later, in November 1928, Mayor Marshall McCormick of Herrin, Illinois; that city's chief of police, John Stamm; and the mayor's brother, Elmer McCormick, were indicted by a federal grand jury on charges of running a protection ring in Herrin. The four collected regularly from Williamson County bootleggers, with sums in the thousands of dollars, Assistant U.S. Attorney Ralph F. Lessemen said. They were convicted of the charges the following February.

Among others charged with liquor-related offenses during the prohibition years were a sheriff and three deputies in Alexander County, Illinois; a sheriff in Ste. Genevieve County, Missouri; and a sheriff and his deputy in Massac County, Illinois, along with thirty-two other Massac County citizens.

RUM-RUNNING IN RICHMOND HEIGHTS

More mysterious was the report in the December 21, 1926, *Post-Dispatch* of a "Suburban Police Chief Accused of Being Bootlegger." The unnamed chief, of "one of the leading incorporated communities in the county," was accused by the city's former mayor, two policemen, and two businessmen of bootlegging whiskey. Cancelled checks bearing the chief's endorsement, said to be from whiskey transactions, were turned over by the former mayor to a St. Louis County grand jury investigating the matter. "The Chief of Police, said the former Mayor, was in modest circumstances when appointed to the job, which pays less than $200 a month," the *Post* reported. "Now he owns his home and other property.

"Two brothers, who own a grocery store in the community, and two police officers were among those who appeared before the grand jury. The grocers, according to the story of the former Mayor, bought whiskey by the case from the Chief of Police, giving checks in payment at the rate of $48 for a case of 24 pints. The whiskey was said to be moonshine, manufactured by rich Italians or their henchmen."

Two months later, during a raid on a still in February 1927, prohibition agents seized a little red leather memorandum book in the vest pocket of Richmond Heights resident Byrd S. Hurt. Marked inside were notations of "Sheriff $150," and "Police $100, $115, $120 and $75." Hurt was arrested with four other men in a house on Mohl Avenue, in unincorporated St. Louis County, where a still was found in operation. Hurt refused to offer any explanation of the book and said he knew nothing about a still. The others arrested were Charles Castelani, Louis Oldani, Jim Congelosi, and John Cherina.

In March 1927, Richmond Heights city officials created a special committee to investigate an alleged protection racket of moonshiners and bootleggers. About five hundred people crammed into the meeting at the Richmond Heights School to hear former Mayor James Jensen present his testimony against Police Chief John Maloney. Jensen produced three checks, two for forty-eight dollars each and one for ninety-six dollars, which he claimed were used to purchase liquor from Maloney by Deputy Constable James Ryan of Central Township. A policeman on the night watch had obtained the checks, Jensen said. Police Officer Tom Brown testified that Maloney had always assisted other police officers in raiding moonshine plants and was a capable leader. Brown also testified that the department had more superior officers than patrolmen and recommended it be disbanded.

At a final investigative meeting March 15, Deputy Prohibition Administrator James Dillon testified that, to his knowledge, the Richmond Heights Police Department had attended to its duty in enforcing liquor laws, and that the city did not have more liquor law violations comparatively than other communities. Two other officers offered similar testimony. The constable's office in Clayton had previously reported that there were more stills in Richmond Heights than in all of the rest of the county.

Maloney, who said the checks in question were for various loans and other personal business dealings he had with a resident of St. Louis County, declined to testify. "No charges have been made, and I don't see the necessity of testifying in view of this fact," Maloney said. "If I had been charged with inefficiency or any other charge I certainly would have taken the witness stand. I have always tried to conduct my office in an efficient manner and I defy anyone to get up and state that I have ever been negligent or taken a bribe."

TIPS AND TRIPS

In July 1928, Deputy Constable John Hanson was at a loss to explain how 271 gallons of whiskey seized six months earlier were inside his garage at Taylor and

Bridgeton roads. Hanson, of St. Ferdinand Township in St. Louis County, explained that the constable and various deputies used his garage for safekeeping. Asked why he did not keep the liquor in his office at Florissant, five miles away, Hanson told authorities the office was too small. Hanson was charged with illegal possession of intoxicating liquors.

In Beardstown, Illinois, George Pharr was the chief of police, and his son Rusty ran Beardstown's largest bootlegging joint, lifelong resident May Carr McNeil recalled in 1987. "Yes, every time the revenue officers would come to town, why, he would let his boy know it and his boy would call all the other bootleggers," McNeil said. "One place had a tunnel from their house to the house next door. That was down here on Seventh Street and when the revenue officer would come to town they'd take all their liquor and take it over in the basement next door. Then they'd put a cupboard up against the opening where they went through. When they'd search the house they'd think he was bootlegging but they wouldn't find nothing."

A St. Louis police officer was hauled away after he gave the secret knock that opened the door of a soft drink establishment at 3848 West Pine Boulevard. Prohibition agents had been watching the place for some time. They hit pay dirt in September 1929 as one patron started to drive away with a box that had been loaded in his car by a man inside the building. The driver turned out to be Detective Oscar W. Soutiea. "You've got beer in that carton and you got it in that place," an agent told him. "Now you show us how to get in."

Soutiea gave three raps on the door, then a single rap. After the agents moved in, Soutiea told them he was using the beer for a party and asked them to "give me a break." Both he and the proprietor inside were arrested, and Soutiea was suspended pending trial before the Board of Police Commissioners on charges of unbecoming conduct and neglect of duty.

Soutiea told a reporter the box was offered to him by the proprietor, and he did not know what was inside. A seven-year veteran of the force, he was found guilty by the board and fired, Miksicek said.

BUYING FROM THE BEST

A month after Soutiea was arrested, the mayor of Valmeyer, Illinois, was sentenced to thirty days in jail and fined one hundred dollars for bootlegging. George E. Lewis pleaded guilty to a charge of violating the federal prohibition laws in October 1929 before Federal Judge Fred L. Wham.

Former Secretary of the Interior Albert Fall had been found guilty of taking bribes from oil companies as, closer to home, newspapers across Missouri told of the bootlegging conviction of the son of late Missouri Supreme Court Judge Arthur M. Woodson. Arch Woodson was sentenced to three years in Leavenworth Penitentiary in 1929 after he pleaded guilty to charges of possession and sale of whiskey at his roadhouse three miles west of Jefferson City following a raid the previous July. A bartender at the roadhouse received a lesser sentence. "We cannot discriminate between the man who comes from the alley to violate the law and the man who has walked in high places," Federal Judge A. L. Reeves said. "My sympathy is with the man from the alley who perhaps does not know better. I served with the defendant's father on the bench and it was my pleasure [as a Missouri Supreme Court commissioner] to appear before him many times. This is the most painful duty that I have ever faced."

ENGLISH LESSONS

Some officials were better than others at protection rackets, and budding bootlegger Edward Dashner probably deserved his money back. In January 1923, Dashner, of Renault, Illinois, pleaded guilty in East St. Louis to charges of sale, possession, and transportation of intoxicating liquor. Dashner told Federal Judge George Washington English he contracted with an East St. Louis man to pay ninety cents a gallon to avoid arrest, but that he had hardly set up his still before he was arrested by prohibition agents and did not have time to make any sales. Prohibition agents disagreed, saying he had been operating for more than a year. English sentenced Dashner to ninety days in jail and fined him six hundred dollars.

English had his own problems with alleged misdeeds (see Chapter 4). Facing impeachment proceedings in the U.S. Senate for "high misdemeanors," English resigned on November 4, 1926, though he denied the charges. These included congressional testimony by Mrs. Grace Thayer, a former employee in the office of Referee in Bankruptcy Charles B. Thomas. Thayer told the committee that on one occasion, two men she understood to be bootleggers facing criminal action handed a roll of bills to Thomas, who immediately divided them with English. "Was the money green?" asked Frank T. O'Hare of Paris, Illinois, chief of counsel for English. "The color did not impress me," Thayer replied. "It was the size of the roll."

The two divided money on other occasions, and it was generally understood that Thomas bought English an automobile, Thayer said. East St. Louis

Police Chief John J. Barry told the committee how, on one occasion, English commanded police to release and restore the pistols of three automobile loads of Herrin vigilantes who had come armed to East St. Louis in connection with liquor raids. It appeared the fighting for which Williamson County was infamous might be continued in East St. Louis, Barry said, and that's why police confiscated their weapons (see Chapter 15).

English also was charged with using profane and obscene language on the bench, disbarring attorneys without cause, showing gross favoritism in his appointments in bankruptcy cases and threatening newspaper reporters, among other allegations. His son was charged to have profited financially from the deposit of court funds in favored banks. The House voted 306–60 for impeachment. "While I am conscious of the fact that I have discharged my duties as District Judge to the best of my ability, and while I am satisfied that I have the confidence of the law-abiding people of the district, yet I have come to the conclusion on account of the impeachment proceedings against me, regardless of the final result thereof, that my usefulness as a Judge has been seriously impaired," English said in his resignation statement.

Shakedowns, Tributes, and Bill the Boob

At least 110 people were indicted by a federal grand jury in Quincy, Illinois, in October 1927 in connection with a bootleg protection graft in Madison County, Illinois. The accused included several minor officials in Madison County, including justices of the peace, constables, deputy constables, and a former police magistrate. They were charged with "shaking down" East Side bootleggers with spurious search warrants and representing themselves as federal officers. At least $170,000 in payments was collected, investigators said. Also indicted were members of the wealthy Italian gang of bootleggers known as the Green Ones.

Shaking down bootleggers was not an easy business. In 1926, Deputy Constable Ohmer Hockett and a friend, John Balke, paid with their lives after they allegedly tried to collect a protection payment from the Green Ones at Horseshoe Lake in Madison County (see Chapter 8). The murders prompted those on the take to be a little more careful, the federal investigation into the graft revealed. One of the constables named in the indictments used a learning-challenged assistant known as "Bill the Boob" to help him collect the payments, the *Post-Dispatch* reported in October 1927. When the constable approached the moonshiners' digs, he stopped the car at a safe distance and dispatched Bill to the scene. If Bill came out safely, the constable, sometimes accompanied by a justice of the peace, would enter. "Sometimes 'Bill' was beaten and thrown out, and sometimes he came out on the run," the *Post* noted. "In these instances the others passed the place up. Even the moonshiners looked upon 'Bill' as a boob, and one of them at Quincy told the *Post-Dispatch* correspondent that 'Bill' would have been slain long ago had the moonshiners not had compassion on him for being such a numbskull."

More than fifty defendants pleaded guilty in fall 1927 before Federal Judge Louis Fitzhenry at Springfield, Illinois, where a grand jury heard the charges and listened to 240 witnesses. A several-month investigation revealed that one hundred people had paid for protection. In Alton alone, population thirty thousand, grafters collected fifteen to one hundred dollars a month from seventy bootleggers. They went to saloons, homes, stores, tire shops, and garages, many of which had liquor only for their private use, investigator Victor J. Dowd told reporters. "I have a list of of about 40 places in Alton which paid a total of about $1,000 a month for protection since April 1925," Dowd told a *Post* reporter. "The fellows who were getting the money frequently double-crossed each other and went around to collect when their pals weren't looking. The $170,000 graft money was shared by a number of men (14 or more)."

Each grafter earned an annual income of about $10,000, Dowd estimated, or more than $114,000 today. "This one man went to a woman who only made homebrew for family use and demanded money," Dowd said. "She said she had none except in her child's bank. He made her give him that, $20. An Alton woman was making homebrew for her husband and they tried to get $30 a month from her. She wouldn't pay, so they raided her house and fined her $162."

Sums were levied on the anticipated business volume for the bootlegger. In one instance, a justice of the peace suspected that a home-brew vendor operating a sandwich shop was doing a greater volume of business than she reported, so he would go daily to the place and munch sandwiches for hours at a time to observe the business. "Certain deputy constables, it has been told, made a practice of entertaining girl friends at roadhouses and other places at the expense of the owners," the *Post* reported. "After dining and drinking they would mark on the check, 'Charge it to your old man.' Several of these girls appeared before the grand jury."

Barrels of confiscated liquor. Courtesy Library of Congress.

TRAPPING THOSE ON THE TAKE

After three prohibition agents and a police officer raided his soft drink bar at 4701 Nebraska Avenue in March 1923, Max Kannapell told authorities he was asked for $250 by the officer, Herbert Lampe, "after which I would be a 'member of the gang' and could do as I pleased regarding the sale of liquor."

Kannapell summoned his friend, former Prohibition Agent Bernard Kwiatkowski, who was at his shoe shop at 506 Bates Street when the raiders arrived at Kannapell's saloon. A woman came to the shop and asked him to come at once. "I asked to see the search warrant and after looking at it, told the agents they had no right to search Kannapell's home, that the warrant related only to the saloon," Kwiatkowski said. "One of the men looked at me and said, 'Keep quiet, Barney, we are shaking this guy down. . . .'"

Kwiatkowski told Kannapell to offer a check, which he knew the agents would refuse. Officer Lampe came back later that day and said his fellow agents had given him the devil for selling out so cheap, and asked for $300. Kannapell agreed to pay $270, and Lampe returned the next day to pick it up.

In the meantime, Kannapell and Kwiatkowski notified General Prohibition

Agent George Bausewein of the scheme, and a trap was laid. The next day, Lampe accompanied Kannapell in his car to the Lafayette South Side Bank of St. Louis, where Kannapell drew out thirteen twenty-dollar bills and one ten-dollar bill. Bausewein, already at the bank with Deputy Sheriff Paul Toelle of St. Louis County and Fred Tate of the Missouri attorney general's office, took down the numbers of the bills.

Lampe admitted taking the money, but said he had come to the saloon only to get a bottle of milk for his baby. He said Kannapell offered money to "fix the case with the agents so they would drop it." Lampe said he intended to return the money and took it only because he had known Kannapell for some years and wanted to keep his friendship. Police and prohibition authorities promised a full investigation.

A similar trap was planned in July 1924 after Frank Kiesling, a saloonkeeper at 1827 S. Second Street, paid ten dollars in protection money to Police Officer Henry Moorkamp of the Soulard Street District. When he was hit up a second time, Kiesling consulted with Inspector of Police James Vasey, who gave the saloonkeeper two marked five-dollar bills, stood behind a partition as Moorkamp entered, and placed him under arrest when he accepted the cash. Moorkamp was dismissed by the Board of Police Commissioners the next month for unbecoming conduct.

A two-mile automobile chase ended an extortion attempt in September 1924 on Sam Fuchs, a saloonkeeper near Sappington in south St. Louis County. Two men awakened Fuchs one night, showed him a bottle of liquor, and accused him of selling it. He denied it and was told to call a certain telephone number the next day and ask for "Jones," who would tell him what to do. Fuchs went to the county prosecutor's office the next day, told his story, and called Jones, who asked for six hundred dollars. Fuchs said he didn't have that much money. "Then bring all you can and meet us at Sappington Road and Lockwood Avenue at 2:30," Jones replied.

Fuchs headed to the meeting point, accompanied by another Jones—the prosecuting attorney, Adam Henry—his assistant, David Russell, Sheriff John Willmann, and Deputy Sheriff Wengler. The officials hid in the bushes. About 3 p.m., a car drove up with two men inside. They refused forty-five dollars in small bills offered by Fuchs and insisted that he follow them to another point. Fuchs signaled to the officers, a car chase ensued, and it ended with their capture on the outskirts of Webster Groves. Authorities took the badge and empty revolver of J. W. Ward, Jr., of Maplewood, who turned out to be a deputy constable from the Central Township. Also arrested was Clifford Jones of University City.

ONE FRANK TOMATO

Some bootleggers assumed the police were on the take, even when they weren't. In March 1927, St. Louis Patrolmen William Eckles, Otto Glaser, and Frank Schwartz were sitting in a patrol car in the 7000 block of North Broadway when one Nathan Amato climbed in. "Fellows, I am playing a losing game unless I can sell more whiskey," Amato said, with an engaging smile. "Of course, it will be all right for me to sell whiskey in my home? You are good scouts—if you let me alone for thirty days I will pay each of you $5 a month. Here is $15 for the first month."

As the smiling bootlegger handed the money to Eckles, Glaser looked at Schwartz. "This fellow Amato is one frank tomato," he said. They arrested Amato and took him to his home at 7925 Oberbeck Avenue, where they confiscated nine quarts of moonshine found inside and another five gallons buried in a thirty-gallon barrel under the goat and chicken yard.

Though many officers turned down payoffs, the temptation always was there. After five years on the job, Prohibition Agent Paul Toelle was one of eleven prohibition agents fired in September 1928 from the St. Louis unit after failing to pass civil service examinations. Only three in St. Louis passed the exam, along with eleven of thirty-eight agents in the district serving eastern Missouri and Arkansas. A disgruntled Toelle told reporters that during his five years as an agent he had been offered many bribes, in one instance two thousand dollars a month by a clique of bootleggers.

"I wish I had taken some of the thousand-dollar bills that have been dangled under my nose," Toelle was quoted as saying. The next day, Toelle told the *Post-Dispatch* he had been quoted erroneously. "I have always resisted such offers," he said. "Perhaps I was foolish, but I don't think so."[*]

In an April 1930 speech in Granite City, Illinois, Judge Louis Bernreuter noted that enforcement of the liquor and gambling laws was not as popular as it used to be. "There are several reasons for this," Bernreuter told patrons gathered at the Presbyterian Man's Brotherhood. "One is that many of the prohibition enforcement officers are crooks who seek and get appointments for what they can make out of it."

---

[*] Agent Toelle got his job back, because he was listed among the temporary appointments in a *Post-Dispatch* article in March 1929. In August 1933, as prohibition was on its last legs, Toelle was listed in the *Globe-Democrat* as one of nine agents who were not reappointed to the force. Only three agents received reappointments.

Pseudo-Agents

Ne'er-do-wells found they could ease their way into criminal opportunities by posing as prohibition agents. On the evening of February 15, 1924, a young couple, Robert L. Kimmel and Melba Hill, were seated in Kimmel's Essex car in Chain of Rocks Park in north St. Louis when three figures approached in the shadows. "Hands up, we are prohibition agents and we are going to search your car," one said.

Kimmel and Hill got out. Instead of searching the car, one of the men got in with the intention of driving it away. The others began searching Kimmel, who sensed something amiss. He grabbed a revolver belonging to one of the men and struck him in the face. The two shot and killed Kimmel and shot and seriously wounded Hill before they got in the car and drove away. Police found her about 9:30 p.m., dazed, seated near Kimmel's body in a pool of blood. Within hours the abandoned Essex was found on St. Cyr Road near Prospect Hill. Detectives arrested John Gardner, John Rou, and John Weisner. "We had a date with two girls and neither of us had any money," Rou told authorities. "We decided to hold up some one and get some money so we could keep the date. When we started to get in the automobile the man grabbed my gun and struck me, we both shot him, and one of the bullets must have struck the girl, then we took the automobile and drove it near to our home and walked the rest of the way."

A Fishy Tale

A soft-hearted store clerk was scammed in February 1923 after he attempted to provide overnight accommodations for some tired Japanese fish. Charles Cowels was feeding the stock in the fish department of the Greater St. Louis Poultry Supply Company, 1100 Market Street, when two men entered the store one evening. "I am an attaché of the Japanese navy," said one, "and I am escorting the fish to Washington. They are a gift from the Mikado to President Harding, and they are tired out from traveling. I would like to put them up for the night."

Cowels went to inspect a tank in the rear of the store for the would-be lodgers. He returned to find the men gone, along with $123.85 from the cash drawer.

Similar shakedowns happened to motorists on the rural roads of St. Louis County, and it was difficult to know whether the culprit was a fake deputy or a corrupt one. "Complaints have reached the Clayton authorities this week that a certain St. Louis County deputy has been in the habit of late of stopping automobilists on the county roads and searching their cars for whiskey, and when some was found it was taken by the deputy," the *St. Louis County Watchman-Advocate* announced in June 1920. "Sheriff Bopp said he has not instructed any of his deputies to stop machines and search for liquor, as by this procedure many an innocent party would be embarrassed." If a bottle was found, the driver might be allowed to go his way with the liquor intact if he came up with a cash tribute, the story noted.

In June 1925, St. Louis Prosecuting Attorney Albert Schweitzer planned to present evidence to a grand jury that a number of homes had been raided by liquor pirates posing as detectives. Recent raids had included the home of a seventy-five-year-old woman in the Angelica police district and that of Edward Raithel, an attorney with offices in the Arcade Building. "I am recommending to private citizens that they defy anyone to enter their homes without a legal search warrant," Schweitzer said. Prohibition officials announced in July 1928 that all agents doing road work would be uniformed with a distinctive blue cap and shield, for identification purposes.

FAKE AGENTS ACROSS THE RIVER

The pseudo-busts continued, several in Illinois. The Mounds Country Club on Collinsville Road was targeted on July 21, 1929, after robbers posing as prohibition agents entered the restaurant about 9:30 p.m. Two of the men covered the doorman while three went into the gambling room, found several persons at the roulette and dice tables, scooped up all the cash they could find, and demanded the cashier open the safe. When he insisted he didn't know the combination, they seemed satisfied and took the clerk's word, the *Edwardsville Intelligencer* reported. The robbers made off with eight to twelve thousand dollars.

Christ Koless, a Macedonian immigrant, gave up saloonkeeping when prohibition began and started a pickled pepper business at 926 Pacific Avenue in Granite City, Illinois. Koless had built up a nationwide trade in pickled peppers, and it was his custom to keep a large amount of cash on hand on Saturdays to cash the paychecks of his customers, the *Post* reported. Phony prohibition agents with guns muscled their way into the establishment at 5:20 on the morning of December 7,

1929, serving a fake warrant, robbing Koless of $1,900, kidnapping his twelve-year-old son, Vasil, and escaping in an automobile. Vasil Koless was thrown out of the vehicle in Madison, Illinois, and suffered lacerations and bruises.

Edward Weise was shelling some corn for his chickens at his farm, on Route 160 north of Edwardsville, when four men approached in February 1931. They identified themselves as prohibition agents and demanded entry. They bound the forty-five-year-old bachelor and placed a rope around his neck. Then they found a can of coal oil, poured it over his clothes, and threatened to light it. Weise told them where he kept his money, which totaled less than twenty dollars. The bandits also ransacked the house for nearly an hour and took about twenty-five dollars worth of gold. While the bandits worked, Weise was able to escape from the ropes and headed to a neighbor's house. By the time Sheriff Peter Fitzgerald and his deputies arrived, however, the robbers were gone.

A half-dozen neighbors came to Joseph Grezzeo's rescue on March 5, 1931. Grezzeo was held hostage in his Maryville, Illinois, home for two hours by five gangsters who posed as federal prohibition officers and demanded money. The gangsters fled after one was injured in an exchange of gunfire with the neighbors, who learned of Grezzeo's plight after he asked them for money. Sheriff Peter Fitzgerald, Deputy Leo Liebler, and others searched around the city but found no trace of the thieves.

CARNIVAL OF CRIME

Every day was a carnival of crime and graft in prohibition-era St. Louis County, if grand jury reports through the prohibition years were accurate. In September 1928, a special grand jury delivered the blame for the county's corruption to its high-ranking officials, including Prosecuting Attorney Fred Mueller, Sheriff Albert Wilmas, and Constable George Roth of Central Township. Professional "fixers" or "fronters" trying to make deals frequented Mueller's office, the jury reported. Mueller denied the charges and claimed he was being persecuted politically by his enemies.

Sheriff Wilmas also failed his duties, the jury noted. "The continued and frequent law violations of lesser character, together with the homicides, gang killings, bombings and other criminal activities in the county, indicate that there is not now and has not been in some time past any effective police work on the part of this official," the jury wrote in its report. "Lack of police experience, antiquated methods, and timidity in dealing with crime and criminals have rendered this office without force or effectiveness in the apprehension of criminals, the solution of crime problems, jail breaks, the proper care of prisoners, and the collection and preservation of evidence."

Earlier in 1928, Wilmas had been forced by the government to pay tax and civil penalties of nine hundred to thirty thousand dollars in income "from mysterious sources which he would not disclose," the *Post-Dispatch* reported. "This exposure put an end to plans of his friends to run him for the Republican nomination for County Assessor."

Constable Roth also took it on the chin. "These officials have abused their power to appoint special deputies," the jury reported. "We find that George J. Roth, Constable of Central Township, for instance, appointed 231 Deputy Constables. This is at least 200 more than is necessary to perform the functions in the township. This privilege to so great a number is but the official sanction to such men to carry weapons, and facilitates their infraction of the laws."

The jury also indicted two deputy constables in connection with an alleged attempt to kill a gangster who charged they did so because he knew too much of their alleged liquor dealings. The jury found no evidence of any dedicated effort by officers to deal with liquor law violations.

"In fact, there is evidence in some cases where the officers charged with the enforcement of the law have been the agents supplying the bootleg liquor to the retailer," the jury noted. "This jury has reason to believe that some of the liquor so confiscated again found [their] way into the channels of the 'trade.'"

The grand jury indicted Tony Foley on charges of conducting gambling resorts. Foley was operator of the Los Angeles Club, 9008 Manchester Road,

A ROUGH RIDE

Corrupt public officials were bad news for bootleggers, but even worse was the condition of some city streets, one local bootlegger complained in May 1924. He dispatched to Clinton Fisk, director of streets and sewers for the city of St. Louis, a letter "couched in painfully phonetic spelling" that decried local street conditions along the route he used to deliver whiskey from his home on Natural Bridge Road, the *St. Louis Globe-Democrat* reported. "In the county, it's fine like Forest Park, but at a place where St. Louis begins there's a patch as gives a terrible impression to my customers about your department," he wrote, and signed his name but did not give an address. Dry agents managed to find him, regardless.

and another gambling establishment in Wellston that served as a gathering place for gangsters. "His places have been conducted for years on a big scale, either in defiance of the law or under the protecting wing of law-enforcement officials," the *Post-Dispatch* noted in July 1928. "From the beginning the grand jury, which was called three weeks ago, has sought the expiation of Foley's immunity."

In 1925, Foley was one of the defendants in a scheme to siphon whiskey from the Jack Daniel Distillery (see Chapter 11). He also was the leader of a notorious group called the Bottoms Gang that flourished in St. Louis from 1900 to 1919, served a term in the Missouri Penitentiary for assault to kill a policeman, and was arrested frequently for various crimes, including larceny. As the grand jury began in July 1928 to investigate reports of official protection of organized crime, Foley closed his clubs and transferred his operations to the gambling house of "No Coat George" on Lemay Ferry Road, just over the border of Jefferson County. Patrons who showed up at the clubs were given admittance cards to No Coat George that also contained a schedule of free automobile service from a Grand Boulevard and Chouteau Avenue gas station and other advertisers.

Things weren't much better by 1929, the grand jury noted in its report that year. It cited a raid by former Constable George Roth and his deputies on a Richmond Heights home in which twenty-five-thousand-dollars worth of liquor was confiscated. "We fail to find a single record at Clayton, or elsewhere, that Mr. Roth or any of his deputies ever made a return on the search warrant indicating the seizure of liquor; nor was any one ever charged by affidavit, information, indictment, or otherwise, with any offense in connection with the case. . . ." Another raid by Roth and the deputies in Pine Lawn resulted in the confiscation of the more valuable liquor "that was conveyed on a truck to the residence of one of Mr. Roth's deputies, and its final disposition has not yet been accounted for."

Chapter 15
The Hooded Ones

There was one summer when they were pretty big. They had parades. My father wrote articles in the newspaper against them and they didn't like that much and threatened him. But nothing ever happened. They had a tremendous event down at what's now the Cahokia Mounds State Park. On one of those small mounds on the south side of Route 40, they set up a huge cross and during the day they had speeches and big crowds. And my father took me down there. And I well remember it was one of the few times I'd ever had hot dogs in those early days, picnic style. They were selling hot dogs and other refreshments. And this was one of my first experiences with something like that. I was a small boy.

That night I wasn't there, but I was told that they burned this huge cross on the mound. And that was sort of the high water mark of the Ku Klux Klan around here. One of their problems was that they didn't have anything really to do except get people mad at somebody else. They didn't have any programs of any kind except hatred. And in Indiana, as I say, they got into politics. Here they didn't, or if they tried, they didn't succeed. And the thing went for I guess two or three years and then drizzled off to nothing much. So much for that one.

—Karl Monroe, Collinsville, Illinois, newspaperman and son of *Collinsville Herald* publisher James O. Monroe, Sr., February 1973

SOME BOOZE-WEARY COMMUNITIES, DISGUSTED WITH THE LACK OF PROHIBITION enforcement, sought help from the vigilante liquor-busters of the Ku Klux Klan. Their tactics were usually corrupt and illegal. Members of the Klan were held in high esteem by many in deep southern Illinois, and they ran liquor raids in out-state Missouri and attempted to gain power in East St. Louis. Although many Klansmen drank and were involved in bootlegging or protection rackets, liquor raids allowed them to persecute Italians, Catholics, African Americans, Jews, and other groups during prohibition. Some of the raids were authorized by the local sheriff or police force, others seemed to have covert approval, and some were soundly denounced by local authorities.

The Klan had grown slowly between 1915 and 1920, but sprang up with a vengeance during the early 1920s. "Echoing the old Populist platform of the 1890s, it was now strongly pro-farmer, pro-working class and anti-Wall Street," Nathan Miller wrote in *New World Coming.* "The Klan was the champion of Prohibition, guardian of the purity of Christian women, and opponent of

The Klu Klux Klan, 1921–22. Courtesy Library of Congress.

international Jewish bankers, who, it was charged, had started the war for their own profit. The typical Klansman lived in a small town or rural area in the South or Midwest." The *St. Louis County Watchman-Advocate* estimated the Klan's St. Louis County membership at three thousand in 1924. "The strongholds of the klan are thought to be in Wellston, Luxemburg [Lemay], Maplewood, Webster Groves and Kirkwood," the newspaper reported.

From the outset, Klansmen faced opposition from many circles, including the Centennial Grand Lodge of Missouri, Ancient Free and Accepted Masons. "An organization that practices censorship of private conduct behind the midnight anonymity of mask and robe, and enforces its secret degrees [*sic*] with the weapons of whips and tar and feathers, must ultimately merit and receive the condemnation of those who believe in courts, open justice and good citizenship," Grand Master William F. Johnston said at the lodge's annual convention in St. Louis in 1921.

Klan members sought to ingratiate themselves through monetary contributions to local Protestant churches they admired, families in need, and charitable organizations, but this did not always work. In November 1922, a fifteen-thousand-dollar Klan donation to a fund to benefit the Boy Scouts in St. Louis was refused by the campaign committee, a joint body of representatives of the American Legion, the Society of Forty, and the Boy Scout Council.

That same year, a group of hooded Klansmen entered the evening service of the First Methodist Episcopal Church in Belleville, Illinois, and presented the Rev. W. H. Whitlock with an offering. The proceedings frightened many in the audience. Klansmen were credited with the fiery crosses found burning on many a night during the 1920s.

SPECTACLE OF FIRE

"The planting of flaming crosses seems to have become a favorite outdoor sport on these warm April evenings," the *Post-Dispatch* deadpanned in April 1925. "Those who have not had a flaming cross in their neighborhood thus far should not get discouraged, as the illuminators may reach them later." The spate of crosses included one on Calvary Hill, between Calvary and Bellefontaine cemeteries, lit by a man wearing blue overalls who drove away in a Ford car; one on the grounds of St. Ann's Catholic Foundling Asylum at Page and Union boulevards; and one in front of the statue of St. Louis on Art Hill.

Patrons leaving the Saturday night moving picture show hosted by the Kirkwood Parent-Teacher Association in April 1924 were met with a cross on the grounds in front of Kirkwood High School, now Nipher Middle School. Another cross was erected at St. Hedwig's Catholic Church in south St. Louis in 1925, and one was planted through the frozen ice of the Missouri River at St. Charles in January 1924. "It was supposed to have been one of the K.K.K. crosses, but what it meant, nobody seems to know," offered a reporter for the *Daily St. Charles Cosmos-Monitor.*

Crosses also were burned across the street from the homes of two Jew-

THE NERVE OF THAT GUY

Herbert Blumer, a sociology instructor at the University of Missouri–Columbia, riled local Klansmen in January 1925 when he addressed a Bible class at Stephens College on the topic of race. Blumer told the class the black race is simply repressed and not really inferior to whites, as many thought at the time.

"The white race is the most hybrid race in the world today," Blumer told the group. "I can see negroid blood through characteristics of this audience."

Klansmen promptly planted a fiery cross in front of Blumer's home.

ish families in St. Charles, Steve Ehlmann noted in *Crossroads.* "Because of the immigrant past of so many St. Charles County families, along with the large percentage of Catholics in the community, the Klan did not prosper in the county," Ehlmann wrote. "Nevertheless, the KKK made several brief appearances in St. Charles, including several donations in 1923 to needy families and worthy causes, including the school district."

A crowd of five thousand attended elaborate services hosted by the Klan on St. Charles Rock Road in June 1924. Some two hundred new members were sworn in; robed members carried torches; and a twenty-five-foot cross, illuminated with electric lights, was erected adjacent to the services. "About 600 feet south of the cross, several hundred robed members of the order formed a living cross, which took on an eerie aspect when the klansmen making up the formation produced flashlights," the *Watchman-Advocate* observed. "To the strains of 'Onward Christian Soldiers' the members of the living cross marched in the direction of the enclosure in which four robed klansmen, seated on robed horses, were in position. Just before entering this enclosure the electric flash lamps were exchanged for flaming torches which the klansmen carried into the enclosure. The torches were alternately green and red." Parking at the affair was 25 cents per car, and Klan officials said proceeds would be given to the poor. Refreshments were available, and decorations included toy balloons emblazoned with the Klan insignia. Copies of the organization's publication, *The Klan Kourier*, were sold, along with a "100 per cent cigar" said to be manufactured and distributed solely by Klansmen.

In March 1923, some eight hundred men and women assembled at the Haven Street Methodist Episcopal Church in the Carondelet neighborhood of south St. Louis to hear the Reverend Charles D. McGehee speak in defense of the Ku Klux Klan. They went away disappointed after the pastor announced he had been ordered, in the interest of peace and harmony, by a church official not to preach such a sermon. In a letter to the *Globe-Democrat,* McGehee said "85 percent of our ministers belong" to the organization. He was one of them.

For a time, the organization enjoyed its day in the sun. By 1926, however, the Klan's 150,000 members in Missouri had declined to fewer than 75,000. Illinois once was home to 287 local organizations or "Klaverns" and 200,000 members in the Chicago area alone. By 1926, internal strife and scandal had splintered the group to a fraction of its former size.

"You'd Better Do Your Duty"

Descendants of the hill people from Kentucky and Tennessee, the fundamentalist Protestant citizens of Williamson County, Illinois, were concerned about the bootlegging, saloons, gambling, prostitution, and corruption prevalent in their county. It seemed Sheriff George Galligan couldn't or wouldn't do much to stop the corruption during the early years of prohibition. They also were dismayed with the many Italian and few French immigrants who had settled in the mining towns, many of whom were Catholic and some of whom bootlegged.

"Many Protestants . . . were vehemently opposed to drinking alcohol in any form and saw the use of wine to toast a wedding, for instance, as a flagrant disregard for law and order," Betty Burnett wrote in her book *A Time of Favor: The Story of the Catholic Family of Southern Illinois*. "Agnes Wiech, a resident of Williamson County, suggested in *The New Republic* in 1924 that it was this antagonism toward alcohol that reignited the anti-Catholic, anti-foreigner prejudice in that area and resulted in the resurgence of the Ku Klux Klan."

In early 1923, a group of prominent citizens formed the Marion Law Enforcement League to help stamp out bootlegging and gambling. "It started out to work in co-operation with the county officers, but soon reached the point where it condemned them as delinquent, and proclaimed that 'as citizens we want the law enforced and . . . if our officers are not doing their duty, we must resort to such measures as will accomplish the end we desire in another way,'" Paul Angle wrote in *Bloody Williamson*. "The Klan offered the other way."

The good-natured Sheriff Galligan, elected in 1922, suffered from a small force of deputies as well as a reluctance to intercede in the bootleggers' operations, Angle noted. On the heels of a massacre of strike-breaking coal miners in Herrin in 1922, the citizens had felt a sense of shame as well as a compelling reason to put the bootleggers and gamblers out of business.

One recipient of the Klan's generosity was the Reverend P. H. Glotfelty, pastor of the Methodist Church of Herrin, who received a thirty-dollar donation to his church. On Monday, August 20, 1923, he helped officiate at a public meeting that brought nearly two thousand people together in the broiling sun at the Marion courthouse yard. He spoke of Americanism and of the need to clean house "if we have to do it ourselves." Then the Reverend L. M. Lyerla of Carterville delivered a grim, prophetic warning: "Mr. Sheriff, Mr. State's Attorney, Mr. Judge, you'd better do your duty. If you don't, something is going to happen, and that little mine trouble out here will be but a drop in the bucket compared to it."

"That night five thousand Klansmen met at near-by West Frankfort to initiate the largest class so far admitted to the order," Angle wrote.

The Klan grew to be a tremendous presence in southern Illinois, retired southern Illinois newspaper editor Henson Purcell recalled in 1972. "The thing that was always surprising to me about it, and still is, was that it got to the place where among the leaders were the outstanding ministers of the area—preachers of various denominations who were among the leaders in this thing," Purcell said. "They were the people who went to the big meetings and spoke. Of course, at the height of this Ku Klux Klan thing, they would have huge meetings out in the fields . . . just thousands of people there. A lot of them were in robes and this kind of thing. There would be people patrolling the highways in the vicinity. The big thing that happened was that the Ku Klux Klan people, because they were unhappy with law enforcement, finally brought in a fellow by the name of Glenn Young."

Two-Gun Glenn

S. Glenn Young was a brash, beetle-browed vigilante brought in by the Law and Order League. He was a former Justice Department agent who had also worked for the Prohibition Unit only a short time before he was dismissed in December 1920 for "unbecoming acts." He had killed a Madison, Illinois, resident, Luka Vukovic, after forcing his way without a search warrant into Vukovic's home in the belief that there was liquor inside. Vukovic, seeing Young and a police officer from Granite City, pointed his pistol at them. The weapon misfired, and Young returned the fire. Young was found not guilty of the murder.

Shortly before his trial in June 1921, Young's first wife, Pearl, filed suit for divorce, alleging he was violent and on one occasion threw her down and kicked her. Pearl Young maintained her husband had failed to support her and their twin daughters for some time. "Well, he actually was just a gunman," Purcell recalled. "He was a real personable guy, a nice guy to talk to and a pretty nice-looking guy. But he was a hired gunman."

Young started his Williamson County work in November 1923 by visiting more than one hundred liquor establishments and collecting evidence with his father-in-law, George Simcox, a former U.S. marshal. Then he went to Washington with John L. Whitesides, a Marion Klan leader; and Arlie O. Boswell, a Klansman, lawyer, and candidate for the office of state's attorney.

They were sponsored in their quest by Richard Yates, congressman-at-large from Illinois, and E. E. Denison, congressman from the Williamson County district (See Chapter 16). They asked Federal Prohibition Commissioner Roy Haynes to send an agent from his force to deputize Young and the men he selected to raid liquor establishments, and Haynes agreed. Young then recruited as his raiders five hundred men, including many ministers and leading citizens of the area.

Many agree that if the raids had stopped at roadhouses and saloons, there would have been no further violence. But Young and his raiders went over the line in their three raids, which resulted in 256 arrests. "Private homes were raided in the dead of night by men counted as members of the Ku Klux Klan," *New York Times* reporter William Chenery wrote in September 1924. "Italian families who possessed a little home-made wine for their own consumption were aroused in the middle of the Winter night. The hours between midnight and 1 o'clock were chosen for the invasion.

"Opponents of the Klan insist that women were subjected to indignities by gunmen employed to act as special policemen under the disputed authority possessed by Young. . . . Little children were roughly awakened and men in whose domiciles wine was found were hurried off to jail."

The raiders credited Young with the brutality. "It was Young—so they said—who used abusive language toward women, turned the contents of cash drawers into his own pockets, and pistol-whipped an occasional victim who failed to raise his hands above his head quite fast enough," Angle wrote.

Among those who retaliated was Ora Thomas, a professional gambler and sometime bootlegger who later served as Galligan's deputy sheriff. Thomas, a friend of gangster Charlie Birger, was the founder of an anti-Klan organization called Knights of the Flaming Circle. "Gambler and bootlegger though he was, Thomas had the pluck of a storybook hero and a delicacy of manner and appearance that is usually found in better men," author Gary DeNeal wrote of Thomas in his book *A Knight of Another Sort.* "His strange combination of misdeeds and assets had won him the enmity of S. Glenn Young and his zealots."

After Young and his men carried a machine gun and weapons into a courtroom following a heated scuffle with Klan opponents in December 1923, Sheriff Galligan asked for—and received—federal troops. Attorney Boswell demanded they be sent home at once. A compromise was reached: The mayor of Herrin agreed to replace his anti-Klan police officers with Klan sympathizers, and Galligan promised to raid any place suspected of selling liquor. The sheriff kept his promise and made eighteen raids. But the Klan didn't leave law enforcement to Galligan. The Young gang on January 20, 1924, arrested sixty-six alleged bootleggers and confiscated seven stills at Weaver, a mining camp near Herrin, and at Spillertown. Presumably the raiders avoided the homes in Weaver that had white cloths tied at the doorknobs, indicating the homes that belonged to Klan members.

On February 1, they followed with the biggest raid of all, involving twelve hundred to thirteen hundred Klansmen armed with warrants issued by justices of the peace. From 9 p.m. until noon the next day they arrested 125 people and seized six stills, twenty-seven barrels of wine, fifty-four gallons of white mule, and two hundred gallons of home brew. "At their destination [in Benton] the prisoners were formed into a column, and with Young, armed with his forty-fives and sub-machine gun, at the head and armed guards on the flanks, marched to the public square," Angle wrote. "Thousands of spectators witnessed one of the most novel parades ever seen in an American city."

In March 1924, a Williamson County grand jury reported on the "so-called raids by the Ku Klux Klan . . . numerous people were robbed, beaten, abused and in many instances imprisoned secretly without any legal process and wholly without justifiable cause."

Hospital Shootout

On Friday night, February 8, 1924, the tension exploded after members of Herrin's new pro-Klan police force stopped in on a meeting of anti-Klansmen at the Rome Club. A short time later Caesar Cagle, active Klansman and Herrin deputy constable, was fatally shot on the street by an unknown assailant. Klansmen issued warrants charging Sheriff Galligan, Ora Thomas, and Herrin Mayor C. E. Anderson with the murder. Young learned Thomas and Anderson were at the hospital with Galligan's deputy, John Layman, who had been injured in a scuffle at the Rome Club. In the wee hours of Saturday morning, Young headed to Herrin Hospital with several hundred Klansmen. Dr. J. T. Black, the hospital superintendent, refused to admit him, so Young smashed the glass of the door, poked a rifle through, aimed it at Black, and pulled the trigger. "I ducked and the bullet sizzled through my hair," Black recalled. "I ran upstairs."

The raiders began shooting into the hospital everywhere, and didn't stop. "We're going to blow the hospital to hell and kill everybody we can get our hands on," one said. They also invaded the nurses' home, a two-story building adjoining the hospital. "Three men came into the room occupied by myself and my sister, Ire," nurse Idell Getter told a reporter. "One of them waved a revolver at us and cried, 'Get out of bed, you women.' We did and they chased us down the hall into a room occupied by Miss Edna Morris. Then they demanded to know where we had hidden Ora Thomas. We convinced them that Thomas was not in the building. 'Well, it doesn't matter,' one of them said, 'we are going to kill you all anyway.' Finally someone outside yelled at them and they left. They came back several times and searched the place."

At least eighteen shots were fired into the room of nine-year-old Helen Baggett, who was recovering from a recent surgery. Her father was in the room at the time, and rolled Helen off the bed to the floor until the attack had ended. Amazingly, no one was injured, although a boy who had been operated on Friday afternoon for appendicitis died the next day.

Deputy Constable Cagle was buried that Sunday following ceremonies at the First Baptist Church in Herrin. Glotfelty referred to Cagle as a martyr to law enforcement and credited the "liquor element" with his death. A huge red cross bearing the letters KKK was held at the head of the grave as the casket was lowered.

While two thousand Guardsmen came into the town early Saturday morning to restore order and secure the hospital, Young set up his own dictatorship and proclaimed himself mayor, chief of police, and magistrate of Herrin. He deputized his henchmen with crude tin stars, set up a heavily armed fortress at the city hall, and patrolled the streets. He arrested Galligan and Anderson and threw them in jail for Cagle's murder. "These policemen had the time of their official lives arresting men, women and children by the score," the *St. Louis Star* reported. "The principal offense was failing to know the klan password which was changed about every twenty minutes by the powers that be. These 'law violators' were hailed before Young and either fined or sent to jail."

Although Young was ousted on February 11, 1924, by Major General Milton J. Foreman and one thousand men of the 132nd Infantry from Chicago, months of tension followed. The Herrin grand jury issued ninety-nine indictments in connection with the Herrin Hospital attack and the murder of Caesar Cagle. Two of the Shelton brothers, Carl and Earl, were indicted for the Cagle murder, not Anderson, Galligan, or Thomas. Young also was indicted on destruction of property and on twenty-three counts pertaining to the recent liquor raids, as well as charges of larceny, robbery with a deadly weapon, assault to murder, and false imprisonment. As a protest against the actions of the grand jury, the Klan hosted a large parade through the streets of Herrin.

Young became even more reckless after an attempt on his life in May 1924. He had taken the job of reorganizing the Klan in East St. Louis in April, and Young and his second wife, Maude Simcox Young, were driving to East St. Louis in his Lincoln touring car, purchased by the Klan. A car passed, and a barrage of gunfire injured Young in the leg and blinded his wife. They were taken to the Catholic-run St. Elizabeth's Hospital in Belleville, where the sisters tended to his wounds and prayed for the Klansman's speedy recovery. His corner room on the ground floor of the hospital was turned into an arsenal with two .45-caliber automatic pistols and a submachine gun with which a Klansman kept watch on the door. Attendants knew to knock discreetly before entering, even when they were summoned by Young himself. Klansmen stood guard outside the hospital.

From his room, Young kept the newspapers running with wild statements, one concerning a letter he had written recently to W. W. Anderson, head of the federal prohibition forces in Illinois. If officials did not clean up the hundreds of saloons and stills operating in Madison and St. Clair counties, he threatened, he and his Klansmen would take care of the problem. He also accused U.S. District Attorney W. O. Potter of being "fixed" by bootleggers (see Chapter 4).

Young skipped out on the hospital bill, after the U.S. Department of Justice refused to pay on the grounds Young wasn't a federal employee. In 1928, a Belleville collection agent still was trying to collect $1,358.70 from Young's wife, by then a widow.

THE GUNSLINGER BITES THE DUST

Young became an embarrassment to the statewide Klan organization, which dismissed him from his position in East St. Louis as soon as he was discharged from the hospital. From that time on, Angle said, he acted with "complete abandon." Among other actions, he brandished weapons and cursed in court. On September 13, 1924, he was officially expelled from the Klan, less than a month after six men were killed in a riot between Klan and anti-Klan factions at a Herrin garage. That same month he and twelve Klansmen were indicted by a federal grand jury in Danville for impersonating government officers during liquor raids. "I slept, performed my duties and ate my meals with my pistols always within reach," Galligan recalled. "There were always riot guns and high-powered rifles available to repel a possible klan attack on the jail, and there were men awake at all hours acting as sentrymen."

In January 1925, Young, two of his men, and Ora Thomas, by then a deputy sheriff, were killed following a gun battle in the Canary Cigar Store of Herrin's European Hotel. Elias Green, an officer of the local miners' union, was talking to store proprietor Mrs. Angelo Biotti when Young entered and began cursing and berating him. Green had gone before certain Williamson County unions and denounced Young as a protector of "scabs" and an enemy of union labor. "Then the door in the rear opened and in came Ora Thomas," Green told the *Post-Dispatch*. "Young whirled about and shouted, half over his shoulder, 'Close the door and lock it.' Ora just stood there and looked at Young. Ora had his hands on his two automatics but didn't make a move.

"Then, Young grabbed me and shoved me between them. I pushed Young a little back, and Young said, 'Don't draw, Ora, or I'll shoot, too.' Then I shoved back at Young and shoved him along the cigar case, and suddenly he drew one of his two guns and fired a shot but didn't hit anybody. Then Ora came out with his guns and fired twice and Young fell. At this time the shooting commenced from the outside and two men ran in with guns in their hands. I got out but the shooting continued until all were down."

Young died at the cigar store after two slugs pierced his heart. Thomas died en route to the hospital. There was no love lost between the two, Galligan recalled. Young was known to bird-dog Thomas's car when he and his wife and two young sons were out, he said.

Both funerals were public events. Thomas's casket was placed on the front porch of his small home, and some one thousand visitors filed past in the January snow. Two hundred and forty-six cars followed the procession to the cemetery. "While entrance to the Presbyterian Church had not been denied the body, it had been intimated that the reception of the body of Thomas in the church might cause discord in the congregation, which has a large proportion of klan sympathizers," the *Post-Dispatch* reported.

Young's body was clothed in full Klan regalia near an incandescent cross during packed services at First Baptist Church. Maude Young stroked the face of her husband in the coffin. Hooded pallbearers rode white-hooded horses, and eighty-six cars proceeded to the Herrin cemetery, where Young was buried in a concrete vault.

The tragedy was Mrs. Young, at twenty-four blind and a widow with a twenty-three-month-old son, Bobby, *Post-Dispatch* reporter Frederick Brennan reported. She had been the private secretary to Federal Judge George Washington English when she met Young, then still married to his first wife and a government witness in a number of cases. The two often were seen walking around town in Cairo with Young's police dog. "To her, whose grief is deepest, no light comes through the tears," Brennan wrote.

After Klan sympathizers announced that Mrs. Young would appear at a local theater in Harrisburg in February, the opposing faction announced that Mrs.

Thomas would speak a few days later. Residents learned the news and disapproved, and city officials spoke with leaders of both factions, who agreed to cancel the engagements. Mrs. Young also was scheduled to speak in Carbondale, but that engagement was canceled by the Carbondale City Council at a special meeting.

The vault that housed Young's body became a target for pistol shots from passing autos, a former member of the Shelton gang told the *St. Louis Star* in February 1927. "His widow has remarried her late husband's chauffeur, and I understand they are now running a barbecue stand at Patoka, Illinois," said the gang member, who planned to go straight and would only use the pseudonym "Ralph Johnson."

Clashes and occasional shootings followed the big shootout that killed Young and Thomas, but the Klan's influence was receding. On April 13, 1926, six were killed in a shootout at the Herrin primary elections, which marked the Klan's last stand. "The Klan organization collapsed entirely in 1926, after the Illinois State Militia effectively destroyed the Klan's stronghold in Williamson County," Andrew J. Theising noted in *Made in U.S.A.*

With Klan support, Arlie O. Boswell was elected state's attorney from Williamson County and took office in 1926. He struck up a friendship with the Birger Gang and was a frequent visitor to their hangout, Shady Rest. In January 1929, he was found guilty of conspiracy to violate the national prohibition act after federal witnesses testified he solicited and accepted "protection" bribes, neglected the duties of his office and connived with Birger's gang and other law violators. Convicted of similar charges were Hezzie Byrn, former Johnston City police chief, and Pete Salmo, a Williamson County bootlegger.

Picking Them Off in Poplar Bluff

Months after the Williamson County liquor raids, a "private citizen" of St. Louis named G. H. Foree led a wholesale series of raids in Poplar Bluff between 3 and 5 p.m. on August 4, 1924. The crusaders, who described themselves as "special deputies of the Ku Klux Klan," arrested two women and thirty men. Indignant friends and relatives of those arrested, assisted by newspaper correspondents and others, learned that federal prohibition officers assisted in the raids. Foree claimed to have been a government investigator during World War I and was said to have conducted a private investigation in March, April, and May, during which he said he bought illicit liquor at Poplar Bluff restaurants and hotels that he and his followers later raided. He was reportedly employed by the Ku Klux Klan and several church groups. Among others assisting him was another St. Louisan, I. E. Palmer. "At one time Foree worked at a shoe factory here [in Poplar Bluff]," the *Globe-Democrat* reported.

U. S. Attorney Allen Curry was incensed. He told the *Globe-Democrat* his office would not tolerate the activities of the Klan in enforcing the dry law and said his office would investigate Foree and two assistants. He did not want a repetition of the liquor law enforcement agitation that caused casualties in Williamson County, Illinois. The person or agency who authorized the agents to work with the Klan raiders was not mentioned in local newspaper accounts. Foree told D. B. Deem, probate court judge in Poplar Bluff, "in the presence of a number of persons that he was a federal officer," Deem said. "Later he told others he was not a federal officer."

Deem assailed "a certain element" in the churches for passing resolutions favoring such raids. "They never issue proclamations approving actions of local officers," he said. "The local officers get more contraband whiskey and make more arrests in most months than Foree brought about in three months' time."

Curry presented the evidence to a federal grand jury that reconvened in September. Foree, Palmer, and A. Booher of St. Louis were charged with possession of some of the liquor seized in their raids.

A GROWING REPUTATION

From time to time Klansmen made the news, but the stories were never good. One of the most brutal incidents involved the murder of Albert W. Saegesser, a thirty-seven-year-old real estate man, in February 1924 at his home in Webster Groves. Saegesser was listening with headphones to a radio set in his living room when Beecher Coleman, a Klan member, fired two shots through a window into the back of Saegesser's head. Saegesser's three-year-old daughter was playing at his feet, and his wife was in the kitchen. When the shots struck, Saegesser was telling his mother he had just tuned in to a good program that he wanted her to hear.

Coleman recently had been discharged from the St. Louis Police Department because of his Klan activities. He gave himself up to St. Louis police and told them he had been discharged from a job being done in Ferguson by the Magray Real Estate Company, of which Saegesser was treasurer. He said Saegesser had no right to discharge him and take the bread and butter from his family. He purchased a shotgun in East St. Louis and proceeded straight to Saegesser's home.

POLITICAL PULL

In Missouri, Klan support generally was more of a liability than an asset, though some local elections early on were carried on Klan-backed candidates and issues. Former Governor Frederick D. Gardner declared the Klan was "dying" in 1924, and both the Democratic and Republican parties denounced the organization. A major scandal that year concerned allegations that Dr. Arthur W. Nelson, the Democratic party's nominee for governor, had once belonged to the Ku Klux Klan in California, Missouri. Nelson denied the charges, though he refused to criticize the Klan. He lost the election to Republican Samuel Baker, who like Nelson had been endorsed by the Klan.

In 1925, similar charges were made against Victor J. Miller, a Republican candidate for St. Louis mayor, who offered twenty-five thousand dollars to any person who could prove he was a member, had signed an application for membership, or attended a meeting of the Klan. He won the race. Miller, who served as president of the St. Louis Police Board from 1921 to 1923, did cozy up to the Klan and temperance types, St. Louis writer and poet Orrick Johns recalled in his memoirs, *Time of Our Lives.* "Miller was an eccentric who sought and obtained the support of the Anti-saloon league, while he himself boasted of his high dingoes in all the live spots in town," Johns wrote. "He was playing the demagogue to a following of silly temperance women, their intimidated following, and the Ku Klux Klan. These forces were organized and well-equipped with money in Missouri, during the Harding-Coolidge era."

Orrick's father, *Post-Dispatch* editor George Johns, bitterly fought prohibition and its allies. Orrick claimed Miller issued an order to the entire police force to "Get George Johns in an embarrassing situation. Follow him and disgrace him, and if you have a good excuse, bump him off."

One night some officers brought in a man they claimed was George Johns. Orrick Johns recounted the reaction: "The precinct Captain looked at the prisoner, and said to the officers, 'Go take a jump for yourself in the river. I've known George Johns all my life. This guy looks as much like him as I look like Vic Miller.' The unidentified victim went home."

The *St. Louis Argus* took the St. Louis Board of Aldermen to task in June 1923 for its recent refusal to endorse resolutions condemning the Klan, and for its role in fostering segregation in the city. "In the face of these facts, we here at St. Louis can't but report that the spirit of the Klan is prevalent in this part of the country," the African American newspaper observed. "We can further report that during a recent initiation of the klansmen near St. Louis, a spokesman let it be known that not only the Negroes, Catholics and Jews are marked by the Klan, but also the Greeks.

"Of course, in a country like this, tolerance goes a long ways. But when the spirit of Ku Kluxism finds its way into high officialdom, then it's time for the people to sit up and take notice. Surely the Negroes, the Jews, the Greeks and the Catholics will answer the Ku Kluxters spirit with their ballots when the time comes."

Some, like the St. Charles City Council, found technical reasons to disallow local Klan groups to meet on city property. The Illinois legislature took matters a step further when it approved a bill in June 1923 that made it "unlawful to appear in public places with evil or wicked purpose while hooded, robed or masked to conceal identity."

Some refused to accept the Klan's bullying tactics. Among them were Martin B. Lohmann, a longtime Illinois state representative and insurance and real estate broker in Pekin. Two Klansmen and a preacher visited his office one day, Lohmann told an interviewer in 1979: "'We are forming an organization,' he says, 'in Pekin and we want you in it' . . . if I didn't join, they'd put me out of business. And I said, 'You mean politically?' 'Oh, no, we won't put you out of that, but we'll put you out of the insurance and real estate business.' He didn't no more get it out—if the lady was living that worked for me—I can hear her scream yet—but I had a club and I took a swing at that guy and the two fellows—one of them owed me five dollars that he had borrowed from me at a bootlegging joint. The other one had his feet under my mother's table. Don't think I didn't tell them! I run them out of that office with that club, all three of them."

Kleaning Up

East St. Louis, Illinois, was a corrupt city before prohibition took its toll, and the graft continued as the Klan and hoodlums such as the Shelton brothers battled for control of the city's bootleg liquor market, author Andrew Theising noted. In 1923, an organization called the Good Government League hosted a meeting at which Alexander Flannigan, a longtime lawyer from East St. Louis, described his home as the worst city politically in the United States, a city governed by bribery. "I have bribed the City Council in the old days, but it is too late to indict me now," he said.

In April 1923, the Klan lost a hard-fought battle to elect its candidates to city commissionerships in East St. Louis. Only one Klan-backed candidate claimed victory, and even he denounced the group. "I am not a Klansman," Ralph Cook said. "I never sought the Ku Klux Klan endorsement, and I repudiate that organization; it will get nothing from me."

But members rode on, and in May 1923 some ten thousand Klansmen met in their white robes near a flaming cross on a farm near Monk's Mound in what is now Cahokia Mounds State Historic Site. Gilbert W. Killinger, journalist and future Collinsville mayor, observed the event with his future wife. "We saw it and there were so many people there," Killinger told an interviewer in 1976. "Traffic along route 40 was blocked for miles and miles." After the meeting, one hundred or more carloads of Klansmen took a midnight tour of downtown East St. Louis, with white handkerchiefs tied to the car doors, Taylor Pensoneau reported in *Brothers Notorious*.

During one Klan parade James O. Monroe, Sr., the publisher of the *Collinsville Herald*, copied down every license number he could get at the corner of St. Louis Road and Main Street. "So the next day he checked with the State Police," said Killinger, then a reporter for the *Collinsville Herald*. "They got the names of the drivers of those cars, the owners of those cars, and published them in the paper the next edition. We had all kinds of telephone calls. All kinds of them. Mr. Monroe had one or two threats but nothing came out of it except that everybody knew who was the head of the Klan who was here then. And they didn't last too much longer after that. It looked like the publicity of the thing . . . I think Mr. Monroe had accomplished that."

East St. Louis Boodle-oo

The Klan's corruption was revealed in March 1924, after Orla H. Cannady, proprietor of a drug store in East St. Louis, claimed that two agents of the Klan tried to extort five hundred dollars from him. Cannady said Jerry Cummings, a shoe store owner in East St. Louis, and Harve McCormick, a clerk formerly employed by Cummings, demanded that he donate five hundred dollars to the Klan building fund or face prosecution for an alleged liquor law violation. L. V. Walcott, assistant U. S. attorney in East St. Louis, said no complaint ever was made of illegal sale of whiskey at Cannady's drugstore.

Cummings told a different story to the *St. Louis Star*. He said he had been approached by some southern Illinois residents who said they had evidence against Cannady for selling liquor, "and [I] said it probably could be settled satisfactorily out of court." East St. Louis businessmen not affiliated with the Klan offered their assistance to any druggist from whom money was demanded. State's Attorney Hilmar C. Lindauer said he would investigate Cannady's charge.

Later in March, eight East St. Louis Klan members were caught in a sweep of liquor violators by investigators hired by a Klan subsidiary known as the St. Clair County Law Enforcement League. Among them was Klansman Thomas J. Anthony, owner of a saloon that was closed as a "common nuisance."

Two days later, authorities learned of a one-hundred-member "Department of Constabulary" operated by the East St. Louis Klan. Borrowing names from prominent public figures who had no idea they were included on the Klan letterhead, the department came to light when two men with revolvers were arrested in an East St. Louis saloon. They had permits to carry revolvers issued by a suburban justice of the peace. At the "constabulary" office, a *Post-Dispatch* reporter found one Ralph G. Deal, who produced the misleading letterhead and said the organization was open to anyone to become a member and receive a "gun toting" permit. The letterhead indicated the headquarters were in Chicago, although the East St. Louis branch had offices in the Metropolitan Building a few doors from the office of Klansman Charles D. McGehee, the Methodist minister who had been defrocked. McGehee was known as the "Great Titan" of the Klan for southern Illinois, and himself wore a constabulary star.

On March 31, the East St. Louis City Council passed a resolution ordering Police Chief John J. Barry to investigate the constabulary, organized under provisions of the city's 1887 anti-horse-thief act. The East St. Louis Chamber of Commerce adopted a related resolution that said members of so-called law enforcement organizations should not be permitted to carry firearms and should be restrained from any operation except that of obtaining evidence. "It is but a short step to anarchy when groups of citizens arm for any purpose and presume to take over the duties of regular public officers," the chamber resolution read in part.

Less than a month later, S. Glenn Young arrived in East St. Louis to conduct a Klan-authorized liquor cleanup of the city. "East St. Louis is a rotten city and has a bad reputation all over the state," Young told fourteen hundred Klansmen who gathered to greet him on April 25, 1924. "It is run by a bunch of corrupt politicians. I am still a resident of Williamson County, and that county is the cleanest in the entire state now."

East St. Louis Mayor Malbern M. Stephens begged to differ. "If the city is rotten it is because of the Klan and not the city officials being corrupt," Stephens said. "As for cleaning up the city, I think he [Young] will only get it dirty."

That same day, a federal grand jury in Danville, Illinois, returned three indictments charging extortion by threat against alleged liquor violators. Charged were Dr. H. F. Killene, exalted cyclops of the East St. Louis Ku Klux Klan; H. A. McCormack, member of the Klan Executive Committee; and A. I. Cummings, a Klansman. Killene was charged with demanding and receiving five hundred dollars from East St. Louis druggist Edward R. Chase, on his promise to stop prosecution for an alleged Volstead Act offense. McCormick and Cummings were charged in the attempted extortion of druggist Orla Cannady. A state grand jury at Belleville returned similar indictments against the three the same day.

ON THE WAY OUT

Otto Turley, a former investigator for the St. Clair County Law Enforcement League, was a shining star for a time. Turley, a paid Klan agent who accompanied S. Glenn Young on his raids, was credited with going undercover and buying liquor in twenty-eight resorts against which charges were made. The league prosecuted more than three hundred dry-law cases in 1924. That August, however, Turley literally was caught holding the bag—or in this case the basket—at a bar at 453 Collinsville Avenue. Federal prohibition agents had been called to serve a permanent injunction against the bar's owner, Max Sonsinski. As they approached the house, there was a scuffling of feet, and U.S. Deputy Marshal

FISH GONE DRINKING

The *St. Louis County Watchman-Advocate* credited the KKK with aquatic mayhem in the River Des Peres in May 1924:

> *You can believe it or not, but 667 River Des Peres carp went home drunk Thursday night and beat their wives. Four hundred and thirty-nine suckers got their scales all turned the wrong way trying to back over the gas company dam. . . . And long, long after their bedtime 19 lonesome catfish were tearfully serenading Maplewood and Shrewsbury singing, "Father, Dear Father, Come Home to Me Now.*
> *". . . Between the hours of 10 a.m. and 1 p.m. the river was treated to 10,000 gallons of hooch by weak-kneed manufacturers of the stuff that cheers because a rumor was circulated that Glenn Young and his flying squadron of Klu Kluxers were about to pay a visit . . . at midnight it is said that some of our dryest citizens were out with expanded nostrils doing the old-time folk dances and praying for a flood . . ."*

Broadway, East St. Louis, Illinois.

Guy M. Wallace stepped up to find a door slammed in his face. The government agents waited and listened, as they heard the telltale clinking of bottles inside. They then hurried around to the back to catch Turley coming over the side of the one-story garage at the rear, the roof of which led to the Sonsinski apartment. Turley was lugging a basket filled with fifteen bottles of home-brewed beer and several whiskey bottles containing a sour substance resembling vinegar. He was charged with violation of the prohibition act and for contempt, based on possession of illicit liquor in a place upon which a temporary "dry" law injunction had been served. Turley expressed surprise on seeing the officers and said he was working in the garage owned by Sonsinski. He did not state how he came into possession of the beer.

Turley's troubles were not over. In January 1928, he was sentenced to four months in jail and fined three hundred dollars for possession of a still. In July 1929, he was charged in a federal warrant with theft of goods in interstate shipment. He and seven others had been arrested earlier that year by East St. Louis police and railroad special agents in connection with the theft of merchandise valued at five thousand dollars from the railroad yards.

In February 1926, the *New York Times* credited internal dissension and external ridicule with the Klan's pending demise. "Outside criticism and the wearing process of time have helped to bring about the decline, the novelty of the movement has lost its appeal and, most important, perhaps, of all, the Klan has not been able to achieve its advertised ends," the *Times* opined. "It has failed of any outstanding accomplishment, even where its strength was greatest."

CHAPTER 16
OUR ELECTED OFFICIALS

The man who votes to send his fellow man to prison for selling a drink of whiskey, and yet buys a drink for himself, is a contemptible coward.
—U.S. Senator James Reed, D-Missouri

ON JANUARY 18, 1929, THE PHONE RANG IN THE OFFICE OF THE PROHIBITION administrator for the District of Columbia. "There's a leaking suitcase in this place, and it smells like liquor," reported Patrick Lynch, an employee of the American Railway Express Company. Basil N. Quinn, an agent of the Prohibition Enforcement Service, proceeded to the express office and learned the dripping suitcase was addressed to Room 411 of the House Office Building. Lynch noted that a trunk, part of the same shipment from New York City, had been delivered to Room 411 two days earlier. Quinn realized he had a member of Congress on his hands, so he contacted his superiors to double-check the search procedure.

This wasn't just any congressman. Room 411 was the office of one the driest members of the House of Representatives, Edward Everett Denison, a Republican from Marion in southern Illinois. A fourteen-year veteran of the Twenty-fifth District, Denison had voted for every law put forth by prohibition advocates. His farming constituents in Little Egypt had voted wet in a 1926 liquor referendum, but Denison never veered from his course. "He was about the last person of those on Capitol Hill expected to run afoul the District bone-dry net," observed the *New York Times*.

Denison was at his desk when Quinn and another agent showed up at the office the next day and glimpsed the trunk. The surprised representative replied he had left at home the key to the trunk, which contained only a set of dishes from a junket to Panama. The skeptical agents met Denison back at the office that evening, but his key didn't fit. He told the agents that if the trunk belonged to him it would have his name on the end. They raised the trunk. "B. B. Dawson," it read.

The agents were sure the name had been written, or changed, on the trunk sometime between their two visits. Denison became angry. Using a screwdriver and pliers, the agents finally snapped the lock. Inside, neatly packed, were eighteen bottles of real Scotch whiskey and six bottles of gin. Denison denied ownership and suggested the express company had delivered a trunk belonging to somebody else, such as the mysterious B. B. Dawson. Denison also would hint, but never actually say, that the spirituous luggage belonged to his nephew, Charles Lane, who also went on the Central American junket. The agents believed the story and went on their way, and that was the end of it, he would later say.

The agents gave a different story: that Denison pleaded for the incident to be kept secret, as newspaper publicity would mean his political ruin and dash his hopes of being appointed to a post by President Herbert Hoover. For reasons never made clear, nothing was done about the case for nearly ten months. Unexpectedly, on November 6, District Attorney Leo A. Rover presented the charges to a District of Columbia grand jury, which promptly indicted Denison for possession of intoxicants. He was the third member of the House that year to face liquor charges.

After some legal maneuvers, the case was tried in the District of Columbia Supreme Court in March 1931. "I never bought any liquor in Panama," the congressman testified at his trial. "Why, I wouldn't know what to do with it because I'm not a drinking man."

Despite the prosecutor's assertion that the story was "a fine fairy tale," a jury acquitted Denison in one hour. He shook hands all around and said he would soon take a trip around the world. He had plenty of time for it. The Anti-Saloon League had supported Denison in his 1930 re-election bid, but the voters

President Herbert Hoover. Courtesy Library of Congress

didn't take so kindly to the scandal and retired him from office in 1931. He ran again for Congress in 1932 and for circuit judge in 1939 but lost both races.

THE "DRINKING DRYS"

U.S. Senator James Reed of Missouri, an unabashed wet, once threatened to publish a list of the legislators he knew who voted dry and drank wet. "It will not be many years before the moral sensibilities of the American people will awake to the fact that the prohibition law is the worst crime in the history of the United States and that the reign of hypocrisy and cant, of false pretense and of chicanery and fraud will have come to an ignominious end," Reed said during debate on the pending Jones Law in 1929.

Reed's threat on a Saturday made for an upsetting weekend for many of his Senate colleagues. On Monday, Reed let them off the hook. "I have made many mistakes and done many wicked things, but I have never fallen to the level of a prohibition informer," he said. "I thought at the time I had perpetrated a joke, but it seems it should have been so labeled."

In the Illinois legislature that same year, State Representative Thomas J. O'Grady lobbied for a bill he co-sponsored to put a statewide referendum on the ballot to repeal the Illinois prohibition law. "There are those members on this floor right now," O'Grady said, "who are going to vote dry on this bill whom I have seen so drunk that they could scarcely walk on the streets of Springfield."

Even a distinguished federal judge like Louis Fitzhenry of the United States Circuit Court of Appeals was said by one source to repair for drinks to a café near his Springfield, Illinois, office. The bane of the wets, Fitzhenry was the first federal judge to uphold the constitutionality of the wartime prohibition act, and he created a sensation with a decision that the buyer of liquor was a felon and was as guilty as the one who sold it. He once ruled that if one was a guest in a home where liquor was served, that person was guilty of a law violation and subject to the same penalty as a bootlegger unless he reported the liquor law violation to the authorities.

Nick Campo of Springfield, a restaurant owner at the time of prohibition, said he knew of a café owner in town who served Fitzhenry whiskey. "Judge Fitzhenry used to go . . . in there for lunch every day and the fellow—he's dead now—he used to serve him whiskey in coffee cups so that people wouldn't see that he was drinking," Campo said in an oral history interview in 1974. "I know. I know what I'm talking about."

William "Smokey" Downey, who later served as assistant to Illinois Governor William Stratton in the 1950s, landed a job at the *Illinois State Journal* in 1928 as a police reporter. He got to know some of the legislators around Springfield. "Well, the bootlegging joints got the legislators that were always voting dry," Downey recalled in 1982. "They hung around the bootlegging joints as much as those who were always voting wet."

LEGISLATIVE MONKEYSHINES

Two years after science teacher John T. Scopes was found guilty of teaching evolution in violation of Tennessee law, educators in Missouri were spared a similar restrictive statute by twenty votes.

A monkey named Joe Scopes watched from the gallery at the Missouri state capitol in February 1927 as principal proponent Sam D. McDaniel of McDonald County argued that since the Bible was not taught in the public schools, Darwinian theory also should be excluded. Tongue-in-cheek legislators offered a flurry of amendments, including one by C. P. Turley of Carter County that the law should apply only to counties where a "majority of the people have rejected and refuse to accept the discoveries and findings of scientific thought and research for the past 400 years, and who believe that the world is flat; that the sun travels daily around the earth; that the storms of the sea are caused by the fury of monsters of the deep; that the gleam of the evil eye is the basilisk of sickness and death; that an epileptic is a wicked person possessed of Satan."

St. Louis legislator Clifford Rens suggested that punishment should be changed from a fine and revocation of one's teaching permit to "imprisonment in the St. Louis Zoo for not less than thirty days or forty nights." They need not be found guilty to be punished, only "suspected of being guilty," he said.

The bill was defeated by 82 to either 61 or 62, depending on the account. "It is said that a newspaper man conceived the entry of the bill as a joke; the 62 votes for it were not so humorous," Frederic Arthur Culmer observed in *A New History of Missouri*.

Hearing the news, the simian chairman of the Saint Louis Zoo's Monkey House Committee on Evolution treated himself to a drink, the *St. Louis Star* reported. "We are pleased that our lobbyist did his stuff yesterday," he was quoted as saying, "and the Monkey House has voted to reward him with a sack of goobers. It was great work."

St. Nicholas Hotel, Springfield, Ill.

During prohibition, the St. Nicholas was the hotel of choice for the Illinois legislators who frequented the bootlegging joints of Springfield, retired newspaperman William "Smokey" Downey recalled in 1982.

POLITICAL CHAMELEONS

Prohibition issues dominated state and federal legislative matters in the late 1920s and early 1930s. These included attempts to modify the law, enforcement methods, and an ongoing debate on the use of additives to make industrial liquor unfit to drink, in many instances poisoning it. Each state legislature and the federal legislature handled hundreds of such bills dealing with prohibition issues. To list them all would take a book by itself.

Voters on either side of the debate were unable to choose their candidate by party affiliation alone. As Frederic Arthur Culmer noted in *A New History of Missouri*, "in Missouri the Democratic party *used to be* the dry party, and the Republican, especially among the Germans in St. Louis, the *wet.*"

If he or she could get away with it, the most expedient tactic was for a politician to mask his views on prohibition. Elmer E. E. McJimsey tried, but failed. McJimsey's race for Missouri governor in the 1920 Republican primary had started out on a positive note. He was the choice of many Republican "wets," and he set a precedent in Missouri campaigning when he made a two-week, whirlwind tour of the state in an army airplane piloted by Ensign Ralph Snavely. In July 1920, he earned plaudits from the *St. Louis County Watchman-Advocate* when he served as principal orator at a picnic to benefit the Meramec Highlands Road and School Improvement Association. The picnic was held at Eden Park, generously donated for the event by proprietor Peter Gounis, who would become known as a notorious liquor law violator.

Shortly before the election, McJimsey was tripped up during a debate with his opponent, Arthur M. Hyde, an admittedly dry Bible class teacher from northwest Missouri, author Jean Carnahan noted in *If Walls Could Talk: The Story of Missouri's First Families.*

Hyde called for his opponent to declare if he was wet or dry and asked him to tell how he voted in the last Springfield, Missouri, election on prohibition. "I have answered," McJimsey replied. ". . . only Mr. McJimsey knows whether he is wet or dry, and he won't tell," Hyde responded. "They taught me when a boy of a toad that takes its color from the leaves of the tree in which it lives, so I guess McJimsey is wet in the city, dry in the country and of varying degrees of humidity in between."

The audience's applause turned into an ovation. Hyde then launched an attack on the "boss regime" in St. Louis and the Central Trade and Labor Union of St. Louis, which Hyde said endorsed McJimsey because he was wet. Hyde, of Trenton, had been angered by longtime Republican committeeman Nat Goldstein's assertion that he didn't stand a chance in St. Louis.

"Does anyone know where Mr. McJimsey stands on the wet and dry question?" Hyde asked at a luncheon in July 1920 at the City Club in St. Louis. Finally McJimsey stood up. "I said in announcing my platform that whether prohibition is constitutional or not is a question for the courts, and not for governors, to decide," McJimsey said. "If that question comes up it will be referred to the legislature, and can be submitted to the people for a referendum. I will not offer any obstacle to the people. Their declaration will be mine." Jeers came from the crowd, the *St. Louis Star* reported. "Are you wet or dry?" "Say it."

"McJimsey already had sat down," the *Star* reported. "He said only half audibly, 'I have given my answer.'"

The *St. Louis Post-Dispatch* denounced McJimsey as "the political chameleon . . . who tries to sneak into office by deceiving everybody." Others readily agreed, and Hyde won the primary and was elected governor in November.

Democrat Martin B. Lohmann, an Illinois state legislator and later a state senator from Pekin, acknowledged it would have been easy to declare himself a "dry" in some areas. Paved roads were a more important issue than prohibition at the time, but prohibition wasn't far behind. "Now, I'll tell you, if I would have lied, it would have been simple," Lohmann recalled in 1979. "Under seventy-five or eighty miles from here, I could have said, 'Yes, I'm for the Anti-Saloon League,' you know, and 'I'm for prohibition.' I could have lied, but I got a father and a mother—your teachings in early life, one of the things is, in German, you '*shalt nicht flugen.*' That means you shouldn't swear or lie. See, I give them the answer whether they was for me or against me."

That worked against him in some places, but his honesty was appreciated in many instances. "I heard a fellow go out of my office one time, they come up to see me about a road, and 'By God,' he says, 'I'm going to vote for that little fellow.' He said, 'He tells the truth.' That's what I heard when he got outside with his gang that had come to see me, you know."

Outstate, it wasn't easy to be a wet through most of the 1920s. A crowd of four hundred walked out on former St. Louis Judge Henry S. Priest, dripping-wet candidate for Missouri governor in 1924, as he gave an address in the Hannibal courthouse. "The atmosphere appears to have cleared somewhat," observed Priest, and he went on with his address. Priest had just concluded an attack on the Ku Klux Klan and was stating his views on prohibition when the members of the audience began leaving. He was running on a clear anti-Klan and anti-prohibition platform; it was unclear where the three other Democratic candidates stood on the issues. Priest was defeated in the Democratic primary race.

There was no shortage of wet legislators, particularly in big-city areas. Where it mattered—in the state legislatures and in Congress—drys (at least dry-voting legislators) beat out wets by resounding margins.

THE REED LEGACY

One of prohibition's fiercest opponents was James Reed of Missouri, who served in the U.S. Senate continuously from 1911 to 1929. He cited a disillusionment with "drinking drys" in his decision to retire from the Senate, which also followed a failed bid in the 1928 Democratic presidential primary. "I have enjoyed many agreeable companionships with Senators, but after a convivial evening with them, during which I was amazed by their capacity for imbibing liquor, I have heard those same Senators make impassioned speeches in favor of prohibition," he said. "I am sick of sitting in the Senate and observing Senators look to Wayne B. Wheeler [chief counsel for the Anti-Saloon League] in the gallery to motion to them how to vote!"

Reed had risen through the ranks as prosecuting attorney of Jackson County and mayor of Kansas City, where he named future political boss Thomas J. Pendergast as street commissioner. He defeated St. Louisan David Francis in

Missouri Senator James Reed. Courtesy Library of Congress.

the 1910 Senate Democratic primary. Never a Progressive, Reed fought women's suffrage and launched an all-out assault on Woodrow Wilson's League of Nations. He bitterly fought the Ku Klux Klan, anti-Semites, protective tariffs, members of the Anti-Saloon League, and, later, President Franklin Roosevelt's New Deal. Author Paul Nagel describes him as a controversial Jeffersonian in *Missouri: A History.*

His opposition to the League of Nations, women's suffrage, and prohibition earned him stiff opposition from women, who formed "Rid Us of Reed" clubs in an unsuccessful attempt to defeat him in the 1922 Senate race. "The 'Rid Us of Reed' club which the ladies said was 'non-partisan,' became the nucleus out of which grew the League of Women Voters in St. Louis," wrote Reed's friend and biographer, attorney Lee Meriwether of St. Louis. "My niece was the President of that nucleus, which had a single purpose, to ruin Reed. As he left the Jefferson Hotel that April day in 1922 . . . he was diverted by a funeral procession passing slowly by; in a hearse was a coffin above which was a banner bearing the words, 'Reed's Political Corpse on the Way to Oblivion.' The happy mourners were members of the ladies' 'Rid Us of Reed' club."

Reed managed to carry both the primary and the general election for the Senate with the help of voters in St. Louis and Kansas City, particularly German American Republicans who applauded his opposition to Wilson's foreign policy as well as to prohibition, author Richard Kirkendall noted in *History of Missouri, Volume V.*

Known more for what he opposed—such as a strong central government—than for what he favored, Reed was able to do little on the prohibition issue because he was one of only a few senators who opposed it from the outset. Others, such as U.S. Representative Harry B. Hawes of Missouri, formerly the attorney for St. Louis brewers, favored modification of prohibition to allow light beer and wine.

Kirkendall published a description of Reed by an unnamed source as "not a nice man, not a kind man, not a fair man or a pleasant one, but an enormously able one, honest, courageous. Also, he can be charming when he wants. His humor and likable traits are often obscured by his tendency to believe nearly everything in the world is rotten, and almost all the people who are not damned fools are damned scoundrels. He goes cursing and damning his way through life, setting fire to his foes, jealously guarding his grudges, of which he has a large accumulation."

He was a good friend to many, including perhaps the only orator in the Senate who was his superior, William Borah, with whom Reed debated on the issue of prohibition. "Jim Reed was one of the most virile men I ever knew," Hawes said. "Vigorous, alert, handsome, he had a carrying voice that in those days before radios and microphones was a great asset. When he was mayor of Kansas City he often visited St. Louis and we became fast friends. When he became a Senator he bought a Ford car in which he often took me on long drives in the Washington area. Sometimes we were accompanied by famous good fellows like Billy Reedy of the St. Louis *Mirror,* and George Johns of the *Post-Dispatch.*"

Reed drank moderately and enjoyed an old-fashioned or a highball, Meriwether said. As much a zealot against the cause of prohibition as some of the drys were for it, he had only contempt for such prohibitionists as Andrew Volstead, author of the prohibition enforcement act. "I never had the pleasure of seeing until the other day the distinguished author of the Volstead act," Reed declared in 1921. "I do not know what his ancestry may be, but I do know that I have seen the pictures of some of the conspirators of the past, the countenances of those who have led in fanatical revolts, the burners of witches, the executioners who applied the torch, and I saw them all again when I looked at the author of this bill."

There was no love lost on the dry end, either, when Reed asked the White House for a stay of sentence for convicted bootlegger George Remus (see Chapter 11). Reed maintained Remus, known by many as the "King of the Bootleggers," had been "too drastically prosecuted"; Justice Department officials disagreed.

Years later, after his retirement in 1929, he sounded off on the Jones Act, which raised maximum penalties for bootleggers to five years and ten thousand dollars. It simply opened the way for large-scale blackmail, he said. He added that

Governor Al Smith of New York.
Courtesy Library of Congress.

he "had cross-examined Volstead and associated with Jones, and neither ever had a thought. "If I had to live a life planned by Jones and Volstead, I would commit suicide," he said. "Just because several hundred jackasses get together and pass it, does not make a law right."

MAKING HAY FOR SMITH

Strange bedfellows shared the Democratic ticket in Missouri in November 1928. They were New York Governor Al Smith, a wet and a Catholic, for president, and Charles M. Hay of St. Louis, said to be the driest Democrat in Missouri, for U.S. Senate. Their Republican opponents were Herbert Hoover and Roscoe C. Patterson, respectively.

Originally from rural Missouri, Hay came to St. Louis to practice law and retained his Methodist and prohibitionist beliefs and his support for the League of Nations, which made him an outcast among city politicians. He was a former dry leader in the Missouri legislature, served as counsel for the Anti-Saloon League, and defended Missouri Labor Commissioner Heber Nations against charges of conspiring to distribute Griesedieck beer (see Chapter 5). Hay's wife was active in Women's Christian Temperance Union (WCTU) affairs. Hay was an ardent foe of Reed, who backed his own, unsuccessful, Senate candidate in the 1928 primary. The *Post-Dispatch* once described Hay as "dry as a covered bridge."

"He is a rather extraordinary-looking man: fairly tall, heavy-set, partly bald," the *New York Times* observed at the Democratic convention in Madison Square Garden in 1924. "He is a new power in Democratic politics in Missouri, very much of a leader in the anti-Reed fight and, according to all the Missourians, a comer who will be heard from in the near future, and may become a figure in the present convention through the advocacy of a mild Klan plank."

Hay refused to budge on the prohibition issue and was adamantly opposed even to modification, a stand that won him the support of the Anti-Saloon League and the WCTU in the primary. As the 1928 presidential campaign wore on, political deals were struck between the Reed and anti-Reed factions of the state Democratic party. "Yet the Democratic wets of Missouri are going to support him because they want the drys in turn to support Smith," the *Post-Dispatch* noted in 1928. "The Democratic organization in St. Louis, one of the wettest cities in the nation, is arranging to trade Hay votes for Smith votes. Let us say that the outcome is the election of both these men. Gov. Smith, as President, proposes modification of the Volstead Act. Mr. Hay, as Senator, says no. Like all the drys, he is adamant. The wets propose compromise, but not the drys. What, then, is accomplished in this difficult matter by choosing the one man to offset the other?

"Nothing, you will say. Precisely. It is where the most amazing hypocrisy that any people ever practiced have landed us."

All the speculation was moot, the *Edwardsville Intelligencer* declared in October 1928. For example, Reed was unable to deliver any changes amid a Senate full of drys. The same would be true of Smith, if elected: His only opportunity to influence the prohibition question would be to fill any vacancies on the Supreme Court. "The United States will remain 'dry' until a majority of congressmen and senators are anti-prohibitionists and there is no present indication that situation will ever arise," predicted the *Intelligencer.*

The lively race of 1928 brought out some nasty slurs against the Catholics. There was talk in some of the rural Democratic areas that the political workers weren't working very hard to get votes for the national ticket, due to Smith's religion and his stand on prohibition.

The national WCTU began a campaign against Smith, saying he worked for more saloons while he rose through the ranks of the Tammany Hall political machine in New York, and would lead the way to legalized liquor. And the

Reverend Parker Shields, superintendent of the Missouri Anti-Saloon League, wrote to four hundred Protestant clergy urging them to write to their local newspapers with various arguments in favor of Hoover. "I do not regard Governor Smith's candidacy for the Presidency a moral menace any more than I consider the record of the Anti-Saloon League in Indiana, New York, Illinois and Missouri a model of Christian citizenship," retorted the Reverend John Thomas Stewart, pastor of the First Congregational Church in Bonne Terre, Missouri, who made the letter public.

Julius W. Reinholdt, a prominent St. Louis businessman and lifelong Republican, said in September 1928 he was leaning toward Hoover. "I am not a Catholic, and I detest to see the religious issue brought into this election," Reinholdt told the *New York Times*. "If the Republican party seeks to capitalize Governor Smith's Catholicism and make it a campaign issue, he certainly will get my vote."

Outstate, however, was a different story. Henry T. Burckhartt, a native of central Missouri who had since moved to Los Angeles, California, wrote his old friend Taylor Kingsbury in New Franklin, Missouri, shortly before the election.

"I could never draw the line on denominationalism so long as a candidate was a Protestant; denominationalism cuts no figure in my mind, whatever," Burckhartt wrote. "But God forbid that America shall ever be under the complete cover of the Roman Catholic Church. . . . Aside from all I have said, if Smith should be elected, it means the setting back of the prohibition movement just 20 years or more."

Hay lost the Senate election to the Republican dry, Roscoe Patterson. Hay once had been characterized by a writer for *Collier's Magazine* as "upright a politician as the State possesses." Likely he would have been elected on his own, but he stood for the whole ticket and lost to Patterson by a 61,177-vote margin.

Nelle Burger, Missouri president of the WCTU, had rallied for Hay in the Democratic primary. Then, saying they could not stand for the views of Smith, many drys turned tail and voted the Republican ticket in November. Nearly two years after the 1928 election, Hay remained bitter over the defeat in a letter to a former campaign supporter C. E. Betts of St. Joseph. "I have started three or four times to dictate a letter to you but every time I have done so, I have become so 'het-up' that I gave up," Hay wrote. "I would be in the Senate today and the Drys in Missouri and elsewhere would have a leader who could, to some extent at least, get the ear of the country had it not been for the failure of some people to stand by me when they should have done so. The result is the Dry cause is floundering today for lack of a leader of national prominence."

St. Louis went Democratic in the 1928 presidential election for the first time in forty years, largely due to Smith's Catholicism and his opposition to pro-hibition. Elsewhere in Missouri, the vote was for Hoover: Even Kansas City went Republican by its largest majority ever. In Illinois, Hoover trounced Smith by 1,770,723 to 1,312,235 votes. Hoover himself was a drinking dry who report-edly asked August A. Busch for a drink while visiting him in Cooperstown, New York, authors Peter Hernon and Terry Ganey recounted in *Under the Influence.*

A New Era

Although the country remained largely rural, radio broadcasts began to supplant old-fashioned political rallies as a source of campaign information for farmers, Louis LaCoss of the *New York Times* noted in June 1930:

> *It started early in the morning when farmers drove long miles over bad country roads to spend the day at an unending feast of oratory. At noon there was a basket luncheon or a barbecue at which thousands partook of chicken and pie and drank barrels and barrels of lemonade. It was a big event, which sweltering sun or driving rain was unable to stop.*
>
> *The last big rally held in Missouri was on the occasion of the visit to the State of John W. Davis when he was the Democratic candidate for President in 1924. It was held at Bunceton, on the estate of Dr. A.W. Nelson, candidate for governor. Extravagant claims of attendance were made, some figures being as high as 100,000. Half that number would be crowd enough to warm the cockles of any politician's heart.*
>
> *But the radio has changed the picture. The old-time rally, glamorous as it was, entailed dis-comfort. First there was the discomfort of getting there, then the accommodations after arriving and finally the long trip home. Now it is so easy for the farmer to draw up his easy chair, flip the dial on his radio and receive the party message in much more direct and distinct fashion than he could were he on the grounds. Ergo, the rally has passed into the limbo of forgotten things.*

The same year, Missouri's Women's Organization for National Prohibition Reform (WONPR) organized, and a group of several hundred women met in St. Louis and approved a resolution asking for a return to temperance, or re-sponsible control of alcohol. And in January 1930, U.S. Representative Leoni-das C. Dyer, R-Missouri, presented at the White House an argument for legal manufacture of beverages containing 2.75 percent alcohol as a means to help enforce the law. Dyer declined to indicate the president's response.

Dissatisfaction with prohibition was growing in Missouri. "There is no doubt but prohibition is the most discussed topic in the State," LaCoss noted in April 1930. "One hears it talked about in hotel lobbies, smoking cars, railroad stations, cafes, street cars, and on the streets. And likewise it may be stated with accuracy that there is a general belief that 'something will be done.' It is probably true that the ardent drys are just as zealous and fervent as before, but it is also true that the wets are more open in their advocacy of repeal, or at least modification, of the Eighteenth Amendment."

The same was true in Illinois, where in 1931 wets began an investigation of the administration of dry Governor Louis L. Emmerson after he vetoed the O'Grady-McDermott Bill to repeal the state prohibition law. Voters had called for repeal in statewide referendums on the topic.

A Casualty of Prohibition

A year earlier, in November 1930, Illinois voters had vanquished U.S. Representative Ruth Hanna McCormick—described as "provisionally wet"—in a race for U.S. Senate and elected "dripping wet" Colonel James Hamilton Lewis by some 700,000 votes. They also approved resoundingly a three-way referendum for repeal of the dry laws with more than 1 million votes in favor. The wet vote carried downstate as well, and even in Evanston—hometown of the WCTU—4,841 favored repeal of the dry laws versus 2,639 against.

McCormick had lived politics: Her father was the late Senator Mark Hanna of Ohio and her husband was the late Senator Medill McCormick. Remarkably liberated for the time, she owned and operated the dairy and stock farm Rock River Farm, served as president and publisher of the Rockford Consolidated Newspapers, and was active in the women's suffrage movement. In 1925, she was widowed with three children, the youngest a year old. Undaunted, she was elected to the U.S. House of Representatives in 1929 and, the next year, defeated her Republican opponent, Senator Charles S. Deneen, in the primary race for U.S. Senate. Deneen, interestingly enough, had defeated her late husband six years earlier.

A woman with strong opinions including an ardent defense of prohibition, McCormick earned the backing of the Illinois Anti-Saloon League early on in the Senate race. In April 1930, she reiterated her agreement with President Hoover's law-enforcement policy. "I have always been a dry, and you've never known me to switch around," she told reporters in Washington, D.C.

In August, however, when Illinois Republicans dampened themselves by agreeing to be bound by the results of the prohibition referendum election on November 4, McCormick followed the plank. In doing so, she angered the drys but declined to express any support for repeal that might have endeared her to the wets.

The Anti-Prohibition Party of Illinois worked to defeat her in a petition drive, and George B. Safford, superintendent of the Illinois Anti-Saloon League, said the organization's officers would support any worthy dry candidate who entered the race against McCormick and Lewis. In September, they threw their support behind Mrs. Lottie Holman O'Neill of Downers Grove, who ran as an independent. Anti-Saloon-Leaguers called McCormick's actions "sheer betrayal." Members of WONPR, some sixteen thousand members strong in Illinois, couldn't bring themselves to support her, either. "If Mrs. Ruth Hanna McCormick abides by her decision to keep silent on the most important issue before the American people, our organization will not be sympathetic toward her candidacy for the United States Senatorship," a spokesman for the organization said.

Lewis drove another nail in McCormick's political coffin when he said he would not worry about the referendum. If the state's voters backed repeal, as he did, they could vote for him. They did.

In March 1931, McCormick celebrated her fifty-first birthday in El Paso, Texas, and, soon after, married a fellow legislator, U.S. Representative Albert Gallatin Sims of New Mexico. "Getting to the 50 mark was a horrible nightmare," she admitted, "but leaving it is not half so bad."

A Waterfall of Wet

For the drys, the legislative events of 1932 were disappointing. For the wets, it brought repeal so close they could taste it. Even the driest Democrat in Missouri moderated his stance. Charles M. Hay, running for the Democratic nomination for U.S. Senate, said he was willing "in view of present public sentiment" to work out some sort of compromise liquor control plan that would be acceptable to both the drys and the wets. Two years earlier, he had characterized prohibition as a condition necessary to modern life. "Prohibition made a social and civic contribution to sobriety and decency at a time when we suffered a moral letdown in all the world," Hay told members of the House Judiciary Committee in 1930. "What would have been the condition in the post-war period with more and not less liquor? I only wish there was some way to go back to the old days for a period of thirty days and see what would happen."

If elected, Hay said in July 1932, he would vote for submission to the states of a repeal measure, then return to Missouri to attempt to defeat it. That stance prompted ridicule from one of Hay's two primary opponents, Bennett "Champ" Clark, who spoke of Hay's "patent reversible, double-back acting, Burger-Simon,

Ruth Hanna McCormick. Courtesy Library of Congress.

now-you-see-it-and-now-you-don't change of front on prohibition."

"Mr. Hay has repudiated the Democratic National platform [repeal]," Clark said in June 1932. "His own present position on the prohibition question is exactly that of the Republican National platform."

Clark added that Henry Kiel of St. Louis, a dripping wet and the Republican nominee for U.S. Senate, was aligned with the Democratic platform on prohibition. "So if Mr. Hay were nominated, we would have the ridiculous situation of the Democratic nominee running on the Republican platform and the Republican nominee running on the Democratic platform," Clark said. "If Charley still adheres to his ancient views of the time when he preached a religious crusade and wanted to jail every man or woman who took a drink, or who had liquor in their possession, he ought to say so openly and frankly. If he has changed his mind, he ought to say so openly and disclose the extent of his change of view. . . . It is unworthy of his reputation as a first-class fighting man for him to remain in his present ambiguous situation."

Hay was not the only candidate to change his stance. Hoover also cast aside his arguments in favor of prohibition in August 1932, when he admitted a breakdown of law and order had occurred through prohibition. He proposed resubmitting the question to the states. "Both sides are wet and the poor old dry hasn't got a soul to vote for," quipped humorist Will Rogers.

Though the national Republican Party didn't exactly come out for repeal, the Illinois state Republicans did so at their state convention in May 1932. They adopted a plank calling for repeal of the Eighteenth Amendment, for a beer and

St. Louis Mayor Henry Kiel. Courtesy Library of Congress.

light wine amendment to the Volstead Act, and repeal of the state search and seizure act. The search and seizure act had been repealed by the legislature but was vetoed by Governor Emmerson.

The state Republican Party in Missouri adopted a plank favoring resubmission of the entire prohibition matter, including the Eighteenth Amendment, to a national convention to be called by Congress as speedily as possible. Some charged the party with "pussyfooting," but that didn't include Kiel's campaign. "Describing him as a dripping wet is stating the facts mildly," commented La-Coss. The three-time mayor of St. Louis, a bricklayer, and a building contractor, Kiel led the drive for civic achievements that included an $87 million bond issue in 1923, Koch Hospital, city jail, and the waterworks filtration plant. He called not only for immediate repeal of the Eighteenth Amendment, but also pledged if elected to request that President Hoover authorize the making of real beer at once. "Put the breweries to work and bring back beer tomorrow," was one of his campaign slogans. In the August primary he received nearly four times as many votes as his five opponents combined.

On the Democratic side Clark handily defeated Hay and another candidate, Charles Howell. Clark was the son of the late Champ Clark, Missouri Speaker of the House. Hay, ever the statesman, appealed for the wholehearted support of Clark and the next year was appointed St. Louis's city counselor.

Drinking To the Democrats

Voter discontent over a growing Depression and concern about the legacy of prohibition helped Democratic wets carry the day just about everywhere in November 1932. Republican wets were swept away, from Fiorello LaGuardia in New York to Henry Kiel in Missouri. In his hometown of St. Louis, Kiel

What Would Lincoln Do?

Prohibition will work great injury to the cause of temperance. It is a species of intemperance within itself, for it goes beyond the bounds of reason, in that it attempts to control a man's appetite by legislation and makes a crime out of things that are not crimes.

This famous quote was attributed to Abraham Lincoln during the wet/dry debate of the prohibition years. Letter writers across the country tried to claim him as a "wet" by using the quote above, which was claimed to have been found in the records of the Illinois legislature in 1840. Others tried to claim Lincoln as a dry. William H. Townsend, in an article in *The Atlantic Monthly*, said original sources indicated Lincoln was a temperate drinker, his father was a moderate drinker, his uncle Mordecai died while trying to cool off his liquor in a snowdrift, and his schoolteacher was indicted for selling liquor at retail without a license. "Liquor shops clustered thick around every court house, but Lincoln seldom drank liquor or wine," Townsend wrote. " 'It always leaves me flabby and undone,' he told Herndon [William Herndon, his law partner].' " The quote attributed to Lincoln was invented in Atlanta in 1887.

Bryon Andreasen, Ph.D., research historian for the Abraham Lincoln Presidential Library in Springfield, Illinois, said he can find no reference to the quotation in the library's database of known Lincoln writings. Another quote that is erroneously attributed to Lincoln, ". . . all attempts to regulate it [the liquor traffic] will aggravate the evil. There must be no attempt to regulate the evil . . ." is from a temperance address made by a friend of Lincoln, the Reverend James Smith, minister at the First Presbyterian Church in Springfield. "Most Lincoln scholars have concluded that Lincoln was no believer in legal compulsion of prohibition, though he was sympathetic to the temperance reformers' concerns and shared a desire to minimize the social and personal damage caused by alcohol," Andreasen noted. "His preferred approach was persuasion rather than coercion."

received only 79,803 votes to Clark's 127,536 votes. Hoover, Kiel's partner on the ticket, did not fare that well. He received 71,304 votes in St. Louis to Roosevelt's 132,280. In the Republican stronghold of St. Louis County, voters elected all but one of the Democratic candidates in national, state, and county races. "In St. Louis beer is not only a beverage; it is an important economic factor," noted the *New York Times*.

Roosevelt beat Hoover by 460,693 votes in Missouri. Four years earlier, Hoover had carried the state by 171,000 votes. Democrat Guy B. Park defeated Republican Edward H. Winter for the governor's race. The state sent a solid block of thirteen Democrats to Congress. "This same vote also finally disposes of a staple argument of the drys that rural Missouri is almost fanatically opposed to any tampering with the prohibition law," LaCoss observed. "Out-state Missouri, which is traditionally Democratic, remained within the party and voted the ticket straight."

In Illinois, the Hoover defeat turned out to be a plurality of more than 450,000 votes, with Roosevelt receiving 1,882,304 to Hoover's 1,432,756 votes. In the governor's race, Democratic Judge Henry Horner defeated Republican rival Len Small by 515,000 votes, 110,000 from downstate voters. In the Senate race, William H. Dieterich, a Democrat, defeated incumbent Senator Otis F. Glenn by 320,000 votes, 170,000 from downstate. Part of the state Republican party's wet plank, Small had supported repeal of the Eighteenth Amendment and the state search and seizure act; Glenn had criticized the interference by federal snoopers in business and family affairs. Due to circumstances beyond his control, Democratic U.S. Representative Charles A. Karch of East St. Louis failed to achieve his re-election bid. An outspoken wet originally from Mascoutah, Illinois, the fifty-six-year-old Karch died two days before the election from complications of a gall bladder operation performed a month earlier.

Of 216 candidates elected to the House nationwide, 183 were in favor of changing the prohibition law. The sweeps gave the Democratic Party complete control of Congress. "No such upset has occurred in recent history," the *New York Times* reported.

Swept into office in April 1933 on the heels of the Democratic landslide was St. Louis Mayor Bernard "Barney" Dickmann, the first Democrat to hold the office in twenty-four years. A lifelong St. Louisan and real estate agent, Dickmann went on to get federal authorization for the Jefferson National Expansion Memorial and to clear forty blocks on the riverfront. He also helped push through the city's first smoke abatement ordinance in February 1937 and set up the Division of Smoke Regulation in the Department of Public Safety. The program was successful enough that by 1941, eighty-three other cities from thirty-one states had sent to the city for information.

Chapter 17

Happy Days Are Here Again

As the Great Depression gripped the St. Louis area, young Vera Niemann of Fairview Heights, Illinois, was thrilled to land a short-lived job going door-to-door and filling out forms for a directory in town. The hours were 6 a.m. to 6 p.m., the walk to work was long, and the pay was one dollar a day. She was warned not to stop at the "sportin' house." "I had read about sportsmen shooting wild animals," Niemann recalled in 1984. "Could this be a sportsman's house? Deciding I had misunderstood her pronunciation, I thought no more about it."

After several weeks on the job, she entered a peculiar, two-story building that housed practitioners of the oldest profession. It had long hallways through the building and many doorways, all open. "Even in the darkness, I noticed strange things. People waved me away, or made me feel like an intruder. But my work had to go on. Forging ahead through two floors, I felt that everyone must be sleeping late. Three o'clock in the afternoon? Going down the stairway to the front door, I saw a man at the table there. He just stared at me for a moment. Then 'What are *you* doin' here?'"

"Waving my clip-board, I said, pretty importantly, 'Getting interviews.' He jumped up from his chair, grabbed my shoulders and pushed me toward the door, saying, 'Did any of them bother you?'"

"I answered, so truthfully, 'No, they wouldn't pay any attention to me.'"

"He got me to the door, opened it, and said, 'Get out of here. Go home. Don't ever come back.' I left, feeling terribly crushed that I had failed my job. . . . I had left without his interview!"

Dejected, Niemann returned to work and reported the incident to her supervisor, who appeared to be ready to have a stroke: "'YE GODS, she got into the sportin' house on _____ Street,'" she said.

Niemann was sent into better neighborhoods in the future. When the directory work finished, she was paid for five extra days' work. "Total $10, which I proudly turned over to Mama."

Hoovervilles and Soup Kitchens

Like Niemann, many St. Louis–area residents found only temporary work. The Great Depression shifted the political balance of power in the United States and ensured prohibition's demise, Kenneth M. Murchison noted in *Federal Criminal Law Doctrines.* Times were hard. Like many cities, St. Louis had a Hooverville, a village of shacks erected by the unemployed along the Mississippi River and named sarcastically for President Herbert Hoover. Floodwaters inundated the shacks in the fall of 1931, forcing residents to flee to higher ground.

Hoover feared that federal relief would lead to reckless spending and recommended that local governments and charities care for their own. They did. According to one estimate the city of St. Louis was feeding one of every ten of its families by 1932. That same year, 92,666 St. Louisans, or 24 percent of the workforce, were unemployed, as opposed to 15.9 percent nationwide, James Neal Primm noted in *Lion of the Valley.* The number grew to more than 30 percent in 1933, when national unemployment figures peaked at 24.9 percent. An estimated 5,000 St. Louisans populated the riverfront shacks. In one week in August 1933, Monsignor Timothy Dempsey served 66,967 meals at his soup kitchen in St. Louis. That number had grown steadily from 14,706 meals served in November 1931 and 36,118 meals in August 1932. In Illinois, some 1.5 million residents statewide of a total population of 7.6 million, or 19.7 percent, were unemployed in 1933.

Spirited Camaraderie

By the time it ended in 1933, prohibition had influenced many private organizations. Even The Boy Scouts of America indulged in a little thrill seeking at Camp Irondale in Washington County near Irondale, Missouri. Irondale was one of the first permanent scout camps in the United States, according to author William J. Brittain in *The Spirit of Scouting '76.*

"George Hall of the *St. Louis Post-Dispatch* recalled a highlight of his own days at Irondale—the big 'Bootlegger Hunt' of 1925, when the entire camp was turned out one night to beat the bushes for some 'local moonshiners' who had eluded the constabulary," Brittain wrote. "Not surprisingly, some Scout mothers took a dim view of this extracurricular activity."

Anheuser-Busch and other local breweries wasted little time delivering kegs to area watering holes.

From 1929 to 1933 the value of manufactured goods in St. Louis dropped 56 percent, while wages declined 53 percent. Seizing their golden opportunity, brewers and related businesses stressed the economic enhancements that liquor production would provide. August A. Busch argued in 1931 that the manufacture of beer nationwide would employ 1.25 million people, would provide $400 million to the government in annual revenue, and would purchase 80 million bushels of grain. "I may be wrong, but it is my belief that the huge quantity of grains formerly used in the brewing industry, thrown into the markets every year in competition with wheat, has contributed much to the farm debacle," Busch said.

It was a debacle. In 1932, farmers received only 56 percent of the prices they received for goods immediately after World War I, according to Duane G. Meyer in *The Heritage of Missouri*.

"Perhaps the lowest point was reached in the early days of 1933, when Missouri poultry farmers sold eggs at ninety cents per case—three cents a dozen," Edwin C. McReynolds wrote in *Missouri: A History of the Crossroads State*. From 1930 to 1934, some eighteen thousand farms were seized in foreclosures; those who stayed became tenant farmers. A statewide public relief program was begun in Missouri in 1932.

Miners On the Rocks

Miners also took a beating. The tiff, or barite ore, farmers of Washington County, Missouri, went on strike in 1935 for better wages. Entire families dug in the fields with picks and shovels for the mineral, which was used in paints, chemicals, glass, and rubber products. At $3.50 a ton, workers earned starvation wages.

Workers in the Illinois mines were left to fend for themselves when on-the-job injuries rendered them unable to work. Between June 30, 1920, and December 31, 1930, 146 people were killed in Illinois mining accidents and another 2,982 injured. An undated letter sent out by Local 2441 of the United Mine Workers of America in Springfield, Illinois, contained two imported "Spanish Lace Handkerchiefs" worth 50 cents each and a request for donations for its beneficiary, H. D. Richards of Springfield, who had been seriously injured in Peabody Mine No. 6 in 1923 while lifting a coal car. "He has a wife and eight children to support," noted the letter, from union president Herman Risse and financial secretary Thomas E. Denton. "His small house is heavily mortgaged; has had four children in the hospital and his personal property burned up. The cup of sorrows of Brother Richards is running over and he is at the mercy of his fellow brothers."

Cost-cutting measures were made to keep everyone working and cash-strapped departments going. St. Louis firefighters agreed voluntarily in April 1932 to take one day off each month, without pay, to pare the department's budget by 10 percent for the next fiscal year. The days off would save the city about $75,000 a year, it was estimated, and replacements would not be hired to fill vacancies.

In Alton, the Owens-Illinois Glass Company reorganized its operating schedule from three eight-hour shifts daily to four six-hour shifts in July 1932, so it could employ a larger number of workers.

"Radio star Eddie Cantor poured his heart into 'Potatoes are cheaper, tomatoes are cheaper,' we made soap from bacon grease and lye, long lines of men waited at plant gates, and signs appeared, 'No Help Wanted,'" Vera Niemann recounted. "Pretty pink and green glassware tried to tempt people to movies and relief lines grew longer and longer."

At a former truck farm on Manchester Road in Ballwin, Missouri, the Citizens Committee on Relief and Employment opened a camp for fifty indigent transients in December 1933 with state and federal funds. The men received 75 cents a week plus food, lodging, and classes on practical subjects. They were

required to work thirty hours a week on projects that included highway beau-
tification from St. Louis to Gray Summit. The Bureau for Homeless Men had
operated the farm the previous summer.

Going, Going . . .

Repeal couldn't come fast enough for a parched member of the St. Louis Board
of Education who wrote Anheuser-Busch in March 1930 and placed an order
for five cases of Budweiser beer "when and if" the law was modified or repealed.
"You may be required to keep this order on file for several years before being
able to fill it, but I hope I am not too optimistic in placing it," wrote Henry P.
Schroeder.

Schroeder wasn't alone. A *Literary Digest* poll in 1932 turned up 106,519
Missouri residents in favor of repeal versus 43,890 opposed. In Illinois 228,972
were in favor of repeal, 53,748 opposed.

A resolution by the St. Louis Board of Aldermen in April 1932 to organize
a "beer parade," in favor of the restoration of the right to make and sell beer,
went over like a lead balloon. Mayor Victor Miller was asked by the board to
send letters to twenty organizations seeking their participation. The St. Louis
Bar Association and the Building Trades Council promptly nixed the idea, although both organizations publicly opposed prohibition. The council suggested
the "drys" hold a parade instead, "to give the legislators concrete evidence of
the actual number of fanatics who would regulate our appetites by legislation,"
council secretary Maurice J. Cassidy replied to Miller.

Methodists and members of the Church Federation of St. Louis objected
strongly to a pro-beer parade, and their thoughts on the idea of a "dry" parade
are not known. In the end, however, there was no parade. At a May meeting on
whether to hold the parade, the vote was 7–4 in opposition.

Buoyed by the November 1932 election of repeal candidate Franklin Delano Roosevelt as president, the Industrial Bureau of St. Louis's Industrial Club
estimated in December of that year that the city's brewing industry was in a
position to recapture 70 percent of its former peak output of 3 million gallons,
to re-employ 70 percent of its former wage-earners, and to pay 70 percent of
its former payroll. In 1919, 3,136 brewery workers received a combined yearly
pay of $4,362,000, according to the bureau. In 1929, 597 workers in the bever-
age industry received $838,669. Talk of repeal—and of liquor taxes that would
help struggling governments—was everywhere by December 1932.

As with its enactment, the repeal of the Eighteenth Amendment required a series of state referendums. On February 6, 1933, Congress submitted the Twenty-First Amendment to the states for ratification. The amendment, which allowed the manufacture and sale of all intoxicating liquor, would become effective December 5, 1933.

To speed the process of legal beer, Congress passed and on March 22 Roosevelt signed the Cullen-Harrison Bill, which amended the Volstead Act to declare 3.2 percent beer and wine non-intoxicating. The amendment allowed sales at one minute after midnight on April 7, 1933, in each state not bound by state prohibition laws. After some wrangling, both the Missouri and Illinois legislatures passed bills that allowed 3.2 percent beer to be sold.

The Women's Christian Temperance Union and the Anti-Saloon League unsuccessfully challenged the wet legislation in both states. "CHEER BECAUSE BEER'S NEAR—NOT NEAR BEER," read the headline in the *Granite City Press-Record* after Illinois Governor Henry Horner signed bills repealing state prohibition statutes from the books.

ROLL OUT THE BARREL

Brewers across the country had been making tentative arrangements to improve their factories since the November 1932 presidential election, much to the pleasure of the Barry-Wehmiller Machinery Company, at 4660 W. Florissant Avenue in St. Louis. Fred E. Busse, vice president of the company, announced in November 1932 the receipt of $60,000 in immediate and $250,000 in conditional orders from two New York breweries. Colonel Jacob Ruppert, owner of the Yankees, placed an order for a $20,000 pasteurizer, and the Fidelio Brewery ordered $40,000 worth of machinery.

Anheuser-Busch placed orders in February 1933 that included 28 million beer bottles and 500,000 beer cases from the Owens-Illinois Glass Company in Alton, the Obear-Nester Glass Company in East St. Louis, the Huttig Sash and Door Company of St. Louis, the Mound City Box Factory, and the Columbia Box Company.

The brewery at first would turn out only about one-third of its pre-war capacity of 1.5 million barrels a year but planned to increase by a million barrels annually, Vice President and Treasurer R. A. Huber told the *St. Louis Globe-Democrat*. Between three thousand and four thousand employees would be added to the payroll after beer was legalized, and veteran employees would be given

This ad for Mound City Beer appeared in the St. Louis Globe-Democrat *on March 27, 1933, and the paper claimed that it was the first beer ad to appear in a newspaper in thirteen years.*

preference, Huber said.

Altogether, the company invested $7 million into renovations and new equipment, Peter Hernon and Terry Ganey reported in their book *Under the Influence.* "So confident was the Anheuser-Busch leadership that Congress would pass the Cullen-Harrison Bill that they made plans for a special promotional gimmick to help celebrate the return of beer," Ronald Jan Plavchan wrote in *A History of Anheuser-Busch, 1852–1933.* "On December 28, 1932, the board of directors approved a motion by [attorney] Charles Nagel to purchase a six-horse team 'for advertising purposes' and appropriated $15,000 to cover the cost. Two months later, August A. Busch, Jr. informed the directors that he had purchased during January (1933) sixteen head of Clydesdales for $21,000 through the Kansas City Stockyards . . . the younger Busch requested an additional sum of $10,000 to finalize the purchase, to buy adequate harnesses and other pertinent equipment, and to build an old-time beer wagon."

Others were preparing, too. The Griesedieck-Western Brewery Company in Belleville planned to spend about $100,000 to prepare for legalized beer, and to hire two hundred new employees, manager Fred V. L. Smith told the *Globe-*

Democrat in February. Once beer was legalized, the company would be ready to "shoot the works," Smith said.

Officials at Schorr-Kolkschneider Brewery, at 2537 Natural Bridge Avenue, contracted for a million pint bottles, 25,000 wooden cases, 60,000 gross of bottle caps, five million labels, 600,000 pounds of ground corn, and 60,000 bushels of malt. They planned to spend $50,000 for plant rehabilitation, $20,000 for new bottling machinery, $13,000 on new automobile trucks, and $15,000 for advertising.

Joseph Hahn, secretary of Brewers and Maltsters Union #6, received numerous applications for work. Many were from men who plied the brewery trade in pre-prohibition days, including Otto B. Herrmann of Indianapolis, Indiana. "Hoping to have a chance to come back to Local Union #6 and good old St. Louis," Herrmann wrote.

Preparing For the Onslaught

Related industries also witnessed a boom. Sales of saloon equipment, from brass spigots to sawdust, enjoyed a 50 percent increase by mid-February 1933. Officials of a downtown St. Louis saloon equipment company reported sales of five or six complete bar sets a week. "Taking a tip from Noah, St. Louisans are preparing against the flood," reported the *Naborhood Link News*. "But they're not building arks, they're buying bars, for it's not a cloudburst they're anticipating, but a foaming, amber deluge of beer."

Joseph K. Nester, president of the Obear-Nester Glass Company, reported in February 1933 he expected to hire several hundred more people, due to substantial bottle orders from local breweries. The company installed additional furnaces to meet the demand. "Before prohibition, we were among the largest producers of beer bottles," Nester said. "The advent of the dry law forced us to curtail operations, releasing several hundred men from work, even though we adopted the expedient of adopting a six-hour [day] plan."

The American Cone & Pretzel Company, at 1721 DeKalb Street, was ready to begin running twenty-four hours a day the minute beer was made legal, if necessary, Vice President and General Manager Charles F. Betz said in March. At the time, the plant ran seventeen hours a day, five days a week. "Our business has kept up because of the large number of homebrew drinkers and the increasing general use of pretzels," Betz explained to the *Star*.

The beer bill's passage meant increased freight tonnage for the Missouri

Pacific Railroad, in rush orders for beer bottles and kegs. Real estate agents received inquiries about "restaurant" sites, and hotels prepared to serve beer in dining rooms, grill rooms, and guest rooms the moment it became legal. The Hotel Mayfair embarked on a fast and furious remodeling effort of what was once the old KMOX radio studio into a rathskeller, decorated as a hunting lodge and equipped with a service bar, adjacent to conference and meeting rooms. By December 1932, real estate agents reported brisk sales of flats and cottages near former breweries to investors in what previously had been a sluggish housing market.

Officials of Bartenders' Local No. 51 were inundated with applications for membership. The St. Louis branch of the International Geneva Association of Hotel and Restaurant Employees called for a pre-prohibition state liquor law provision to be retained that forbade women or waitresses from serving alcoholic drinks. They were unsuccessful.

Hucksters also joined in the merriment. In February 1933, the Better Business Bureau of St. Louis warned would-be investors of fake brewery stocks making the rounds.

CELEBRATION

Midway through the afternoon of April 6, 1933, patrons began to gather at the entrance to Anheuser-Busch to celebrate the return of 3.2 percent beer. Company officials hired a brass band to entertain the crowd, which by one minute past midnight on April 7 numbered twenty-five thousand strong. A *Post-Dispatch* reporter described the scene:

When the clock in the brewhouse tower began striking 12, only the first stroke could be heard. The rest were drowned by the roar of the crowd, the shriek of sirens, the blaring of bands and the din of motor horns.

Within a minute after the clock struck, a scarlet-hued truck came out, carrying to Lambert-St. Louis flying field the case of beer addressed to President Roosevelt, Vice-President Garner, Speaker Rainey, former Gov. Alfred E. Smith, and Gov. Park. Airplanes waited at the field for these souvenir shipments.

Other trucks, some of them loaded since morning, followed on their way to downtown hotels and to outside communities. Springfield and Peoria, Ill., and Hopkinsville, Ky., were among these places whose stenciled names showed the trucks' points of destination.

About 300 trucks were loaded with cases and ready to go, while about 1200 others were in line, along Arsenal street, as far west as Jefferson avenue. They moved in a steady line through the Seventh street entrance, and came out on Broadway, laden with closely packed cases. Among the trucks were those of chain stores and industrial establishments, some of them borrowed by beer retailers.

August A. Busch, Jr., vice president and general manager, estimated forty-five thousand cases and three thousand thirty-one-gallon barrels had been sent out by daylight. He told the crowds the brewery had added seventeen hundred employees in the previous sixteen days, bringing the number on the payroll to twenty-six hundred. He praised "the wisdom, foresight and courage of a great president" before he retired to host his own private gathering of prominent citizens.

At Falstaff, the only other St. Louis brewery ready to turn out finished beer, several thousand spectators gathered around the bunting-draped building at Spring and Forest Park avenues. They cheered as the trucks departed. Seventy-five trucks were waiting at the Falstaff gates before midnight, and additional trucks arrived throughout the night.

Al Zenthoefer, a filler operator at the brewery during prohibition, handed Papa Joe Griesedieck the first bottle of real beer made after prohibition ended, recalled Zenthoefer's son, Alexander "Fritz" Zenthoefer of Chesterfield. "Papa Joe went to the bank and got a whole bag full of nickels and dimes," said Zenthoefer. "He was throwing the nickels and dimes out to the crowds as they watched the first beer come out. Harvey Beffa [the company secretary] told him, 'Put that money back in your pocket. We'll need it.' They did."

Many on the streets didn't get their drink, the *Post* noted:

Some of those who waited around the breweries went to hotels or restaurants in time to share in the drinking there. But the greater part of the sidewalk throng went to bed without a taste of the legalized product. It could be seen that this was a disappointment to some, who had carried tin "growlers" in the hope that a free distribution might occur. They waved these pails at the drivers, some of whom called back, "I haven't had any, either."

Thousands attempted to slake their thirsts from a half-hour to two hours past midnight at various stops, depending on the distance from the breweries or the efficiency of the delivery service. A carnival atmosphere prevailed, almost like a Mardi Gras celebration, Zenthoefer recalled. "I remember in the neighborhoods they had parades in the street," he said. "All the old speakeasy saloons, why, they had parades and big parties, you know. I lived down by the Bevo Mill. I can remember when the first beer came back at one saloon, you got a 15-ounce glass for a nickel. That was at Schiller and Morganford."

Some in the crowd had ulterior motives, including East St. Louis gangster Frank "Buster" Wortman, who was arrested with three other men after they allegedly attempted to hijack two Anheuser-Busch beer trucks at Kingshighway and Delmar boulevards. Wortman's accomplices were Felix F. McDonald, Wincel Urban, and Eugene Tebeau. Police had kept a close watch on the beer trucks at the order of St. Louis Police Chief Joseph Gerk, and they arrested the suspects after a car chase through the Central West End.

Sellout Crowds

Waiters at hotels or restaurants found themselves clearing glasses containing "beverages not yet having legal sanction," and their patrons happily shelled out from 10 cents for a glass or schooner to 35 cents for a twelve-ounce bottle for the legal stuff. The crowds just kept coming:

> *Hundreds who did not wait up ordered it for breakfast, at luncheon, or in the interim. . . . Waitresses were swamped with orders for beer at the luncheon period. They struggled to acquire the knack of opening bottles and found themselves deluged with orders for sandwiches, customers neglecting other items on the menus. Along with that, [servers] found themselves unskilled in serving beer in the best pre-prohibition manner.*

Emmet Pearson was finishing his internship in medicine at Washington University at the close of prohibition. "In fact, the first night that beer was available I went with a group of people to Anheuser-Busch's place in St. Louis and you'd think they'd give you a free beer, but they didn't that night," Pearson recalled in 1983.

Across the river in Collinsville, the celebration was anything but wild, recalled Gilbert W. Killinger. "The first load of beer, I remember, that came into town was delivered by a man named Ed Bertram," Killinger recalled in 1976. "I think the first delivery was made to the Collinsville Park Ballroom, tavern or nightclub, and to Blaha's Tavern . . . at the corner of Clay and Center street. There was nobody waiting in line," he said, and laughed. "Everybody had been making home brew."

In Granite City, the evening was designated "New Beer's Eve," and Cline's Barbecue was the place to be, with beer priced at 10 cents a stein and 20 cents a bottle. They were out of stock by noon. The city's own signature brewery,

Wagner, was scheduled to start selling beer the following September, brewery historians Kevin Kious and Donald Roussin noted.

In Boonville, Missouri, retailers sold out of the new beer by 9 p.m. that first day, April 7. "Local supplies were replenished early today and beer was yet available this afternoon," the *Boonville Daily News* reported April 8. "One or two retailers expected their supply to last well into tonight and perhaps even tomorrow."

Beer had arrived in the central Missouri town at 9:25 a.m. April 7, and it was "on tap" a few minutes later at Cassing & Thoma's sandwich shop, followed by other venues. When the beer truck arrived, a shout came up from the street: "The new beer has arrived!" and a crowd soon gathered, according to the *Boonville Daily News*:

> *Sparkling steins, sandwiches and pretzels were provided as fast as agile hands could supply the demand. Throughout the day the crowds continued to patronize the retailers of beer. New money came into circulation. Men in business suits, men in overalls, men with soft hands and men with calloused hands ordered up the new 3.2 drink. A man dug down down into his overalls and obtained a well worn pocketbook. He peeled off an old "blanket" $5 bill. He had kept the bill in hiding for years.*
>
> *"Give me a beer," he said. "I've been saving that bill for this particular occasion."*

For the campus crowd at Mizzou in the early 1930s, the action could be found at a hangout in Columbia called Jack's Shack, Clarissa Start observed in *I'm Glad I'm Not Young Anymore*. "I was not in school that year but was told that the day beer became legal, a line many blocks long formed in front of Jack's Shack," Start wrote.

St. Louis's supplies were exhausted less than twenty-four hours after they began, much to the chagrin of crowds who took advantage of the sunshine and seventy-degree spring weather to stop by their favorite restaurant or cafeteria for a cold one. Some country clubs planned beer parties on the evening of April 8. Observed the *Post*:

> *South St. Louis restaurants with beer were crowded all day. Eating went with the drinking. The proprietor of an inn famous for its mint juleps in other days declared he'd 'never sold so many sandwiches before.' His old garden, after a few years in the unaccustomed role of a miniature golf course, is about to become a garden again.*
>
> *A downtown night club offering music and dancing from noon through the evening was packed with afternoon family parties. The proprietor, whose standing before prohibition changed to wider fame under the slogan "Nothing worries Joe" when prohibition agents gave him plenty to*

After repeal, Anheuser-Busch Clydesdales toured the Northeast, eventually leading the antiquated horse-drawn beer cart to become an international icon.

worry about, commented that the return of beer had brought out evening crowds of a sort he hadn't seen since prohibition.

"Finest people in St. Louis," he insisted. "I hadn't seen some of them for 20 years."

The first night of legal beer in St. Louis resulted in only four "drunk on the street" cases on the police court docket the next day, all of them in the area south of Washington Avenue. Judge James G. Blaine, seeking to know more about the effects of 3.2 beer, quizzed the defendants about their consumption. The first man insisted his trouble with police followed the drinking of only two and a half bottles of the stuff. The second, an Irishman, said he consumed twelve bottles before becoming drunk. The third said he lost count before passing out, and the fourth said he had not tried the beer: He was drinking hard liquor. Because none of the defendants had been arrested before, Blaine let them go with a warning.

Due to the aging process for beer, it took a while for brewers to catch up with demand. Alvin Griesedieck, vice president of Falstaff, said orders were on hand for more than four times the brewery's production capacity. "We still only had two bottling units—the combined total capacity of which was approximately 4000 cases per day (without breakdown)," Griesedieck wrote in *The*

Falstaff Story. "For instance, a retail tavern proprietor placed an order for 100 cases of beer. He was lucky if we could allot him five cases."

THE ROAD TO REPEAL

With 3.2 beer now legal, states voted individually to repeal the Eighteenth Amendment. Illinois was the ninth state to ratify repeal on June 5, 1933, by a margin of 3–1. Downstate, where the Anti-Saloon League once held sway, the vote easily was 2–1 for repeal. Of sixty-eight downstate counties, only eighteen returned dry majorities. Governor Henry Horner said he was "immensely gratified and happy in the knowledge that Illinois holds its place in the forefront of the forward-looking and progressive commonwealths of our nation."

Josef Roman Wingen of Staunton, Illinois, also was gratified. "We voters consider this Prohibition system is an unfair and contrary act to live with, because we did not vote for it," Wingen wrote in a letter to Governor Park earlier that year. "The Prohibition Party ruled the people of the United States for the last fourteen years and made some people into Rummies and Dummies. Now let us Democrats stick together, throw out Prohibition people, who are the Soda water drinkers."

The WCTU was less than pleased. "Undoubtedly the President's popularity is responsible for much of the repeal enthusiasm, but we believe the administration will regret its policy with respect to prohibition before this fight is over," WCTU officials said in a statement from the national headquarters in Evanston, Illinois.

In Missouri, the Anti-Saloon League and WCTU challenged the validity of the repeal effort and the legalized beer amendment. It lost one of the battles right away, which centered on the law that set up the machinery for the repeal vote in August 1933.

On August 19, Missouri became the twenty-second state to vote for repeal, with a majority of more than 3–1. St. Louis voted 20–1 in favor; St. Louis County, 14–1; Jefferson City, 10–1; Boonville, 5–1; St. Charles, 13–1; Maryville, all 46 votes for repeal; Columbia, 2–1; Carthage, 3–2; and Eureka, 6–1. The little German community of Westphalia cast all of its 237 votes in favor of repeal. Still, 55 of Missouri's 114 outstate counties voted dry.

The "dry" strongholds of Webster Groves and Kirkwood also went wet, Webster by a vote of 2,336–397, Kirkwood by 1,442–120. Only three of Florissant's 235 voters were dry, as were 16 of 349 in Rock Hill Village, 20 of 393 in Shrewsbury, 8 of 303 in Des Peres, 20 of 471 in Brentwood, 106 of 1,823 in Richmond Heights, 102 of 2,013 in Clayton, 7 of 202 in Grover, 369 of 4,698 in University City, and 130 of 1,696 in Overland.

Both the Anti-Saloon League and the WCTU sought to postpone final action by the state on the repeal of the Eighteenth Amendment to the next general election. They were unsuccessful.

Soaring Sales of Suds

With the legal sale of all kinds of liquor imminent, the industry took off like a big bird in 1933. Of twenty-one new companies established in the St. Louis industrial district during June, July, and August, thirteen were beer and liquor concerns, the Industrial Bureau of the Industrial Club reported in October. The bureau predicted that the production capacity of St. Louis's breweries would be more than twice the amount of the yearly output before prohibition, 6.5 million barrels produced by twenty-six breweries.

In April, prospective purchasers had agreed to pay $750,000 for the old American, Columbia, and Central breweries, subject to contingencies. The three were among eight that had been operated before prohibition by the Independent Brewing Company, which had gone into foreclosure; three of the eight had been dismantled. By June, the Schott Brewing Company in Highland, Illinois, was newly renovated to produce five hundred barrels daily, nearly twice the old Highland Brewery's pre-prohibition output. The Wagner Brewing Company in Granite City also reopened in the fall of 1933, and by the end of July seven breweries in the St. Louis area were producing at a rate of 1,492,000 barrels per year, with plans underway to increase production to 2,537,000 barrels per year. They included Anheuser-Busch, Falstaff, Schorr-Kolkschneider, Griesedieck-Western in Belleville, Bluff City Brewery in Alton, and the Mound City Brewing Company in New Athens.

Four other breweries also set up shop: Fischbach Brewing Company in St. Charles; Griesedieck Brothers Brewing Company on Shenandoah Avenue; Obert Brewing Company on S. Twelfth Street; and the Stifel-Union Brewing Company on Gravois Avenue, which was operated by Falstaff. The four planned to employ 550 and produce 1,535 barrels per day, and plans were in the works to reopen additional breweries.

There was a problem, at least at Anheuser-Busch. Used to the sweet concoctions they had been imbibing during prohibition, customers and salesmen began complaining about the taste of Budweiser and asking for a sweeter beer. August A. Busch refused to change the formula and reasoned they'd be back in time. The prediction came true, August Busch, Jr., recalled in 1955. "The trend back to Budweiser was as sudden as the trend away from it," Busch wrote. "It was *our competitors* who finally changed their formulae in a frantic effort to duplicate the matchless Budweiser taste!"

Although many brewers would claim their beer formulas were unchanged over the years, that wasn't always the case, Roussin and Kious noted. "During prohibition some people cheated and drank bootleg, but a lot of people followed the law and didn't drink beer," Kious said. "When repeal came, the breweries brewing beer in the old style, which was heady and maltier, didn't do as well as the taste shifted to sweeter, lighter beverages. People's tastes changed."

"Even to this day, a single brand of beer may be brewed differently in different parts of the country, to appeal to regional tastes," added Roussin.

A SECOND CELEBRATION (SORT OF)

Missouri Governor Park called a special session of the Missouri legislature October 17, 1933, to repeal the McCawley "Bone Dry" law and pass a liquor control law. Then, as today, the legislature couldn't get its act together—liquor taxes were the bone of contention in early December. Illinois didn't have its new liquor control law drafted, either, but it had the foresight the previous February to repeal the old prohibition and search and seizure laws. "The Volstead law is one with the dodo bird," the *Post* sputtered on December 11, 1933, six days after nationwide repeal took effect. "But the McCawley bone-dry law, which, in St. Louis, at any rate, was always honored more in the breach than in the observance, is still on the books. Reputable liquor dealers, bending backward in an effort to avoid any shadow of criticism, are impatiently waiting for the gentlemen at Jefferson City to do something. As for the public, its mood might be described as sulphuric."

The celebration on Repeal Day, December 5, 1933, was a disappointment. Major hotels pledged not to sell the stuff until a state law made it legal, though some drugstores sold whiskey and champagne. Reported the *Globe*: "The joker was that East St. Louis saloonkeepers had depended on St. Louis distributors to furnish the old-time liquor, but the distributors were not willing to violate the Missouri dry law by sending the product from this state to wide-open Illinois . . . the only liquor available was the bootleg stuff sold in prohibition days."

Judge Edward E. Butler of the Court of Criminal Correction shared in the scorn of the average customer. "I absolutely will discharge every person coming before me charged with liquor law violation, because I refuse to allow any citizen to be penalized because of the negligent Governor and Legislature," Butler said.

Circuit Attorney Franklin Miller said he would handle each case on its merits, and Prosecuting Attorney Harry Rosecan said he would view "any present violations of the bone-dry act with even more liberal attitude" than he used previously. Soon after nationwide repeal, reports began circulating that St. Louis liquor dealers were obtaining huge supplies from Illinois, via trucks carrying distilled, blended whiskey over the Mississippi River into St. Louis.

Without a state liquor law on the books, Illinois liquor dealers could have roamed the streets peddling baskets full of bottles, but this didn't happen, the *Post-Dispatch* reported. The Illinois state legislature remained deadlocked December 22 on a liquor bill, but many East Side drinkers were sticking to familiar favorites such as whiskey and beer.

The price of bootleg liquor plummeted, with a pint of liquor that would have been described as "excellent" four years earlier priced at 50 cents. Blended whiskey sold at the bars for 15 to 25 cents a drink, and $1.50 by the pint. Bonded whiskey cost 25 to 50 cents at the bar, and $2.50 to $3.75 a pint. Domestic champagne was $2.50 a pint. This was at a time when a small cottage with a bath in south St. Louis rented for $18 to $20 per month. The prices were about half of what patrons had paid in speakeasies, and proprietors of the latter told the press they planned to reduce their prices.

WE'RE NOT WAITING

As Christmas 1933 approached, storekeepers in St. Louis with liquor in stock were tired of waiting for the state legislature to act. At a meeting of the St. Louis Hotel Men's Association on December 21, some suggested the association continue to follow the "Bone Dry" law, while others pointed out the hotels were losing large amounts of revenue. When they returned to their hotels, some instructed their wine stewards to proceed openly, while others continued their policy of serving to "friends of the management" only. "And the managements have few enemies," the *Post-Dispatch* reported.

Liquor stores popped up all over town, and chain drugstores displayed whiskies, wines, and cordials prominently in their front windows with a price card on each bottle. Prices were high, with whiskey ranging from $1.50 a pint for the cheapest blended stuff to $5 for eighteen-year-old bourbon. Wines ranged from $1.75 for the cheapest imported varieties to $8 or more for the best champagnes.

Prosecuting Attorney Rosecan refused to prosecute one Hyman Nudelman, who was arrested by police on December 19 for operating his new liquor store at 305 N. Seventh Street. "This man has committed no crime," Rosecan said. Curiously, this lack of law enforcement was okay with the Carthage, Missouri, resident who sponsored the "Bone Dry" law ten years earlier. "St. Louisans, it is quite apparent, are going to proceed as though the McCawley bone dry law had been erased from the statutes," the *Post* noted. "This, incidentally is what former State Senator A. L. McCawley recommends. He told a Post-Dispatch reporter two weeks ago that the delay of the Legislature in repealing the bone dry law and providing proper licensing of liquor sales was depriving the State of revenue at the rate of $800,000 a year."

On December 20, 1933, the Illinois legislature approved a fifty-cent-per-gallon state tax on the manufacture of liquor, intended to raise $6 million annually for the state. It also set a ten-cent gallonage tax on the manufacture of wine, and early in 1934 passed its own liquor control law.

New liquor legislation finally was passed by the Missouri legislature on January 12, 1934, and was signed by Park the following day. It set state licenses for liquor by the drink at three hundred dollars and in the package at fifty dollars per year and allowed cities with more than twenty thousand population to sell liquor by the drink. Those of between five hundred and twenty thousand population were required to vote at a special election whether to sell liquor by the drink, and those of under five hundred population were forbidden to have taverns or saloons.

Despite concern among reformers about a return to the old-fashioned saloon, the main concession in the state law seemed to be a requirement of stools over the brass rails—ostensibly to prevent standup drinking in bars. The situa-

First Permit

Missouri State Permit No. 1 for wholesalers or distributors of intoxicating liquor was issued on January 26, 1934, by the State Department of Liquor Control to the Dan Becker Distributing Company in St. Louis and cost five hundred dollars.

The first state license to sell package liquor was issued to Columbia, Missouri's Peck drugstore for fifty dollars.

tion was no better with St. Louis's liquor control ordinance, the *New York Times* reported in March 1934. "In fact, the saloon has been back in St. Louis ever since the Eighteenth Amendment was repealed, and a new interpretation of the State liquor law by Supervisor [state liquor control supervisor E. J.] Becker has all but told the saloonkeepers to install swinging doors, scatter sawdust on the floor and install a player piano," noted the *Times*. The St. Louis Board of Aldermen had to please many different tastes, including hundreds of St. Louis saloonkeepers and others who pleaded during hours of hearings for a return to the old-time saloon. The city ordinance required license applicants to have petitions signed by a majority of property owners and first-floor tenants within two hundred feet of the location. There was no limit on the proximity of a liquor establishment to a school, church, or park, and there was no prohibition on sales to minors. In St. Louis County, the League of County Municipalities approved a uniform ordinance for licensing and control of liquor sales in incorporated suburbs.

BACK TO BOOTLEGGING

In Illinois, State Senator Martin Lohmann warned that high liquor taxes would prolong the life of the bootlegger, a prediction also made by Colonel James W. Byrnes of the Missouri Association Against Prohibition. They were right. In February 1934, the United States Brewers Association passed a resolution urging the federal government to lower its excise taxes on liquor and urging the states to abandon excise taxes entirely, to discourage bootlegging. But the wheels had been set in motion. Missouri collected $6,536,156 in various liquor taxes for the Bureau of Internal Revenue in the first seven months following complete repeal, while Illinois made the third-highest haul in the country, with $21,634,937.

The bootlegging problem was particularly pernicious in Missouri, where abuses were tied to those holding 3.2 percent beer licenses. When the state approved the sale of 3.2 beer, it set a license fee of only ten dollars—there was no city fee—and many of these establishments sold strong beer and whiskey on the side. St. Louis's excise commissioner, Colonel Harry Scullin, estimated in December 1934 there were five thousand or more 3.2 beer taverns in the city alone, with a considerable majority selling strong beer and liquor as well. "In fact, a drink of 3.2 beer in St. Louis is pretty hard to locate," observed the *New York Times*.

Missouri's liquor revenue in 1934 was about $2 million, half of what state officials had predicted. Illinois's take was $7 million, also less than expected. Retailers with full-drink licenses, which paid six hundred dollars more in state and local fees than the 3.2 percent establishments, were angry. "Inasmuch as they have not had to pay the high state and city license fees, [3.2 establishments] naturally could undersell the legitimate, established retail tavern," wrote David B. Gibson, editor of the *Western Brewer.*

In June 1935, Missouri officials began enforcing a new liquor control law that set closing hours for taverns at 1:30 a.m. weekdays and midnight Sundays, forbade sales of liquor or beer with more than 3.2 percent alcohol on Sundays, and added search and seizure, nuisance, and abatement clauses. Holders of hard liquor and 5 percent beer permits could not open their doors on the closed days, even if they planned to sell only 3.2 beer.

Illinois's liquor law also was fraught with problems, and by December 1934 some six hundred precincts in Illinois used local option to vote out saloons. Because the new law forbade establishments to maintain a bar of any kind at which beverages could be sold for consumption, "standeasies" were cropping up for the comfort of "vertical drinkers." Brewers pushed for legislators to exempt beer from restriction on the methods of sale, but Horner maintained that would mean a return of the saloon and violate party pledges.

Various provisions designed to prevent a return of the saloon failed to work, *Times* editorial correspondent E. J. Duncan-Clark declared in December 1934. From politics and patronage to vice and bootlegging, "every evil that attended the institution in pre-prohibition days is conspicuously present under the tavern's thin disguise. . . . Governor Horner did his best to create a tavern that would be readily distinguished from a saloon," Duncan-Clark wrote. "But the liquor traffic rode the Legislature and the law that emerged was such as even to provoke reasonable wets to say that it was the worst liquor control law to be adopted by any State in the Union. . . . Efforts to obtain a strong state liquor control board failed."

There were other problems, Duncan-Clark noted. "Many credit the alarming increase in automobile accidents to a combination of liquor and the new light, high-powered, speedy cars. The fact that the increase has been notable in a number of down-State counties, where the number of fatalities per 100,000 population has exceeded—for the first time—the rate in Cook County [Chicago area], is regarded as significant."

WE'RE BACK

The ink was scarcely dry on the repeal legislation when the drys announced they would seek a return to prohibition. One of the WCTU's first post-repeal efforts from the Evanston, Illinois, headquarters was a "measuring stick" in October 1933 to determine the various stages of intoxication from 3.2 percent beer.

In December 1935, leaders at the Anti-Saloon League's annual convention in St. Louis launched a new drive with the goal of bringing back prohibition in ten years. They lambasted the wets for, among other things, failing to keep their pledge against the return of the saloon. "Prohibition is on its way back and it is coming sooner than any of us thought," General Superintendent F. Scott McBride said. "When it is here it will be stronger than it ever has been."

Accompanied by the hand clapping of Bishop W. N. Ainsworth of the Methodist Episcopal Church, evangelist Homer Rodeheaver sang his new song, "Repeal Has Failed":

Repeal has failed, It was all in vain, The old saloon is back again. Tho' it's called another name, it's a hell-hole just the same, for it damns men in their shame.

We've been down that road before, Mary E. Ryder, president of the Joint Council of Women's Auxiliaries Welfare Association, replied to the drys in her own public flier. The Joint Council had worked for repeal as part of the WON-PR. "But, we would not like to see our industries that manufacture liquor and that are made up of Union men again supplanted by gangs of the underworld," Ryder wrote. "If liquor is used moderately it is a boon to the soldier in battle, to the sick in our hospitals, to the aged and to all who work hard mentally or physically, because it is a gift that nature and God would never have given to man if it was not intended for man's use."

LIFE GOES ON

Some traditions received a new lease on life after prohibition, while others faded into the dust. "For thirteen years St. Louisans have said if the Eighteenth Amendment was ever repealed there were two spots that were certain to be revived," the *New York Times* noted in November 1933. "One was Tony Faust's Cafe, known all over the world for the excellence of its cuisine; the other was the Southern Hotel, likewise renowned for its wines and food. Both have lain idle since prohibition came in.

"Wreckers received orders this week to raze both structures. Too far off the beaten path, was the explanation."

In the predominantly German American stronghold of St. Charles, resi-

Tony Faust's restaurant was located at Broadway and Elm Street in downtown St. Louis. Elm Street no longer exists.

dents returned to a "continental Sunday" tradition with church picnics every week, Steve Ehlmann noted in *Crossroads*. In contrast to the Sunday stuffiness of Anglo-Americans, the Germans' Sunday activities included such delights as bingo, beer gardens, and dances.

From April 1933 to April 1938, St. Louis breweries produced approximately 13.5 million barrels of beer, paid approximately $60 million in taxes, purchased approximately $50 million in materials and supplies, paid approximately $35 million in salaries and wages, and spent about $20 million improving plants and equipment, according to Jules R. Field, secretary and counsel of the Missouri Brewers' Association. By May 1938, St. Louis breweries employed about ten thousand workers.

In the face of stiff competition and high upgrade costs, many venerable breweries didn't make it back for long. The Obert family, for example, issued public stock to help raise the funds to renovate the brewery and begin full-scale operations. They began brewing again in October 1933, but by the following February the brewery faced 162 creditors with claims of more than $150,000. In August 1934, Obert brewed its last batch of beer.

The Central Brewing Company in East St. Louis managed to stick around until the late 1930s. Its owners accepted an offer from William J. Lemp, III, to license his name and brew and sell Lemp Original Lager and Lemp Pale Ale, and

DRUNKEN DRIVING ARRESTS IN ST. LOUIS

From the annual report of the St. Louis Board of Police Commissioners:

Year	Men	Women
1924*	206	0
1925	256	5
1926	466	5
1927	464	7
1928	681	7
1929	696	12
1930	660	20
1931	627	13
1932	357	3
1933	483	15
1934	470	14
1935	409	8
1936	595	31
1937	544	29

*First year DWIs mentioned in report

in 1939 changed the brewery name. A year later, however, the William J. Lemp Brewing Company declared bankruptcy, and attempts to save it failed. Lemp himself died suddenly in March 1943 at age forty-two.

Wagner in Granite City was another brewery that lost its original name with a 1939 sale and, as the American Brewing Company, barely made it to the end of 1940. Others survived and prospered, among them Fischbach in St. Charles, Griesedieck Western [Stag] in Belleville, and Griesedieck Brothers and Falstaff in St. Louis, Kious and Roussin said. Mound City, formerly New Athens, was destroyed by a suspicious fire in 1950, and Bluff City in Alton made it to the early 1950s.

The Women's Christian Temperance Union also survived and has chapters today.

So, What's the Diff?

The abuses were flagrant, the parties wild, the enforcement pathetic, the graft grimy, and the battles between wets and drys cutthroat. So did prohibition really accomplish anything? One might deduce from the newspaper accounts and many oral histories that most people drank like W. C. Fields. Experts, however, say that drinking declined during prohibition. "A notorious and chronically unemployed drunkard of the Speed [Missouri] community 'took the cure' with the onset of prohibition," Louis Geiger wrote. "He remained sober and mostly employed throughout the dry years, only to return to his old ways after repeal. This doesn't prove anything, but it is fairly certain that many people did indeed drink less during prohibition than they had before, if only because most illegal products were not very good and took some trouble to obtain. Besides, many people undoubtedly obeyed the law because they believed it was a good citizen's duty to do so."

One exception was the number of female drinkers, who increased their ranks, to the chagrin of saloonkeepers in post-prohibition St. Louis. "The question—whether a lady, free, twenty-one and thirsty, has an inalienable right to toss off a gin fizz in public with her boy friend—has aroused the greatest dissension here since short skirts were an issue instead of a memory," rhe *New York Times* described the controversy in July 1935.

St. Louis Excise Commissioner Thomas L. Anderson started the battle by asking the St. Louis Board of Aldermen to prohibit the sale of liquor to women in barrooms. "The new saloon is just the old saloon hiding behind women's skirts," Anderson said. "Mothers used to have to worry over the sobriety of their sons. Now they are faced with a greater problem, the sobriety of their daughters." A committee of saloonkeepers maintained women were a menace to their business. "They're moochers," said one. "They buy one drink and expect the men at the bar to buy the rest. That drives the men into buying package liquor and taking it home to drink in peace."

Mrs. Joseph T. Davis, president of the Federated Women's Clubs, seconded the ban. "I do not think his idea is to discriminate against women but to protect them for their own good," she said. "To my mind there is nothing more pathetic than an intoxicated woman." Another civic leader, Mrs. Sidney Maestre, didn't buy that argument. "You deny women the front door and they will go around to the back door or up an alley to a speakeasy or out to a beer flat where there isn't even a pretense of regulation," Maestre said. "You can't keep the wrong kind of women out, so you might as well let the right kind of women in."

Kitty Amsler, secretary-treasurer of the Waitresses' Union, Local 249, agreed. "It is any woman's privilege to enter a respectable tap room," Amsler said. "Let's be 1935! Women are equal to men and every one knows it." As the controversy raged, the *Times* observed "no decrease in the number of feminine oxfords parked along the brass rail."

A TOAST

The prohibition experiment began with good intentions by some of its proponents, but it was an ill-conceived law from the beginning. It took away honest livelihoods and stripped every American of the legal right to enjoy an alcoholic refreshment. It required residents to uphold a morality that many public officials had no intention of fulfilling and fostered violence through inadequate enforcement and opportunities for crime and corruption.

On a sultry July night in 1936, U.S. Representative Thomas C. Hennings Jr., D-Missouri, told members of St. Louis's Ninth Ward Democratic Organization of the need for "constant vigilance . . . to prevent the rise of more Andrew Volsteads and Wayne B. Wheelers."

BIBLIOGRAPHY

Chapter 1

Bartley, Mary. *St. Louis Lost: Uncovering the City's Lost Architectural Treasures.* St. Louis: Virginia Publishing Co., 1998.

Carondelet News, June 1, 1928.

Faherty, William Barnaby, S.J. *A Gift to Glory In: The First Hundred Years of the Missouri Botanical Garden (1859–1959).* Ocean Park, Wash.: Harris & Friedrich, 1989.

The First Fifty Years: The Racquet Club. St. Louis: The Racquet Club of St. Louis, 1956.

Friedman, S. Morgan. The Inflation Calculator. http://www.westegg.com/inflation/.

Hay, Charles Martin. Papers (1879–1945), Western Historical Manuscript Collection, Columbia, Mo.

Jefferson City Tribune, February 14, 1925.

The Minute Man, Missouri edition, March 1923, published by the Association Against the Prohibition Amendment, St. Louis, Mo., from the collections of the Missouri Historical Society, St. Louis.

New York Times, January 2, 1923.

O'Connor, Candace. *Meet Me in the Lobby: The Story of Harold Koplar and the Chase Park Plaza.* St. Louis: Virginia Publishing Co., 2005.

St. Louis County Watchman-Advocate, January 9, 1925; April 14, 28, 1925.

St. Louis Globe-Democrat, January 1– 3, 6, 8, 11, 1923; December 12, 1930.

St. Louis Post-Dispatch, January 5, 1920; January 2, 5, 8, 26, 1923; February 1, 9, 12, 16, 18, 21, 1923; March 17, 1923; July 19, 1923; October 28, 1924; February 5, 1926; January 2, 1927; September 4, 6, 1928; January 2, 1929; October 19, 1929.

St. Louis Star, January 6, 8, 11–12, 14–17, 19–20, 22–23, 25, 28, 29, 31, 1923; February 2–4, 7, 9, 12, 13, 15, 1923; March 17, 1923.

Spytek, Sue. "A Stroll Through Memory Lane." In *Memories of Southern Illinois: Stories Written by Senior Citizens,* by Belleville Area College Programs and Services for Older Persons. Belleville, Ill.: Belleville Area College, 1984.

Chapter 2

American Brewer Magazine, 1901 and 1910, months unknown.

Andrews, Gregg. *City of Dust: A Cement Company Town in the Land of Tom Sawyer.* Columbia: University of Missouri Press, 1996.

———. "The War on Booze." *Gateway Heritage* (Spring 1996).

Anheuser-Busch Co. "Epoch Marking Events of American History," promotional brochure, 1914. Western Historical Manuscript Collection, St. Louis.

Baker, James F. *Glimpses of Meramec Highlands: "St. Louis' Only Exclusive Health and Pleasure Resort."* Kirkwood, Mo.: Meramec Highlands Books, 1995.

Bevo Area Historical Society. *History of the Bevo Area, Book Two.* St. Louis: Bevo Area Historical Society, 1986.

Borland, Bruce, ed. *America Through the Eyes of Its People.* New York: Longman Publishers USA, 1997.

Brown, Robert L. *Saloons of the American West: An Illustrated Chronicle.* Silverton, Colo.: Sundance Publications, 1978.

Carnahan, Jean. *If Walls Could Talk: The Story of Missouri's First Families.* Jefferson City, Mo.: MMPI, 1998.

Collinsville, Ill. "Because Community Counts," promotional brochure, 2007.

Coyle, Elinor Martineau. *Old St. Louis Homes: 1764– 1865.* St. Louis: The Folkestone Press, 1979.

Decatur Review, January 17, 1920.

Detjen, David W. *The Germans in Missouri, 1900– 1918: Prohibition, Neutrality, and Assimilation.* Columbia: University of Missouri Press, 1985.

Friedman. The Inflation Calculator.

Geiger, Louis G. "In the Days of Prohibition, Cooper County (Mo.) 1919–1934." Paper presented at the meeting of the Cooper County Historical Society, West Boonville Church, May 11, 1992.

Gregory, Ralph. *A History of Washington, Missouri.* Washington: Washington Preservation, Inc., 1991.

Harrison, Samuel F. *History of Hermann, Missouri.* Hermann: Historic Hermann, 1966.

Hay. Papers.

Hernon, Peter, and Terry Ganey. *Under the Influence: The Unauthorized Story of the Anheuser-Busch Dynasty.* New York: Avon Books, 1991.

Howard, Robert P. *Illinois; A History of the Prairie State.* Grand Rapids, Mich.: William B. Eerdmans Publishing Co., 1972.

Jensen, Richard J. *Illinois: A Bicentennial History.* New York: Norton, 1978.

Kingsbury, Lilburn A. Papers, 1816–1983, Western Historical Manuscript Collection, Columbia, Mo.

Kious, Kevin, and Donald Roussin. "The Breweries of Alton, Illinois." *American Breweriana Journal*

(July–August 1998).

Krebs, Roland, with Percy J. Orthwein. *Making Friends Is Our Business: 100 Years of Anheuser-Busch*. St. Louis: Anheuser-Busch, 1953.

Kyvig, David E. *Daily Life in the United States, 1920–1940: How Americans Lived Through The "Roaring Twenties" and the Great Depression*. Chicago: Ivan R. Dee, 2004.

———. *Repealing National Prohibition*. Kent, Ohio: Kent State University Press, 2000.

Magnan, William B., and Marcella C. Magnan. *The Streets of St. Louis: A History of St. Louis Street Names*. St. Louis: Virginia Publishing Co., 1996.

Merz, Charles. *The Dry Decade*. Seattle: University of Washington Press, 1969.

Meyer, Duane. *The Heritage of Missouri: A History*. St. Louis: State Publishing Co., 1963.

"Missouri's Largest Industrial Institution," Anheuser-Busch ad, *Chicago Tribune*, October 10, 1918.

Mormino, Gary R. Telephone interview with author, April 2007.

"Mr. Busch." *Time Magazine*, August 27, 1928.

Murchison, Kenneth M. *Federal Criminal Law Doctrines: The Forgotten Influence of National Prohibition*. Durham, N.C.: Duke University Press, 1994.

Muzzey, David Saville. *The American Adventure*. New York, Harper & Brothers, 1927.

New York Times, September 19, 1918; November 22, 1918; March 9, 10, 1919; June 26, 1919; July 1, 2, 1919; November 23, 1919; December 26, 1920; May 15, 1927; February 21, 1930.

Odegard, Peter H. *Pressure Politics: The Story of the Anti-Saloon League*. New York: Octagon Books, 1966.

Olson, Audrey Louise, C.S.J. "St. Louis Germans, 1850–1920: The Nature of an Immigrant Community and Its Relation to the Assimilation Process." Ph.D. diss., University of Kansas, 1970.

Primm, James Neal. *Lion of the Valley, Saint Louis, Missouri*. Boulder, Colo.: Pruett, 1981.

"The Prohibition Record of Congress 1917 to 1932." *Congressional Digest* (January 1933).

Renner, G. K. "Prohibition Comes to Missouri, 1910–1919." *Missouri Historical Review* (Summer 1968).

St. Charles, Mo. Bicentennial celebration program, August 15–23, 1969.

St. Louis County Watchman-Advocate, May 16, 1919; January 30, 1920; April 30, 1920; August 13, 1920.

St. Louis Globe-Democrat, June 2, 1920.

St. Louis Post-Dispatch, June 29, 30, 1919; July 1, 1919; October 29, 1919; January 2, 5– 8, 10, 11, 14–18, 20, 23–25, 28, 1920; February 1–3, 6–11, 13, 1920; August 1, 1920; September 29, 1920; March 17, 1923; December 8, 1929;

July 1, 1982, September 10, 1995.

St. Louis Star, July 1, 1919; September 24, 1929.

Schmeckebier, Laurence F. *The Bureau of Prohibition: Its History, Activities and Organization*. Washington, D.C.: The Brookings Institution, 1929.

Stern, Ron. *A Centennial History of Madison, Illinois, 1891–1991*. St. Louis: Bunn Winter Associates, 1999. From paper originally presented by Ron Stern, M.S. in Educational Administration, Southern Illinois University at Edwardsville.

Streissguth, Tom. *The Roaring Twenties*. New York: Infobase Publishing, 2007.

Taft, William H., comp. *Wit & Wisdom of Missouri's Country Editors*. Columbia: Pebble Publishing, 1996.

Taylor, Samuel Mills. Memoir, Oral History Collection, Archives/Special Collections, Norris L. Brookens Library, University of Illinois at Springfield.

Terry, Dickson. *Clayton: A History*. Clayton, Mo.: City of Clayton, 1976.

Theising, Andrew J. *Made in USA: East St. Louis*. St. Louis: Virginia Publishing Co., 2003.

Time Magazine, August 27, 1928.

Tingley, Donald Fred. *The Structuring of a State: The History of Illinois, 1899–1928* Urbana: University of Illinois Press, 1980.

Tobias, Henry. Papers, Brewers and Maltsters Union No. 6, 1873–1990, Western Historical Manuscript Collection, St. Louis, Mo.

Waal, Carla, and Barbara Oliver Korner, eds. *Hardship and Hope: Missouri Women Writing About Their Lives, 1820–1920*. Columbia, Mo. University of Missouri Press, 1997.

Webster News-Times, January 9, 1920.

The Western Brewer and Journal of the Barley, Malt and Hop Trades (May 1882).

Wheeler, Adade Mitchell, with Marlene Stein Wortman. *The Roads They Made: Women in Illinois History*. Chicago: Charles H. Kerr Publishing Co., 1977.

Chapter 3

Alexander, Charles. *Rogers Hornsby: A Biography*. New York: Henry Holt & Co., Inc., 1995.

Andrews. *City of Dust*.

Antweiler, Richard. "A Land Flooded by Change." *Missouri Life*, July–August 1981.

Baker. *Glimpses of Meramec Highlands*. Also telephone interview with author, April 2007.

Carondelet News, June 1, 1928.

Clayton, John. *The Illinois Fact Book and Historical Almanac, 1673–1968*. Carbondale: Southern Illinois University Press, 1978.

Coffman, Lloyd E. "Dude." Memoir, Oral History Collection, Archives/Special Collections, Norris L. Brookens Library, University of Illinois at Springfield.

Collinsville, Ill., City of. "Because Community Counts," promotional brochure, 2007.

Columbia Missourian, November 27, 1929.

Conrad, Jennifer, deputy Webster Groves city clerk. E-mail correspondence, May 2008.

Crist, Helen Valle. *They Was Frenchmans: The Vallee Family Legacy.* Columbia, Mo.: Author, 2003.

Dahl, June Wilkinson. *A History of Kirkwood, Missouri 1851–1965.* Kirkwood: Kirkwood Historical Society, 1965.

Daily St. Charles Cosmos-Monitor, March 16, 1925.

Darst, Katharine. "The Girls Kept Their Shoes On." *Bulletin of the Missouri Historical Society* (October 1957).

Eberle, Jean Fahey. *A Starting Point: A History of the Oakville-Mehlville-Concord Village Community.* St. Louis County, Oakville, Mehlville and Concord Village Chamber of Commerce, 1993.

Ehrlich, Walter. *Zion in the Valley: The Jewish Commmunity of St. Louis, Volume II, The Twentieth Century.* Columbia: University of Missouri Press, 2002.

Fox, Jim. Telephone interview and e-mail correspondence with author, April 2007.

Friedman. The Inflation Calculator.

Geiger. "In the Days of Prohibition."

Golenbock, Peter. *The Spirit of St. Louis: A History of the St. Louis Cardinals and Browns.* New York: Avon Books, 2000.

Guggenheim, Charles, producer. "The Flamboyant Years: St Louis in the Twenties," commissioned by Laclede Gas. St. Louis: KETC/Channel 9, 2006.

Hagood, J. Hurley. *The Story of Hannibal: A Bicentennial History.* Hannibal: Standard Printing Co., 1976.

Hall, John. "Westphalia: 'It's a Solid Place.'" *Missouri Life,* September–October 1979.

Harris, NiNi. *Bohemian Hill: An American Story.* St. Louis: St. John Nepomuk Parish, 2004. Also telephone interview with author, April 2007.

———. *Legacy of Lions.* University City, Mo.: The Historical Society of University City, 1981.

Hensley, Glenn. E-mail correspondence with author, April 2005 and October 2007.

Hoelzel, Norma J. *Valles Mines, Missouri and Vicinity: A Pictorial History.* Vineland, Mo.: Author, 1998.

Hunter, Julius. *Honey Island: A Broadcaster's Search for His Mississippi Roots.* St. Louis: Virginia Publishing Co., 1999. Also telephone interview with author, spring 2005.

Johns, Orrick. *Time of Our Lives: The Story of My Father and Myself.* New York, Octagon Books, 1973.

Keil, Matilda "Til." E-mail correspondence with author, April 2005.

Kirkendall, Richard S. *History of Missouri, Vol. V: 1919–1953.* Columbia: University of Missouri

Press, 1986.

Kirkwood-Webster Journal, October 26, 2005.

Kirschten, Ernest. *Catfish and Crystal: The Bicentenary Edition of the St. Louis Story.* Garden City, N.Y.: Doubleday & Co., 1965.

Kodner, Barbara. *Olivette: Chronicle of a Country Village.* Gerald, Mo.: Patrice Press, 1979.

Kyvig, David E. *Repealing National Prohibition.* Kent, Ohio: Kent State University Press, 2000.

Lang, Della. *On the Road to History (A Sequel to Along Old Gravois).* High Ridge, Mo.: Jefferson County Genealogical Society, 2004.

———. "The Prohibition Era: Moonshine in Jefferson County." Presentation to local groups, 2002.

———. *River City: The Story of Fenton, Missouri.* Fenton: City of Fenton, 1992.

Little, Judy, with assistance from Esley Hamilton. *University City Landmarks and Historic Places.* University City, Mo.: The Commission, 1997.

Lohmann, Martin B. Memoir, Oral History Collection, Archives/Special Collections, Norris L. Brookens Library, University of Illinois at Springfield.

Mallinckrodt, Anita M. *Augusta's Harmony: The Harmonie-Verein Cultural Society, 1856–1922.* Augusta, Mo.: Mallinckrodt Communications, 2005.

Miller, Nathan. *New World Coming: The 1920s and the Making of Modern America.* New York: Scribner, 2003.

Monroe, Karl. Memoir, Oral History Collection, Archives/Special Collections, Norris L. Brookens Library, University of Illinois at Springfield.

Mormino,. *Immigrants on the Hill.* Also telephone interview with author, April 2007.

Naborhood Link News, September 19, 1930.

Olson, James, and Vera Olson. *The University of Missouri: An Illustrated History.* Columbia: University of Missouri Press, 1988.

Park, David G., Jr. *Good Connections: A Century of Service by the Men and Women of Southwestern Bell.* St. Louis: Southwestern Bell Telephone Co., 1984.

Plavchan, Ronald Jan. *A History of Anheuser-Busch, 1852–1933.* North Stratford, N.H.: Ayer Company Publishers, 1976.

Polk's St. Louis County Directory. St. Louis, Polk & Co., 1926.

Renner. "Prohibition Comes to Missouri."

Richmond Heights, City of. *Down Memory Lane.* St. Louis: City of Richmond Heights, 1988.

Rose, Kenneth D. *American Women and the Repeal of Prohibition.* New York: New York University Press, 1996.

St. Louis County Watchman-Advocate, May 14, 1920; June 25, 1920; December 23, 30, 1921; January 6, 1922; April 7, 1922; May 4, 1923; August 3,

24, 1923; January 9, February 10, April 14, July 17, 21, 1925; December 14, 1928; August 30, 1929.

St. Louis Globe-Democrat, May 24, 1924; August 5, 1924; July 21, 1925; April 6, 1926; March 3, 11, 1927; August 20, 1933.

St. Louis Post-Dispatch, February 5, 1920; March 30, 1921; December 1, 1921; September 1, 1922; February 19, 1923; July 19, 1923; October 2, 22, 28, 1924; February 5, 1926; September 5, 6, 1928, October 17, 1928; September 10, 1929; February 13, 1989; April 28, 1994; May 27, 1998; July 30, 1998.

St. Louis Star, August 30, 1920; January 6, 1923; February 8, 14, 18, 20, 28, 1923; February 27, 1924; October 16, 1924.

Schuppe, George. Memoir, Oral History Collection, Archives/Special Collections, Norris L. Brookens Library, University of Illinois at Springfield.

Smith, Steven D. *Made in the Timber: A Settlement History of the Fort Leonard Wood Region.* Fort Leonard Wood, Mo.: U.S. Army Maneuver Support Center, 2003.

Speer, Lonnie R. *Meacham Park: A History.* St. Louis: N.P., 1998.

Sperino, Floyd J. Interview with author, March 2007.

Spytek. "A Stroll Through Memory Lane."

Start. *I'm Glad I'm Not Young Anymore.*

Stern. *A Centennial History of Madison, Illinois, 1.*

Swift, Wilda, and local history class at Webster Groves High School. *In Retrospect* series. Webster Groves, 1978.

Taylor, Irene. Papers, 1891–1986, Western Historical Manuscript Collection, Columbia, Mo.

Terry. *Clayton.*

Terry, Dickson. "Nostalgia." *Saint Louis Magazine* (May 1964), files of Missouri Historical Society.

Theising. *Made in USA.*

Tingley. *The Structuring of a State.*

Toigo, Avinere. Memoir, Oral History Collection, Archives/Special Collections, Norris L. Brookens Library, University of Illinois at Springfield.

University of Missouri Botany Department. Papers, 1894–1956, Western Historical Manuscript Collection, Columbia, Mo.

Vexler, Robert I. *Chronology and Documentary Handbook of the State of Illinois.* Dobbs Ferry, N.Y.: Oceana, 1978.

Volunteer Committee, City of Hillsboro, Mo. *Hillsboro, Missouri, 1839–1989.* Hillsboro: Author, 1989.

Wayman, Norbury L. *History of St. Louis Neighborhoods: Old North St. Louis & Yeatman.* St. Louis: St. Louis

Community Development Agency, 1976.

Webster News-Times, selected articles, and notes from *In Retrospect* series by local history class of Wilda Swift at Webster Groves High School, from the files of the Webster Groves Historical Society.

Wilke Book Committee, Washington (Mo.) Historical Society, comp. *I Didn't Know That!,* articles by Stanley Wilke. Washington, Mo.: Missourian Publishing Co., 1989.

Wittmond, Carl. Memoir, Oral History Collection, Archives/Special Collections, Norris L. Brookens Library, University of Illinois at Springfield.

Chapter 4

American Brewer, The, January 1916.

Anheuser-Busch Companies. "Brewing Our Future." 2006 annual report.

Bartley. *St. Louis Lost.*

Belleville Daily Advocate, December 10, 1920; April 1, 1924; September 5, 1928. Courtesy of Kevin Kious.

Brewer and Maltster, The, February 15, 1919.

Brewers' Journal, The, December 1921.

Busch, August A., Jr. "'Budweiser': A Century of Character." Henry Tobias, Brewers & Maltsters Union #6 records, 1873–1990, Western Historical Manuscript Collection, St. Louis, Mo.

Charleston (W. Va.) Gazette, November 29, 1926.

Coffey, Thomas M. *The Long Thirst: Prohibition in America, 1920–1933.* New York: W.W. Norton & Co., 1975.

"Corporations." *Time Magazine,* October 1, 1934.

Daily St. Charles Cosmos-Monitor, January 27, 1925.

Decatur Daily Review, March 22, 1924.

Decatur Sunday Review, May 8, 1921.

Eberle, Jean Fahey. *A Starting Point: A History of the Oakville-Mehlville-Concord Community.* St. Louis: The Oakville, Mehlville and Concord Village Chamber of Commerce, 1993.

Edwardsville Intelligencer, October 18, 1922; April 2, 1924.

Ehlmann, Steve. *Crossroads: A History of St. Charles County, Missouri.* St. Charles: Lindenwood University Press, 2004.

Evening State Journal, Lincoln, Nebr. April 8, 1924.

Fischbach Brewery, newspaper clippings and other items from the archives of the St. Charles County Historical Society.

Fitchburg (Massachusetts) Sentinel, January 28, 1926.

Friedrich, Manfred, and Donald Bull. *The Register of United States Breweries, 1876–1976.* Stanford, Ct.: Holly Press, 1976.

Gould's Red Book/Blue Book for the City of St. Louis. St. Louis: Gould Directory Co., 1919.

Griesedieck, Alvin. *The Falstaff Story.* N.P.: Simmons-Sisler Co., 1951.

Hannibal Courier-Post, April 15, 2004.

Henry Tobias, Brewers & Maltsters Union #6 records, 1873–1990, Western Historical Manuscript Collection, St. Louis, Mo.

Hernon and Ganey. *Under the Influence.*

Hyde, Arthur Mastick. Papers, 1913–1954, Western Historical Manuscript Collection, Columbia, Mo.

Jeffries, Jerry W. *From Hog Alley to the State House: A History of the Jefferson City Police Department, 1836–1997.* Marceline, Mo.: Walsworth Publishing Co., 1998.

Johns, Orrick. *Time of Our Lives: The Story of My Father and Myself.* New York: Octagon Books, 1973.

Kious, Kevin, and Donald Roussin. "Bootlegging, Boxing, and Benny's Bottled Beer Drinking Mule." *American Breweriana*, March-April 2004.

———. "The Breweries of Alton, Illinois." *American Breweriana Journal* (July-August 1998).

———. "The Breweries of Belleville, Illinois." *American Breweriana Journal* (November-December 1997).

———. "The Breweries of St. Charles, Missouri." *American Breweriana Journal* (January-February 2005).

———. "Brewing in New Athens, Illinois." *American Breweriana Journal* (March-April 2006).

———. "Central Brewing Co., East St. Louis, Ill." *American Breweriana Journal* (November-December 1999).

———. Interview and archival materials provided to author, May 2007.

———. "The Louis Obert Brewing Company." *American Breweriana Journal* (March-April 2001).

———. "Mascoutah Brewing Co.: The Brewery That Refused to Die." *The Breweriana Collector* (Winter 1998–1999).

———. "Rudolph Stecher Brewing Co." *American Breweriana Journal* (January-February 2007).

———. "Wagner Brewing Company: Bringing Beer and Baseball to Granite City, Ill." *American Breweriana Journal* (May-June 1999).

Kirkendall. *History of Missouri.*

Krebs. *Making Friends Is Our Business.*

Lemp, William J., Jr. Death certificate, Missouri Secretary of State website, http://www.sos.mo.gov/archives/resources/birthdeath/.

Mexia (Texas) Daily News, April 8, 1924.

Naborhood Link News, October 3, 1930.

New York Times, March 9, 1921; October 25, 26, 1921; November 19, 24, 1921; December 8, 1921; February 11, 1926; March 31, 1926; August 10, 1931.

Plavchan. *History of Anheuser-Busch.*

(Dolton, Ill.) Pointer, The, April 11, 1924.

Primm. *Lion of the Valley.*

Renner. "Prohibition Comes to Missouri, 1910-1919."

Rother, Hubert, and Charlotte Rother. *Lost Caves of St. Louis: A History of the City's Forgotten Caves.* St. Louis: Virginia Publishing Co., 2004.

St. Louis Globe-Democrat, May 13, 1921; January 5, 1923; August 5, 1924; December 25, 1932; February 29, 1964.

St. Louis Post-Dispatch, August 4, 1920; September 12, 1924; January 15, 1925; April 27, 28, 1925; May 25, 1925; June 26, 1926; December 13, 16–18, 1926; October 18, 1928; January 10, 1929; October 24, 1929; April 19, 1970; September 25, 1988; October 19, 1997.

St. Louis Star, August 19, 20, 28, 1920; January 29, 1922; December 29, 1922; November 7, 1924; January 22, 1925; March 7, 1928; October 2, 10, 1929.

Schibi Brewery, newspaper clippings and other items from the archives of the St. Charles County Historical Society.

Sikeston (Mo.) Herald, March 18, 1948.

Stifel, Otto F., death certificate, Missouri Secretary of State website, http://www.sos.mo.gov/archives/resources/birthdeath/.

Tobias. Papers.

Trampe, Stephen L. *The Queen of Lace: The Story of the Continental Life Building.* St. Louis: Virginia Publishing Co., 2003.

Walker, Stephen P. *Lemp: The Haunting History.* St. Louis: Mulligan Printing Co., 2004.

Washington Post, October 16, 1921.

Western Brewer and Journal of the Barley, Malt and Hop Trades The, (August 1907).

"Where the Budweiser Flows." *Time Magazine,* April 3, 1950.

Woman's Society of Christian Service, Methodist Church. Papers, Western Historical Manuscript Collection, Columbia, Mo.

Zenthoefer, Alexander "Fritz." Telephone interview with author, January 2008.

Chapter 5

Church Bell, January 11, 1946, First Christian Church in Jefferson City, Mo., from State Historical Society of Missouri reference library, Columbia, Mo.

Columbia Missourian, December 4, 1929; February 7, 1988.

Douglas, Robert Sidney. *History of Southeast Missouri.* Chicago, Ill.: Lewis Publishing Co., 1912.

Fitchburg (Mass.) Sentinel, February 12, 1925.

Griesedieck, Raymond. Death certificate, Missouri Secretary of State website, http://www.sos.mo.gov/archives/resources/birthdeath/.

Hyde, Arthur Mastick. Papers, 1913–1954, Western Historical Manuscript Collection, Columbia, Mo.

Jefferson City Daily Capital News, February 12, 15, 23,

1924; June 20, 1924; February 2, 1927; March 12, 1948

Jefferson City Daily Democrat-Tribune, May 13, 1922; February 16, 1924.

Jefferson City Daily Post, January 21, 1925; February 3, 6, 7, 9–14, 1925; June 1, 3, 6, 10, 1925; September 23, 1925; July 1, 9, 12, 16, 17, 26, 30, 1926; August 4, 19, 20, 1926; January 3, 1927; February 1, 1927.

Jefferson City News Tribune, September 23, 1945; March 12, 1948.

Jefferson City News and Tribune, October 17, 1971.

Jefferson City Post-Tribune, January 3, 15, 1930; August 16, 1937; June 1, 1938; July 18, 21, 1938; March 11, 12 1948; July 25, 1951; November 4, 1968; April 14, 1972.

Jefferson City Tribune and Democrat-Tribune, May 2, 3, 1917; October 6, 1917; December 18, 1920; February 27, 1922; April 16, 1923; February 15; May 2, 3, 1917; October 6, 1917; December 18, 1920; February 27, 1922; April 16, 1923; February 15, 1924; March 22, 1924; May 7, 8, 1924; December 17, 1924; January 27, 1925; February 5, 9, 10, 11, 14, 1925; April 15, 1925; May 21, 22, 1925; June 1, 2 5, 1925; September 23, 1925; April 19, 26, 1926; November 19, 22, 1926.

Kansas City Star, December 22, 1942.

Kirkwood-Webster Journal, August 10, 2005.

Missouri Historical Review, April 1943, July 1948.

Missouri Republican, February 12, 1942; April 16, 1942.

Nations, Gilbert, family, Missouri Federal Census records, St. Francois County, 1910. From "Prohibition, Missouri" vertical file, State Historical Society of Missouri, Columbia.

Nations, Gilbert. T*he Protestant Who's Who in Congress; Blight of Mexico, or Four Hundred Years of Papal Tyranny and Plunder; The Canon Law of the Papal Throne; The Papal Guilt of the World War; Papal Sovereignty, the Government Within Our Government; and The Political Career of Alfred E. Smith.* From the reference library of the State Historical Society of Missouri, Columbia.

Nations, Heber. Death certificate, Missouri Secretary of State website, http://www.sos.mo.gov/archives/resources/birthdeath.

Nations, Heber. Draft registration card, World War I. From World War I Draft Registration Cards, 1917–1918 (online database). Provo, Utah: The Generations Network, Inc., 2005. Accessed through Ancestry.com.

Nations, Heber, Missouri Federal Census records, Cole County, 1920. Accessed through Ancestry.com.

Nations, Heber. Missouri National Guard records.

From Graden, Debra, ed., *Missouri National Guard, the Mexican Border, 1916* (online database). Provo, Utah: The Generations Network, Inc., 1999. Accessed through Ancestry.com.

"Nations V. Willebrandt," *Time Magazine*, September 2, 1929.

New York Times, February 15, 1924; May 28, 31, 1925; February 21, 1928; August 14, 20, 21, 1929; January 17, 1930; June 19, 1930; September 24, 1930; April 12 1933; June 22, 1933; April 9, 1963.

Ogden [Utah] Standard-Examiner, September 15, 1929.

Phillips, V. E. Papers, Western Historical Manuscript Collection, Columbia, Mo.

St. Louis Directory. St. Louis: Polk-Gould Directory Co., 1923 and 1924.

St. Louis Globe-Democrat, March 15, 1924; May 29, 1924; May 31, 1925; December 22 1942.

St. Louis Globe-Democrat, December 22, 1942, from St. Louis Mercantile Library collection.

St. Louis Post-Dispatch, July 19, 1923; February 14, 21, 1924; September 22, 1924; May 25–28, 30, 1925; June 2 1925; October 16, 1933, December 22, 1942.

St. Louis Star, January 19, 1922; March 10, 1924; May 25–27, 29–30, 1925.

St. Louis Star, January 29, 1922, from St. Louis Mercantile Library collection.

Stone, Kimbrough. Papers, 1875-1958, Western Historical Manuscript Collection, Columbia, Mo.

Willebrandt, Mabel Walker. Biography from *Library of North American Biographies—Volume 7: Scholars and Educators* (1990). WilsonWeb, the H.W. Wilson Company, http://0-vnweb.hwwilsonweb.com.iii.slcl.org.

Wilson, Francis M. Gubernatorial campaign papers, Western Historical Manuscript Collection, Columbia, Mo.

Chapter 6

Baker. *Glimpses of Meramec Highlands.* Also telephone interview with author, April 2007.

Bishop, Elmer. Interview from the archives of the St. Charles County Historical Society.

Chillicothe [Mo.] Constitution-Tribune, March 13, 1929; January 22, 1930.

Coffman, Lloyd E. Memoir, Oral History Collection, Archives/Special Collections, Norris L. Brookens Library, University of Illinois at Springfield.

Columbia Missourian, May 30, 1929; August 9, 12, 1929; September 26, 1929; November 26, 1929.

Conlon, J. Willard. Memoir, Oral History Collection, Archives/Special Collections, Norris L. Brookens Library, University of Illinois at Springfield.

Decatur Daily Review, January 10, 26, 1929; February 9,

1929; October 6, 1929; May 3, 1930.

Decatur Evening Herald, January 3, 1931.

Decatur Review. July 23, 1923.

Drake, Bill. Oral history interview, Negro Baseball League Project, Western Historical Manuscript Collection, St. Louis.

Ellis, Mary Margaret. "That's the Way It Was, 1914–1930." Western Historical Manuscript Collection, St. Louis.

English, Tom. Memoir, Oral History Collection, Archives/Special Collections, Norris L. Brookens Library, University of Illinois at Springfield.

Favignano, John. Oral history interview, Immigrant Project, Italian, Western Historical Manuscript Collection, St. Louis.

Friedman. The Inflation Calculator.

Gegg, Paul. Interview with author, April 2007.

Geiger. "In the Days of Prohibition."

Harrison, Samuel F. *History of Hermann, Missouri.* Hermann, Mo.: Historic Hermann Inc., 1966.

Hyde, Arthur Mastick. Papers, 1913–1954, Western Historical Manuscript Collection, Columbia, Mo.

Jefferson County Record, January 1, 1924; October 31, 1929, courtesy of Della Lang.

Jeffries. *From Hog Alley to the State House*, 1.

Killinger, Gilbert. Memoir, Oral History Collection, Archives/Special Collections, Norris L. Brookens Library, University of Illinois at Springfield.

Krebs. *Making Friends Is Our Business.*

Kyvig, David E. E-mail correspondence with author, May 2007.

Lang, Della. Interview with author, April 2005.

Mantowich, Larry. Memoir, Oral History Collection, Archives/Special Collections, Norris L. Brookens Library, University of Illinois at Springfield.

Massaro, Anthony. Memoir, Oral History Collection, Archives/Special Collections, Norris L. Brookens Library, University of Illinois at Springfield.

McNeil, May Carr. Memoir, Oral History Collection, Archives/Special Collections, Norris L. Brookens Library, University of Illinois at Springfield.

Meriwether, Lee. *Jim Reed, "Senatorial Immortal."* Webster Groves, Mo.: The International Mark Twain Society, 1948.

Merz, Charles. *The Dry Decade.* Seattle: University of Washington Press, 1969.

Morgan, John P., and Thomas C. Tulloss. "The Jake Walk Blues: A Toxicologic Tragedy Mirrored in American Popular Music." *Annals of Internal Medicine* (December 1976).

Mormino. *Immigrants on the Hill.* Also telephone interview with author, April 2007.

Naborhood Link News, August 8, 1930.

New York Times, April 7, 1926; May 17, 1926; September 25, 1927; July 17, 1928; March 4, 1929; April 5, 12, 1931; December 19, 1924; December 31, 1926; January 4, 1927; March 19, 1930; April 8, 1930; May 1, 28, 1930; June 11, 19, 1930; July 30, 1930; March 10, 1931; May 17, 1931; March 26, 1932.

Ottolini, James. Telephone interview with author, January 2008.

Pearson, Emmet. Memoir, Oral History Collection, Archives/Special Collections, Norris L. Brookens Library, University of Illinois at Springfield.

Police Journal, June 20, 1923, from the St. Louis Police Department archives.

St. Louis County Watchman-Advocate, September 15, 1922; December 29, 1922; December 7, 1923; September 25, 1925.

St. Louis Globe-Democrat, November 11, 1875; March 11, 18, 19, 1927; March 16, 1934; April 19, 1934; February 29, 1964; March 1, 1964.

St. Louis Post-Dispatch, January 2, 8 , 14, 1920; February 6, 10, 1920; May 15, 1920; August 1, 1920; October 4, 25, 31, 1920; February 15, 1923; March 3, 1923; May 18, 1924; October 29, 30, 1924; April 29, 1925; December 30, 1926; January 2, 1927; September 24, 1927; October 20, 1927; November 10, 29, 1927; July 10, 1929; October 30, 1929; March 21, 1933.

St. Louis Star, April 23, 1925; May 20–29, 1925; January 17, 1927; December 20, 1927; March 6, 1929; August 2, 1932.

Smith. *Made in the Timber.*

Terry. "Nostalgia."

Tobias. Brewers & Maltsters records.

Victor, Benjamin. Memoir, Oral History Collection, Archives/Special Collections, Norris L. Brookens Library, University of Illinois at Springfield.

White, Mahlon N. *Farmin' in the Woods during Prohibition Days.* Clinton, Mo.: The Printery, 1976.

Winkler, Albert. Telephone interview with author, April 2007.

Chapter 7

Adams, Leon D. *The Wines of America.* New York: McGraw-Hill, 1990.

April, Tom. *Taste Missouri Wine Country.* Chesterfield: Missouri River Trading Co., 1991.

Baggerman, William. "Historical Series—Wine Industry in St. Charles County." *St. Charles Heritage* (October 1996). Previously published in the *St. Charles Journal* in four parts, October 11–November 1, 1962.

Baxter's Vineyards. http://www.nauvoowinery.com/history.htm.

Bek, William G. *The German Settlement Society of Philadelphia, and Its Colony, Hermann, Missouri.* Boston:

American Press, 1984.

Columbia Missourian, August 16, 1929.

Decatur Herald & Review, August 2, 2000.

Decatur Review, May 11, 1926.

Edwardsville Intelligencer, October 5, 1929.

Ehrlich. *Zion in the Valley.*

Fuller, Robert C. *Religion and Wine: A Cultural History of Wine Drinking in the United States.* Knoxville: The University of Tennessee Press, 1996.

Geiger. "In the Days of Prohibition."

Gray, James. *The Illinois.* Urbana: University of Illinois Press, 1940.

Harrison, Samuel F. *History of Hermann, Mo.* Hermann: Historic Hermann, 1966.

Held-Uthlaut, Patty. E-mail correspondence with author, January 2008.

History of Hermann, Missouri, Home of the "Maifest." Booklet, n.p., n.d.

Hooker, H. D. "George Husmann." *Missouri Historical Review* (April 1929).

Illinois Grape Growers and Vintners Association (IGGVA). http://www.illinoiswine.com/about.html.

Ketchum, Bruce. Telephone interview with author, May 2007.

"Lasting Impressions: German Americans in St. Louis." Exhibit, St. Louis Public Library, 2005.

Mallinckrodt. *Augusta's Harmony.*

Missouri Department of Agriculture—Agriculture Business Development Division, Wine & Grape Board. http://www.missouriwineorg.default.html.

Monroe, Karl. Memoir, Oral History Collection, Archives/Special Collections, Norris L. Brookens Library, University of Illinois at Springfield.

Muehl, Siegmar. "Isidor Bush and the Bushberg Vineyards of Jefferson County." *Missouri Historical Review* (October 1999).

———. "The Wild Missouri Grape and Nineteenth-Century Viticulture." *Missouri Historical Review* (July 1997).

———. "Winegrowing in the Hermann Area: Early Years' Chronicle." *Missouri Historical Review* (April 1993).

Murchison. *Federal Criminal Law Doctrines.*

National Association of American Wineries. http://www.wineamerica.org.

National Commission on Law Observance and Enforcement on Prohibition Laws of the United States [Wickersham Commission] Report on Prohibition, The, *New York Times,* January 21, 1931.

Nauvoo, Ill. http://www.nauvoo.net/history.

New York Times, July 30, 1923; November 19, 1923; July 24, 1925; October 28, 1925; November 23, 1925; December 2, 1925; November 16, 1926; November 15, 1930.

Orth, Kim. E-mail correspondence with author, January 2008.

Pinney, Thomas. *A History of Wine in America, From the Beginnings to Prohibition.* Berkeley: University of California Press, 1989.

Puchta, Adam & Son Wine Company. http://www.adampuchtawine.come/vineyard/ourStory.asp.

Puchta, Lois. Telephone interview with author, May 2007.

Randolph County, Ill. Genealogical Society. *Randolph County, Illinois.* Paducah, Ky.: Turner Publishing Co., 1995.

Repplinger, Raymond. Memoir, Oral History Collection, Archives/Special Collections, Norris L. Brookens Library, University of Illinois at Springfield.

Rolla New Era, December 20, 1884; November 17, 1888.

St. Louis County Watchman-Advocate, August 6, 1920; March 18, 1921.

St. Louis Globe-Democrat, November 28, 1931.

St. Louis Post-Dispatch, January 9, 1920; May 15, 1920; February 14, 1924; March 10, 1924; June 21, 1926; July 14, 1928; September 4, 6, 1928; July 2, 3, 5, 13, 1929; October 30, 1929; May 10, 2002; September 17, 2006.

St. Louis Star, March 10, 1924; October 30, 1929.

Scheef, Robert F. "Prohibition Vineyards: The Italian Contribution to Viticulture in Missouri." *Missouri Historical Review* (April 1994).

———. *Vintage Missouri: A Guide to Missouri Wineries.* St. Louis: The Patrice Press, 1991.

Sperino, Floyd J. Interview with author, March 2007.

Terry. "Nostalgia."

Victor, Benjamin B. Memoir, Oral History Collection, Archives/Special Collections, Norris L. Brookens Library, University of Illinois at Springfield.

Wilke Book Committee, Washington (Mo.) Historical Society, compiler. *I Didn't Know That!,* articles by Stanley Wilke. Washington, Mo.: Missourian Publishing Co., 1989.

Chapter 8

American Medical Association. *Saint Louis: What to See and How to See It.* Convention tour guide, 1922.

Angle, Paul. *Bloody Williamson: A Chapter in American Lawlesness.* New York: Alfred A. Knopf, 1952.

Beelmann, Aloys. Death certificate, Missouri Secretary of State website, http://www.sos.mo.gov/archives/resources/birthdeath/.

Boehm, Rose Marguerite. Memoir, Oral History Collection, Archives/Special Collections, Norris L. Brookens Library, University of Illinois at Springfield.

Carondelet News, January 27, 1928.

Chillicothe Constitution, June 30, 1925.

Columbia Missourian, January 22, 1929.

Courtaway, Robbi. *Spirits of St. Louis II: Return of the Gateway City Ghosts.* St. Louis: Virginia Publishing Co., 2002.

CourtTV Crime Library. www.crimelibrary.com/gangsters_outlaws/family_epics/louis/1.html, -2.html, -5.html.

Coyle, Elinor Martineau. *Saint Louis Homes, 1866–1916: The Golden Age.* St. Louis: The Folkestone Press, 1971.

Decatur Daily Review, May 2, 1927; October 11, 1929; April 19, 20, 1930; May 3, 1930; June 6, 1930; December 28, 1930.

Decatur Evening Herald, September 23, 1930.

Decatur Herald & Review, September 26, 1999.

DeNeal, Gary. *A Knight of Another Sort: Prohibition Days and Charlie Birger.* Carbondale: Southern Illinois University Press, 1998.

Edwardsville Intelligencer, February 24, 1930; May 5, 1930; May 14, 1930; June 23, 1934.

English, Tom. Memoir, Oral History Collection, Archives/Special Collections, Norris L. Brookens Library, University of Illinois at Springfield.

Favignano. Oral history interview.

Frankfort Area Historical Society. *History of West Frankfort, Illinois.* Utica, Ky.: McDowell Publications, 1978.

Friedman. The Inflation Calculator.

Gould's St. Louis City Directory. St. Louis: Polk-Gould Directory Co., 1928.

Hallwas, John E. *The Bootlegger.* Urbana: University of Illinois Press, 1998.

Hannibal Courier-Post, October 5, 1935.

"Kippered Herrin." *Time Magazine,* November 8, 1926.

Kirschten. *Catfish and Crystal.*

Kodner. *Olivette,* 1.

Machi, Mario, Allan May, and Charlie Molino. "St. Louis Family." American Mafia. http://american-mafia.com/Cities/St_Louis.html.

McNeil. Memoir.

Mogler, Joseph. Death certificate, Missouri Secretary of State website, http://www.sos.mo.gov/archives/resources/birthdeath/.

"Moneymaker." *Time Magazine,* May 2, 1927.

Monroe. Memoir.

Mormino. *Immigrants on the Hill.*

New York Times, October 27, 1926; November 8, 13, 28, 1926; December 13, 1926; January 11, 1927; February 8, 1927; June 14, 16, 1927; July 7, 25, 28, 1927; August 14, 1927; December 3, 1929; May 27, 1930; October 3, 1930; April 29, 1931; May 9, 1931; July 7, 1931; September 19, 1931; November 11, 1931; April 16, 1932.

Niemann, Vera. "My Association with Gangsters." In *Memories of Southern Illinois,* 1.

Nixon, Nancy. "Bootlegging in Illinois." *Illinois Country Living* (April 2001). http:www.lib.niu.edu/ipo/ic010410.html.

Nunes, Bill. *Southern Illinois: An Illustrated History.* Glen Carbon, Ill.: Author, 2001.

O'Toole, Monsignor Joseph M. *My God, What a Life.* St. Louis: O'Toole, 1981.

Palazzolo, Nick. Death certificate, Missouri Secretary of State website, http://www.sos.mo.gov/archives/resources/birthdeath/.

Pensoneau, Taylor. *Brothers Notorious: The Sheltons, Southern Illinois' Legendary Gangsters.* New Berlin, Ill.: Downstate Publications, 2002.

Purcell, Henson. Memoir, Oral History Collection, Archives/Special Collections, Norris L. Brookens Library, University of Illinois at Springfield.

Ross, Charles G., and Carlos F. Hurd. *The Story of the St. Louis Post-Dispatch.* St. Louis: Pulitzer Publishing Co., 1944.

St. Louis County Watchman-Advocate, October 1, 1920; December 30, 1921; April 13, 1923; June 19, 22, 1923; September 11, 21, 1923.

St. Louis Globe-Democrat, October 6, 1922; August 14, 20, 1924; April 25, 1925; October 31, 1925; October 14, 1926; November 22, 1926; March 2, 1927; April 2, 1978.

St. Louis Post-Dispatch, September 29, 1920; November 1, 1921; December 1, 1921; September 1, 4, 1922; February 22, 23, 26, 27, 1923; March 10, 15, 1923; February 14, 20, 21, 1924; September 4, 12, 1924; October 30, 31, 1924; November 6, 1924; April 23, 27, 30, 1925; May 1, 1925; January 6, 1926; February 6, 7, 1926; December 13, 14, 29, 1926; January 2, 1927; October 27, 1927; April 19, 1928; July 5, 7, 8, 30, 1928; January 8, 9, 18, 19, 22, 28, 1929; September 5, 1929; October 30, 1929; December 2–5, 7–10, 13, 15, 21, 28, 1929; February 9, 1934; August 16, 1963; November 2, 1996; April 8, 1997.

St. Louis Star, March 9, 25, 28, 29, 1923; February 13, 1924; April 1, 1924; June 19, 1924; November 1, 1924; March 9, 18, 20, 22, 25, 30, 31, 1925; April 1, 1925; May 28, 1925; January 18, 1927; February 2–5, 7–10, 1927; November 11, 21–23, 25, 26, 28–30, 1927; December 1–5, 7–10, 1–17, 19, 1927; July 26–28, 30, 1928; September 26, 1929; October 10, 19, 23, 1929.

St. Louis Star and Times, August 4, 11, 1932.

Schuppe. Memoir.

Sgro, Samuel A. Memoir, Oral History Collection, Archives/Special Collections, Norris L. Brookens Library, University of Illinois at Springfield.

Sutter, Orval C. *My Memoirs.* Presented to the Historical Society of University City, 1980.
Theising, Andrew. "The Beginning of Organized Crime in East St. Louis." http://www.eslarp.uiuc.edu/ibex/archive/nunes/esl%20history/organized_crime.htm.
———. *Made in USA.*
Tingley. *The Structuring of a State.*
Waugh, Daniel. *Egan's Rats: The Untold Story of the Prohibition-Era Gang That Ruled St. Louis.* Nashville, Tenn.: Cumberland House Publishing, 2007.
"Worst Man." *Time Magazine,* April 6, 1931.

Chapter 9

Boonville Central Missouri Republican, October 16, 1924.
Burnett, Elizabeth Ann Detweiler."Thy Kingdom Come: The History of the Church Federation in St. Louis, 1909–1969." Ph.D. diss., Saint Louis University, 1984. From the files of the Western Historical Manuscript Collection, St. Louis, Mo.
Cairns, Anna Sneed. Obituary, from an undated 1931 *Post-Dispatch,* from collections of Kirkwood Historical Society.
Carondelet News, March 16, 1928.
Columbia Missourian, February 4, 6, 1929.
Daily Constitution, Chillicothe, Mo., August 30, 1921.
Daily St. Charles Cosmos-Monitor, June 29, 1925.
Davis, Ralph E. *Webster Groves Christian Church, Disciples of Christ: 100 Years of Service and Witness, 1895–1995.* Webster Groves, Mo.: Webster Groves Christian Church, 1995.
Friedman. The Inflation Calculator.
Hagood. *The Story of Hannibal.*
Hay. Papers.
Hensley, Glenn. E-mail correspondence with author, April 2005 and October 2007.
Hyde. Papers.
Hyndman, Virginia. Memoir, Oral History Collection, Archives/Special Collections, Norris L. Brookens Library, University of Illinois at Springfield.
Jefferson City Tribune, December 10, 1926. Kingsbury. Papers, 1.
Kirkendall. *History of Missouri.*
Kirschten. *Catfish and Crystal.*
Kyvig. *Repealing National Prohibition.*
Lohmann. Memoir.
Mendelson, Anne. *Stand Facing the Stove: The Story of the Women Who Gave America the Joy of Cooking.* New York: Henry Holt & Co., 1996.
Minute Man, The, Missouri Edition, December 1922 and March 1923, published by the Association Against the Prohibition Amendment, St. Louis. From the files of the Missouri Historical Society.

Montano, Betty. Research, December 2007.
Mormino. *Immigrants on the Hill.*
Murchison. *Federal Criminal Law Doctrines.*
New York Times, August 31, 1921; March 28, 1926; February 19, 1929; March 29, 1929; August 14, 1929; January 2, 1930; March 16, 1930; September 8, 26, 1930; February 11, 1931; January 16, 1932.
Odegard. *Pressure Politics.*
Park, Guy Brasfield. Papers, 1932–1937, Western Historical Manuscript Collection, Columbia, Mo.
Renner. "Prohibition Comes to Missouri."
Rose, Kenneth D. *American Women and the Repeal of Prohibition.* New York: New York University Press, 1996.
St. Louis County Watchman-Advocate, January 30, 1920; August 6, 1920; February 22, 1924; June 17, 1924; January 18, 1929.
St. Louis Globe-Democrat, January 17, 1925; May 31, 1925; April 6, 1926; August 30, 1933.
St. Louis Post-Dispatch, January 25, 26, 28, 1920; January 31, 1923; February 12, 13, 18, 1923; March 3, 1924; January 18, 1924; November 28, 1927; December 15, 1927; July 19, 1928; March 19, 1929; December 7, 1929.
St. Louis Star, January 25–29, 1923; February 2, 4, 8, 9, 12, 13, 15, 1923; March 6, 13, 17, 1923; January 30, 1924; September 2, 1924; May 29, 1925.
Tobias. Papers.
Tyler, Helen E. *Where Prayer and Purpose Meet: The W.C.T.U. Story, 1874–1949.* Evanston, Ill.: The Signal Press, 1949.
Woman's Society of Christian Service, Methodist Church. Papers, Western Historical Manuscript Collection, Columbia, Mo.

Chapter 10

Andrews. *City of Dust.*
Baker. *Glimpses of Meramec Highlands.*
Bartley. *St. Louis Lost.*
Belleville News-Democrat, December 29, 2002.
Bopp, Orville, and Clinton Bopp. Interview from Kirkwood Historical Society archives.
Carondelet News, March 23, 1928.
Clayton. *The Illinois Fact Book.*
Conlon. Memoir.
Daily St. Charles Cosmos-Monitor, April 18, 1925; May 7, 11, 1925.
Decatur Herald & Review, April 13, 1999; April 3, 2000.
Edwardsville Intelligencer, March 24, 1930.
Elz, Ron (Johnny Rabbitt). Telephone interview with author, May 2007.
Finney, Chick, and Martin Luther Mackay. Oral history interview, Jazzmen Project, Western Historical Manuscript Collection, St. Louis, Mo.
Friedman. The Inflation Calculator
Goins, Robert H. Oral history interview, Black Com-

munity Leaders Project, Western Historical Manuscript Collection, St. Louis, Mo.

Gould's St. Louis City Directory. St. Louis: Polk-Gould Directory Co., 1928.

Grimes, William. *Straight Up or On the Rocks: A Cultural History of American Drink.* New York: Simon & Schuster, 1993.

Hammerstone's. History. www.hammerstones.net.

Hunter. *Honey Island.*

Jefferson City Post, January 17, 1925.

Jefferson County Record, August 31, 1922; undated issue, 1927; undated issue, 1929; April 18, 1935.

Kirkendall. *History of Missouri.*

Lang. *On the Road to History.*

———. *River City.*

Logsdon, Harley Edgar. Memoir, Oral History Collection, Archives/Special Collections, Norris L. Brookens Library, University of Illinois at Springfield.

Mantowich. Memoir.

Maplewood, Mo., city of. Council proceedings, Vol. 3, April 25 and May 2, 1923; Vol. 4, August 15 and 22, 1923.

Maschmeier, Earl. Telephone interview, spring 2007.

Massaro. Memoir.

McNeil. Memoir.

Mendelson. *Stand Facing the Stove.*

Metz, Jerred. *Drinking the Dipper Dry: Nine Plain-Spoken Lives.* St. Louis: K. M. Gentile Publishing Co., 1980.

Meyer, Raymond F. "Peg." *Backwoods Jazz in the Twenties.* Edited by Frank Nickell. Cape Girardeau, Mo.: Center for Regional History and Cultural Heritage, Southeast Missouri State University, 1989.

Monroe. Memoir.

Mormino. *Immigrants on the Hill.*

Naborhood Link News, July 18, 1930; September 26, 1930; July 28, 1932.

New York Times, March 16, 1930; October 10, 1931.

Nickell, Frank. E-mail correspondence, January 2008.

Owsley, Dennis. *City of Gabriels: The History of Jazz in St. Louis, 1895–1973.* St. Louis: Reedy Press, 2006.

Pearson. Memoir.

Perryman, Gus. Oral history interview, Jazzmen Project, Western Historical Manuscript Collection, St. Louis, Mo.

Press Journal, April 28, 2004.

Roussin, Donald. Interview with author, May 2007.

St. Louis County Watchman-Advocate, January 16, 1920; June 25, 1920; July 8, 1921; August 19, 1921; December 2, 1921; October 17, 1922; April 13, 1923; May 8, 22, 1923; July 6, 1923; August 31, 1923; April 8, 18, 1924; June 17, 1924; August 19, 1924; November 7, 1924; March 3, 1925; June 26, 1925; September 1, 1925; August 3, 1928; October 4, 1929.

St. Louis Globe-Democrat, August 18, 1924; July 20, 1925; November 21, 1926; March 9, 13, 18, 1927; May 29, 1928; May 2, 1935; February 29, 1964; March 1, 1964.

St. Louis Post-Dispatch, January 10, 25, 1920; February 4–6, 10, 11, 13, 1920; August 1, 1920; October 31, 1920;February 26, 27, 1923; February 20, 1924; April 3, 1924; February 17, 1925; April 23, 29, 1925; May 18, 27, 29, 1925; January 2, 1927; April 16, 1928; July 16, 19, 1928; October 17, 21, 31, 1928; January 2, 7, 1929; March 14, 16, 1929; July 3, 6, 8, 11, 1929; September 1, 1929; December 19, 1929; December 16, 1988; November 19, 1989; January 31, 1996; November 15, 1997; May 6, 1999; August 11, 2002; February 27, 2003; December 2, 2004.

St. Louis Star, August 16, 17, 1920; January 11, 16, 22, 1923; February 5, 27, 1923; March 12, 21, 1923; February 27, 1924; March 1, 3, 1924; June 19, 1924; October 18, 1924; December 15, 1924; March 7, 1925; December 20, 1927; November 28, 1928; March 9, 1929; October 29, 1929; July 27, 1932.

Shyne, Millicent Petrov. *2943: An Immigrant Girl's Childhood in St. Louis.* Alamogordo, N.M.: Six Sisters Publishing, 2002.

South County Journal, July 20, 1988.

Souther, Howard. Memoir, Oral History Collection, Archives/Special Collections, Norris L. Brookens Library, University of Illinois at Springfield.

Sperino, Floyd J. Interview with author, March 2007.

Stern. *A Centennial History of Madison,* 1.

Sullivan, Frank R. Memoir, Oral History Collection, Archives/Special Collections, Norris L. Brookens Library, University of Illinois at Springfield.

Wesley, Doris. *Lift Every Voice and Sing: St. Louis African-Americans in the Twentieth Century.* Columbia: University of Missouri Press, 1999.

White. *Farmin' in the Woods During Prohibition Days..*

Zenthoefer, Alexander "Fritz." Telephone interview with author, January 2008.

Chapter 11

Campo, Nick. Memoir, Oral History Collection, Archives/Special Collections, Norris L. Brookens Library, University of Illinois at Springfield.

Columbia Missourian, June 19, 1929.

Decatur Daily Review, November 21, 1922; January 26, 1923; September 8, 1924; December 9, 1925.

Geiger. "In the Days of Prohibition."

Ilch, O.B., M.D. Records and obituary from archives of St. Charles County Historical Society.

Killinger. Memoir.

Kingsbury. Papers, I.

Lang. *River City*, I.

National Commission, *New York Times*, January 21, 1931.

New York Times, July 8, 28, 1923; November 19, 1923; April 4, 7, 1926; August 22, 1926; July 28, 1929.

Olson, Edna McElhiney. "The Noble Experiment, Prohibition." St. Charles County *Heritage*, St. Charles County Historical Society, January 2001.

Pavlige, Betty. *Growing Up in Soulard*. St. Louis: Knight, 1980.

Perkins, Marlin. *My Wild Kingdom: An Autobiography.* New York: E. P. Dutton, 1982.

Rosenberg, Albert, and Cindy Armstrong. *The American Gladiators: Taft Versus Remus*. Hemet, Calif.: Aimwell Press, 1995.

St. Louis County Watchman-Advocate, November 7, 1924.

St. Louis Globe-Democrat, June 2, 1920; May 17, 22, 1924; October 31, 1925; November 3, 1925; March 8, 16, 1927; March 4, 8, 1928; April 11, 1944.

St. Louis Post-Dispatch, January 25, 1920; February 1, 1920; August 1, 1920; July 19, 1923; April 1, 1924; September 28, 1924; January 2, 3, 5, 7, 11, 12, 1926; December 21, 1926; July 19, 1927; November 9, 13, 16, 1927; July 3, 1928; January 6, 20, 1929; March 21, 23, 1929; January 27, 1952.

St. Louis Star, August 20, 1920; March 18, 1921; January 29, 1922; April 27, 1922; January 23, 27, 1923; March 11, 1923; March 10, 1925; November 14, 26, 30, 1927; December 1, 1927; September 19, 1929.

Sullivan, Herbert. Memoir, Oral History Collection, Archives/Special Collections, Norris L. Brookens Library, University of Illinois at Springfield.

Terry. "Nostalgia."

Victor. Memoir.

Webster News-Times, January 1, 1926.

Chapter 12

Angle, Paul M., ed. *Prairie State: Impressions of Illinois, 1673-1967, By Travelers and Other Observers.* Chicago: University of Chicago Press, 1968.

Brown, Daniel. *Small Glories: A Memoir of southern St. Charles County and the formation of the Francis Howell School District.* St. Charles: the Howell Foundation, Inc., 2003.

Carondelet News, March 16, 1928; December 21, 1928.

Clayton. *The Illinois Fact Book.*

Columbia Missourian , October 22, 1929; November 27, 1929.

Dahl. *A History of Kirkwood, Missouri.*

Daily St. Charles Cosmos-Monitor, March 6, 1925; May 2, 25, 1925.

Decatur Evening Herald, March 21, 1930; December 25, 1930.

Decatur Review, November 2, 1923; January 21, 1934.

Edwardsville Intelligencer, May 19, 1930.

Ehlmann. *Crossroads*.

Friedman. The Inflation Calculator.

Geiger. "In the Days of Prohibition."

Gould's St. Louis City Directory. St. Louis: Polk-Gould Directory Co., 1928.

Howard. *Illinois*.

Hyde. Papers.

Illinois State Police: A Division of the Department of Law Enforcement. Springfield, Ill.: State Police Benevolent Group, Inc., 1972.

Jefferson County Record, March 26, 1925; January 15, 1926; September 12, 1929.

Jeffries. *From Hog Alley to the State House.*

Jones, J. Elbert. *A Review of Famous Crimes Solved by St. Louis Policemen.* St. Louis: Moinster Printing Co., 1924.

Kirkendall. *History of Missouri.*

Knez, Cecilia, and Mary Oldani. Oral history interview, Immigrant Project (Croatia), Western Historical Manuscript Collection, St. Louis, Mo.

Kyvig. *Repealing National Prohibition.*

Mallinckrodt. *Augusta's Harmony.*

Massaro. Memoir.

Miksicek, Barbara. Interview, e-mail and telephone correspondence, February 2007, December 2007.

Miksicek, Barbara, David McElreath, and Stephen Pollihan. *In the Line of Duty.... St. Louis Police Officers Who Made the Ultimate Sacrifice.* St. Louis: St. Louis Metropolitan Police Dept., 1991.

Missouri State Highway Patrol. *Missouri State Highway Patrol, 1931–1981.* Jefferson City: Missouri Department of Public Safety, 1981.

Mormino. *Immigrants on the Hill.*

Murchison. *Federal Criminal Law Doctrines.*

Naborhood Link News, November 14, 1930; October 27, 1932; March 2, 1933.

National Commission, *New York Times*, January 21, 1931.

New York Times, July 23, 1923; August 24, 1923; November 29, 1929; March 23, 1931; August 25, 1931; January 16, 1932; May 25, 1932.

Popp, Bill. E-mail correspondence, July 2008.

St. Louis County Watchman-Advocate, September 3, 1920; February 24, 1922; June 9, 1922; September 1, 22, 1922; October 6, 1922; May 11, 18, 25, 1923; July 27, 1923; October 2, 1923; November 23, 1923; December 18, 1923; January 15, 1924; March 7, 28, 1924; April 8, 1924; September 9, 1924; December 19, 1924; May 1, 26, 1925; September 8, 1925; September 3, 1926.

St. Louis Globe-Democrat, January 6, 12, 1923; August

20, 1924; March 6, 1927; September 28, 1927; January 11, 1931.

St. Louis Police Journal, June 20, 1923.

St. Louis Post-Dispatch, January 14, 1920; February 4, 6, 7, 1920; August 1, 1920; February 6, 7, 19, 1923; April 3, 1924; September 14, 25, 26, 1924; May 15, 16, 30, 31, 1925; October 1, 1925; December 4, 12, 20, 21, 1926; January 2, 1927; July 2, 3, 5, 6, 9, 1928; September 5, 12, 18, 1928; January 2, 24, 1929; March 14, 18, 24, 1929; May 2, 1929; July 10, 1929; September 5, 1929; October 3, 19, 1929; December 22, 1929; December 16, 1933; February 21, 1999.

St. Louis Star, August 25, 1920; January 29, 1922; February 21, 1922; April 27, 1922; December 31, 1922; March 13, 20, 21, 1923; February12, 27, 28, 1924; March 5–7, 10, 1924; June 26, 1924; September 25, 29, 1924; October 17, 1924; May 1, 9, 29, 1925; July 10, 1925; January 2, 1927; November 25, 1927; July 27, 1928; March 8, 9, 22, 1929; October 10, 22, 23, 1929.

Schmeckebier, Laurence F. *The Bureau of Prohibition: Its History, Activities and Organization.* Washington, D.C.: The Brookings Institution, 1929.

Sperino, Floyd J. Interview with author, March 2007.

Stern. *A Centennial History of Madison, Illinois,* 1.

Taylor, Roger W. *Stories and Songs: Vol. 1: Born in the County.* Ballwin, Mo.: Kestrel Productions, 1995.

Tingley. *The Structuring of a State.*

Washington Post, November 23, 1921; August 10, 1923.

Chapter 13

Baker. *Glimpses of Meramec Highlands.* Also telephone interview with author, April 2007.

Benson, Joseph Fred, and Bernard L. Lewandowski. *One Hundred Years of Justice: A History of the Circuit Court of St. Louis County, Missouri, 1877–1978.* St. Louis: N.p., 1994.

Campo. Memoir.

Carondelet News, March 16, 1928; December 21, 1928.

"Cattle-Herding." *Time Magazine,* August 19, 1929.

Collinsville Herald, undated clipping, spring 2007.

Columbia Missourian, January 9, 21, 29, 1929; February 8, 1929; March 23, 25, 1929; April 13, 1929; May 10, 13, 1929; August 19, 1929; September 14, 1929; October 24, 1929.

Daily St. Charles Cosmos-Monitor, March 6, 1925; May 2, 25, 1925; June 7, 1925.

Decatur Evening Herald, March 21, 1930; December 25, 1930.

Decatur Review, November 24, 1924; February 21, 1927.

Jefferson County Record, March 26, 1925; January 15, 1926; September 12, 1929.

Killinger. Memoir.

Kirchner, L. R. *Robbing Banks: An American History, 1831–1999.* Edison, N.J.: Castle Books, 2003.

Kirkwood-Webster Journal, April 11, 2007.

Murchison. *Federal Criminal Law Doctrines.*

Naborhood Link News, November 14, 1930; October 27, 1932.

National Commission, *New York Times,* January 21, 1931.

New York Times, February 19, 1922; June 27, 1923; September 15, 1924; February 17, 1929; February 21, 1930; April 13, 1930; July 26, 1931; September 27, 1931; June 17, 1933.

Polk's St. Louis County Directory. St. Louis, R.L. Polk & Co., 1926.

St. Louis County Watchman-Advocate, February 7, 1920; January 7, 1921; May 23, 1923; November 25, 1924; March 31, 1925; March 22, 1929.

St. Louis Globe-Democrat, January 28, 1923; May 22, 28, 1924; December 5, 1931.

St. Louis Police Journal, June 20, 1923.

St. Louis Post-Dispatch, August 1, 1920; October 26, 27, 31, 1920; March 30, 1921; November 1, 1921; February 15, 22, 1923; May 18, 1924; September 6, 7, 21, 1924; February 7, 1926; July 17, 1928; March 8, 13, 15, 21, 22, 1929; July 7, 1929; September 6, 1929; October 22–25, 1929; December 16, 1929; September 19, 1932; May 6, 1992.

St. Louis Star, January 22, 25, 1923; February 7, 9, 1923; March 22, 1923; February 11, 28, 1924; March 1, 3, 4, 1924; June 5, 1925; January 24, 1927; March 4, 1929; October 3, 21, 1929.

Schmeckebier. *The Bureau of Prohibition.*

Schreiber, Mark S., and Laura Burkhardt Moeller. *Somewhere in Time: 170 Year History of Missouri Corrections.* Marceline, Mo.: Walsworth Publishing Co., 2004.

Tuttle, Mae. Memoir, Oral History Collection, Archives/Special Collections, Norris L. Brookens Library, University of Illinois at Springfield.

Wallis, Michael. *Pretty Boy: The Life and Times of Charles Arthur Floyd.* New York: St. Martin's Press, 1992.

Washington Post, November 23, 1921; August 10, 1923.

Chapter 14

Clark, Bennett Champ. Papers, 1890–1954, Western Historical Manuscript Collection, Columbia, Mo.

Columbia Missourian, January 26, 1929; October 25, 1929.

Conlon. Memoir.

Decatur Review, May 21, 1928; October 11, 1929.

Edwardsville Intelligencer, July 23, 1929; April 17, 1930; February 21, 1931; March 5, 1931.

Friedman. The Inflation Calculator.

Green, Harvey. *The Uncertainty of Everyday Life, 1915–1945.* New York: Harper Collins Publishers, 1992.

Hyde, Arthur Mastick. Papers, 1913–1954, Western Historical Manuscript Collection, Columbia, Mo.

Jones. *A Review of Famous Crimes.*

Killinger. Memoir.

Kirkendall. *History of Missouri.*

McNeil. Memoir.

Miksicek, Barbara. Interview, e-mail, and telephone correspondence, February 2007, December 2007.

National Commission, *New York Times,* January 21, 1931.

New York Times, June 28, 1923; November 18, 1923; March 9, 1924; March 26, 1925; May 4, 1926; June 17, 1926; November 5, 1926; April 24, 1927; February 5, 1928; November 21, 1931; December 19, 1933.

Randolph County Genealogical Society, comp. *Randolph County, Illinois, Commemorative Edition.* Paducah, Ky.: Turner Publishing Co., 1995.

Ross and Hurd. *The Story of the St. Louis Post-Dispatch.*

St. Louis County Watchman-Advocate, June 25, 1920; November 25, 1921; June 10, 1924; September 19, 1924; December 26, 1924; January 30, 1925; April 17, 1925; May 10, 1929; June 21, 1929.

St. Louis Globe-Democrat, August 7, 1924; February 23, 1927; March 9, 18, 1927; September 28, 1927; August 12, 1933.

St. Louis Post-Dispatch, August 3, 1921; February 6, 1923; February 22, 1924; September 5–7, 14, 1924; October 5, 1924; January 23, 24, 26, 29, 1925; February 1, 2, 1925; December 21, 1926; January 4, 1927; March 13, 1927; July 19, 1927; August 5, 1927; October 12, 23, 26, 1927; November 26, 27, 1927; July 2, 17, 18, 22, 1928; September 5, 10, 12, 14, 16, 20, 24, 1928; January 22, 1929; March 21, 24, 1929; October 25, 1929.

St. Louis Star, January 24, 1923; February 7, 1923; March 29, 1923; February 13, 1924; March 3, 1924; June 19, 1924; June 3, 1925; February 17, 1927; March 11, 1927; March 19, 20, 1929; September 24, 25, 1929; October 10, 1929; December 7, 1929.

Schmeckebier. *The Bureau of Prohibition.*

Chapter 15

Angle. *Bloody Williamson.*

Burnett, Betty. *A Time of Favor: The Story of the Catholic Family of Southern Illinois.* St. Louis: Patrice Press, 1987.

Chalmers, David M. *Hooded Americanism: The History of the Ku Klux Klan.* New York: New Viewpoints, 1976.

Cornwell, Charles H. *St. Louis Mayors: Brief Biographies.* St. Louis: St. Louis Public Library, 1965.

"Decline," *Time Magazine,* March 1, 1926.

DeNeal. *A Knight of Another Sort.*

Ehlmann. *Crossroads.*

Green, Harvey. *The Uncertainty of Everyday Life, 1915–1945.* New York: Harper Collins, 1992.

Harris, NiNi. Telephone interview with author, April 2007.

Jefferson City Daily Post, January 30, 1925.

Johns. *Time of Our Lives.*

Killinger. Memoir.

Kirkendall. *History of Missouri.*

Lohmann. Memoir.

Miller, Nathan. *New World Coming: The 1920s and the Making of Modern America.* New York: Scribner, 2003.

Monroe. Memoir.

New York Times, September 21, 23, 1921; November 11, 1922; April 3, 5, 1923; January 21, 1924; February 15, 1924; April 3, 26, 1924; September 2, 14, 1924; August 3, 1925; February 21, 1926; November 7, 8, 1926; February 5, 1928; November 17, 1928.

Pensoneau. *Brothers Notorious.*

Purcell. Memoir.

St. Louis Argus, June 15, 1923.

St. Louis County Watchman-Advocate, February 19, 1924; March 18, 1924; April 8, 1924; June 17, 1924.

St. Louis Globe-Democrat, May 29, 1924; August 5, 6, 15, 16, 1924.

St. Louis Post-Dispatch, March 12, 1923; February 14, 1924; March 25–27, 1924; April 1, 1924; September 4, 1924; October 21–23, 1924; January 27, 28, 1925; February 3, 4, 5, 7, 1925; April 24, 1925; January 30, 1927; February 6, 1927; January 23, 26, 1929; July 2, 1929.

St. Louis Star, February 27, 1923; February 11, 12, 1924; March 5, 6, 1924; June 18, 1924; October 28, 1924; November 5, 1924; April 4, 1925; February 3, 1927; August 10, 1932.

Theising. *Made in U.S.A.*

Totten, Grant, and Carrie Waldvogel. "A Question of Legitimacy: The Ku Klux Klan in St. Charles in the 1920s." *St. Charles Heritage* (April 1993).

Chapter 16

Albany (Ill.) Review, February 6, 1930.

"America is Dry," *Time Magazine*, November 19, 1928.

Andreasen, Bryon. E-mail correspondence with author, October 2007.

Basler, Roy P., editor. *Collected Works of Abraham Lincoln, Vols. I and II.* New Brunswick, N.J.: Rutgers University Press, 1953.

Brewers Journal, May 1936.

Campo. Memoir.

Carnahan. *If Walls Could Talk.*

Cashman, Sean Dennis. *Prohibition: The Lie of the Land.* New York: The Free Press, 1981.

Clark. Papers.

Clayton. *The Illinois Fact Book.*

Columbia Missourian, March 27, 1929.

Cornwell. *St. Louis Mayors.*

Culmer. *A New History of Missouri.*

Decatur Evening Herald, February 20, 1930.

Downey, William "Smokey." Memoir, Oral History Collection, Archives/Special Collections, Norris L. Brookens Library, University of Illinois at Springfield.

Edwardsville Intelligencer, October 2, 1928; December 6, 1930.

Hay. Papers.

Hernon and Ganey. *Under the Influence.*

Howard. *Illinois.*

Hyde. Papers.

Kingsbury. Papers.

Kirkendall. *History of Missouri.*

"Little Egypt's Dry," *Time Magazine*, December 2, 1929.

Larsen, Lawrence H. "Reed, James Alexander." American National Biography online, 0-www.anb.org.iii.slcl.org/articles/06/06-00549.html?a=1&f=reed%2C%20james&ia=-at&ib=-bib&d=10&ss=8&q=12.

Lohmann. Memoir.

Meriwether. *Jim Reed.*

The Minute Man, Missouri Edition, December 1922, published by the Association Against the Prohibition Amendment, St. Louis. From the files of the Missouri Historical Society.

Morel, Lucas E. "Lincoln Among the Reformers: Tempering the Temperance Movement." *Journal of the American Lincoln Association*, Winter 1999.

Naborhood Link News, July 28, 1932; November 24, 1932; December 8, 1932; May 3, 1934.

Nagel, Paul C. *Missouri: A History.* Lawrence: University Press of Kansas, 1977.

New York Times, June 25, 1924; September 15, 1924; August 5, 1926; October 19, 1926; November 4, 1926; May 19, 1927; May 27, 1928; August 7,

1928; September 30, 1928; October 22, 1928; November 28, 1928; February 17, 19, 1929; April 14, 24, 1929; June 9, 1929; November 20, 21, 28, 1929; January 26, 1930; March 14, 30, 1930; April 10, 12, 27, 28, 1930; May 17, 1930; June 22, 1930; July 1, 1930; August 23, 1930; August 30, 1930; September 7, 8, 15, 17, 1930; October 23, 1930; February 11, 1931; March 28, 1931; April 15, 1931; April 24, 26, 1932; May 28, 1932; July 17 1932; August 7, 28, 1932; September 18, 1932; November 3, 6, 7, 9, 20, 1932; November 19, 1935.

"Real Sentiments," *Time Magazine*, March 23, 1931.

Reed, James A. Biography. Arizona State University. http://www.public.asu.edu/~icprv/courses/hst315/secret315/biographies/1920%20to%201950s/Reed,%20James%20Sen.txt.

———. Scrapbook, 1920–1922, Western Historical Manuscript Collection, Columbia, Mo.

St. Louis County Watchman-Advocate, July 23, 1920; June 10, 1924; January 30, 1925.

St. Louis Globe-Democrat, July 25, 1924; August 20, 1924; November 15, 1926; November 9, 1932.

St. Louis Post-Dispatch, February 8, 1920; July 28, 1920; September 21, 1924; July 17, 19, 1928; undated, 1928; March 21, 1929; September 7, 10, 1929.

St. Louis Star, July 28, 1920; June 17, 21, 1924; February 9, 1927.

State Master statistical database, www.StateMaster.com.

Stevenson, Burton, arranger. The Home Book of Quotations Classical & Modern. New York, Dodd, Mead & Co., 1956.

Chapter 17

"April Beer," *Time Magazine*, March 27, 1933.

American Brewer, May 1938.

Brewers Journal—The Western Brewer, February 1935.

Brittain, William J. *The Spirit of Scouting '76.* St. Louis Area Council, Boy Scouts of America, 1976.

Burnett. "Thy Kingdom Come."

Busch, August A., Jr. "'Budweiser': A Century of Character." From Henry Tobias, Brewers & Maltsters Union #6 papers, 1873–1990, Western Historical Manuscript Collection, St. Louis, Mo.

Clayton. *The Illinois Fact Book.*

Edwardsville Intelligencer, March 25, 1933; April 21, 1933; June 8, 1933; July 5, 1933; October 20, 1933; December 20, 1933.

Ehlmann. *Crossroads.*

Falstaff Brewing Corp. "Brewed in St. Louis: The

Story of an Industry." St. Louis: Author, 1966.

Geiger. "In the Days of Prohibition."

Griesedieck. *The Falstaff Story.*

Hernon and Ganey. *Under the Influence.*

Howard. *Illinois.*

Killinger. Memoir.

Kious, Kevin, and Donald Roussin. Interview with author, May 2007.

———. "The Breweries of Alton, Illinois." *American Breweriana Journal* (July-August 1998).

———. "The Breweries of Belleville, Illinois." *American Breweriana Journal* (November-December 1997).

———. "Brewing In New Athens, Illinois." *American Breweriana Journal* (March-April 2006).

———. "Central Brewing Co., East St. Louis, Ill." *American Breweriana Journal* (November-December 1999).

———."The Louis Obert Brewing Company." *American Breweriana Journal* (March-April 2001).

———."Wagner Brewing Company: Bringing Beer and Baseball to Granite City, Ill." *American Breweriana Journal* (May-June 1999).

Kirkwood Monitor, May 5, 1933.

Lang. *On the Road to History..*

Lemp, William J. III. Death certificate, Missouri Secretary of State website, http://www.sos.mo.gov/archives/resources/birthdeath/.

McCandless, Perry. *The Missouri Experience: A History of the State.* Iowa City, Iowa: Sernoll Division, Effective Communications Inc., 1972.

McReynolds, Edwin C. *Missouri: A History of the Crossroads State.* Norman: University of Oklahoma Press, 1962.

Meyer. *The Heritage of Missouri.*

Mormino. *Immigrants on the Hill.*

Murchison. *Federal Criminal Law Doctrines.*

Naborhood Link News, January 28, 1932; April 7, 21, 1932; September 15, 1932; November 17, 1932; December 1, 1932; February 2, 9, 16, 1933; March 23, 1933; April 6, 1933.

New York Times, March 18, 1930; August 10, 1931; April 29, 1932; July 25, 1932; November 13, 1932; February 16, 1933; March 16, 22, 23, 1933; April 7, 1933; June 6, 1933; July 30, 1933; August 15, 21, 26, 27, 1933; November 9, 19, 1933; December 3, 1933; January 28, 1934; March 11, 25, 1934; April 8, 1934; May 6, 1934; July 15, 22, 1934; August 9, 1934.; December 2, 1934; February 17, 1935; June 12, 30, 1935; July 8, 1935; December 3, 8, 1935.

Niemann, Vera. "I Was There, Charlie." In *Memories of Southern Illinois: Stories Written by Senior Citizens,* by Belleville Area College Programs and Services for Older Persons. Belleville, Ill.: Belleville Area College, 1984.

Park, Guy Brasfield. Papers, 1932–1937, Western Historical Manuscript Collection, Columbia, Mo.

Parrish, William E., Charles T. Jones, Jr., and Lawrence O. Christensen. *Missouri: The Heart of the Nation.* Arlington Heights, Ill.: Harlan Davidson, 1992.

Pearson. Memoir.

Plavchan. *A History of Anheuser-Busch.*

Primm. *Lion of the Valley.*

St. Louis Board of Police Commissioners. Annual Report, 1918–1937.

St. Louis Globe-Democrat, April 26, 1932; May 5, 1932; May 8, 1932; December 25, 1932; February 23–25, 1933; March 15, 27, 1933; June 28, 1933; July 23, 1933; August 12, 20, 1933; October 1, 1933; December 6, 9, 13, 1933; January 11, 1934; February 8, 10, 1934; March 16, 17, 1934; April 19, 20, 1934; May 1, 8, 1934; June 8, 1934; January 14, 1935; July 23, 1936; November 21, 1936; February 2, 1938; April 2, 3, 1983.

St. Louis Post-Dispatch, April 7–9, 1933; December 5, 6, 11, 19, 22, 1933; January 13, 16, 20, 27, 1934; February 9, 1934; May 26, 2002; December 14, 2003; May 9, 2004.

St. Louis Star-Times, April 7, 1933; January 13, 1934.

Start. *I'm Glad I'm Not Young Anymore.*

Tobias. Papers.

Tyler, Helen E. *Where Prayer and Purpose Meet: The WCTU Story, 1874–1949.* Evanston, Ill.: The Signal Press, 1949. Vogel, Edward H., Jr., et al. *The Practical Brewer: A Manual for the Brewing Industry.* St. Louis: Von Hoffmann Press, 1946.

Zenthoefer, Alexander "Fritz." Telephone interview with author, January 2008.

INDEX